Pensions:
A Practical Guide

Fourth Edition

J S D Seres, MA (Oxon)
Solicitor

LAW & TAX

ISBN 075200 2465

Fourth Edition 1997

First edition written in 1980 by
J S D Seres and J W Selley

Published by
FT Law & Tax
21–27 Lambs Conduit St
London WC1N 3NJ

A Division of Pearson Professional Limited

Associated offices
Australia, Belgium, Canada, Hong Kong, India, Japan, Luxembourg, Singapore, Spain, USA

First published 1980.

A CIP catalogue record for this book is available from the Britsh Library

Printed and bound in Great Britain by
Hartnolls Ltd, Bodmin, Cornwall.

Stop Press

Budget Speech—2 July 1997

The Chancellor of the Exchequer announced in his Budget speech of 2 July 1997 that payment of tax credits on UK dividend income will be abolished for pension schemes from that date.

Details are set out in the Inland Revenue press release which states that pension providers, eg insurance companies and unit trusts providing exempt funds, will also cease to be entitled to tax credits. The cost to pension schemes, including personal pension schemes, will be over £5 billion in a full year.

This dramatic change in the tax system, if fully implemented in the Finance Act, alters the balance between approved pension schemes and other shareholders that has applied since 1921. UK dividend income will be reduced by 20 per cent. The total reduction in income will depend upon the proportion of investment in UK companies and any change in the rate of distribution and improvement in capital gains. The latter may arise from the reduction in the corporation tax rate from 33 per cent to 31 per cent (23 per cent to 21 per cent for smaller companies) but long term market changes may move either way.

The tax change will put up the cost of salary related schemes and reduce the benefits from money purchase (defined contribution) and personal pension schemes.

Pages 78, 257 and 262 of this book should be read accordingly.

Contents

Preface to the Fourth Edition

Pensions law is dominated by two areas: tax legislation and protection for members. The previous edition of this book followed the innovative tax changes of 1987 and 1989 which, by their effect, revolutionised pension provision for the highly paid. They introduced restrictions that, on the whole, applied only to new members. At a stroke the uniformity of the tax code was destroyed and transfers between jobs took on a pensions dimension.

Sex equality judgments were awaited from the European Court leaving most employers uncertain whether there would be a huge past service bill arising from unequal retirement ages. These matters have now been resolved (apart from the part-timers' issue) and are included here.

This new edition is, however, dominated by the Pensions Act 1995 which together with the earlier legislation consolidated into the Pension Schemes Act 1993, sets out the detailed protection for members that has been added to trust law. The 1993 Act is a consolidating statute bringing together 20 years of developing legislation with three main themes: protection of the early leaver, contracting-out from the upper tier of the State scheme, and inexpensive complaints' procedures via OPAS and the Ombudsman.

The Pensions Act 1995 arose out of the 'Maxwell' scandal, which involved theft from pension funds on a grand scale. The Act does not lock funds away from villainy, but it does create a minimum funding requirement and a Compensation Board that, if the employer is also insolvent, will make good theft that has reduced a fund significantly below the minimum requirement. The Act also creates a panoply of compliance requirements enforced by obligations on advisers to 'whistle-blow' to the Occupational Pensions Regulatory Authority ('OPRA').

Divorce has disentitled a rapidly expanding population of former spouses from the possibility of sharing pension or receiving widows/widowers' benefits. The Pensions Act 1995 authorises the courts to 'earmark' a member's pension for the benefit of a divorced spouse, and the Family Law Act 1996 provides for 'pensions splitting' when the practical difficulties, outlined in a White Paper, have been resolved.

As before, the book does not attempt to be an encyclopaedia. It is intended as a guide setting out accepted answers to the main practical questions where they are available.

On the complexities of recent regulations, I am indebted to a number of my colleagues, particularly Pauline Sibbit.

The kind permission of the Controller of HM Stationery Office is acknowledged in permitting reproduction of extracts from Memoranda issued by the Pension Schemes Office.

JSD Seres
April 1997

Table of Cases

Table of Statutes

Table of Statutory Instruments

Introduction

Although pensions have been the subject of much lengthy legislation in recent years, the most important statute remains Chap 1 of Pt XIV of the Income and Corporation Taxes Act 1988 (ICTA 1988), as amended. The older types of scheme were phased out by 1980 (see Chapter 17), leaving this as the only statute conferring on an employer's occupational scheme all four tax advantages of:

(*a*) full relief on an employer's ordinary annual contributions;
(*b*) no tax on the employee in respect of contributions;
(*c*) relief on an employee's own contributions (which may not exceed 15 per cent of annual remuneration);
(*d*) freedom from income and capital gains tax on the investments of the fund.

Personal pension schemes obtain similar tax advantages under Part XIV, Chapter 4 of the same Act. As employers can contribute to these, while avoiding the more regulated areas of administration, their popularity is increasing. However, they cannot provide a conventional defined benefit structure, nor (yet) effective employer sanctions for poor investment performance. Chapter 2 describes them briefly, including group personal pension schemes which may become serious competitors where a defined contribution structure is desired. Other than that section, the book relates entirely to occupational schemes.

Occupational schemes that meet certain requirements automatically fall within the tax approval conferred by the Act. The majority, however, take advantage of s 591 which enables the Commissioners of Inland Revenue (in practice the Pension Schemes Office ('PSO') of the Inland Revenue) to grant approval at discretion even though not all these requirements are met. Either way schemes seeking investment income tax relief must be established under 'irrevocable trust'.

Revenue practice for discretionary approval follows published guidelines, amended from time to time. The importance of obtaining and retaining Revenue approval cannot be too strongly stated: it forms the framework of this book. Nonetheless, the book is not a manual of Revenue practice, and the practitioner will find the published practice notes essential. Brief references are included here in Chapter 17.

Unapproved schemes play their part in executive pension provision since the Finance Act 1989 restricts new members of *approved* schemes to pensions based on the first £84,000 (the 1997/98 figure) of their annual earnings. While unapproved schemes are outside the scope of this book, their salient features are briefly described in Chapters 2 and 17.

The second dominant feature of legislation is protection for members, both against loss of expectation and loss of security. The bedrock of this protection has always been trust law, so statute has added to this base rather than removed it. Trustees play a key role and, like company directors, can now face statutory penalties for breach of specific provisions.

Legislative protection is now consolidated into the Pension Schemes Act 1993 ('PSA 1993') and the Pensions Act 1995. The PSA 1993 consolidated legislation (other than tax statutes) of the previous 20 years. The Pensions Act 1995 is entirely new; it adds a new protective structure in five major areas and a host of minor ones. These are described within the appropriate chapters of this book and are drawn together in Chapter 25.

The five major areas are:

(1) OPRA (Occupational Pensions Regulatory Authority).
(2) Member nominated trustees.
(3) Investment duties.
(4) Minimum funding requirement.
(5) Compensation Board.

Reference is also made throughout the book to the requirements for contracting-out of the upper tier of the State pension scheme.

Additionally, the book attempts to outline the legal matters which arise from the conventional (and occasionally unconventional) ways of meeting the wishes of employer or employee within the statutory constraints. These wishes may simply be for a particular level of retirement benefit (Chapter 8 describes the drift towards defined contribution schemes). They may, however, arise for totally different reasons, such as takeovers or redundancies, unexpected deaths or matrimonial situations, or even the need to provide for retirement out of the profits of an employer in a cyclical trade.

Many areas of law are necessarily touched upon. The most important remains equity, primarily trusts. The funds of every exempt approved scheme (save for the rare 'Hancock' arrangement mentioned in para 1.1(*b*) in Chapter 17) are held on trust so that the powers of the trustees, apart from those implied by equity or conferred by statute, are those set out in the instrument governing the scheme, usually a deed. This may cater for tens, hundreds or even thousands of beneficiaries (and, in an industrial group having many subsidiary or allied companies, a large number of sponsoring employers). The deed must confer wide administrative powers and, equally, must specify precisely the normal benefits to which the beneficiaries (the members and their families or dependants) will become entitled.

The short section on personal pension schemes has been included to give the practitioner an outline of their structure and application. They are operated by regulated providers (insurance companies, banks, building societies and the like) and are therefore not the subject of mergers, closure by employers or discretionary benefits. They have therefore not yet of themselves given rise to daily legal questions affecting the general practitioner.

On the other hand, the mis-selling of those schemes from 1987–1992 (and perhaps later) to persons wrongly advised to leave their occupational schemes, has led to regulatory requirements for compensation that are costing the providers several billion pounds.

The book has always been a guide for practitioners. Statutory sources are therefore given wherever they are thought helpful, but the book is not an encyclopaedia. Much guidance material is now available from the three sources cited (Inland Revenue, DSS London, Contributions Agency), and more is promised from OPRA. The practitioner should check the sources and guidance before embarking on specific action.

The law relates to England and Wales only and is stated as at 6 April 1997.

Chapter 1

What you are faced with in a hurry

1 The client's demands

All too often you will receive a telephone call claiming that a scheme *has been* established and the broker will be sending documents for engrossment. The matter is normally very urgent. For the exception of unapproved schemes see para 6 below.

2 How urgent is it?

If a scheme is not established under irrevocable trust by the date of an employee's first contribution, he will not obtain tax relief on it (except in certain circumstances). If the employer wishes to make a payment before the end of a profitable year, the date may be crucial.

Further, if the scheme is to be contracted out of the State scheme (see Chapter 3, para 12), and employers and employees are to be relieved from the higher National Insurance contributions, notices will have to be given, usually one month in advance (three months if there are relevant trade unions, and they must, by statute, be consulted). If the union agrees, the notice may be one month, and exceptionally, with the agreement of the Contributions Agency, retrospective.

3 Information you must have

A checklist of information required could be very long but the following main headings (given here with cross-references to chapters of the book) will usually suffice:

(*a*) date of intended first premium (Chapter 3, para 1);
(*b*) date of intended first employees' contributions, if any (Chapter 3, para 9);
(*c*) whether contracted out of the State scheme (Chapter 3, para 12);
(*d*) list of participating companies (Chapter 5);
(*e*) list of trustees (Chapter 3, para 7);
(*f*) whether the insurer (if any) has supplied drafts (Chapter 3, para 13);
(*g*) whether the benefits have been outlined to employees (Chapter 3, para 10 and Chapter 8);
(*h*) the categories of membership, if more than one (Chapter 9);
(*i*) name of the broker, consultant or other person who has organised the scheme (para 4 below).

4 Communication with the insurance company and/or broker

Your client may be establishing a scheme with its own fund. If so, he will probably have engaged a consultant who will either be or employ an actuary. More likely the scheme is to be insured. There will still be a consultant but he may be the broker or even the insurer's representative.

The scope of the scheme and its costings will have occupied so much of the preliminary discussion that the likelihood of draft documents having been considered will be small. The stage will be precisely the same as that reached by an estate agent and a house purchaser. The solicitor is rarely thought of until negotiations are complete. He is then asked to agree the documents.

The difference is that here he may be up against an inflexible timetable (see para 2 above) and an inflexible insurer (Chapter 3, para 13). It is therefore essential to get together with the broker/consultant/insurer as soon as you are instructed. It rarely takes long to demonstrate that you are trying to push a matter through, not delay it indefinitely.

Obtaining the broker's respect does not, however, extend to giving up your professional integrity. It may be true that all you need do is engross the drafts which he forwards to you, but you must first be satisfied that this will not tie your client forever to an unadaptable arrangement or grant rights of far wider scope than intended.

5 The inland revenue, the contributions agency and the former occupational pensions board

The importance of meeting Inland Revenue requirements cannot be too highly stressed (see Chapter 17). The majority of schemes fall within the scope of Revenue statutory discretion rather than mandatory approval. The discretion follows published guidelines. The revenue therefore have a department, the Pension Schemes Office (PSO) formerly called the Superannuation Funds Office (SFO), devoted to the question of approval and to communication with employers or their professional advisers.

Unlike other branches of the Inland Revenue, the PSO are generally willing to advise on hypothetical questions. Their primary function is to confer approval which results in relief from tax, and not to gather tax. If you are in any doubt as to a matter of practice, telephone (from 10 am) or write:

Inland Revenue Pension
Schemes Office
Yorke House
PO Box 62
Nottingham
NG2 1BG
Tel: 0115 9740000

The Contributions Agency is relevant if the scheme is to be contracted out of the upper tier of the State pension (Chapter 3, para 12). If so, a certificate from the agency must date from the establishment of the scheme. The agency (established in 1991) is an executive agency of the Department of Social Security (DSS), and operates the national insurance scheme. Unlike the PSO, which does not need to be advised in advance (if you know your way about their requirements), the agency will normally require an election before the relevant date.

The election cannot be made before the expiry of the notices to employees mentioned in para 2 above. For document packs and enquiries, contact (generally from 8.30 am):

Contributions Agency
COEG (Contracted-out Employments Group—Elections Section)
DSS Longbenton
Newcastle-upon-Tyne
NE98 1YX
Tel: 06451 50150

The Occupational Pensions Board (dissolved 6 April 1997) operated the contracting-out procedures from their establishment in 1978. Their main (former) statutory functions are set out in Chapter 18. Some, including its office for compulsory registration of pension schemes, have been taken over by OPRA (Occupational Pensions Regulatory Authority) whose main functions are also described in Chapter 18.

6 Unapproved schemes

Unapproved schemes are mainly relevant to highly paid employees. They will usually be contractual arrangements, often unfunded. The acronyms that will come up are UURBS and FURBS (unfunded/funded retirement benefits schemes). If acting for the employee the crucial differences are that the former usually have no security, and the latter entail an immediate tax charge.

In the rare case where an unapproved scheme is to be established with a significant initial contribution, or a past service liability, there may be an urgent need to put the contract in place before the employer's financial year-end.

While outside the main scope of this book, Chapter 2, para 10 gives outline information and Chapter 17, paras 3.3 and 4 sets out the statutory background.

Chapter 2

Types of scheme

1 Benefits

Pension schemes can provide pensions and lump sums for members and, on their deaths, for surviving dependants. The amount of pension normally varies according to the earnings of the member and his length of service. The method of calculation is usually one of the following:

(*a*) final salary (or 'defined benefit')
(*b*) average salary (now fairly rare);
(*c*) money purchase (or 'defined contribution')

Chapter 8 describes these further. It is enough here to say that, although it is essential for the employer to understand the nature of the commitment (Chapter 8, para 1), it is perfectly possible to establish the scheme on any of these bases.

All were capable, and (*a*) and (*c*) still are, of contracting out of the State earnings-related scheme (Chapter 20), although in the case of (*a*) and (*b*) above until 6 April 1997 this required guaranteed minimum pensions (GMPs) to be included or, more rarely, a money-purchase underpin.

Under (*a*), contracting-out now includes the definition 'salary related' or rather 'salary-related contracted-out scheme'—see PSA 1993, s 8(1) as amended.

Benefits may also include lump sums on retirement or death, spouses' pensions (mandatory for contracting out), children's allowances and special ill-health provisions. The latter differ from 'permanent health' schemes, which are mentioned in para 8 below.

Payment for the scheme may be exclusively by the employer or may include employees' contributions. However, employees have a statutory right to opt out and also, while members, the right to pay voluntary contributions (for additional benefits) either to the scheme or to a free-standing scheme offered by, for example, a different insurance company.

2 Individual policies for key people

A scheme, or even just a single retirement benefit, for one person comes within the tax legislation. There is no difficulty in obtaining Revenue approval provided the normal limitations are included. See also Chapter 17, para 4 regarding unapproved schemes.

For a small company, there is much sense in making such an individual arrangement, for the employee may have already been with the company for many years and may require far different benefits from younger staff. Indeed, a small company may not wish to become involved with pensions until it becomes clear that an individual is likely to stay for the rest of his working life.

Such a scheme will usually be insured although it may be self-administered or, less commonly, an unfunded contractual arrangement. At its simplest (and safest for the company) it is a money purchase arrangement (para 1(*c*) above).

Such a scheme should not be confused with a 'key man' policy for the benefit of the company. The latter pays a lump sum to the company in the event of the employee's death. It does not come within revenue pensions approval at all as it confers no benefit on the employee or his family.

The rules for a one-man insured scheme are usually as long as those for a group scheme, and are therefore costly to consider (Chapter 13, para 5). The alternative of a personal pension scheme (para 9 below), will also have long rules, but as the employer's commitment will be limited to payment of contributions the legal involvement may be minimal. In either case the broker should be asked to advise on the surrender and transfer terms.

3 Twenty or thirty employees

It is likely that even a scheme for twenty or thirty employees will be insured, although some such schemes are invested directly by trustees (para 5 below). Older schemes will be final or average salary types (paras 1(*a*) and (*b*) above) but modern ones are more likely to be money purchase (para 1(*c*) above). A warning about final salary is mentioned in Chapter 8, para 1. However, the warning does not extend to the technicalities of establishing the scheme, which are no more difficult than those for any other type.

4 Managed fund—say, 200 employees

To describe a scheme as having a 'managed fund' (or 'deposit administration', to mention another type) is only to describe the means by which its funds accumulate within the insurance company and to give a clue as to the broad approach to contribution rate.

In other words, the description tells you nothing about the benefits or about the approval of the PSO or Contributions Agency. It may not even be necessary to reflect the type of funding in the documents establishing the scheme (although the investment power must be sufficiently wide). Eventually, and quite separately from these documents, there will be a policy (Chapter 4, para 1) which will specify the method by which premiums are assessed and value accrues.

However, it is useful to know that the expression 'managed fund' is universally applied in the pensions industry to a particular type of arrangement with an insurance company and should not be confused with self-administered schemes (para 5 below) even though the latter have investment 'managers'. The insurance company issues a policy to which units (of identifiable but variable value) in the managed fund are allocated.

5 Privately invested (or 'self-administered') schemes—large and small

Once the assets of a scheme have grown to sufficient size the scheme will probably cease to be insured, except perhaps for its death-in-service benefits. The investment powers of the trustees become crucial (Chapter 13, para 3). The initial documents should always include provision for these to be enlarged in the future (Chapter 3, para 8 and Chapter 15). Further changes can often be left until that time comes (Chapter 26).

Some small schemes are self-administered. A few are even 'self-invested', that is, are invested back into the employer company within the permitted exceptions under the Pensions Act 1995—see Chapter 16, para 13). The two phrases should not be confused as their meanings are totally different. Traditionally, investments should be diversified (see also Chapter 24, para 5). The security for pensions should not depend on the viability of the employer. However, the employer may not be able to afford the capital to establish a scheme for elderly employees unless self-invested to the maximum proportion permitted by the Revenue (small non-insured schemes representing one of the few areas where the Revenue are concerned as to the manner of investment see also Chapter 17, paras 6 and 7). Alternatively, the scheme may be limited to controlling directors who accept the risks (but see Chapter 17, para 7).

6 Lump-sum schemes—group life and retirement nest eggs

A scheme is permitted by the Revenue to give any type of benefit within the approved range. Some schemes are limited to lump sums on death-in-service. They constitute a very inexpensive and useful form of life insurance. If suitably drawn, their benefits need not form part of the employees' estates for inheritance tax purposes, most commonly by providing for the distribution under a discretionary trust between the deceased's dependants and/or nominees (which can include charities).

Another popular benefit is a lump sum on retirement. The employer may pay this *ex gratia* but this has the following disadvantages, both of which are avoided if a suitable pension scheme is established:

(*a*) the 'golden handshake' on retirement is now generally considered by the Revenue to be taxable even if there is no advance commitment (see Chapter 10, para 5);
(*b*) an unfunded sum is payable just when the expense of finding a successor may also have to be met.

7 Retirement annuity contracts

Self-employed people such as partners in professional firms taxed under Schedule D have never been able to establish traditional style tax-approved pension schemes (except for their employees). Further, many employed people are not provided with such schemes. A person in either category may keep up (but may no longer start) a retirement annuity contract approved under Chap 3 of Pt XIV of the Income and Corporation Taxes Act 1988. These are generally in the form of life office policies.

The history of these policies dates back to the Finance Act 1956. It is enough to say that they have all the tax advantages of exempt approved schemes and only two major disadvantages:

(*a*) there is no longer power to diversify by adding new policies (but further premiums to existing policies can still be paid);
(*b*) pension cannot, except in cases of ill-health or professions with normal earlier retirement dates, be taken before age 60.

While such policies may be kept up no new policies have been permissible since July 1988 (when personal pension schemes became available—see para 9 below—but unlike these premiums to retirement annuity contracts are still not limited by an earnings cap). They were occasionally taken out for employees in non-pensionable employment. Their main function was to provide pensions for professional people—and, until 1973, for controlling directors who were not, until then, permitted to join the normal type of company scheme.

8 'Permanent health' schemes

The difference between pension schemes and permanent health schemes established by employers is that the former provide benefits for those who have left service (or reached normal retiring age) while the latter enable those who are absent through illness to be treated for remuneration purposes as continuing in employment. In other words the payment of salary or wages continues, in whole or in part, and either the employer is reimbursed by the insurer for the salary he pays out or the employee is paid from the scheme to recompense for lack of or abated salary.

Frequently such continued service counts towards pension, and in some cases the employee continues to contribute to the pension scheme.

Such arrangements are normally insured. Either way there is no tax relief on the investment income of the fund (if any) set aside to finance the scheme. Unlike ill-health pensions, they may reduce an employer's liability in industrial cases (see Chapter 10, para 9).

The main practical differences are:

(1) Pension schemes can only provide a large ill-health benefit if the member entered service sufficiently early in his career, for while the Inland Revenue permit potential service to be taken into account, the calculation can only start from the date that service with that employer (or an associated employer) began; by contrast the insurer of a 'permanent health' scheme will normally underwrite up to 75 per cent of the net salary.

(2) The medical assessment of a 'permanent health' scheme will be carried out by an independent doctor appointed by the insurer; this reduces the likelihood of argument, but on the other hand may be an embarrassment where an employer would like to favour a borderline case.

9 Personal pension schemes

9.1 Concept and tax reliefs

The modern concept of a personal pension scheme was introduced by the Social Security Act 1986 (now PSA 1993, ss 1, 7) which, in this respect, came into force on 6 April 1988. Such arrangements are particularly useful for an employee whose work is likely to last only a short period with each of his successive employers.

The provisions for Inland Revenue approval and tax relief on the scheme's investment income and members' contributions are set out in Income and Corporation Taxes Act 1988, Chap IV Pt XIV. The investment income exemption is to be found obscurely in s 643(2). The capital gains tax exemption is in s 271(1)(*h*) of the Taxation of Chargeable Gains Act 1992.

Unlike the old retirement annuity contracts that could be taken out by self-employed individuals or those in non-pensionable employment before 1988 (in some cases still being kept up), a personal pension scheme has a collective structure although for practical purposes the individual 'members' may be unaware of this, since the membership is simply the collection of all persons to whom the scheme has been sold. (There are also 'Group' personal pension schemes—see para 9.5 below).

The personal pension concept was created for two purposes:

(*a*) to provide a range of investment choice for individual retirement provision;
(*b*) to encourage contracting out of the State scheme (Chapter 20, paras 4 and 14) in order to reduce its long-term liabilities.

Despite (*a*) above the tax requirements limit providers to insurance companies, unit trust managers, building and friendly societies and banks.

Regarding (*b*) above, the attraction for members is the absence of a contribution requirement; they can accrue a personal pension without making any direct payment since the State will make the contribution if the member chooses to contract-out of the State scheme (see para 9.3 below).

Members may contribute to a personal pension scheme and obtain tax relief on up to 17.5 per cent of net relevant earnings (20 per cent at age 36 increasing to 40 per cent at age 61). As with occupational schemes there is a statutory cap on relevant earnings. Basic tax rate is received by the scheme and added to the investments; the individual obtains higher rate relief. An employer may also contribute (and will ordinarily obtain tax relief under the usual rules of Schedule D) albeit reducing the member's maximum correspondingly (s 640(4) of the 1988 Act). While a member of a contracted-in occupational scheme may simultaneously be a member of a contracted-out personal scheme for the purpose of receiving from the DSS minimum contributions only, no tax deductible contributions can be paid to a personal scheme out of his earnings from the pensionable employment unless the occupational scheme provides only death benefits (ss 644(3) and 645(1) of the 1988 Act).

Unlike the Social Security legislation, tax approval under the 1988 Act is not restricted to 'employed earners' and therefore is available to the self-employed (ss 630, 639 and 644).

The Inland Revenue's requirements are set out in their IR76 booklet, issued in 1988 and subsequently updated, available from the PSO. The Social Security requirements are set out in Memorandum

92 issued jointly by the SFO and the Occupational Pensions Board in January 1988 and subsequently updated.

A former member of an occupational scheme can take a transfer payment to a 'self-employed pension arrangement' approved under the legislation (Memorandum 92, para 491 together with para 12(*g*) which reproduces the definition in SI 1987 No 1112, reg 2A).

9.2 Differences from occupational pension schemes

The essential features distinguishing personal from occupational schemes are:

- (*a*) personal schemes are established by the provider, not by a member's employer;
- (*b*) membership is thus available to individuals without any link of common employment—the individuals tend to regard their own arrangement as a separate scheme;
- (*c*) there cannot be cross-subsidy between members so that benefits are invariably money-purchase rather than based on final salary (see para 1 above);
- (*d*) in practice the employer rarely contributes, except for group schemes (para 9.5 below), although highly mobile senior employees sometimes negotiate such contributions.
- (*e*) the member can choose a flat-rate pension or an increasing pension, whereas an occupational scheme has to provide that the pension accrued from or after 6 April 1997 increases annually at a certain rate—for the consequences, and also the exception, see below.

The definition 'personal pension scheme' in the PSA 1993, s 1, differs very little from the definition 'occupational pension scheme', the two differences being that there need not be a link with a particular employment and that benefits are payable 'on death or retirement' rather than also on termination of service. There is no definition of retirement. However, a member may choose any pension date between age 50 and 75, except for protected rights (see below) which cannot be taken earlier than age 60—PSA 1993, s 28(4).

The arrangement between the provider and the member may, as with an occupational scheme, be made under trust but may alternatively be contractual so long as protected rights (see below) are enforceable eg by spouses.

Insurance companies frequently issue clustered policies to enable parts of the benefit (apart from protected rights) to be taken at different ages and to take advantage of the rules relating to lump sums.

Paragraph (*e*) above mentions that personal pensions can generally be paid at a fixed rate whereas occupational pensions have to include provision for certain increases. The exception is that where a personal pension is contracted-out of the State scheme (see para 9.3 below) the resulting pension, or proportion, must increase at the same percentage rate as the retail prices index, up to 5 per cent (formerly 3 per cent) per annum; where the member or employer pays additional contributions, only the protected rights must be increased in this way (while the balance may be flat rate or increasing, as desired). In the case of an occupational scheme the whole pension accrued from or after 6 April 1997 must increase annually in line with the index, subject to a limit of 5 per cent per annum.

The effect is to make the occupational pension more expensive, and therefore of a lower initial amount, than a flat rate personal pension, for a given accumulated fund. When comparing value, the occupational pension may be better, but the member may prefer a flat rate amount.

9.3 Contracting out (protected rights)

Section 43 of the PSA 1993 provides for the Secretary of State to pay minimum contributions to an 'appropriate' scheme, ie a scheme that satisfies the requirements of s 9(5). Schemes are certified by the Secretary of State (through the Contributions Agency), under s 7, and must be governed by rules whereby, in broad terms, either the whole of the benefits or such parts, which, on a money purchase basis, are derived from 'minimum contributions' (known as 'protected rights'), are subject to detailed provisions specifying the date of commencement of benefit, commutation of small pension and details regarding a compulsory 50 per cent surviving spouse's benefit where the member dies in receipt of pension.

It should be stressed, however, that the certification gives no comfort as to the value of the benefits. These depend on investment return and expenses. The purpose of certification is to ensure that non-commutable pension (with spouse's pension) is payable from approximately the age when the State pension (reduced by the contracting out arrangement) is paid.

9.4 Contracting out (rebates)

If a personal pension scheme is contracted out of part of the State scheme, a partial rebate of national insurance contributions is paid by the Department of Social Security (DSS) directly to the trustees or managers of the scheme, as detailed below. The employee's share of the rebate is paid as a grossed up amount (s 649 of the 1988 Act). Additionally an *incentive* has until 5 April 1997 been paid to encourage contracting out.

During the five years from April 1988 to 1993 an additional 2 per cent of earnings between the lower and upper limits was paid (save where the individual was in certain circumstances formerly a member of a satisfactory contracted-out occupational scheme). From 6 April 1993 to 5 April 1997 the incentive was 1 per cent of that band of earnings and was limited to those aged 30 or over. The aggregate of the rebate and the incentive payments is defined as the 'minimum contributions'.

The 2 per cent incentive was also available to an occupational scheme which between 1 January 1986 and 5 April 1993 contracted out for the first time provided the relevant employments had not previously been contracted-out. The 1 per cent incentive did not apply to such schemes from 6 April 1993. Interested parties observed that, not having the incentive, occupational schemes were at a disadvantage in competing with personal schemes.

Apart from these incentives, the rebate of National Insurance contributions, paid directly by DSS to the personal pension scheme, was until 5 April 1997 at a single percentage rate of band earnings, regardless of the individual's age. In the four-year period to 1997 the rate was 5.8 per cent (ie 5.8 per cent for those aged 30 and over, effectively including the 1 per cent incentive mentioned above).

From 6 April 1997 the rebate is age-related, the same principle being simultaneously introduced for contracted-out *occupational money purchase* schemes (COMPs). The purpose is to minimise the likelihood of individuals contracting back into the State scheme on attaining age 40/45 when the flat-rate percentages would have become poor value by comparison with the earnings-related part of the State pension for which they substituted. Fixed percentages still apply to the reduction in National Insurance contributions for members of *salary-related occupational* schemes—Chapter 20, para 4.3).

For the five years to 5 April 2002 the rebate will start at 3.4 per cent of the relevant band of earnings for an individual aged 15, rising to 9 per cent at age 46 (and all ages through to 63). At the intermediate ages there are slight variations in each of the five years, so that 9 per cent is not reached in the last year until age 50 (SI 1996 No 1056).

The rebate to an occupational COMP scheme is almost identical, but slightly smaller by between 0.3 and 0.1 per cent until 9 per cent is reached initially at age 47, and in 2002 at age 50 (SI 1996 No 1055). The small difference is intended to cover the additional expenses of personal pension scheme providers, and also to reflect the investment advantage of COMPs mentioned below so that personal pension schemes should be competitive with COMPs.

The rebate is paid to the providers after the end of the relevant tax year. By contrast a COMP scheme has the investment advantage that part of the rebate is technically a reduction in the weekly (or monthly) national insurance contribution, and the employer is obliged to pay to the COMPs within 14 days of each pay period an equivalent amount. This reduction is a fixed percentage (starting at 3.1 per cent at age 15, allocated as to 1.6 per cent to the employee and 1.5 per cent to the employer). The *balance* of the age-related rebate is, as with personal pension schemes, paid by the DSS to the COMPs after the end of the tax year ie for a 15-year old the balance is zero and for a 50-year old it is 5.9 per cent of the relevant band of earnings.

9.5 Group personal pension schemes

The purpose of a Group personal pension scheme is to combine the attractive features of a personal pension with the lower expense-rates normally associated with occupational schemes. Technically the Group scheme is simply a collection of individual personal pension arrangements, but they are all taken out with a single provider on favourable terms to which the members have been introduced by a financial adviser under facilities made available by the members' employer.

There are several advantages to the employer, the importance depending upon their own priorities. Further, the introduction for *occupational* schemes of expensive and complex compliance with the Pensions Act 1995 offers a new incentive to establish Group personal schemes.

The main points are:

(*a*) low cost; the employer need not contribute at all, and obtains significant recognition for contributions that it does make;
(*b*) avoidance of fluctuating salary-related liabilities; for an *occupational* scheme this can also be obtained through a money purchase structure, and if contracted-out through a COMP, but see (*c*) below;
(*c*) unlike a COMP, the employer does not have to make a separate deduction from remuneration at each pay period;
(*d*) if contracted-out, there is no employer involvement in the collection of the rebate after the year end;
(*e*) portability; if an employee leaves service, his personal pension automatically travels with him; while the same effect can be obtained by a transfer from an *occupational* scheme, it necessitates the employee seeking a quotation from the scheme, and then obtaining advice regarding the available providers, and their different expense rates for individual policies;
(*f*) avoidance of Pensions Act 1995 requirements, eg the imposition on *occupational* schemes of member-nominated trustees, investment obligations upon the trustees (for whom the employer in effect provides professional support), the provision of expensive communication material, the funding of annual reports (either directly or through the contributions to the pension scheme) etc;
(*g*) indeed, the absence of Group trustees—reliance on the provider (which may or may not operate through a trust) in place of in-house support;
(*h*) no *regulatory* liability on employer for stolen assets.

The employer will have negotiated favourable terms with the provider of the Group personal pension scheme. Nonetheless, there are downsides, particularly the following:

(1) If the employer (as is usually the case) is to contribute too, the forms are lengthy.
(2) New members must be introduced through a person authorised under the Financial Services Act 1986; this must be arranged, and has a cost (usually met by the employer).
(3) Providers tend to offer a large range of funds, involving choice by the individual; investment allocation should be left to

experts, and while in practice very few members go outside the broadly managed fund, there is room for concern.

(4) The employer is in a difficult practical position if he becomes aware that the particular provider has ceased to deliver a good investment performance.

Group personal pension schemes are clearly useful for the small employer who may wish to make just a modest contribution to pensions, and wishes to minimise the chance of staff choosing a variety of providers, each with its own unfamiliar forms and procedures. Larger employers may be concerned at the practical difficulty of monitoring investment performance and changing investment managers. New products are addressing the latter question, with segregated investment managers. Sophisticated employers can probably combine Group schemes with separate provision of risk benefits (life cover and ill-health pensions). Group personal pension schemes are therefore likely to become increasingly popular. They cannot provide a salary-related benefit structure but, for money purchase provision, are already a competitive option to a money purchase occupational scheme.

A significant downside for all personal schemes, and for the larger employer particularly looking at a Group scheme, is the application of the accumulated fund to the purchase of an annuity at pension age. The cost of annuities is linked to Government-issued fixed interest stock and, if past experience is repeated, is a more expensive way of providing pension than payment from an equities-based investment fund. Personal pensions have begun to meet this criticism by 'income withdrawal' facilities. An *occupational* money purchase scheme faces the same difficulty unless it contains a reserve to meet fluctuations in investment returns and mortality. Effectively, therefore, new products are developing in both areas which make it increasingly difficult to generalise as to the future attractiveness of the alternatives, but it seems likely that Group personal pension schemes will become increasingly popular.

9.6 Comparison with alternatives

Comparisons may be made in three ways:

(*a*) if the member has chosen to contract out of the State scheme, the comparison is between the likely value of the protected rights (para 9.3 above) and the loss of State benefits;

(*b*) if the member could alternatively join his employer's scheme the outcome of the comparison between them will usually depend on whether the employer contributes significantly to the personal scheme; in only one case can he be a member of both, viz where the occupational scheme is contracted in and the personal scheme is joined for minimum contributions (ie just for contracting-out purposes);

(*c*) the particular personal pension scheme can of course be compared with other schemes on the market; assuming that all are designed for maximum flexibility this is a comparison of investment potential. (As to Group schemes, see para 9.5 above).

As to (*a*) above, it should be appreciated that the *amount* of the protected rights is entirely dependent upon the investment proceeds of the State rebate (para 9.4 above). There are likely to be general views expressed by independent financial advisers (IFAs) from time to time. Further, only an IFA can advise on the suitability of particular personal pension schemes, although the lawyer should be aware that the expenses (and commission) deducted from the contributions may vary substantially.

As to (*b*) above, at the time of writing it appears that few if any, of the larger employers having occupational schemes contribute to personal schemes (with the two categories of exception mentioned below). Therefore an occupational scheme is likely to be substantially better value to the member unless it requires an unusually high rate of contribution or the member is very young and expects to leave the job soon.

The broker or agent selling the personal scheme should have asked the potential member for a copy of the occupational scheme's booklet or the address at work where it could be obtained (the broker or agent's obligation arising under the Financial Services Act 1986, and the regulatory rules pursuant to it commonly cited as 'Know your client'). While there may be some areas where the occupational scheme could be improved, eg additional life cover, these can usually be arranged either by ordinary insurance or on a tax-advantageous basis by voluntary contributions; all occupational (and personal) schemes must include provision for such contributions to provide extra benefits (PSA 1993, s 111) and there are also available to occupational scheme members free-standing additional voluntary contribution schemes, commonly known as FSAVCs (see Chapter 17, para 11.2), marketed by a number of providers under the Finance (No 2) Act 1987 (now s 591 (2) (*h*) of ICTA 1988).

The two exceptions to the general refusal of employers to contribute are:

(*a*) where an individual who has been head hunted negotiates a specific arrangement or a continuation of an existing personal pension scheme;
(*b*) where a group personal pension scheme is promoted by an employer—see para 9.5 above.

In broad terms personal pension schemes have been a great success in reaching young members without occupational schemes who sought to contract-out of the State scheme when the (former) flat-rate rebate favoured their age group. On annual renewal members should check whether there may be reason to contract back in.

Schemes have also been a success in providing a replacement for the former retirement annuity contracts where individuals do not already have such policies which can be maintained. Those who do have such policies may find it advantageous to convert to personal pensions when their relevant earnings are unlikely to exceed the personal pension limit under s 640A of the 1988 Act (£84,000pa for the tax year 1997/8) as the permissible percentage contribution is likely to be substantially higher. However, specialist advice should be sought before conversion as there are also implications affecting the maximum part of the benefit that may be taken in lump sum form.

9.7 Misselling—SIB requirements

The scandal of missold personal pensions arose from a number of factors, but chiefly from two options introduced by statute with effect from 1987 and 1988 respectively. These were:

(*a*) the option to contract-out of the State pension through an individual insurance policy to which the *State* would contribute and which did not require *any* contributions from the individual (now PSA 1993, ss 7, 43—see paras 9.3 and 9.4 above);
(*b*) as part of the above option, the provision of a significant

additional incentive payment to contracted-out arrangements, (para 9.4 above);

(*c*) the option to leave, or not join, an occupational scheme, as *compulsory* membership was prohibited from 6 April 1988 (now PSA 1993, s 160).

There was a separate scandal regarding the success of (*b*) above, for the number who took up the individual contracting-out option was double the Government estimate, with a short-term cost running into several billion pounds to the national insurance fund. The incentive furthered Government policy to reduce the prospective cost in the 21st century of State pensions. Nonetheless the poor estimate, and the short-term poor value for this expenditure, was heavily criticised by the National Audit Office.

There were a number of other factors. Personal pensions had originally been proposed by Government supporters in 1984 as a means of enabling individuals to fund their own businesses. After a lengthy enquiry, the Minister adopted the concept of an individual personal portable pension, while restricting investments to the secure providers (banks, building societies, friendly societies, insurance companies). Nonetheless, the Government encouraged the development of personal pensions as a means to introduce competition into what was then regarded as a closed and uncompetitive industry. Government-sponsored advertisements encouraged individuals to free themselves from the restrictive membership of an occupational scheme. Possibly it was assumed that a significant number of employers would be willing to contribute to personal schemes, but in the event very few did (partly as it would have been administratively costly to contribute to a diverse number of arrangements, all requiring individual study).

Secondly, for totally different reasons the Government legislated in 1985 to enable occupational scheme members who left service to require a transfer of their cash equivalent to a scheme of a subsequent employer or to an individual insurance policy (Chapter 10, para 12). The coal-mining industry was contracting viciously, and the redundant miners were only too pleased for the opportunity to leave the pension scheme which was regarded as an employer's institution after the bitter strike of 1984. Possibly this feeling was increased by the loss by their trade union secretary, Arthur Scargill, of a Court action in which he, as a committee member of the pension fund, was prohibited from the social direction of its investments (Chapter 24, para

10). The miners lived in closed communities where insurance company agents found a ready hearing.

The Financial Services Act, introduced in 1986, required the sellers of investments to know their client. The Act surrounded the agents and brokers with an aura of independence, but the detailed requirements proved totally beyond the ability of a hastily trained workforce. Many did not ask for details of the alternative *occupational* scheme before selling a personal pension. The two chief areas of loss were:

(1) future accrual in an employer's scheme, by comparison with a personal scheme to which the employer did not contribute;
(2) transfer of accrued rights from an occupational scheme where the cash equivalent (in some cases) made no allowance for the value of annual discretionary awards to pensions in payment, whereas in practice these awards were frequently made; the transfer sum would, apart from the cost of the provider's expenses, purchase a similar initial pension but without the increases.

The scandal was investigated by the Securities and Investments Board (SIB) that produced in October 1994 a massive programme for review by personal pension providers of the sales that had taken place, primarily between 1988 and 1993.

The SIB review required that those cases of greatest short-term risk ie individuals who had already retired or were close to retirement, or had died leaving dependants, should be identified by the end of 1995, and action taken by the end of 1996. The requirements for review, established by SIB and implemented by the subordinate regulators, were too complex for this timetable to be achieved. Only a small proportion of cases had been reviewed by the end of 1996. Accordingly, SIB commissioned an actuarial study which indicated that far simpler procedures could 'dramatically reduce' the information needed for review, while statistically satisfying the main purposes of the enquiry. SIB announced simplified procedures in November 1996. The key purpose of the simplification was to enable information to be obtained quickly from the occupational schemes from which individuals had opted out or taken transfers. It remains to be seen whether the advisers regulated by the Personal Investment Authority will in fact cope with a significant proportion of the backlog during a reasonable period.

The purpose of the review is to seek reinstatement into

occupational schemes where it is available, and for the advisers or providers to compensate cases (no doubt the majority) where reinstatement is not available.

The effect of the misselling scandal was to damage the reputation of personal pensions, at the very time that the 'Maxwell' scandal was damaging the reputation of occupational pensions (Chapter 24, para 12).

It is likely that Group personal pensions will be unaffected by the misselling scandal as they have the support of the employers and are not seen as a product being 'pushed' by the providers. It is also likely that highly paid earners who seek their own personal pension arrangements will not associate these with the low-contribution products that were the primary subject of misselling. By contrast, the mass-market for the cheaper products has probably come to an end with the termination of flat-rate rebates for personal contracting-out, as these offered strikingly good value at the younger ages. Quite apart, therefore, from the lesson of experience, it seems unlikely that there will be a repeat of the scandal.

9.8 Scope of this book

It is not part of this book to advise on the financial comparison of the above alternatives. It is also beyond the scope of this book to guide the practitioner to establish personal schemes or FSAVCs, as existing providers will have done this and only a small number of new providers are likely to come to the market each year. However, the practitioner should be aware that insurance companies usually issue individual policies to members of a personal pension scheme but alternatively may issue a group policy to a trustee who then issues membership certificates. Either way, basic information must be supplied concerning the scheme at commencement of membership and about the individual's contributions annually; certain other information must be supplied on request (Personal Pension Schemes (Disclosure of Information) regulations 1987 (SI 1987 No 1110) as amended).

10 Unapproved schemes

10.1 General

Until the passage of the Finance Act 1989 there was a severe tax penalty for an employee with prospective pension rights that had not been submitted to the Inland Revenue for approval.

That Act:

(*a*) removed the tax penalty where the rights were unfunded;
(*b*) enabled unapproved schemes, whether funded or not, to lie on top of approved schemes (whereas previously this would have prejudiced the latter's approval); but
(*c*) prohibited approved schemes from pensioning (for new members) earnings above the first £60,000 per annum (now £84,000) known as the 'earnings cap'—see Chapter 17, para 3.

The purpose of the Finance Act 1989, regarding pensions, was to limit tax reliefs—(*c*) above.

The changes at (*a*) and (*b*) above enabled the 'capped' earner to receive top-up pension without penalising the basic provision. The practical effect was to give a choice of 'unapproved' top-up schemes, *viz* funded or unfunded, known colloquially as FURBs and UURBs.

10.2 FURBS and UURBS—tax differences

FURBS still carry the penalty that the member is taxed on the employer's contributions (albeit an emerging lump sum can then be tax free). The tax basis is described in Chapter 17, paras 3.3 and 4. It is also set out in detail in an Inland Revenue booklet published in August 1991 entitled 'The Tax Treatment of Top-Up Pension Schemes'.

10.3 Practical aspects

Unapproved schemes can take any convenient form. UURBs are usually contractual although trust schemes are sometimes established so that the employers' obligations to dependants of deceased members can be enforced by a trustee of the covenant. However, unlike FURBs, there is no security if the employer becomes insolvent. It is possible to provide security over existing assets without a tax charge (until the security is called) but this is rarely done and would pose a tax problem if assets were acquired for the purpose of giving such security. It is advisable to include, on the establishment of a trust scheme, a power of alteration and provision for novation if the business is sold or for some other reason the obligation is to be transferred.

FURBs are frequently established to provide insured lump sum death benefits. The employee pays tax on the (usually) modest premium but the emerging lump sum is free of income tax and, if arranged under trust or limited power of nomination, can be free of inheritance tax.

A FURB to provide retirement benefits will not be attractive to an employee unless accompanied by sufficient additional salary to meet, after tax on that salary, the tax on the employee arising from the employer's annual contribution to the scheme.

Some of the PSA 1993 and Pensions Act 1995 protections applicable to tax-exempt pension schemes will apply equally to unapproved schemes. For example the Department of Social Security has in the past expressed the view that an UURBs member has a right to transfer the cash equivalent to another scheme (Chapter 10, para 10) albeit there would be a heavy tax charge on the member if the employer made such a payment. Unapproved schemes have obvious drawbacks. Salient practical points are:

(*a*) FURBS entail an immediate tax charge on the employee (Chapter 17, para 4).

(*b*) UURBS offer no security; a young member may still be in receipt of benefits 50 years after the employment began, a spouse even longer;

(*c*) it may be difficult to keep the benefits identical with those payable from an approved scheme for pre-June 1989 members because of the different tax treatment of lump sums; further the question may arise whether the parallel should not be with the pre-17 March 1987 members, and in an executive scheme the difference could be significant;

(*d*) the unapproved scheme may give rise to a demand by some executives for additional remuneration equal to the cost of (and in substitution for) the funding or reserve for the accruing benefits;

(*e*) unless a recognisable scheme is established there is a danger of:
   (i) proliferation of non-standard letters of engagement;
   (ii) uncertainty whether a trust has been created for the current spouse (with potential problems of irrevocability in the case of divorce);
   (iii) equal uncertainty whether a surviving spouse has an enforceable claim, and concern either way whether such independent right would be desirable.

The questions under (*c*)–(*e*) can be met by the establishment of a uniform scheme for the employer, perhaps with eligibility at discretion. If desired the employer's covenants could be made with a trustee. Life cover could be limited to a panel of insurers with whom standard documents could be agreed. Funding would be a matter of choice (having regard to the tax issue); either way a reserve would be required under the accounting standard SSAP 24 (Chapter 16, para 11.4). The scheme could provide for the release of the employer's liability on the assumption of a parallel liability by another employer (albeit taking care to avoid the taxable payment of a 'transfer' sum).

Chapter 3

The first documents

1 Deadlines

1.1 First premium date

You will have seen from Chapter 1, para 2 that it is essential to establish the scheme by a particular date.

Most schemes that are brought to you in a rush will be insured schemes. The one case where you may have a little time to relax is an individual arrangement for a single employee that is secured by an insurance policy. However, current Revenue practice would need to be checked as the former practice is unknown to the PSO Enquiries desk. Formerly such an insured arrangement for a single employee could be recorded in an exchange of letters within a reasonable time after the establishment of the scheme so long as an application to the Revenue for approval was made within the fiscal year of establishment or, if later, within a six-month period of grace after establishment.

In all other cases, and perhaps even in the above case, the scheme should be established before the first contributions are paid by either the employer or the employee. Failure to do so may result in adverse tax consequences, as well as much correspondence. However, there may be a practical solution in respect of employees' contributions—see para 9 below.

1.2 Contracting-out notice

The second deadline relates only to schemes which are to be contracted out of the State scheme (see para 12 below). If the notice to employees of intention to contract out is submitted to you for consideration, remember that (except where the Contributions

Agency otherwise permit which they will only do in special, or certain specified, circumstances) the scheme cannot be contracted out until a little over one month (or three if there are recognised trade unions) from the issue of the notice and the effect of not being contracted out is to require from employees, as well as the employer, larger national insurance contributions. It is therefore essential to consider the notice without delay (but see below regarding retrospective effect). If the notice has expired, it is necessary to despatch the election to the Agency within the required period if payment of the reduced national insurance contributions is to be commenced on the due date. Fortunately a notice can specify a retrospective effective date which will then apply to the contracting-out certificate, once issued, provided the Agency consider it appropriate. (Chapter 20, para 4.4). Their published material, however, regards this as exceptional.

Trade unions recognised for collective bargaining must be consulted regarding the decision to contract out, albeit consultation often comprises a single exchange of letters (Chapter 15, para 4).

1.3 Contracted-in scheme

An employer establishing a contracted-in scheme no longer has to give employees and trustees specific notice of intention to abstain from contracting out. The basic information issued to members merely has to state that the employment is contracted-in.

1.4 Registration

It is the duty of the trustees to supply within three months of commencement of the scheme (or rather, of application to the Inland Revenue for approval) certain details to the Registrar of Pension Schemes (ie the Occupational Pensions Regulatory Authority—see Chapter 18).

2 Document establishing scheme

A list of the most common types of document used during the life of a scheme is set out in Chapter 14.

In order to obtain Revenue approval initially, many provisions will have to be included in the scheme, and they must apply to it as from the date of its establishment. The most common way of achieving this result is to set up the scheme by a relatively short document that incorporates power to tack on subsequently the other provisions with effect from the date of the initial document. Such an initial document is commonly known as an interim deed (or interim resolution etc). It will always refer to a separate announcement or booklet outlining the benefits (see para 10 below) or else set out the major benefits in a schedule.

3 Is it an interim document?

If the scheme is to be insured, you will usually receive draft documents (Chapter 1, paras 1 and 4). These are discussed more fully in para 13 below. The document is in an interim form if it provides for a definitive deed or rules to be executed or adopted at a later date. The normal provision is adoption within 24 months. The Revenue announced in August 1995 that they will normally treat this as a limit.

4 Is a deed necessary?

A deed has the practical advantages mentioned below but it is not a requirement for the purpose of obtaining Revenue approval. The Revenue requirement for exempt approval (which is statutory) is that the scheme must be established under irrevocable trust. Not too much hinges upon the word 'irrevocable' since it is permissible to include powers of alteration and winding up. The crucial word is 'trust'. If the terms of the arrangement are such that an employee's rights can be enforced only by an action in contract, the scheme is not acceptable (save in the exceptional circumstances referred to in Chapter 17, para 1.1(2). In other words, the employee must be a beneficiary under a trust.

A trust can, of course, be established orally. However, the declaration will have to be recorded in writing if it is to be approved by the Revenue. The normal method of establishing a scheme is therefore one of the following:

(*a*) interim trust deed;
(*b*) resolution of the board of directors (provided that it is within their power) or, in the case of a partnership, of the partners;

(*c*) in the case of a single employee, an exchange of letters incorporating the trust.

The likelihood is that the form favoured by the life office will be that of a deed. It has the necessary permanence and a formality that usually ensures that it is properly prepared and is not casually amended. It also offers a convenient format for setting out in a schedule to any deed of amendment the dates of all intermediate supplementary amendments.

5 Is it a deed?

Since the Law of Property (Miscellaneous Provisions) Act 1989, draft deeds usually contain the word 'deed' in the testatum. However, if the testatum is not included in the draft, it may be necessary to check whether the life office had sent the broker instructions for execution, assuming that the life office procedures are to be followed. It should be remembered, however, that it is not essential for the document to be in the form traditionally found where deeds are prepared by solicitors (so long as it complies with the Act). Equally, it does no harm to adapt the document to that form.

A witness is required to the execution of a deed by an individual.

The company's articles of association will indicate whether a seal is still required for execution of a deed. A very practical matter is to ascertain that the company seal is available. If not, establishment of the scheme by a board resolution may be the way out of the difficulty.

6 Who is your client?

The interim deed will contain important powers that may be vested either in the employer or in the trustees (or in the employer as trustee). See the following paragraphs but particularly para 21 below.

It is essential to know whether you are advising the employer or the trustees. Normally on the establishment of the scheme it will be the former as it will have initiated the provision of pensions, but occasionally it will be the trustees who (for example) have negotiated a successor to an existing scheme.

Standard drafts provided by a life office will necessarily strike a balance from that office's experience and therefore, regarding the distribution of powers between the employer and the trustees, will need discussion with the client (see also Chapter 24, para 9).

If the trustees are to receive copies of your advice, they will be in breach of the Pensions Act 1995 (s 47(3)(*a*)) if they rely upon it unless *they* appoint you to advise. There is no prohibition on a simultaneous appointment by employer and trustees, but both the Law Society and the regulations (SI 1996 No 1715, reg 5(2)) require you to notify the trustees of any conflict of interest. Ordinarily on the voluntary establishment of a scheme by the employer a conflict would not arise, but if the balance of power provisions (para 21 below) are not settled in advance by the employer as a condition of the creation of the scheme, they become an obvious source of conflict.

7 Trustees (and employee participation)

7.1 General

The draft will frequently reach you with instructions from the broker as to the initial trustees. Such instructions should be treated with caution. It is rare for the life office to make suggestions as to trusteeship. It is more likely that the broker will have had a brief discussion with the employer and accepted the first suggestion made by the employer. That suggestion will usually be a conservative one (such as solicitor or accountant and one other) but may not be the most practical for the subsequent administration of the scheme. See also para 7.5 below regarding legislative requirements.

It is probably wise for the initial trustees (or trustee directors) to be persons who can readily meet one another. It is certainly not wise to include the bank manager, since trusteeship entails obligations that do not fit readily with his occupation. If the solicitor or accountant is to be included, he should understand that, unlike private settlements of which he may be trustee, this particular trust will require attention to a regular flow of documents. There may also be a regular need for decisions, but this will depend upon the ages of the members (ie whether they are approaching retirement) and the nature of the investment. Legislation necessitates annual reports and other information (Chapter 16, para 6). Professional trustees should be offered a charging clause; there is much to be said for its inclusion anyway, subject to the consent of the employer to any actual payment.

7.2 Corporate trustee

Ideally a £100 company would be incorporated to act as trustee (Chapter 24, para 8) but the initial expense, including consideration of the articles of association, may rule out this course. It is rarely adopted for small insured schemes although it would provide greater constitutional permanence and provide a better platform for subsequent enlargement of the pension scheme. While the need for statutory books may be regarded as a disadvantage they would increase the likelihood that trustees (ie trustee directors) who cease to be connected with the employer would be replaced in good time.

7.3 Employer as trustee

It is common for the company itself to be the trustee, avoiding the need for succession if executives appointed as trustees leave the company. There is no inherent objection to this apart from the need to reassure members that the scheme funds (being held on trust) are not available to creditors of the company. On the whole, however, the obligations of trusteeship fall better on individuals or on a subsidiary company established for the purpose of being trustee. While an employer in receivership may be faced with a conflict of interest, and the position of a liquidator as regards trusteeship is uncertain, the Pensions Act 1995, ss 22–26, provides (as originally enacted in 1990) for the appointment additionally of an independent trustee in such circumstances to exercise all discretionary (fiduciary) powers and discharge the employer if it had been the sole trustee. See also Chapter 16, para 10, and Chapter 24.

7.4 Power to appoint and remove

It is generally prudent to retain in the employer power to appoint and remove trustees (but remember that if a corporate trustee is not appointed initially there may be technical difficulties in a subsequent appointment—see Chapter 24, para 8.4). Occasionally a conscious choice is made by the employer, as settlor, that the trustees should be self-perpetuating, either as individuals or as directors of a trustee company in which they hold the shares, in which event there will be no express power, but perhaps a reference to flag the statutory power (under the Trustee Act 1925) for them to appoint successors, plus the statutory procedure regarding member nominated trustees (para 7.5 below)

7.5 Member-nominated trustees—legislative choice

The Pensions Act 1995 requires the appointed trustees to arrange for at least one-third of their number subsequently to be member-nominated trustees (with a minimum of two where the scheme has 100 or more members) unless the employer obtains the members' approval to an alternative proposal (Chapter 24, para 7).

The appointed trustees have to follow the statutory procedure unless the employer gives them written notice within six months of the commencement of the pension scheme that it intends to propose alternative arrangements (SI 1996 No 1216, reg 7(2)(d)). There is no restriction on the alternative which could simply be that the first trustees continue and that the employer will appoint replacements if they cease to be trustees. However, the regulations contain detailed requirements for informing members of their entitlement to the member nominated route if they object to the employer's alternative (Chapter 24, para 7).

It is clearly essential to advise the employer *before* the establishment of the scheme that this question will shortly arise.

8 Limited forever to one insurance company?

Many life office drafts provide that the scheme assets shall be invested in a policy with that particular office. Such provisions should never be accepted. On the other hand, it might entail unnecessary aggravation to strike them out. A simple solution is to add to the end of the clause words such as 'or such other investment as authorised by clause . . . hereof as the trustees may from time to time decide'. One can then add a normal investment clause ('. . . in all respects as if the trustees were beneficially entitled thereto') and also include in it a general power to take out policies of assurance for the purpose of the scheme.

There is now a wide investment power under the Pensions Act 1995, s 34, but since statutory powers are modified or re-enacted from time to time this should be regarded as a supplement rather than an exclusive source in such a key area as investment.

9 Employee contributions

One attraction of approved pension schemes is that employees' permitted contributions are totally tax-deductible.

Except for the one case mentioned in 1.1 above, there will be no tax relief at all on contributions paid to the scheme before the trust is established. There is a limited way round this difficulty (as mentioned below) but it is essential to establish from the client when the first contributions will be paid by the employees if all difficulty is to be avoided. It is also not possible for a scheme that is to contract out (para 12 below) to obtain a certificate that predates the establishment of the scheme; thus the reduced rate of national insurance contribution will not be available.

A solution to the tax relief problem is to delay employee contributions until the scheme is established and then provide for the first contributions to be an amount calculated by reference back to that which would have been paid had the scheme been established at the earlier date; it is prudent to check that the Revenue will approve such a provision as they usually do if relating to the same fiscal year. It may then be practical to deduct employees' contributions from their remuneration, holding them as the employees' agent, with authority to pay them to the trustees when the scheme is established. Clearly, the employees' agreement is necessary. The PAYE paid in the early months will in effect be recovered in the month of payment.

Employees' contributions are limited to 15 per cent of remuneration (Chapter 17, para 3.1).

If the delay crosses a 5 April or the employer's year end it remains possible (for a contracted-in scheme) to adopt the above procedure (regarding member' contributions) but the accounting becomes difficult, particularly if tax rates change. In practice delay beyond a 5 April should be avoided.

Always ensure that all employees who are expected to contribute sign application forms authorising the deduction of their contributions directly by the employer from their remuneration and indicating their agreement to be bound by the trust deed and rules relating to the scheme.

10 Adequate reference to benefit outline—employee announcements

If the scheme is insured, you will be provided with a draft announcement to employees. You should also ask for a copy of the quotation given by the life office (Chapter 4, para 1). A simple check will reveal whether the two tie in with one another. Alternatively, ask for written confirmation that the benefits conferred by the outline are fully covered in the quotation (subject, in a final salary scheme, to stated assumptions regarding salary progression and scheme profits or yield). This will certainly have been the life office's intention but the outline may have been amended, in which case your enquiry will concentrate the minds of those who have amended it.

The announcement itself is referred to in para 11 below. It is fairly common for the interim deed or resolution to refer to the scheme 'details of which have been or will be announced in writing to those affected thereby'. This is useful emergency wording. It is preferable to annex a copy of the announcement and use words such as 'details of which are set out in the announcement a copy of which has been initialled by . . . for the purpose of identification and is annexed hereto'.

The importance of the announcement cannot be stressed too highly. In substance (even if not in form) it is part of the interim deed. It can also impose, quite independently, a contractual obligation upon the employer. It should therefore be clearly identified. By annexing it to the interim deed or resolution, subsequent uncertainty is avoided.

11 Points to watch in the employee announcements

The usual drafting techniques apply to an employee announcement as much as to any other document intended to confer legal entitlement. It must not be ambiguous (except perhaps where the actual benefit to be conferred is the more favourable of those implied by the ambiguity). It should indicate to whom (and by whom) it is addressed. It should bear a date or at least a reference to avoid doubt as to its identification subsequently (and the reference to it in the deed or resolution suggested in para 10 above could usefully include the words 'dated . . . 1997, reference . . .').

Where death benefits are insured, any restrictions on life cover pending medical examination should be mentioned. Even where not insured, the trustees may be advised to include or reserve the right to require medical examinations.

Above all, the anouncement should include references to the limitation of benefits to comply with Inland Revenue criteria for approval as an exempt approved scheme, the power of alteration, the power of termination, the constitution of the scheme and its trustees. Apart from these points, it is rarely wise to alter the life office draft.

The announcement (or any booklet to be issued to members shortly afterwards) should comply with the statutory disclosure requirements set out in Sched 1 to the Occupational Pension Schemes (Disclosure of Information) Regulations SI 1996 No 1655. The schedule sets out a list of points that are easily checked but if time is short it may be more practical to ask the broker to confirm that the anouncement and/or a follow-up will comply with the Disclosure Regulations. The regulations are not part of the tax legislation. They are enforceable by OPRA or, on a complaint, by the Pensions Ombudsman (Chapter 18). The PSA 1993, s 168 as amended, provides for penalties up to prescribed levels.

12 Where contracted out of the state scheme

Firstly, to clear one possible area of confusion, it should be explained that there have been two State pension schemes from which contracting out has been possible. Both have provided additional pension *on top of* the basic State pension. The first of these was the old State graduated scheme (Chapter 19) which closed to further contributions on 5 April 1975, and provided a tiny, additional pension. No new schemes now being established will (unless incorporating existing schemes and desiring to refer to the old arrangement) include contracting-out provisions relating to that old arrangement, but many existing schemes will still include reference to it.

The present state additional scheme began on 6 April 1978. It, and contracting-out arrangements, are described in Chapter 20, para 4 where it will be seen that they have been radically altered with effect from 6 April 1997. It is enough here to say that if a scheme provided 'guaranteed minimum pension' (GMP) or, from 6 April 1988, was in the alternative form known as COMP ('contracted-out money purchase') providing benefits in the form of 'protected rights', employment by reference to it could (if the employer so elected) be contracted out of part of the State scheme. From 6 April 1997 COMPs (ie the provision of 'protected rights') continue. However, for salary-related schemes the provision of GMPs has ceased (for future service) and is replaced by a requirement to meet an overall quality test known as a 'reference scheme'—but the latter is unlikely to require a specific reference in the documents, or at least the initial documents.

Contracting-out results in lower national insurance contributions by both the employer and the employee. The notice of intention to elect to contract out and the election itself are essential if a certificate is to be obtained. They are mentioned in para 1.2 above.

If a COMP is being established, the trust instrument must contain provisions specifying the 'protected rights' to be provided. If a draft has been supplied, it should be enough to enquire whether the contracting-out provisions conform with a standard issued or approved by the Contributions Agency. In 1997 this will still be in the form issued by the former Occupational Pensions Board (Chapter 18) whose Memorandum 93 set out their requirements and, in Appendix 1, their model rules.

13 Life office drafts approved by revenue

In most cases of insured schemes, a draft will be submitted by the life office. The draft will usually be in interim form. It is then possible to limit one's task to establishing from the insurer that the draft is based on a standard approved by the Inland Revenue for the purpose of exempt approval (and contains model rules if contracted out on a COMP basis—para 12 above) and to ensuring that:

- (*a*) it states that definitive documents will conform with Chapter I of Pt XIV of ICTA 1988 (as amended), the preservation requirements (see below) (and, if the scheme is to be contracted out, the matters mentioned in para 12 above);
- (*b*) it contains a suitable power of alteration (see para 15 below);
- (*c*) it contains some of or all the interim provisions referred to in paras 17–20 below giving particular consideration to winding-up (para 20);

(*d*) its provisions for balance of power have been discussed with the client (see para 21 below);
(*e*) it provides for the right persons to be trustees;
(*f*) it adequately refers to the announcement to employees; and
(*g*) it establishes an 'irrevocable trust' (see para 4 above).

Since the establishment of the scheme is usually required as a matter of urgency, it is prudent to make as few amendments as possible to the draft, subject to the above points and to the very important points mentioned in paras 8 and 16. Further, as the draft will normally have been approved by the Inland Revenue as a standard, the Life Office will require you, rather than themselves, to submit it to the Revenue if it departs too far from the original, even if the changes are not material to approval. Since an interim document is expanded at a later date, deletions are preferable to additions. However, if there is any possibility that such a deletion or alteration may affect any of the matters mentioned in (*a*) above, it would be wise to add a short clause enabling further amendments to be made with effect from the establishment of the scheme for the purpose of compliance with those requirements or else, if a general power of alteration is present (para 16) additional text such as '. . . and in particular (but without prejudice to the generality of the foregoing) for compliance with any of the purposes stated in . . . and . . . above'.

The requirements for preservation of benefits for early leavers are long and complex (Chapter 10, para 1). However, SI 1991 No 167, reg 27, provides that it is sufficient for an interim trust deed (or other interim instrument) to require the trustees to operate the scheme in accordance with the preservation requirements provided that members are notified of the general effect of the intended definitive provisions of the scheme ie that the announcement will refer to the qualifying conditions for preservation. The regulations have been further amended by SI 1996 No 2131 in a number of ways, including the deletion from reg 27 of the previous requirement for the OPB (now dissolved) to be satisfied in effect that the announcement is in order.

It is helpful to the life office to supply with the executed deed a copy of their draft on which your amendments are shown, since this will facilitate submission by them to the Inland Revenue (Chapter 13, paras 2 and 4).

14 Where no drafts supplied

If the scheme is to be insured, it is normal and reasonable to telephone the broker or insurer and state that it is general practice for the life office to supply drafts and enquire from him whether they are available. If you are informed that proposed standard draft rules are with the Inland Revenue for approval at that time, enquire whether a draft interim document approved as a standard by the Revenue is available. If it is not available, it is worth advising your client to reconsider the choice of life office. This is not simply because of the cost of your preparation of specimen documents. It is also because such documents may not be suited to the methods of administration intended to be adopted by the life office.

Further, the practice of supplying drafts is so common that a life office which does not do so may well be unfamiliar with all the other matters which commonly arise from time to time in the continuation of a scheme.

If the scheme is to be self-administered (ie not insured) you will have to prepare the first draft documents yourself (or, if you are the company secretary or accountant, bring in the solicitor to do so). There are various encyclopaedias of precedents for the use of the legal profession. Any of those published after the Finance Act 1970 came into force should include a precedent for an interim deed establishing the scheme, albeit to be updated to refer to Chapter I of Pt XIV of ICTA 1988. The precedent should, as a minimum, be checked for the matters listed in para 13 above. As Inland Revenue practice may have changed since the publication of the precedents, it would be prudent, if time permits, to submit the draft to the Revenue for approval. This is so even if an additional clause is included permitting subsequent alteration to meet Revenue approval, since there is always the danger that for some reason the Revenue will claim that a particular power cannot effectively (or at least, tax effectively) be exercised retrospectively. The draft should also state that the definitive rules will be in such form as to ensure compliance with preservation (Chapter 10, para 1).

Ideally the draft should flag a number of points in the Pensions Act 1995, by brief cross-references. However, since Part I of the Act (which contains the relevant provisions for drafting purposes) will anyway have overriding effect (s 117), this approach is not essential.

15 Power of alteration

It is essential to include a power of alteration in the document establishing the scheme, and if possible to ensure that the announcement to members mentions the power.

It may be said that the existence of the power will give rise to suspicion. This can be avoided by providing that the power can be exercised only by or with the consent of the trustees. The normal provision is 'by the Company with the consent of the Trustees'. In considering whether to consent, the trustees must act in a fiduciary manner. Failure by the trustees to act in the interests of the beneficiaries could result in an action for breach of trust.

Frequently, the draft will include a power of alteration but will limit it so that it cannot be exercised so as to affect 'accrued rights'. It is wise to remove all such hedges, for they can give rise to argument later (albeit see below regarding the Pensions Act 1995). A pension scheme has to run on for several generations and may have to be adapted to unforeseeable circumstances (mergers with other schemes, takeovers etc). It would be as well, on sweeping away any restrictions that are in the draft, to include a clause specifically enabling further amendments to be made with effect from the date of establishment of the scheme for the purposes mentioned at (a) of para 13 above.

The Pensions Act 1995, s 67, limits the power of alteration where accrued rights are affected. As this is an overriding qualification, and indeed may be altered by later statute, theoretically no action is required in the draft, but some practitioners may wish to flag the existence of this qualification with text such as '. . . subject to s 67 of the Pensions Act 1995 so long as it is in force'.

Finally, it is arguable that the power of substitution described in Chapter 13, para 3.16 must be set out or referred to in the interim document if it is to be used in connection with the power of alteration in the definitive deed, ie if a substituted company is to be able to exercise the power of alteration. Whether this is so may depend upon the manner in which the interim deed provides for the definitive deed; it is therefore safer to include it in the earlier deed.

16 Guarantee of solvency—to be avoided

If the scheme is of the final salary type (Chapter 8, para 1), and even occasionally with other types, the effect of inflation or adverse investment returns can be to require further injections of funds from time to time in respect of past pensionable service. For final salary schemes there are now two statutory requirements, although not quite a guarantee of full solvency. In some cases, a requisite payment could be beyond the financial capability of the employer. If the scheme incorporates a guarantee that the employer will pay such sums (or the balance of such sums) as are required to maintain the solvency of the scheme, the employer may be put into liquidation as a result of the commitment. The security which the commitment was intended to confer on the members would in fact be the cause of the termination of their jobs. There is also the problem that an express guarantee may not be drafted clearly.

It follows that express guarantees of solvency are to be avoided (but see below regarding the statutory guarantees). On the other hand it is normal for the employer to undertake to pay such contributions as the trustees on the advice of the actuary or life office may recommend. So long as there is an overriding provision for the employer to give notice terminating its liability to make further contributions, this is acceptable albeit some employers will insist on complete discretion as to their rate of contribution (but not, the Revenue will insist, to be greater than required for the solvency of the scheme).

If a scheme was contracted out before 6 April 1997, the employer could not avoid a guarantee of solvency in respect of certain 'guaranteed minimum pensions'.

The Social Security Act 1990 as amended, now the Pensions Act 1995, s 75, introduced (for salary-related schemes) with effect from 29 June 1992, an important but to some extent uncertain type of guarantee on employers. The guarantee (which does not apply to money-purchase schemes—but see below) is triggered by the winding up of the scheme or the liquidation (or bankruptcy) of the employer. The critical question will be the nature of the liabilities to be valued; by SI 1996 No 3128 the value of the liabilities is to be calculated by the actuary appointed for Pensions Act purposes by the trustees of the scheme in question in accordance with Guidance Note 19 issued by the Institute of Actuaries (revised edn effective 6 April 1997). By reg 2(2) any provision of the scheme which limits the amount of its liabilities by reference to the amount of its assets is to be disregarded.

Although the deficiency provisions do not apply to a money purchase scheme, an employer may still be liable to make good losses to such a scheme arising through fraud or theft—Pensions Act 1995, s 89(2) which provides for regulations to apply all or any part of the general deficiency obligations, with modifications.

The employer's contribution rate to a defined benefit scheme is now governed by a statutory schedule of contributions which aims to keep the fund at (or bring it to) a statutory funding level. This is not a guarantee that scheme benefits can actually be purchased from insurance companies on winding-up, but nonetheless is an important test. The contribution obligation is called the minimum funding requirement (MFR), and is more fully described in Chapter 16, para 17.

17 Interim powers

Although the interim document will provide that the definitive document, when executed, will relate back to the date of establishment of the scheme, it is clearly undesirable for there to be no guidance during the interim period as to day-to-day matters that will arise. It is a question of preference as to the amount of detail that should be set out in the interim document. It should at least include the powers of investment, alteration (preferably including substitution), appointment of new trustees and (if appropriate) delegation. Consideration should also be given to the matters in paras 18–21 below. It is helpful, both for administration purposes and for the avoidance of inheritance tax, if the initial document also sets out the death benefit trusts (see Chapter 13, para 4.7).

18 Trustee liability insurance

It is not common for trustees initially to seek liability insurance (Chapter 24, para 11) as, save on the reconstruction of an existing scheme, there will be no fund or accrued liabilities at that stage. There may, however, be a claim in connection with the alleged wrongful distribution of an insured death benefit or other contingent liability for which indemnity insurance is sought. More importantly, it may be argued that the trustees should not, by a later alteration, benefit themselves by inserting power to pay liability insurance premiums from trust funds; it is therefore useful to incorporate the power in the interim deed even if no insurance is sought (or available at reasonable rates) at that stage. In case a question of public policy arises, it would be preferable for this to be expressed as power to insure against loss to the trust fund by reason of breach of trust (or default of agents) with additional words authorising such insurance to include indemnity to the trustees for personal liability for breach of trust. Some insurers split the premium, attributing a very small proportion to the personal indemnity, the latter being paid by the employer.

19 Refunds to the employer

As the method of funding a final salary type of scheme necessarily results in a surplus or prospective deficit on each valuation (assuming the current rate of contribution) the Inland Revenue permit refunds to the employer. There must be a substantial surplus, and the refund is subject to 40 per cent tax (which is not offset by trading losses). The governing provisions are to be found in ICTA 1988, ss 601–603, regulations made thereunder and the Inland Revenue's Memoranda 82 and 86.

Refunds, however, require authorisation by the trust instrument. If the power is added by an alteration the trustees are likely to require improvements to the pension scheme in order that the overall package be in the interests of beneficiaries. An employer may therefore wish, on establishing a scheme, to include provision for refund should a subsequent valuation show a surplus (if the approval of the scheme would not be prejudiced and the employer directs that there be a refund).

If a scheme is to receive a transfer payment containing a surplus arising from the earlier scheme the transferring trustees may require limitations on the exercise of the refund power.

The Pensions Act 1995 provides by ss 37, 76 and 77 that no refund can be made from a salary-linked scheme unless provision is made for pensions in payment (and future pensions) to receive certain annual increases. Section 37(2) also provides that where the power to make a payment to the employer is conferred on anyone other than the trustees, it may nonetheless only be exercised by the trustees (subject to any restriction imposed by the scheme itself under its original power). All three sections also contain other requirements for notification, and in some circumstances the involvement of OPRA. However, for newly established schemes the basic requirement to make provision for pension increases will not be a particular hurdle unless there has been a transfer relating to accrued rights in an earlier scheme, since all accruals from 6 April 1997 must, anyway, provide for such increases.

20 Winding up (and sale of subsidiaries)

Traditionally interim deeds did not set out the winding-up provisions. They simply stated that the definitive deed should provide for winding-up. In the light of numerous recent cases that have reached the courts where application of surplus is disputed, it is now essential to spell out the winding-up provisions in the interim deed (of a salary-related scheme) unless:

(*a*) instructions have been obtained that the definitive deed is to be prepared forthwith thereafter;
(*b*) there is no contemplation of receipt in the short term of a substantial transfer payment, and
(*c*) the rate of funding is considered by the actuary unlikely (on a winding-up in the interim) to throw up a surplus sufficient to meet the requirements for increases referred to in para 19 above.

If time is short this will be a difficult provision on which to obtain adequate instructions. Some of the factors on which to advise are:

(1) A discretion to the employer can always be reversed at the definitive stage, if the directors have good reason, whereas a discretion to the trustee cannot (without good reason or a benefit improvement, or perhaps the application of a reserved power to the employer).
(2) The Board of the employer company must consider the provision to be in the company's interest.
(3) A final salary scheme is usually funded to include a 'salary reserve', ie an allowance for the effect of future salary increases on accrued pension; this becomes surplus on an unexpected winding up (and may or may not be absorbed by the expenses and annuity rates at winding-up). A compromise may be to permit the application of surplus to increase prospective pensions in line with the retail prices index during the period from winding up to the commencement of pension—at present

there is a statutory requirement for such increases (before making a refund to the employer) but only up to 5 per cent per annum. Such application of surplus should not be drawn so as to create a potential debt on the employer under the Pensions Act 1995, s 75 or regulations made under its predesessor, in the event that assets are not sufficient for full index-linking (a drafting trap that needs care to be avoided).

Where the scheme is arranged with an insurance company and the draft interim deed is silent on the above points the insurer can be asked for a specimen definitive deed so that the winding up clause can be studied and, if appropriate, extracted for use (with modifications) at the interim stage.

Similar questions arise on the sale of a subsidiary (after the establishment of the scheme by interim deed) where a purchaser may expect a transfer payment that includes a share of surplus. It is recommended that in the absence of detailed discussion with the client, the interim deed provides that (save with the principal employer's consent) the transfer payment be limited to the minimum cash equivalent—see also Chapter 13, para 3.15).

21 Balance of power

A funded pension scheme necessarily contains a number of powers to decide upon the assets to be applied in a given situation. In each case the key question is whether the power lies with the company in its own interests, or with the trustees.

There may be intermediate positions providing for consultation, or for advice (or objective guidance) from the actuary, but the actual power has to be vested one way or the other. In some situations it can be exercisable jointly but not where a decision must (as opposed to 'may') be taken.

An essential task in advising on the scheme documents is to identify and seek instructions on these points. Outstanding examples are:

(*a*) assessment of employer's contribution rate (subject to the MFR mentioned in para 16 above);
(*b*) discretionary increase in, or award of, benefits;
(*c*) split of fund on withdrawal (or sale) of a subsidiary;

(*d*) application of surplus revealed on a valuation (a provision that can be omitted if (*a*) above is sufficiently flexible); but see para 19 above;
(*e*) application of surplus on winding up the scheme, and conversely whether, apart from statutory requirements, the employer has an obligation to make up a deficit;
(*f*) the power of alteration, as it enables the above powers to be varied;
(*g*) the power to appoint (and perhaps remove) trustees, as it might be used to appoint more compliant trustees or remove obstructive trustees; while this has always been held to be a fiduciary power nonetheless it can be of importance in any restructuring or to give effect to an agreement, eg with members or trade unions.

Numerous other powers will have a cost implication, for example the power (if present) to increase the accrued pension on ill-health retirement.

The power of delegation brings with it the power to appoint an investment manager. For a scheme that is not managed by an insurance company it may be appropriate that exercise of this power require the consent of the sponsoring employer. This provision for consent does not appear to be restricted by the Pensions Act 1995 s 34(2) nor by s 47(2), but the latter is subject to s 47(8) which will require consideration (and which, at the time of writing, necessarily has not been the subject of judicial construction).

Some of these powers will be left to the definitive deed but agreement on them may be advisable at the interim stage.

At para 3 above it is mentioned that the definitive deed is normally to be adopted within 24 months. An important choice is whether its terms are to be decided exclusively by the employer or jointly by the employer and the trustees. Since the terms must be consistent with the interim deed, subject to any agreed alteration, the question may be less important if much of the detail is included at the interim stage.

The Board of the employer company cannot lightly vest these powers in the trustees. However, where there is employee concern over the security of pensions or other appropriate reason it may be proper to do so, to a greater or lesser extent (see also Chapter 11, para 14).

Chapter 4

The insurance policy

1 Have you been shown the quotation?

The quotation (including the proposal to which it relates) is the most important document vis-à-vis the insurer until the policy itself is in an agreed form. The quotation forms the basis on which the insurer is underwriting the benefits.

If the insurer subsequently issues a policy, without having agreed it in draft, that conflicts with the quotation or contains additional restrictions, the trustees can (and should) point to the quotation in seeking an amendment to the policy. The policy will rarely emerge until the definitive documents relating to the scheme have been executed. It has already been stated (Chapter 3, para 10) that the benefits announced to employees must tie in with the quotation. If, exceptionally, they do not do so no harm will result if the employer and the trustees appreciate that part of the benefit is uninsured and make arrangements to enable it to be provided (but this may inadvertantly import a requirement to meet a minimum funding requirement under the Pensions Act 1995).

2 Surrender values

There are several reasons why it may be desirable to surrender a policy at a future date. The most obvious is if the scheme grows to such a size that the decision is taken to cease insurance.

Some policies contain provision for surrender. Some provisions are eminently reasonable; others may appear penal. One should therefore ask the client if consideration has been given to the question.

3 'Free' life cover

Most schemes provide benefits on death in service. The level of benefit that is provided before a medical examination of an employee is required varies from scheme to scheme. It is wise to find out the practice of the insurer and, if relevant, include a caveat in the employee announcement.

4 Cover while waiting for medical examination?

It is also wise to establish whether the insurer is on risk during the period that an employee is waiting for the medical examination.

5 With profits?

Where a scheme is invested through an insurance policy, apart from the important details two broad questions arise:

(*a*) the nature of the investment; and
(*b*) the nature of the benefits.

The two may be inter-woven, for the policy may be intended to provide precise levels of annuity benefit. Alternatively, it may simply be a form of investment, linked to the value of a type of portfolio, or possibly may offer relatively small guaranteed accrual, with bonuses estimated to enable larger benefits to be paid.

The investment may provide a pool of assets from which sums are allocated for annuities as members approach retirement age.

Regarding (*b*) above, the policy and the announcements must be clear whether pensions depend upon the investment proceeds ('money purchase') or comprise 'defined benefits'. In the latter case, a shortfall on estimates will be made up to, or at least targeted towards, the level of the Minimum Funding Requirement (MFR) by the employer at regular contribution reviews, probably entailing a significant administrative charge by the insurance company. The point should be checked in case a caveat is needed in the employee announcement. Until the Pensions Act 1995, a mere obligation to make up a shortfall on a winding-up could lead to disappointment if the employer was then insolvent, and even now the point may not be clear if a money purchase scheme aims at a target pension.

6 The nature of the insured risk

The crucial question to establish for a client is whether the liability ends when the premium is paid, ie whether all the liabilities under the scheme will be met by the insurer for a given level of contributions. Usually death-in-service lump sums (and sometimes enhanced widows' benefits) are fully insured. The amount of the fund from which members' pensions are paid normally depends on the investment performance of the insurance company's underlying assets. With older schemes, where the pension benefit was dependent upon the number of years at a given salary level (ie an average salary type of scheme—see Chapter 8, para 5) it was common to establish a precise level of contribution guaranteed to produce the required benefit. Similar security for the employer is available from a 'money purchase' type of scheme, where the benefit itself depends precisely upon what the policy produces (Chapter 8, para 6).

However, a final salary type of scheme (Chapter 8, para 1) will never give the employer the same comfort. The solicitor or client should establish what salary increases and what rates of return on investments have been assumed in the contribution level set by the insurer. The client, with the help of an authorised adviser, is then able to judge more clearly the nature of his commitment. Substantial rises in percentage contribution rates may occur where salary increases are granted towards the end of an employee's working life. On the other hand, after a period of inflation the benefits from an average salary or money purchase scheme may be woefully inadequate, leaving a moral commitment on the employer to supplement them. These matters are more fully considered in Chapter 8.

Chapter 5

Subsidiary and associated companies participating in the scheme

1 Participation

1.1 General

The Inland Revenue will always allow a UK subsidiary company to participate in the scheme in respect of its employees. They will also often allow associated companies to participate. A telephone call will usually indicate whether or not participation is likely to be allowed.

Participation means the admission to membership of employees of companies other than the principal employer, generally those within the same group. Where there are participating employers, the Inland Revenue refer to such schemes as 'centralised schemes' (see their Practice Notes, para 21.1).

1.2 Insurance company draft

Frequently, the life office draft for the interim document establishing the scheme will provide for all the intended participating companies to be parties to the document. There is no requirement for this whatever. If it proves inconvenient, it is perfectly in order to delete the participating companies from the parties and to make the consequential changes throughout the document. Either way, it may well prove highly inconvenient (and in some cases inadvisable, for example if a disposal may occur) if the subsidiary and associated companies are required to be parties to the definitive documents and to alterations to the scheme.

It remains essential to ascertain, either immediately or in due course, which companies will participate in the scheme. The purpose of the life office draft in the form mentioned above would be to focus attention on the question at the outset. The alternative is the widespread use of separate documents to adhere the subsidiaries (Chapter 14 para 3).

1.3 Inland Revenue

Although the Revenue will insist on the document establishing the scheme being executed by the date of the scheme's commencement, they do not normally object to the execution at a later date of a document by which a subsidiary participates in the scheme, even though the covenant in it by which the subsidiary undertakes to contribute to the scheme is stated to have effect as from a date earlier than that of execution (but not preceding the commencement of the scheme). It is preferable not to deal with subsidiaries in this retrospective fashion, but the ability to do so will often enable the interim document establishing the scheme to proceed more quickly. If the retrospection runs into a preceding chargeable accounting period, difficulties can arise, but the Revenue will usually permit these to be overcome.

1.4 Contracting out

If the scheme is to be contracted out, it is essential that all the participating companies be mentioned on the holding company's notice (or issue notices of their own) and that it can be demonstrated that their participation in the scheme is legally binding (Chapter 20, para 7).

2 Cessation

2.1 General

Participation may end on a date to be specified, eg the expiry of a notice by the participating employer or, unusually, a date specified in the originating document of participation.

2.2 Sale of subsidiary or business

Where a subsidiary is sold, the Revenue will permit continued participation (at least for existing members, and sometimes also for new employees) for a period of 12 months or until the next 5 April beyond that period. If a business is sold, the purchaser may participate for a similar period in respect of the transferred employees; here the participating document may well specify the expiry date.

The trust deed may specify that an agreement to extended participation after a sale is required between the former subsidiary and the trustees (perhaps with the consent of the original holding company); alternatively it may simply permit continuation. Either way, the date of eventual cessation (which may be capable of alteration) is rarely adequately minuted or documented.

While there is advantage in leaving the date open (or capable of alteration) it is advisable to document the date in due course, and to provide a mechanism for closing it off.

2.3 Transfer payment

The purchaser of a subsidiary may seek a transfer payment that includes a share of surplus or ignores a deficit. These are matters for the commercial agreement. The position under the scheme documents is considered in Chapter 13, para 3.15. It is essential that they provide sufficient flexibility to cover a range of possible commercial agreements and that the trustees, if their consent is required, agree or ratify the commercial arrangements.

Chapter 6

Partnership

1 The employer

A trading partnership cannot establish an exempt approved scheme for the benefit of the partners (Chapter 2, para 7) but can do so for its employees. In this case the 'employer' consists of the profit-sharing partners. Salaried (ie employed) partners are in an anomalous position. So far as the outside world is concerned the firm's notepaper sets out the names of all partners, no distinction being drawn between those who share profits or losses (and are truly the proprietors) and those who are employed on a salary, whether with or without bonus. An employed partner who is assessed to income tax under Schedule E is, in the eyes of the Revenue, an employee. As such he would be permitted membership of the scheme. It sometimes happens that a 'salaried partner' is remunerated by way of a fixed amount of the profits (subject for example to a bonus) on which he is assessed to income tax under Schedule D. Such a partner would not be permitted to join his firm's pension scheme. In some such cases the Revenue will assess under Schedule D, in others under Schedule E. It is the taxation status of a partner which renders him eligible or ineligible for membership of the pension scheme; his status for national insurance purposes—which is not always consistent with his status for tax purposes—is irrelevant.

2 The trustee

If partners are establishing a scheme for the benefit of their staff the choice of a trustee is important, particularly since the constitution of a partnership can change radically over the space of a few years. If the partnership operates its own trustee or service company it is probably convenient to make that company the sole trustee of the scheme (Chapter 24, para 8). In the case of the service company the memorandum of association should be considered and if necessary altered so as to ensure that the company has power to act as trustee.

3 The effect of the partnership deed

The interim trust deed of the pension scheme can be executed for the employer by one partner if he is specifically authorised or is authorised by the terms of the partnership. It is generally advisable for the partners to minute their approval of the pension scheme deed or for them all to execute it. This has the merit of bringing home to each partner that the establishment of a scheme is a personal commitment to financial outlay, particularly if the scheme is to be contracted out (see para 4 below). In addition the form of the partnership deed may require consideration so as to ensure that contributions to the pension scheme constitute a deduction against gross profits before net profits are distributed to partners. Provision should be made both in the pension scheme deed and the partnership deed for an incoming equity partner to contribute to the scheme in his capacity as an employer, and for an outgoing partner to be released (if appropriate) from his liability. It may well be advisable for a valuation to be made or estimated on the accession or retirement of a partner, on the lines adopted for leasehold liabilities.

4 Contracting out

If it is intended that the firm's scheme should be contracted out (other than by money purchase), and generally if the benefits are of the final salary type the partners must bear in mind that, in their capacity as employers, they underwrite the solvency of the scheme. For schemes contracted out before 6 April 1997 there are specific guaranteed minimum benefits (Chapter 20, para 4). Liability in respect of a period when a person was a partner may not (vis-à-vis the employee) be discharged by retirement from the partnership.

5 Service company

If the partnership operates a service company which employs some of the staff, that company can adhere to the pension scheme. It is sometimes suggested that profit-sharing partners (who are debarred from scheme membership in their capacity as partners) can become members by virtue of their directorships of the service company. However, the Revenue have indicated that if a full-time working partner draws director's fees from a service company, they would normally not permit his 'pensionable salary' to exceed a nominal figure of some £250 per annum (as to Revenue discretion, see Chapter 17, para 3). It might perhaps be otherwise if the director could demonstrate that a large proportion of his working time was spent as a director rather than as a partner.

Nevertheless it may be possible to restructure the business of the firm and provide a worthwhile level of pensionable salary from the service company (see para 7 below). The question became less significant following the relaxation (progressively from 1976 to or about 1980) of contribution limits to retirement annuity contracts, and for newer partners the earnings cap is the same for personal and occupational pension schemes (although benefit limits are different). See also para 6 below.

6 The salaried alternative

A profit-sharing partner in his mid-fifties might become an employed partner with a normal retiring age some years thereafter. He could then receive a pension based on one-thirtieth per annum (of Schedule E employment) of his final remuneration (Chapter 17, para 3). It may be argued that if he remains a profit sharing partner he could after retirement receive a pension out of current profits. However, there would be little security for this pension, while if he had become a salaried partner taxed under Schedule E, the pension could have been funded in advance.

By contrast the presently available methods of funding a pension in advance for a profit-sharing partner, on a fully tax deductible basis, involve personal pension contributions (or continuation of pre-1987 retirement annuity contracts) made by the partner himself (and limited in their contribution rates—see Chapter 2, para 7). Less efficiently, there may be old endowment policies.

The decision to 'step down' from profit-sharing to salaried partner is a personal and commercial decision for the individual and his partners. It is also affected by the 'pensionable earnings cap' introduced by the Finance Act 1989 which leaves some partners with the ability to keep up existing retirement annuity policies unaffected by the cap.

Whether as a partner or an employee an unfunded pension may be a solution, albeit lacking in security and subject to arrangements between incoming and outgoing partners from time to time.

7 Conversion of partnership to company

If a firm is converted to a limited or unlimited company special considerations apply. It is prudent to seek the advice of the PSO before taking any irrevocable steps but in general:

(1) Employees of the firm who become employees of the company may aggregate both periods of service for the purpose of determining 'pensionable service'.

(2) Salaried partners who have been assessed to income tax under Schedule E and who become employees or directors of the company may do the same.

(3) Profit-sharing partners—or any salaried partner who has been assessed to income tax under Schedule D during his period of partnership—cannot aggregate time spent as a partner with pensionable service as a director or employee of the company. On the other hand a relaxation introduced by the PSO Memorandum 108 (para 12) excludes partnership annuities from retained benefits, thus increasing the permitted pension from the later period—it is assumed that this relates to annuities and prospective annuities that are a liability of the former partnership and that insured retirement annuity contracts, mentioned in (4) below, must still be referred to the PSO for a ruling.

(4) 'Retained benefits' arising from premiums paid to approved retirement annuity contracts may have to be considered, although a distinction should be drawn between those paid in relation to a period of receipt of Schedule E salary (which can rank as pensionable service and may enable a larger overall pension to be paid) and those paid in relation to a period which cannot be aggregated with pensionable service.

Chapter 7

Foreign element

1 Scope

In this chapter the term 'foreign employer' means one who is not treated as resident for tax purposes in the United Kingdom. To the extent that any trading profits are liable to UK tax they arise through the medium of a branch or agency in this country.

A 'UK employee' is one whose earnings are chargeable to UK tax under Case I or Case II of Schedule E but excluding earnings in respect of which a 100 per cent deduction is allowable under s 193, ICTA 1988.

A large number of permutations can arise in respect of foreign employers, UK employees, foreign employees etc. Excluding multinational companies, the problems most likely to be faced in practice relate to:

(*a*) a foreign employer setting up a scheme in the United Kingdom;
(*b*) a foreign employer that includes UK employees in its foreign scheme;
(*c*) an employee who is a member of an approved UK scheme and works overseas either temporarily or on secondment;
(*d*) a UK employee with some emoluments from an overseas subsidiary of a UK employer.

These four aspects are looked at in paras 2–5 below.

This chapter is not intended to cover the even more specialised topic of transfers to overseas schemes. The reader is, however, referred to paras 10.35–10.36, and Appendix VI, of the Inland Revenue's practice notes IR 12 (1991) 2nd edn 1995 but subsequently updated by looseleaf inserts specifically referable to part 15 dealing with foreign element.

Few source references have been given in this chapter. The relevant law is primarily to be found in s 591(2)(*f*) of ICTA 1988. The whole of s 591 is set out in Chapter 17, para 3. It will be seen that the section confers a wide discretion on the Inland Revenue's current practice as set out in part 15 of the above IR 12 or indicated (as generally applicable) in cases referred to the Revenue by the author. The practitioner is advised to refer to the Revenue unless the particular case falls squarely within part 15.

2 Foreign employer with UK scheme

There is no objection to a foreign employer establishing a scheme in the normal way under irrevocable trust (see Chapter 17). Where membership is restricted to UK employees (as defined in 1 above and thus including persons working overseas but chargeable to UK tax because the overseas work is less than 365 days in any year) and a majority of the trustees are resident in the United Kingdom no special provisions apply; the employees will normally be working at a UK branch. If membership is open to employees not chargable to UK tax under Case I or II of Schedule E, the arrangement will be treated as two schemes (as mentioned in para 3.1 below), the proportion relating to taxable employees being calculated actuarially for the purpose of tax relief on the investments. Where the trustees are non-UK resident the same practical result can be achieved—see para 3 below. In effect only paras 3.3–3.5 are special to non-UK schemes.

The following requirements need consideration.

2.1 Administrator

The administrator (Chapter 17, para 1.4) of the scheme must be a person resident in the United Kingdom, or else there must be a person so resident who is responsible for his duties—para 15.4 of IR 12 (see also para 2.4 below). Where the UK resident trustees are the administrators no question arises. Where the overseas employer is the administrator a UK resident must be appointed to act for it. If the administrator or such person defaults, dies or disappears, the UK branch or agent becomes responsible for the duties of the administrator. In practice the Revenue will normally accept one of the professional advisers to the scheme as administrator, provided that he is resident in the United Kingdom. Regarding an indemnity, see para 3.2 below.

2.2 Trustees

Since this heading relates to UK schemes a majority of the trustees will be resident in the United Kingdom, thus confirming that the scheme is a UK scheme for tax purposes. The residence of the trustees may also be relevant to the enforceability of the overriding liabilities regarding revaluation, transfers and disclosure see para 3.5 below.

2.3 'Earnings cap'

The important limitation on pensionable earnings described in Chapter 17, para 3 applies to new members of an employer's UK approved scheme ie persons who join on or after 1 June 1989. It will therefore be helpful for a high earner (who is non-domiciled but comes to the UK) to remain in the foreign employer's overseas scheme provided that the Revenue will treat it as 'correspondingly approved' (see para 3.4 below) which at present they are prepared to do even though it contains no equivalent of the earnings cap. (On the other hand where remuneration is higher than the cap it appears that tax relief for employees' contributions may be limited to 15 per cent of the cap).

The foregoing does not assist a member of an Irish scheme (employed by an Irish employer) who moves to the UK because his emoluments cannot be 'foreign emoluments' within s 192(1) (which specifically excludes emoluments from an Irish-resident employer) and therefore the scheme cannot fall within s 596(2)(*b*) ('corresponding approval'). Prior to 6 April 1994, the Irish and UK Revenues operated reciprocal arrangements under which (broadly) the UK Revenue would treat as approved in the UK that part of an Irish approved Scheme which related to employees working and tax-resident in the UK. The Irish Revenue would extend the same treatment in reverse to UK Schemes. The reciprocal arrangements ceased to operate from 6 April 1994, but Schemes which were approved under those arrangements before then continue to have the benefit of that approval.

The reciprocal arrangements have been replaced by a new Article inserted into the Double Taxation Treaty between the UK and Ireland under a Protocol of 7 November 1994. In broad terms, the effect of the protocol is that a UK employee of a UK employer who is sent to work in the Republic of Ireland for the same or an associated employer may retain membership of the UK Scheme for up to 10 years (if working in the UK before being sent to Ireland) or up to 5 years (if working in a third country before being sent to Ireland). The UK Revenue have made it clear that the requirements referred to in para 4.1 below must also be met. The same treatment applies in reverse for Irish employees of Irish employers who are sent to work in the UK, except that the Irish Revenue's own requirements about (essentially) the retention of a connection with the Republic of Ireland are somewhat differently framed.

2.4 UK representative

If the scheme is to be contracted out under the State pension scheme (see Chapter 20, para 4) a 'UK administrator/representative' will be required (see para 3.2 below). The Contributions Agency should be consulted.

2.5 Foreign law

Confirmation should be sought (perhaps from the foreign employer's overseas lawyers) that the employer is empowered by its country or state of incorporation to establish a pension scheme for UK employees. The formal requirements for executing documents may differ from those laid upon a UK company. In such a case if a deed is desired (eg to avoid doubt whether overseas supplemental documents have been made from time to time) the scheme may be established by the UK trustees executing a deed poll which recites the intention of the foreign employer to establish the scheme. The intention should be confirmed, most conveniently by indorsement on the deed by an officer of the foreign employer or alternatively by one of its UK representatives. A certified copy of the letter of authorisation or the board minute may be scheduled to the deed.

3 Scheme of foreign employer established abroad

3.1 Treatment as two separate schemes

A scheme of a foreign employer is treated as established abroad if it has non-resident trustees. In these cases the Revenue will exercise their power under s 611(3) of ICTA 1988 and will treat the scheme as two separate schemes, the first relating to UK employees, the second to employees whose earnings are not chargeable to UK tax under Case I or Case II of Schedule E. If the scheme is operated under a single trust the appropriate proportions of assets and income may need to be calculated.

Paragraph 15.2 of the Revenue's practice notes IR 12 refers to the scheme of an overseas employer that applies exclusively to UK employees but does not mention a scheme actually established abroad. So long as there is a UK-resident person representing the administrator, objection seems unlikely (but advance enquiry should be made). See also para 2.1 above.

3.2 UK administrator/representative

If the scheme is split under s 611(3) a UK administrator/representative (see paras 2.1 and 2.4 above) will be required. The prudent administrator/representative will seek an indemnity from both the trustees and the foreign employer since the trust assets are unlikely to be under his control. The indemnity should provide that the trustees and/or the foreign employer agree to submit to the jurisdiction of the English courts and that the indemnity provisions be construed according to English law.

3.3 Duties performed wholly abroad

A scheme in effect cannot be approved by the Inland Revenue under ss 590 or 591 in respect of employees whose duties are performed wholly outside the United Kingdom for a non-resident employer except in the special circumstances mentioned in 4.1 below.

If those circumstances do not apply, consideration should be given to establishing a scheme under s 615(6) of ICTA 1988, which gives many of the tax advantages of an exempt approved scheme—see ss 614(5) and 615(3). The section applies only where the trade or undertaking is carried on wholly or partly outside the United Kingdom and the employments to which the scheme relates are wholly outside the United Kingdom. The provisions of such a scheme are outside the scope of this book.

3.4 Corresponding approval

The term 'corresponding approval' is used informally by the Inland Revenue to refer to an overseas scheme of an overseas employer to which a non-UK domiciled UK employee belongs, where the scheme satisfies the Revenue's requirements under s 596(2)(*b*). The approval relates to the individual employee, so each employee must make a claim. Where the claim is accepted, the employee is exempt from a charge to tax under s 595, Chapter 17, para 1.1. Further, the employee will be able to obtain UK tax relief on his own contributions to the overseas scheme under s 192(3)—the position being confirmed in para 15.13 of IR 12 (as updated).

The Revenue are to be satisfied that the retirement benefits scheme (in practice an overseas scheme since a UK scheme would be submitted for exempt approval) 'corresponds' to an approved scheme (or a statutory scheme etc). The correspondence does not relate to any particular approved scheme and therefore confers considerable latitude. In practice, the Revenue's requirements are not onerous although somewhat more so since 23 February 1995. Arrangements submitted since that date must fall within paras 15.13–15.16 of IR 12 (as updated), but earlier approval is not disturbed. In particular see para 3.6 below.

3.5 Effect of UK early leaver legislation

There are five areas where the above question applies:

(*a*) preservation (Chapter 10, para 1.1)
(*b*) revaluation (Chapter 10, para 1.2)
(*c*) anti-franking (Chapter 10, para 1.3)
(*d*) transfers and buy-outs (Chapter 10, paras 10 and 11)
(*e*) disclosure (Chapter 16, para 6)

Contracting-out and funding requirements are also mentioned briefly below.

The basic principle is that a UK statute will not normally apply to non-resident foreigners. To the extent therefore that the above matters confer upon members rights against non-resident trustees or administrators the question is governed by parliamentary intention, the presence in the UK of assets that may be attached and the attitudes of the trustees' domestic courts.

In practice the need for Inland Revenue approval to avoid a charge to tax on UK employees under s 595 (Chapter 17, para 1.1) ensures that the foreign employer has an incentive to procure that his trustees or administrators meet the Revenue's expectations in these areas. These expectations apply to the preservation requirements to the extent stated in reg 25 of Sl 1991 No 167 (mainly consolidating previous regulations). Under that regulation, preservation applies only to a scheme with an overseas element if it is established in the UK or a UK representative has been appointed (see para 3.2 above—but, less formally than under ICTA 1988, for preservation purposes any UK managerial function will trigger the provision—reg 25(4)); in that event preservation applies if, in addition to the usual requirements, on the termination of employment either:

(*a*) that employment is in the UK; or
(*b*) the most recent payment of earnings gave rise to liability for primary Class 1 national insurance contributions or would have done so had the level of earnings not been below the lower earnings limit. (Since reg 25(1) defines overseas element to include non-UK employment, the requirement regarding Class 1 contributions applies equally to overseas members of UK-established schemes. The scope of reg 25 is authorised by what is now PSA 1993, s 165(6)).

Since the preservation legislation does not have direct effect on schemes' rules, it is necessary for the foreign scheme to adopt preservation rules in respect of UK employees.

Revaluation, transfers and buyouts apply when preservation applies and (SI 1991 No 168 reg 11 and SI 1996 No 1847, reg 17) but as these provisions have direct effect the question arises whether the overseas trustees or managers will be in breach of their domestic law in implementing them. Where a scheme has a substantial number of UK members it may well adopt a specific reference to revaluation, transfers and buyouts, but where it does not do so it may well be that the trustees' domestic courts would, in relation to UK employees, reject for reasons of comity a claim that the trustees or managers had been in breach of their own provisions, particularly as it seems unlikely that, in respect of UK employees the UK legislation would be repugnant to the overseas managers' domestic law. Repugnancy appears unlikely in respect of pension accrued in the UK. Alternatively the foreign employer may consider it prudent, as a matter of employment policy, to adopt within its rules the UK provisions in respect of UK employees, assuming there to be adequate properly exercisable power. A further reason would be the avoidance of debate over the trustees' discharge from claims by members' dependants disentitled by buyouts, for otherwise the discharge depends on the efficacy of the UK statute.

Indexation of pensions in payment, under s 51 of the Pensions Act 1995, only applies to a tax-approved scheme. On a straightforward construction this would not apply to an occupational scheme of which part was treated as a separate approved scheme under ICTA 1988, although possibly in due course the Revenue may, as a condition of approval (under s 591) require the approved UK part to provide indexation (for post-5 April 1997 accrual).

Anti-franking should present no problem since it is only relevant to employment where UK national insurance contributions are payable and therefore will presumably automatically apply and be enforceable against the required UK representative. It is a matter of choice whether to contract out, so that the employer need not exercise that choice if he is not able to procure compliance with any such undertaking. Schemes administered wholly or primarily outside the UK can contract out and are subject to a modified resources requirement—SI 1996 No 1172, reg 48. The regulation requires a UK administrator, an appointed actuary and that the notice of intention to contract out informs members that it is an overseas scheme—an important point having regard to the exclusion from the disclosure regs (see below). Unfortunately, reg 48 has been amended by SI 1997 No 786 requiring for a salary-related scheme priorities on a winding-up which may be impossible for an overseas scheme to fulfil.

The disclosure regs do not apply to a scheme unless it is established in the UK or has one or more trustees resident in the UK—SI 1996 No 1655, reg 2(2).

The minimum funding requirement (MFR) does not apply to unapproved schemes (SI 1996 No 1536, reg 28(1)(c)) and therefore not to a totally overseas scheme. However, Sched 5 applies the MFR where within the scheme a *segregated* fund has UK approval (but segregation is rare). Paragraph 5 of Sched 5 applies the MFR to a part that is treated as approved under s 611(3) of ICTA 1988, with a strange provision that the MFR valuation and other forms 'may be modified appropriately'.

3.6 Long overseas service

Extra-statutory concession A10 (revised October 1991) exempts from income tax (including s 596A) lump sum relevant benefits received from a foreign 'retirement benefits scheme' where the employee's overseas service had comprised:

(*a*) not less than 75 per cent of his total service in that employment; or
(*b*) the whole of the last ten years of his service in that employment, where total service exceeds ten years; or
(*c*) not less than 50 per cent of his total service in that employment, including any ten of the last 20 years, where total service exceeds 20 years.

There are tapering provisions where overseas service is less than described above.

A10 also concedes tax relief to an employer for payments made to an overseas (and thus non-approved) scheme which is accepted as 'corresponding' (see para 3.4 above). The concession also extends to payments to a UK s 615(3) scheme (see para 3.3 above). Otherwise s 76 of the Finance Act 1989, would have prevented a deduction for tax as the employee would not have been simultaneously charged to income tax.

In broad terms the above concessions return the tax treatment to the position that prevailed before the Finance Act 1989 was enacted and made amendments to ICTA 1988.

4 Overseas Employees in UK Scheme

4.1 UK employees working overseas

A UK employee as defined in para 1 above of a UK employer may be a member of an exempt approved scheme, notwithstanding that he is working overseas.

Employees whose duties are performed wholly outside the United

Kingdom for a non-resident employer, eg a foreign subsidiary of the UK company, may become (or remain) members of an exempt approved scheme where either:

(*a*) there is a definite expectation, evidenced in writing, that the employee will return to the UK either to take up employment with an employer participating in the scheme or to retire; or
(*b*) the employee's earnings remain effectively chargeable to UK income tax (Case I or II) because the employee only works overseas for periods which total less than 365 days in any year;

and the following conditions are fulfilled:

(*c*) the UK employer must continue to pay any employer contributions due, and be reimbursed by the overseas employer (unless the Pension Schemes Office (PSO) specifically agree otherwise—which they will generally only do if reimbursement is not possible because of local exchange control difficulties); and
(*d*) the pension in respect of the service abroad must be calculated and funded by reference to the rate of remuneration appropriate for similar employment in the UK; and
(*e*) the period of service abroad should not exceed ten years. For this purpose periods of service abroad must be agreggated unless separated by at least one year's UK employment, but periods served abroad for a UK employer are ignored.

There may be local tax arising by reason of UK scheme membership (particularly in the USA) and this question should be raised for reference to the client's local advisers.

These provisions reflect the revised Revenue practice announced in November 1995 and now set out in the updated part 15 of IR 12.

4.2 Other overseas employees

A UK employer may admit to its UK scheme its own employees, world-wide, but not those of its overseas subsidiaries (save for UK employees, as defined in para 1 and those falling within para 4.1 above). It is rare for this to happen in practice since the local employment market will generally expect local-type arrangements. Further, the local tax question raised near the end of para 4.1 above may be applicable. Nonetheless, there are some UK companies that admit overseas employees to their UK schemes.

The Revenue will require that the deed of participation for the subsidiaries is limited to the above two categories, and provides that where membership is dependent on an expectation of return to the UK accrual should cease if that expectation terminates.

5 Part of salary from overseas subsidiaries

A UK employee who is a member of an exempt approved scheme may receive from an overseas subsidiary part of his remuneration for services performed abroad. If his overseas emoluments are chargeable to UK tax under Schedule E there is no objection to them (apart from the exception referred to in para 1 above) being included in the scheme's definition of final remuneration (Chapter 17, para 3.2), provided that:

(1) The overseas subsidiary participates in the UK pension scheme, usually by an agreement of adherence. The agreement should be drafted so as to avoid making other employees of the overseas subsidiary eligible to join the scheme. The matters set out in para 3 above must be considered.
(2) The uplifted sixtieths and eightieths tables (Chapter 17, paras 3.4 and 3.6) may be applied only to that part of the pension based on overseas emoluments after five and eight years' 'foreign part-time service' respectively notwithstanding the fact that the member has potentially in the one case ten, and in the other 20 or more, years' service with the UK employer. This is because the Revenue treat pensions based on overseas emoluments as arising from separate employments. Since these tables are only applicable to members who joined a scheme before 1 June 1989, or where the transitional regs apply, the Revenue should be asked to confirm that they are applicable to the overseas emoluments (where UK service began before that date).

Chapter 8

Advice on benefits

1 Nature of final salary commitment

The three main types of pension calculations have been mentioned in Chapter 2, para 1 and are described more fully here and in para 5 and para 6 below. Until the late 1950s or even the early 1960s, it was most unusual for an insured scheme to provide benefits calculated on the basis of the employee's salary at the time of retirement. This was because such salary would by its nature be unknown until the eve of the retirement. However, the larger, self-administered, funds frequently provided such a benefit. The intention was that after a career lasting a whole working life with a company, the employee should not have to accept too great a fall in remuneration when retiring on pension. The modern final salary ('defined benefit') scheme adopts that intention, subject to limitations required by the Inland Revenue for schemes seeking their approval. The limitations themselves strongly resemble those applicable under the tax code in force before the Finance Act 1970 (itself the starting point for the current tax code).

As a result the normal type of final salary scheme provides for a pension of one-eightieth or one-sixtieth of final pensionable salary for each year of service with the company, the maximum years that count usually being limited to forty. The definition of 'final pensionable salary' will vary. It may be based on salary earned in the last twelve months before retirement, or on an average of salary earned over the last three or, more rarely, five years (or on any of a number of other possibilities). It may also be reduced by a proportion of the basic (flat-rate) State pension so that, taken together with the basic State pension, the total benefits for a member with 40 years' service will not exceed two-thirds of actual final salary (see para 4 below).

It follows that in a final salary pension scheme a pay increase in the last year before retirement may result in a proportionate increase in pension payable for life and a disproportionate increase in the cost of funding it (see para 2 below).

2 Nature of insured risk

No insurance company will underwrite the rate of salary increase. The insurance company will simply undertake to invest the trustees' money and provide either a guaranteed or with-profits (or unit-linked) fund from which to pay the pensions. It will recommend a rate of contribution which is intended to enable the expected benefits to be paid. If an employee's salary is, as described in para 1 above, increased in the last year before retirement, the whole of the additional pension will be unfunded unless some provision for increase has been built into the recommended contribution rate.

The importance of this point is so fundamental to the obligations taken on by an employer establishing a final salary scheme that no apology is made for including it in this book even though it may not directly affect the initial documents relating to the scheme. If the employer does not understand the nature of the commitment he can justly claim that the rest of the advice he has been given is completely wasted.

An example may be useful. A scheme provides for pension at age 65 to be one-sixtieth of the last year's salary for each year of service. An employee is with the company for 20 years, so that his pension will be 20-sixtieths, ie one-third, of his last year's salary.

The insurer has set the level of contribution on the assumption that salaries will increase at 5 per cent per annum (it will also assume a long-term investment yield of the fund of say 8 per cent per annum—see Chapter 11, para 4 regarding the yield/salary assumption). Every three or four years the insurer will look at the actual salaries then being paid and the performance of the fund to date and will adjust its recommendations as to the future contribution rate. It may make a recommendation three years before this particular individual retires. It may assume that by his last year his salary will have risen to £15,000 per annum. The expected pension would then be £5,000 per annum.

However, in the last year the individual might have been promoted and given a pay rise of 20 per cent. Final pensionable salary would have increased to £18,000 and pension to £6,000 per annum. The additional £1000 per annum of pension would be unfunded. At current annuity rates, the capital cost of purchasing it might be approximately £7,000. Effectively, therefore, the last year's pay rise of £3,000 would have cost the employer, apart from the salary, an additional £7,000, making a total of £10,000. If there is a prospective spouse's pension, the cost would be even higher.

It is essential, therefore, to realise that the insurer does not underwrite the pension cost of pay rises. That is why a company, particularly a small company, must think very hard before undertaking a final salary type of pension scheme.

On the other hand, a higher than expected turnover of staff (or redundancies) may reduce the demands on the fund by releasing a salary reserve for which provision has been made (Chapter 10, para 4).

A further aspect of the insured risk is price inflation, mentioned in para 3 below.

3 Inflation

Final salary schemes protect the accrued pension from inflation (assuming wages keep up with prices) while the member is in service but may not do so in retirement. Some schemes provide for increases to pensions in payment, in line with the retail prices index, but others do so only partially or not at all. Some adopt the middle path of funding for such increases but awarding them annually at discretion. In this last case the scheme may have an apparent surplus which would disappear if the exercise of discretion continued. Funding for such increases usually assumes a long-term return on the fund of 3–5 per cent above the percentage rate of inflation, and at the time of writing this ties in with the market return on index-linked gilt-edged stock.

Final salary schemes are obliged by statute to provide a limited degree of protection against price inflation. For persons who leave service before normal retirement date this is described in Chapter 10, para 1.2, and for pensioners in Chapter 16, para 3.

It may be thought that the profits declared by the insurance company will be increased in times of inflation because their funds will be partly invested in equities which, traditionally, are expected to rise in line with the real value of company assets. It is enough to say that even if this proposition were to prove correct, it would still be possible for individual pensions to be secured (by purchase of annuities) before the relevant bonus was declared, in which case the fund relating to those pensions would not participate in the bonus.

4 State pension offset ('integration')

This heading includes the offset mentioned in 1 above under which final pensionable salary is often reduced by part of the basic component of the State pension. The rationale is that employer and employee contribute to the State provision of the flat-rate pension and that this provision would be duplicated if the occupational pension scheme made no offset. Where the intention is to provide an overall pension equal to two-thirds of final salary (for a person remaining in the scheme for 40 years) a common deduction from 'final pensionable salary' is one and a half times the basic component of the State pension. Thus forty-sixtieths or two-thirds of final pensionable salary will be two-thirds of final actual salary less two-thirds of one and a half times the basic component. Since $2/3 \times 1\frac{1}{2} = 1$, the deduction would equal the basic State pension precisely.

There are many permutations on such an arrangement.

It is normal to provide, in contributory schemes, that a similar deduction is made from salary before calculating contributions.

For offset in relation to the State earnings-related pension (SERPS), see Chapter 20, para 2. For equal treatment considerations, see Chapter 22.

5 The average salary scheme

An average salary scheme provides a pension that is built up according to the period served at each salary level. SERPS (see Chapter 20, para 2) is a variant of this type. In the private sector the contributions of the employer (and possibly of the employee too) vary according to the latter's age at a given salary level. If the scheme is insured, the benefits can be guaranteed by the life office since they can be forecast. This type of scheme has the advantage that its cost can be calculated precisely (if a deferred annuity policy is chosen, albeit often regarded as a poor investment). It has three disadvantages:

(*a*) the pension of an employee who is promoted will be a smaller proportion of his salary at retirement than the pension of a person whose level of salary is unchanged;

(*b*) general rises in salaries (whether through price inflation or real increases) cause the pension to be smaller by comparison with salary at retirement (except in SERPS were there is revaluation by reference to a wages index until pension begins, and thereafter by reference to price inflation).

(*c*) fixed deferred annuities are no longer perceived as competitive investments, albeit a variation that revalued each year's salary in line with price inflation has been adopted and might conceivably be fully insured if the range of index-linked gilts (in which the insurer could invest to match its liability) were sufficiently wide.

This type of scheme is rarely now established, but may still exist (often in paid-up form) in relation to service before April 1978 when benefit structures were generally altered to meet the requirements for contracting out of the new State scheme.

Such schemes are sometimes known as 'salary grade' schemes.

6 Money-purchase scheme ('defined contribution')

A money-purchase (or 'defined contribution') scheme resembles a conventional endowment insurance policy in that the level of contribution is chosen, and the benefit depends on the interest (or bonuses) earned by the fund, and in the case of unit-linked funds on the current market level, as well as annuity rates at retirement.

Defined contribution schemes have always been attractive to small employers because they enable a precise cost to be established. Increasingly, large employers have turned to them, since regulation has increased the cost and disruption of salary-related schemes (see para 7 below).

There are innumerable variations of the money purchase type of scheme. Some link the benefit to bonuses, some to money-market rates, others to units (property units, gilt units etc). Increasingly, members have a choice of units, with a basic 'lifestyle' fund which places contributions for younger members in equity units with a phased transition to gilts as they approach pension age (as the price of annuities closely follows gilts).

An attractive feature of defined contribution schemes is that the employer's contribution is a percentage of the employee's salary, so that its immediate value is known and easily understood by both parties.

A disadvantage is that the benefit may bear no relation to the employee's needs at retirement, ie the scheme will either be inadequate or wastefully costly. Age-related contributions can alleviate but not entirely remove the difficulty. This disadvantage is of less significance (for those earning less than the State upper earnings limit—see Chapter 20) if the scheme is in addition to the earnings-related State scheme ie contracted-in. It may then also be possible for a significant proportion of the benefit to be taken as a tax-free cash sum at retirement age. If contracted out, part of the benefit, or all in the case of minimum contributions, will necessarily be taken as 'protected rights' in pension form (Chapter 20).

Money purchase schemes are readily available as policies for single individuals, often entitled 'Executive Retirement Plan' although such a plan is no different in its legal or tax status from any other insured occupational pension scheme. The choice of life office can even be left to the member, although if there is more than one relevant employee this results in a proliferation of documents and correspondence for the employer.

It is now a statutory requirement that the pension provided in respect of contributions paid since 6 April 1997 should include an element of inflation proofing (Chapter 16, para 3). This requirement does not apply to personal pension schemes (so that for a given accumulated fund the initial amount of the pension is larger, albeit without subsequent increases) and therefore Group Personal Pension Schemes are sometimes preferred, both for this and other reasons (Chapter 2, para 9.5).

Age-related contributions

A number of money-purchase schemes are being introduced to replace defined benefit schemes, and often have age-related contributions (from the employer) to enable a reasonable similarity of benefit accrual for members at older ages. Where a consultant recommends this approach it is important, in order to conform with the preservation regulations (see Chapter 10, para 1), to ensure that an actuary certifies either that the higher rate is designed to produce a uniform accrual of benefit on the assumptions specified in reg 16 or that the scale of rates will produce a notional fund in accordance with the PSA 93, s 74(6B) as inserted by reg 14A (SI 1991 No 167 as amended by SI 1996 No 2131 which also preserves the effect of approval by the now-dissolved Occupational Pensions Board).

Investment choice and information

Trustees have new investment duties under the Pensions Act 1995, including a requirement in some cases to consult the employer—which may expose the employer to criticism too if investment returns are poor. Chapter 16, paras 16.2 and 16.4 set out a number of requirements under the Act, but some will not be relevant where the assets are invested exclusively in an insurance policy *provided that* it falls within the exemptions mentioned in 16.1 and 16.2.

There is a remote but increasing risk of litigation by members if the selected investment manager is poor, whether selected by the trustees or the member. The risk is reduced if there is a choice of provider, so long as members are given sufficient information to make an informed choice—but some employers may consider that choice will engender anxiety.

In the United States of America, where consumers are more investment orientated, vast investment choice is often given to individual members (through the purchase of units in different pooled funds), partly to avoid the risk of litigation if trustees have made the selection and it turns out to be poor. Employers too may be sued as fiduciaries in the USA, if they have a role in decision taking. The requirement in the UK obliging the trustees to consult the employer regarding the statement of investment principles, under s 35 of the Pensions Act 1995 (see Chapter 16, para 16.4), may lead to similar litigation although it would be difficult to pursue successfully. There is already a noticeable trend in the UK to offer a choice of, say, three types of fund, often with different investment managers. Such choice should be adequately explained when drafting members' booklets, and may necessitate ongoing information.

It may be thought that the employer can avoid these matters by sponsoring a Group Personal Pension Scheme (see Chapter 2, para 9.5). However, pensions are long-term investments, and it is possible that any trend to impose liability on employers in respect of occupational money-purchase schemes could apply similarly to employers who sponsor Group Personal Pension Schemes, and it is also possible that if the latter become popular, regulatory requirements may be imposed to parallel those in the Pensions Act 1995. An employer sponsoring a Group Personal Pension Scheme will therefore be well advised to seek expert opinion on the provider and to procure standard documents that enable a switch of provider without excessive complexity or penalty. In both occupational and personal schemes, there may be advantage to the employer in arranging at low cost, or in subsidising, the provision to members of independent investment advice on, say, an annual basis. This may have the collateral advantage of raising the profile of the pension arrangements and extending the employees' appreciation of the value of what is provided.

7 Defined benefit: defined contribution—choice

7.1 Background

A significant move away from defined benefit schemes has taken place since:

(*a*) the introduction in 1988 of an accounting standard, SSAP 24, to recognise in the employer's accounts a pension cost for a defined benefit scheme notwithstanding a current cessation of contributions by reason of surplus (unless the surplus would fund benefits over the full service lives of employees)—Chapter 16, para 11.4.

(*b*) the introduction by the Social Security Act 1990, with effect from 1992, of a potential liability for employers (which does not apply to money purchase schemes except in the case of theft or fraud) triggered by the winding up of a scheme which reveals an inadequacy of assets to meet its defined benefits—now, with slight amendments, Pensions Act 1995, s 75.

The tendency has been greatly exacerbated by the constant increase in complexity, and thus cost, imposed by law, highlighting the perceived simplicity, of a defined contribution scheme—para 7.2 below. The key reasons for this tendency are therefore defined cost and simplicity.

7.2 Further factors: Defined Benefit ('DB')—Defined Contribution ('DC')

Apart from (*a*) and (*b*) above, the most significant further factors have been equal treatment and the Pensions Act 1995. Each has had a major financial impact on DB schemes (not on all, but on the majority), but far less on DC. A third factor may be tax changes—see para 7.5 below.

Equal treatment as a design requirement can easily be accommodated in both—see Chapter 22 regarding this and the cases mentioned below. Nonetheless, its practical impact, arising from the uncertain period between 1990, the year of the *Barber* judgment, and

1994 (*Coloroll*), was far greater on DB schemes. (There remains an uncertainty whether DC schemes will be subject to claims arising from unequal purchased annuities, but the logic of the *Neath* and *Coloroll* judgments regarding DB schemes suggests that the DC equality of contributions will suffice).

The Pensions Act 1995 grew out of the 'Maxwell' affair, viz the theft of pension funds (Chapter 24, para 12 and Chapter 25). If the Act had been limited to the narrow question of security of funds, it would not have impacted on the DB/DC choice. However, for two allied reasons (security of the benefit promise and assessment of compensation) the Act has introduced a minimum funding requirement (MFR) for DB schemes. After three years of debate and adjustment since the original proposal, the requirement will have far less an effect on contribution or investment policy than first envisaged, but the initial public impact was considerable, and the requirement (with its allied regular actuarial assessments) remains a complexity that DC schemes avoid.

7.3 Comparison

Any comparison depends upon the starting point. If existing staff (or transferees under an acquisition) have a DB scheme, and consideration is being given to DC, either great care will be needed to meet their legal or industrial relations expectations or the review should be limited to new staff. The following addresses only the latter.

The chief reasons generally given for DB are:

(*a*) certainty for employees;
(*b*) more efficient provision of target benefits;
(*c*) ease of early retirement provision; and
(*d*) surpluses benefit the employer;
Some downsides are:
(*e*) fluctuating cost, exacerbated by MFR;
(*f*) exposure to tax changes (see para 7.5 below);
(*g*) expectation of '60ths' scale (see below);
(*h*) short service in conflict with career design;
(*i*) rare for staff to appreciate full cost.

Item (*d*) above is important as most pension projections are conservative, so that surplus often emerges. In a DB scheme it can then reduce the employer's contribution rate. By contrast, in a DC scheme members (and not the employer) will benefit from good investment returns. However, the DB will probably have a higher long-term cost anyway as most benefit scales, eg 60ths mentioned in (*g*) above, require a higher long–term contribution rate than the DC rate chosen by most employers.

The chief reasons generally given for DC are:

(*a*) known cost;
(*b*) cost recognised by employees;
(*c*) easier benefit administration—but see (*h*) below.
(*d*) good for motivational extras (eg matching contributions);
(*e*) exclusion from the deficiency (on winding up) provisions of the Pensions Act 1995, s 75 (but note the employer's liability, in respect of a tax-exempt scheme of more than one member, to restore, immediately on discovery, stolen assets, other than an unallocated float—SI 1996 No 3128, reg 7).

Some downsides are:

(*f*) possibly inadequate pensions—depends upon chosen contribution rate;
(*g*) investment risk, for members, including risk of tax change (see para 7.5 below);
(*h*) poor early retirement provision;
(*i*) need to record members' individual accounts;
(*j*) close employee concern with fund management;
(*k*) costly purchase of annuities (see Chapter 2, para 9.5, last para).

These lists are not exhaustive. DC schemes link benefits to investment returns ie to the success of industrialised economies. Extending this further, the downside in (*k*) above could be met by equity-based fluctuating pensions if Revenue rules and design practice were to develop that way.

If schemes moved away from annuities, DB might provide a basic pension, and DC the gilt on the gingerbread, but for individual employers that concept has not at present emerged. Nonetheless it may become important in the future to estimate basic pension provision from DC schemes; para 7.4 below indicates the importance for the UK as a whole.

7.4 General comments

The increase in complexity, mentioned in paras 7.1 and 7.2 above, has kept pension awareness high in executive circles. Inevitably, this raises the question whether value is obtained (in staff perception) for the very significant annual expenditure. Reviews constantly show a lack of appreciation by employees of the cost or value of accruing DB pensions. It may be that the existence of *any* pension scheme would be sufficient to satisfy industrial relations. While DC *can* produce large pensions, the temptation is strong for the employer to contribute at a modest level. Staff disappointment may only set in when retirement quotations are obtained. The provision of annual benefit statements may bring forward the age at which the amount of prospective pension is recognised, but probably not in the early years after the establishment of a scheme.

UK occupational pensions are funded at about £600 billion. In the European Community, only the Netherlands (and on a smaller scale Ireland) are comparable. These funded pensions are regarded by other EU countries as an example, since the falling ratio of working population to retired, makes the unfunded pension liabilities of other national systems unsustainable in the future, as the following examples indicate, but the question may arise whether the DC contribution rate is sufficient.

	*Unfunded** *Percentage GDP (1994)*	*Ratio: working age (15–64)** to elderly (65 and over)*	
		1980	2040
UK	19	4.3	3
France	98	4.5	2.6
Italy	113	4.7	2.4
Germany	139	4.2	2

*House of Commons Social Security Committee report, 23 October 1996, 'Unfunded Pension Liabilities in the European Union', citing an OECD study. *NB:* The above figures depended on 'middle assumptions' as to pensions payable until the year 2070 and to productivity growth and discount rates. The alternative figure of just 48 (nonetheless high) was shown for both France and Germany in a footnote.

**Government Report Cm 1723, December 1991. *NB*: Actual support ratios are smaller as many are in full-time education, unemployed or have pension before 65. If females had retained a State retirement age of 60, the UK ratio was projected at 2.2 by 2030—source Cm 2594, June 1994. Figures at 2040 are subject to significant imponderables such as birth rate and immigration (and in Germany's case, the effect of unification). The above figures are multiples, eg 4.3:1.

These figures cannot indicate the sufficiency of the pension, whether funded or unfunded, for the individual. No doubt social research will indicate different needs in retirement, perhaps for those in good health a smaller percentage of final salary than at present (as rising real incomes bring larger personal savings and lower increase in purchase of consumer goods) with an insured basis to meet residential care for those in poor health. A key question regarding DC schemes is whether the perception of either the employer or the workforce is governed by pension estimates. For those employing a highly mobile workforce, the headline factor is more likely to be the contribution rate, in which case the move towards DC will continue.

In due course an awareness by DC members of resulting benefits will emerge, so that employers and workforce have a common interest in the benefit out-turn. Already, age-related contributions and other design features address this question, but the key common interest will be in investment results. Trustees also have a particular responsibility here, and over time may come to review the appointment of their investment managers on a regular basis. While change of investment manager can be costly, as portfolios are often restructured by the incoming manager, the need to demonstrate that the possibility has been kept under review may emerge quite strongly.

Some of these factors affecting DC schemes, and also the alternative of Group Personal Pension Schemes, are mentioned in the concluding paragraphs of para 6 of this Chapter.

7.5 Effect of changes to ACT and tax credits

Although exempt approved pension schemes recover tax on their UK dividend income, the change in 1993 to the rate of tax credits and the associated advance corporation tax (ACT) broke the link with basic rate tax. Tax credits fell from 25 per cent to 20 per cent. The effect of grossing up was a reduction of 6.25 per cent in the expected return on UK dividends—see Chapter 17, para 1.6.

The effect on DB schemes was dramatic. As valuations are based on income flows, and most schemes are heavily invested in UK equities, up to 6.25% was wiped off actuarial asset values. Increased contribution rates were therefore required (subject to other variations).

While the rate of tax credits had previously been falling, in line with changes to basic rate, the 1993 alteration demonstrated that tax credits could alter arbitrarily (or be abolished).

The adverse effect applies equally to DB and DC schemes, but exacerbates the difference in risk, as—

(a) for DB the extra contributions are payable by the employer; the arbitrary nature of this risk is immediately plain to finance directors;
(b) for DC the reduced tax credits mean lower benefits; there is no cost to employers and a strong likelihood that members will not be aware of the risk; employers may *wish* to contribute more but will rarely be *obliged* to do so. (Regarding trustees, see below).

Since 1993 there has been an annual Budget scare that tax credits will fall, particularly as basic rate taxpayers were sheltered from the effect. If the system is altered a second time the trend away from DB is likely to accelerate significantly.

Trustees of DC schemes, providing money-purchase benefits, are obliged to provide annual benefit statements (see Chapter 16, para 6.3). While these have to show the value of *accrued* rights, they sometimes include projections on stated assumptions including the return on the fund. Further, voluntary contribution arrangements (which are obligatory for both DB and DC schemes—see Chapter 17, para 11.1) are often illustrated with income projections. It may now become appropriate to include a warning that the return is dependent upon the tax regime as well as investment performance. Trustees will anyway endeavour to minimise the risk of members relying on projections, and are unlikely to be seriously exposed to a claim in (for example) negligence, but the possibility should be in mind when drafting or commenting on illustrations.

8 Inland revenue limits

The tax advantages of approved schemes are based on the principle that they should provide genuine retirement benefits and not a means of tax avoidance. The discretion exercised by the Revenue on approving schemes is based on this principle. Thus the limits laid down apply to the age at which benefits can be taken as well as to their amount and form. Most insured schemes will be so arranged that they are well within such limits. It is nonetheless always important to include references to such limits in any employee announcement. Further details are given in Chapter 17.

9 Pension mortages, loanbacks etc

The marketing of pensions by insurance companies and intermediaries often focuses on attendant advantages, such as tax relief if a company's first contribution coincides with a year of high profits.

There was a period, in and around the year 1987, when 'pension mortgages' were marketed heavily. The intention in taking out an Executive Retirement Plan (see the penultimate paragraph of 6 above) was that the lump sum available at retirement should be sufficient to repay the capital on an associated house purchase loan. The Inland Revenue pointed out that an overt link in the documents establishing the pension scheme could prejudice its tax approval since its sole purpose was not the provision of retirement and death benefits (see para 8 above). The Revenue's position was broadly similar for personal and occupational pension schemes and was set out in a letter from the Controller to the Association of British Insurers dated 25 April 1988. To adjust to this position, the existence (or simultaneous establishment) of the pension scheme then became a status confirmation that satisfied the lender of the likely ability to repay, where an interest-only mortage was granted. In practice there was no difference in the arrangements since it had never been possible for the borrower to give security over the prospective lump sum from an occupational pension scheme, as Inland Revenue requirements for approval had always included a prohibition on alienation; the standard prohibition is akin to a protective trust, comprising a forfeiture combined with a discretion for the trustees of the pension scheme to pay an equivalent benefit to the member, or his dependants. (The Pensions Act 1995, s 91(1)(*b*) renders a charge unenforceable unless the type of scheme is excluded by regulations under s 94).

Loans from small self-administered pension schemes (Chapter 17, para 8), if permissible under the Pensions Act 1995, (see below), are governed by SI 1991 No 1614 which is fully described in Inland Revenue Memorandum 109 (now restated in Pt 20 of the Revenue's current Practice Notes). Regulation 6 (para 13 of the Memorandum) prohibits loans to, or to anyone connected with, a scheme member (other than an employer—see below). Paragraph 15 of the Memorandum states the serious consequences of attempts to circumvent the regulation by loans to third parties on the understanding that they will make onward loans to members.

Loans to the employer (from a 'small' scheme) must be for the purpose of the latter's business and be—

(*a*) for a fixed term;
(*b*) at a commercial rate of interest; and
(*c*) evidenced by a written agreement containing various provisions (reg 6 and also para 14 of Memorandum 109).

During the first two years of the scheme's existence, the total amounts lent to the employer (and the market value of any shares in the employer held within the scheme's fund) must not exceed 25 per cent of the value of the scheme's assets, excluding received transfer values.

After the first two years the figure increases to 50 per cent, without the exclusion of transfer values (reg 7).

New loans to the employer would be forbidden by the Pensions Act 1995, s40, and SI 1996 No 3127, reg 5, but for the exemption in reg 2(2), reproducing an exemption in SI 1992 No 246, for schemes which:

(a) have fewer than 12 members each of whom is a trustee; and
(b) have rules providing for each member to agree in advance in writing.

Where (a) or (b) does not apply, reg 7 sets out transitional arrangements for loans existing on 6 April 1997.

Loans to employers connected with insured schemes are, in one type of situation, governed by Memorandum 112, viz where the lender takes security over the insurance policies held by the pension fund trustees. The provisions were stated, in para 2 of the Memorandum, to coincide with the above new provisions for small self-administered schemes (but see below regarding the Pensions Act). For example the 25 per cent (excluding received transfers) and 50 per cent figures mentioned above are reproduced in para 2e of the certificate that must be given to the Revenue in accordance with the specimen attached to Memorandum 112.

The Pensions Act 1995 now prohibits any such loans, except where the above 'small schemes' exemption applies or a member has paid voluntary contributions and agreed in writing to the loan (SI 1996 No 3127, reg 6(5)) or a director's ordinary benefits arise under an insurance policy and he has agreed in writing to his interest being used as security, reg 6(8) (as substituted by SI 1997 No 819 and exempted from s 91(1)(*b*) by SI 1997 No 785)—or certain specialised situations arise such as deposits with a bank or building society that is the employer, reg 6(4). The principal regulations were laid on 18 December 1996. Accordingly loans which are not exempt and were in existence on that date (which in effect means that they were within SI 1992 No 246) may be retained until the earliest date on which repayment can be enforced—reg 7(2)(a) and (d) as amended by SI 1997 No 819.

There are numerous other provisions of interest in Memoranda 109 and 112. However, the practitioner should remember above all the duties of the trustees in making such loans. Unless made at the request of all persons prospectively entitled under the trust (in practice rarely possible as there are usually contingent beneficiaries) or all persons who might be affected by a default, the loan can properly be made only if specifically authorised by the trust instrument (unlikely in view of the Revenue's above-mentioned concern that the initial documents avoid an overt link with an intended loan) or comprising a particularly advantageous investment. The latter would entail first class security and a better than market rate of interest. It may be held that a standard market rate of interest would suffice; this must be a matter for legal advice at the time.

Chapter 9

Senior executives

1 Separate scheme?

It is often desired to give additional benefits to employees who carry exceptional responsibilities, referred to generally as senior executives, even though they will in any event, under a final salary scheme, have larger benefits than others because of their higher remuneration. It is possible to achieve this end by a separate section within a scheme, or by a separate scheme which may stand on its own or may be a top-up scheme (see para 3 below). The choice may depend upon the question of trusteeship mentioned in para 2 below.

These arrangements are not to be confused with so-called Executive Retirement Plans (see the last paragraph of Chapter 8, para 6), the distinction being that the senior executives are offered a wider range or more favourable scale of benefits than is available from the employer's standard scheme. In both cases, however, the legal and tax status of the arrangement is no different from any other exempt approved pension scheme.

2 Trusteeship (and employee participation)

In some companies, the benefits available to senior executives are well known, whereas in others it is often desired to keep them confidential. If the latter is the case, it may be preferable to have a separate scheme for senior executives because:

(*a*) any beneficiary under a scheme is entitled under general trust law (the principle in *Re Londonderry* [1964] 3 All ER 855, CA) to see all its provisions, including those governing the benefits available for others; additionally the disclosure regulations under the Social Security Act 1985 confer certain rights of inspection (Chapter 16, para 6); it is possible, while complying with the regulations, to provide in the trust documents that members may only see the rules applicable to their own category, but in practice the actuarial valuation and possibly other documents may refer to the remaining sections;

(*b*) the new statutory requirements for member-nominated trustees (or a member-approved alternative) will make available to such trustees information regarding the senior category that the employer may wish to keep confidential from them (notwithstanding that details of individuals may possibly be kept confidential); however, in principle the published accounts of a stock exchange listed company will now make it impossible to retain close confidentiality regarding the value of such benefits (Chapter 16, para 11.5, and also para 3 below).

Sometimes a senior executive scheme has discretionary benefits. Even if funds are adequate, this can impose a considerable burden on the trustees who have to exercise their power of discretion treating all beneficiaries fairly. Usually, however, such exercise is conditioned entirely by the funds that the employer is willing to make specifically available to the trustees, or else the discretion is vested in the employer provided the actuary certifies that the security of other beneficiaries is not materially affected.

Eligibility is usually at the discretion of the employer.

3 Top-up scheme

A useful mid-way course is the top-up scheme whereby standard benefits for the members are still paid from the main scheme, while additional benefits come from the top-up scheme.

The chief advantages, by comparison with a totally separate scheme, both relate to funding. Firstly, the standard benefit will have built up in the main fund over the years before promotion (and will not be followed by a transfer payment to the separate scheme). Secondly, the funding cost of large salary increases is shared with the main fund where its effect on the overall percentage contribution rate will be much smaller. Both aspects have, until 1997, reduced the rate disclosed in the company accounts for overall emoluments of directors, assuming that the main fund contributions were calculated by reference to the total membership rather than on an individual basis. For accounting periods ending on and after 31 March 1997, new provisions are in force, following the *Greenbury* report—see Chapter 16, para 11.5. However, for unlisted companies the disclosure regarding defined benefit schemes may still be obscured by a top-up arrangement.

The top-up scheme can provide a fixed or discretionary range of additional benefits. It may also have a different standard normal retirement age (although it is then necessary to consider the ability under the main scheme's rules to take its pension at that age and the effect on combined death-in-service benefits in the event of postponed retirement). For Inland Revenue limits purposes the top-up scheme governs the normal retirement age(s) of its members.

For employers whose senior executives are partly promoted from within and partly recruited externally, a top-up scheme is particularly flexible, since the extra accrual required for the former category may be very small.

Where non-standard benefits are agreed under a service contract (Chapter 12) it is important to be clear whether they are also, from the outset, terms of the pension scheme in which case they should be minuted by the trustees (unless the scheme gives the employer the appropriate power and the ability to enter the arrangement in the scheme records).

4 Retained benefits or transfers

Almost invariably the additional benefits for senior executives will require a record to be made of pension accrued with a previous employer, in order to check for Inland Revenue limits when benefits come in to payment. However, even when some curtailment is needed it may not be as great as the pension from the previous employer's scheme, either because full advantage was not previously being taken of the permitted Inland Revenue scale or because there are substantial non-pensioned bonuses or the like. The question then arises whether, as a matter of policy, there should be a complete offset (in the current scheme) for the retained benefits anyway.

There is no standard answer. Frequently, however, the current scheme in effect provides each individual with a target pension at normal retirement age. This often includes the value of transferred-in benefits (whether transferred to the main scheme or the top-up scheme). If this is the general design it is important to recommend a similar offset for benefits retained with the previous employer for otherwise there is an unexpected disadvantage to the members who brought a transfer. In practice the drafting of the offset involves decisions regarding increases to the retained pension and ancillary benefits.

5 Early Leavers

Senior executive schemes are obliged to follow the same preservation rules for the benefit of the early leaver as any other scheme (see Chapter 10, para 1.1). Prior pensionable service in the main scheme is generally aggregated for the purpose of finding two years' qualifying service but the two schemes may, depending on their terms, be treated separately when calculating the preserved pensions.

In practice the more serious problem is the common occurrence of a letter to a potential new senior employee promising uplifted benefits and omitting to state that the accrual will arise proportionately over future service to normal retirement date. On premature dismissal there can be an expectation of the full uplift (subject to Inland Revenue limits). It is helpful to offer clients a standard letter that covers the point, or to suggest a follow-up from the pensions department at commencement of the employment.

A technical but important preservation problem arises where the scheme provides additional sixtieths subject to an aggregate limit of 40-sixtieths. For those who could, but for the limit, attain more than 40-sixtieths (eg persons promoted from the main scheme) the benefits from the top-up scheme should, in the rules, be expressed as an individual target at normal retirement age (which will be less than sixtieths in the top-up scheme) to avoid conflict with the view (expressed at one time by the now dissolved Occupational Pensions Board) that otherwise the early leaver is entitled to sixtieths so long as, on leaving, 40 sixtieths has not been attained.

Chapter 10

The employee who leaves service

1 Preservation and revaluation

1.1 Basic purpose of preservation

The basic purpose of 'preservation' is to ensure that if a member of a scheme leaves service before his normal retirement age he will not forfeit his right to pension. The requirements were introduced with effect from 6 April 1975 by the Social Security Act 1973, s 63—now PSA 1993, s 69. The Occupational Pensions Board (OPB) were established with power to determine whether a scheme conformed with those requirements. The determination of the OPB was final, except on a point of law (PSA 1993, ss 172, 173—now repealed). The OPB issued several memoranda relating to preservation (consolidated in the revised Memorandum 78 of May 1992, see Chapter 13, para 3.20). The OPB was dissolved by the Pensions Act 1995 s 150, with effect from 6 April 1997 (Chapter 18) but its Memoranda remain of interest. The basic requirement of preservation is set out in PSA 1993 s 71.

Unlike the later legislation (paras 1.2 and 1.3 below) preservation does not apply directly to a scheme's rules, ie it constitutes a requirement (addressed to the trustees) that the rules, if necessary, be brought into conformity with the legislation (PSA 1993, ss 131, 132).

The preservation requirements originally did not apply unless the member leaving service had attained the age of 26 and had five years' pensionable service, except in circumstances where he rejoined service or brought a transfer payment from another pension scheme.

The age requirement was removed with effect from 1 January 1986 by the Social Security Act 1985 (s 1). The five-year qualifying period was reduced to two years with effect from 6 April 1988 by the Social

Security Act 1986, s 10. The net result is in PSA 1993, s 71 which requires preservation if:

(*a*) the member has at least two years' qualifying service; or
(*b*) a transfer payment for him has been made to the scheme from a personal pension scheme; or
(*c*) a transfer credit rises from a payment made from another occupational scheme (directly or via a buyout policy which has been surrendered) in which, together with the current scheme, the member has in aggregate two years qualifying service—PSA 1993 s 71(7) and, for 'linked qualifying service', s 179.

Prior to 6 April 1997, if their rules so provided, trustees could compulsorily buy out from interested insurance companies the small preserved benefits of those having between two and five years' qualifying service, subject to adequate notice and other stringent conditions (SI 1991 No 167 reg 9(4) and (5)(b)). The author is not aware of any general exercise by trustees of this buyout power, perhaps because at least 12 months must first elapse after the member has left pensionable service (reg 9(6)(b)) by which time considerable expense might be entailed in giving notice to and corresponding with the member regarding his own right to a transfer or buyout (paras 10 and 12 below). As reg 9(5) referred to the now-dissolved OPB, it has been amended with effect from 6 April 1997 to confer instead on the scheme's trustees the decision as to reasonableness—SI 1996 No 2131, reg 2.

Where the preservation requirements apply, a member leaving service must be entitled to 'short service benefit', generally a pension payable from normal pension age based on scheme service to the earlier termination date and with corresponding surviving spouse's and dependants' rights. Where retirement pensions accrue unevenly (eg on a more favourable scale after, say, twenty years) the principle of uniform accrual must apply to the early leaver.

Detailed provisions regarding transfers, schemes with overseas members and numerous other aspects of preservation are set out in SI 1991 No 167. The OPB's Memorandum 78 (May 1992 edition) remains a useful and comprehensive guide. See also Chapter 9, paras 5 and also 11 below. Paragraph 273 of the Memorandum refers to helpful checklists, for rule drafting, contained in App 3.

The preserved benefit additionally has revaluation rights (see para 1.2 below).

1.2 Revaluation

A member whose pensionable service ended on or after 1 January 1986 has the further protection that his deferred pension cannot be 'frozen'—PSA, s 84. Initially, from 1 January 1986, the protection was partial, the full protection becoming applicable to persons leaving pensionable service on or after 1 January 1991—PSA, Sched 3, para 1. For persons who left between those dates the part of a final-salary type of pension that accrued from 1 January 1985 (or, in the case of a contracted-out scheme, the excess over the guaranteed minimum pension so accrued) must be revalued during the period of deferment by the rate of increase in prices, subject to a cut-off of 5 per cent per annum compounded from approximately the date of leaving until commencement of pension.

The statute was retrospective to 1985 for calculation purposes but applied only to those leaving service in or after 1986. The link is not to the Retail Prices Index as such but to a corresponding rate specified by the Secretary of State—PSA 1993, Sched 3, para 2(3) and (4).

The extension to full pensionable service for those leaving on or after 1 January 1991, now in the PSA, was made by the Social Security Act 1990.

For a money purchase scheme (Chapter 8, para 6) including the protected rights of a contracted-out money purchase scheme, the revaluation is on a different basis, ie that the accrued capital must share in the same investment yield as the capital referable to employees who remain in pensionable service.

Revaluation does not apply to prescribed alternatives to short service benefit (eg early pension), curiously called 'protected provisions' by PSA 1993, s 129 (2) and (3).

Since revaluation, by s 129(1) and its predecessor, the statute has direct effect (unlike the preservation requirements). Many standard documents omit all reference to it although increasingly a 'flag' is included to clarify the scope of other increases eg those to guaranteed minimum pensions or those awarded at discretion.

There are other detailed provisions for average salary and so-called flat-rate schemes and specific provisions covering the award of past service in respect of transfer payments received by the scheme. It is beyond the scope of this book to enlarge on these, but the reader may refer to Sched 3 cited above and to SI 1991 No 168.

Part 7 of the Memorandum 78 cited above helpfully restates the statutory provisions.

1.3 Anti-franking

Anti-franking is a statutory prohibition relevant to guaranteed minimum pensions (GMP) which have ceased to accrue as at 5 April 1997 but which remain a protected obligation of salary-related contracted-out schemes. The protection is re-enacted in the PSA 1993, Pt IV, Chap III (ss 87–92), where the heading is followed by the label 'Anti-franking'.

GMPs are revalued between date of leaving the scheme and the date when they begin to be paid. As the scheme invariably provided a larger pension, of which the GMP was part, anti-franking required that the revaluation to the GMP was additional to the total pension, for otherwise the member would not benefit until the revalued GMP climbed above the total pension.

GMPs were introduced in 1978, and anti-franking was enacted in 1984. The following year, the obligation was introduced to revalue (by a different amount) the balance of the total pension above the GMP—see para 1.2 above. Further, it was thought necessary to make provision to follow through the protection to the GMP of the surviving spouse of the member. The subject therefore became highly technical, and rules that endeavoured to incorporate the full provisions became extremely long. However, as the statute had, and still has, direct effect (now the PSA 1993, s 129(1)) many rules omit the provision or, more helpfully, contain just a short cross-reference.

The subject is complex but it suffices that the practitioner understands the general purpose, if only to recognise such a provision where it occurs in an insurer's draft.

There were two ways in which franking might, before 1985, have occurred, simply as a by-product of the pension scheme's design. First, a scheme providing for a member a scale pension of one-sixtieth (and for a widow one-hundred and twentieth) of final salary for each year of service almost always thereby conferred a benefit significantly greater than the GMP unless the compulsory revaluation of the latter between date of leaving and retirement (Chapter 3, para 12) produced a higher result. It is now necessary to add the revaluation of the GMP to the scale pension (and the excess over the GMP must also be revalued as stated in para 1.2 above).

Secondly, if a member had lengthy pre-1978 pensionable service, his (and his widow's) overall scheme pension was generally far in excess of the GMP revalued (because the GMP accrued only from 1978 onwards). Again, the revaluation of the GMP now has to be added to the overall pension.

Although the anti-franking legislation applies only to persons who left service on or after 1 January 1985, PSA 1993 s 87(7), it is for those members and their widows fully retrospective in that the revaluation of the whole of their GMP accrued in that pension scheme (which could be applicable from 6 April 1978) has the benefit of the statutory protection.

1.4 Refunds of contributions

Until 5 April 1980, transitional arrangements enabled employees who qualified for preservation nonetheless to receive (with their consent) a refund of contributions (if permitted under Revenue approval) in place of their preserved pension rights. Since that date refunds of contributions have been permissible alternatives to short service benefit in respect only of service up to 5 April 1975. It is now rarely good value to exchange this pre-1975 pension for a refund.

It should be noted that any refund to a member from an exempt approved scheme gives rise to a liability to tax (currently at 20 per cent or 33 per cent in the special case of surplus voluntary contributions returned at a later date) on the trustees (ICTA 1988, s 598 as amended). Some schemes provide that this is deductible from the refund (but the tax is chargeable on the amount before the refund—s 598(4)). The refund is not treated as income for any other purpose of the Taxes Acts (s 598(4)).

The Revenue permit (but do not require) interest to be added to refunds of contributions.

The effect of preservation (see para 1.1 above) was to remove the refund of contributions from the range of 'benefits' save for those with under two years' qualifying service or with pre-1975 service (or the special case of surplus voluntary contributions mentioned above, and in SI 1991 No 167 reg 23).

1.5 'Value for money'

The preservation regulations formerly contained a provision requiring contributory schemes (ie schemes under which members contribute) to include one of the following alternative provisions in their rules relating to the prospective pension (or other short service benefit) of an early leaver entitled to preservation to whom a lump sum option was not available in respect of the period to which the pension related:

(*a*) the pension (or other benefit) was to be increased by 3 per cent per annum for each year between the date of leaving service and that of commencement; or
(*b*) such benefit was to be so increased at a rate equivalent to that applicable to certain public service pensions—this alternative was rarely adopted; or
(*c*) the value of the benefit had to compare reasonably with the value of the member's contributions other than any refunded to him; for a young member this usually increased the benefit (if it was not otherwise revalued in deferment) as the contributions were worth more than the capital value of the pension discounted to the date of leaving service.

The foregoing provisions were revoked by reg 2(4) of SI 1985 No 1926. The revocation was intended to avoid excessive complexity in the light of the other calculations to be made for an early leaver under the revaluation and anti-franking regulations (see paras 1.2 and 1.3 above). It was also stated that the value for money provision was no longer necessary in the light of revaluation and anti-franking. However, many schemes have retained the value for money rule as full statutory revaluation applies only to leavers from 1 January 1991 onwards, and anti-franking is relevant only to contracted-out schemes (and then only to the benefit accrued from 6 April 1978).

There remains a 'value' regulation of a different type, ie that the alternatives mentioned in para 1.6 below (including the amount of an annuity premium where the member is not exercising a statutory right to a buy-out and the amount of a transfer payment where the transfer is made without the member's consent other than on a winding up—regs 11, 12 of SI 1991 No 167) must in effect be at least equal in value to the short service benefit that they replace (and in the case of the foregoing reg 12 transfer there must be an actuary's certificate taking account of various factors).

1.6 Other 'alternatives to short-service benefit'

The prescribed alternatives to short-service benefit are referred to in reg 7 (and see also reg 22) of SI 1991 No 167. They include early payment of a benefit, postponed payment of a benefit (under reg 22) and benefits under an insurance policy or annuity contract (which may be an off-loading of liability by the trustees or may be a buy-out chosen by the member as described in para 12 below). Regulation 7(2) requires the member's consent save where the relevant reg specifies to the contrary.

In addition, PSA 1993, s 73 permits a transfer to another scheme in place of short-service benefit. Such transfer may, by s 73(4), be only with the member's consent save in prescribed cases (see para 11 below).

See also the final paragraph of para 1.5 above.

1.7 Foreign schemes with UK employees etc

The intention regarding preservation, revaluation and transfers, and its effect on foreign trustees or managers is now clear. These matters, and the position of the UK scheme member who leaves service while abroad, are fully considered in Chapter 7, para 3.5.

1.8 Generally

The preservation requirements are well known to the insurance industry, so it is likely that any scheme being established with the help of a broker or consultant will comply in its major terms. It would be prudent to include in the interim document establishing the scheme a provision to enable further changes to be effective from the date of establishment if needed to enable the scheme to conform with the preservation requirements of the PSA 1993.

The revaluation and anti-franking provisions need not be written into the rules (see paras 1.2 and 1.3 above), although there may be greater clarity if a brief cross-reference is included, particularly to revaluation if the rules contain other provisions for increases to benefits.

2 Continued life cover

Some schemes include an arrangement with the relevant life office to permit a member, on leaving service, to take out a policy (at his own expense) without a medical examination for life cover up to the amount provided either for him while in service or even for members generally. This may also be negotiated on a bulk withdrawal, eg on the sale of part of a business.

It is rare for the scheme itself to provide continued lump sum life cover for members with preserved pensions but this may be permissible under Inland Revenue practice—see below.

For members who joined the pension scheme before 1 October 1991 there is considerably more scope than for subsequent entrants. (The date reflects a change of practice announced in the Revenue's Memorandum 108 and incorporated subsequently in their revised practice notes at paras 7.26 and 7.38/39). If the sum becomes payable (from the scheme) before the deferred pension begins, it may comprise a continuation of the cover in force before the member left service. If payable after commencement of pension, three requirements apply save on exceptional ill-health retirement when, if the scheme's rules so apply to all members, the first can be ignored unless the whole pension has been commuted and the second applies only once normal retirement age is eventually reached. Firstly, the notional premium cost must (save for trivial exceptions) be included as a lump sum retirement benefit, thus reducing the maximum permitted commutation and reducing by the pension equivalent of the sum the maximum permissible pension. The notional cost is likely to be low. Secondly, the lump sum (save in some circumstances where it does not exceed £2,500) must be payable to the member's estate or surviving spouse to prevent the avoidance of inheritance tax.Thirdly, where the life cover continues in retirement and after normal retirement age, either it must be insured under a policy that does not qualify as 'pensions business' or the employer must undertake to provide the lump sum to the trustees in the event of a death, the intention being to avoid the benefit building up out of tax exempt funds.

Leavers who joined the pension scheme on or after 1 October 1991 may also be given the (comparatively rare) continuation of lump sum life cover, and other survivors' benefits on death before deferred pension begins (see the Revenue's practice notes, para 10.19). However, life cover for pensioners (apart from a five-year guarantee of pension under para 12.10), including leavers who draw their pension early, cannot be available to this category except for the period before normal retirement age where the early commencement of pension arose from exceptional ill-health (para 7.26).

3 Transfer of undertaking

The Transfer of Undertakings (Protection of Employment) Regulations 1981 (SI 1981 No 1794) now referred to by trade unions (and employers) as TUPE, provide that the contract of employment is treated as if originally made between the employee and the purchaser (reg 5). However, reg 7 provides that reg 5 'shall not apply . . . to so much of a contract of employment . . . as relates to an occupational pension scheme . . .' (see below). In the event that the purchaser does not provide similar pension arrangements it is not clear whether the employee has a remedy against the vendor or the purchaser. On balance, it is likely to be against the vendor. Frequently sale agreements include an indemnity from the purchaser.

If both parties to a sale and purchase wish to avoid a difficulty in relation to pension arrangements, they may agree that the trustees of the vendor's pension scheme will provide a transfer payment to the trustees of the purchaser's scheme sufficiently generous to enable the latter to provide full continuous pensionable service either having obtained the trustees' prior approval or being confident that they will obtain it—or agreeing to use their best endeavours to obtain it. It will be necessary to consider whether the transfer should be compulsory or at the employee's option (para 11 below).

Complexities arise where the purchaser's scheme has a different benefit structure from the vendor's. Chapter 11 outlines many aspects of such transfer arrangements. Where only the vendor's scheme is contracted out, a partial transfer could, until 6 April 1997, be effected. The liability for guaranteed minimum pension or protected rights (Chapter 20) would be retained by it, or purchased from the State by payment of a transfer premium, and the purchaser's scheme would provide a smaller past service benefit that made some allowance for that retained accrual. The statutory provision for a transfer premium is no longer available (Pensions Act 1995, Sched 5, para 50). Further, as the contracted-out accrual from 6 April 1997 no longer contains a guaranteed minimum underpin, there is no 'excess' above it which can be transferred to a contracted-in scheme, so the likelihood of the parties bothering to negotiate *any* transfer, ie for pre-6 April 1997 accrual only, is now remote. In any event, the employee will have a right to an insurance buy-out (para 12 below).

Where the parties are not able to make arrangements for continuity of pensions, or the terms of their schemes are very different, the question arises whether the employee can effectively claim to have been constructively dismissed. There is little authority on the subject. There may be a parallel in the redundancy cases, although this would not be redundancy. If the parallel applies, where a term of employment (such as membership of a pension scheme) is different, the question of suitability (and reasonableness of the employee in accepting or refusing the offer) would fall to be dealt with by an industrial tribunal. It is considered that the lack of comparable pension benefits creates a strong doubt as to suitability. In 1967 it was held in a Scottish case (in the Court of Session) that the loss of a sick pay scheme was 'a serious blow' to the relevant household (*Carron Co v Robertson* 1967 SC 273; [1967] ITR 484); the *Carron* case illustrates very clearly that the question of an employee's reasonableness in accepting or refusing the offer of suitable employment is subjective and dependent on his circumstances (see pp 489 and 491 of the ITR report). The extent to which the new pension arrangements must match the old, and to which the employers must provide continuity of pensionable service, will depend upon the facts of each case and, no doubt, the opinion of the tribunal.

The above contractual questions only arise if TUPE does not transfer pension rights. Regulation 7, quoted at the beginning of this section, plainly excludes pension rights, but has been challenged as in breach of the EU Directive on Business Transfers 77/187 in *Adams v Lancashire CC and BET Catering* [1996] IRLR 154 Ch D. The court noted the gap in full protection of pension rights (because preservation protects accrued rights to the extent only of salary at the date of transfer, plus revaluation) but concluded that the Council of the EU must have intended this, and that the meaning of the Directive was sufficiently clear to make it inappropriate to request a ruling from the ECJ. Upheld in the Court of Appeal in 1997, the case may go to the House of Lords. (An earlier case that came to the same conclusion and is frequently cited is *Walden Engineering v Warrener* [1993] IRLR 420 EAT.)

4 Effect on funding

A final salary pension scheme will usually include a reserve to allow for the effect of future salary rises on past pensionable service, subject to an allowance for an assumed percentage of employees leaving service ('withdrawals', in actuarial jargon). It is sometimes observed that a fund makes a profit when employees are redundant. This is not strictly the case, for the retained liability is the same for any employee who leaves service. Nevertheless, if the employer has made advance provision for future salary increases, and more employees leave than had been assumed by the actuary, the assets will be available to enable a reduced future contribution rate or to be treated in some other way as surplus. However, increasingly, redundant employees over the age of 50 are awarded an immediate pension which does not suffer an actuarial reduction on account of its early commencement. This will be an additional liability for the scheme.

5 *Ex gratia* payments

Retirements or death in service are sometimes accompanied by *ex gratia* lump sum payments from the employer. The Revenue will now generally regard the payment as a retirement benefits scheme (except where due solely to redundancy or death/disability caused by accident) and, being unapproved, chargeable to tax under s 596A of ICTA 1988. However, where the recipient is not already a member of an approved pension scheme, and the lump sum does not exceed the amount normally approvable from such a scheme, the Revenue will normally (on an application from the employer) approve the *ex gratia* arrangement as a scheme. Many recipients of *ex gratia* sums will, however, be members of approved schemes; in their case the unavailability of the usual £30,000 tax relief may be unexpected.

The foregoing represents two changes in Revenue practice, brought into effect together on 1 November 1991. They are set out in a Statement of Practice (SP 13/91) and a PSO (then SFO) Memorandum No 111.

The first change is to treat a decision to make an ex gratia payment as an 'arrangement' and therefore within s 611(2) which defines retirement benefits scheme. The second change is the willingness, where there is no membership of an approved scheme, to confer approval on the *ex gratia* arrangement (although, surprisingly, paragraph 16 of Memorandum 111 indicates that some payments will be non-approvable and yet taxable as payments from a scheme).

Any applications for approval are necessarily made after *ex gratia* awards. Form SF 60, attached to Memorandum 111, sets out the time limits.

By concession no application need be made in respect of small sums which will not be taxable if the recipient is not a member of an approved scheme. This applies to sums not exceeding one-twelfth of the earnings cap prescribed under s 590C (currently £84,000 so that such sums do not exceed £7,000).

Membership of an exclusively death benefit scheme can be ignored if the payment is on retirement.

An entirely separate question can arise, usually on redundancy. Where an employer voluntarily provides lump sums exceeding the statutory requirement, and outside the terms of the employee's contract, the excess over the tax-free £30,000 is frequently paid into the pension scheme or to provide enhanced benefits. There is usually scope for such enhancement since pension can be taken at any time from age 50 onwards (earlier in cases of extreme ill-health, but this is hardly likely to apply on redundancy). The value of an early pension is clearly higher than that of the normal pension; for this reason, the standard benefit usually provides for actuarial reduction. That reduction can be waived without infringing Inland Revenue limits. Clearly such a payment must be entirely separate from an employee's entitlement to receive a lump sum if he is not to be taxed on it as monies due which he has directed to the pension scheme.

6 Maternity rules and family leave

6.1 Maternity leave

Statutory maternity leave, and its effect on pensions, altered radically in 1994. The former has been consolidated in the Employment Rights Act 1996, ss 71–85 (and see ss 66–68 where pregnancy or recent childbirth can give rise to suspension on full pay on medical or health and safety grounds). Section 71 may of itself give rise to pension rights (see below) but, where there is simultaneously maternity pay, specific provision for pension is made by the Social Security Act 1989, Sched

5, brought into force (partially) after a five-year delay by SI 1994 No 1661—see para 6.3 below.

The first period—14 weeks

The ERA, ss 71 and 73 provide, without qualification as to service or any other material qualification, for 14 weeks maternity leave. Section 71(2) states that the provision 'does not confer any entitlement to remuneration' (but see below regarding statutory maternity pay). The 14-week period was introduced, effective 1994, to comply with an EU Directive 92/85 EEC (and, exceptionally, is extended if the child is born after the period would have expired or return to work is 'prohibited' under a statutory requirement by reason of the recent birth).

By contrast s 79 in effect re-enacts the long-standing right, where the woman has had two or more years' continuous service, to return to work at any time up to 29 weeks after childbirth (measured from the beginning of the week of birth).

Most commentators regard the first period (ie the 14 weeks) as a continuation of the contract of employment, and the balance of the second period as outside that contract unless (as often implicitly happens) brought within it. For example, the ERA 1996 does not, for the first period, confer a specific 'right to return' but instead s 71 which is labelled '. . . maternity leave' refers to an employee 'who is absent'. It provides that, other than for remuneration, an employee who is absent 'during her maternity leave period is . . . entitled to the benefit of the terms and conditions of employment which would have been applicable . . .'. This view is supported by the provision, in s 76, for an employee wishing to return *during* the 14 weeks to give notice, and in particular the provision of s 76(3) whereby the employer cannot require her to delay her return beyond the 14 weeks, and further supported by s 79(2) which refers to the person who was her employer before the end of her maternity leave period.

The second period—26 weeks

The second period begins at the end of the 14 weeks—s 79(1). As the first period cannot begin until 11 weeks before expected childbirth (s 74(2)), and this second period ends 29 weeks after childbirth, the total period of absence is normally up to 40 weeks of which up to 26 weeks will be the second period. Some commentators label the second period 'the extended period'.

Section 79(2)(*b*) re-enacts the existing provision that where a woman exercises her right (ie by due notice etc) to return by the end of the second period, her pension rights are to apply as if her employment prior to the end of her maternity leave period (the 14 weeks) were continuous with her employment after her return to work. The same is provided for preservation purposes by SI 1991 No 167, reg 21(3)(b) so long as the member returns to pensionable service within a month after returning to work. Unlike reg 21(5), there is no requirement for the earlier period to have been sufficient to qualify for preservation (see para 1.1 above) ie the two periods together can make up the two years qualifying pensionable service.

The SI uses the term 'confinement', as did the old employment legislation, but since 1993 (and in particular in the 1996 Act) this has been abandoned in favour of the more modern 'childbirth' eg the expression 'expected week of childbirth'.

Section 79(2)(*b*), in treating the return to work after the second period as continuous with the first (14-week) period, adds 'but subject to the requirements of paragraph 5 of Schedule 5 to the Social Security Act 1989 (credit for the period of absence in certain cases)'—see para 6.3 below.

6.2 Statutory maternity pay

If the woman on maternity leave had been in the particular employment for 26 weeks ending in the fifteenth week before expected childbirth she will normally be entitled, under the Social Security Contributions and Benefits Act 1992, s 165 and SI 1986 No 1960, as amended, to 'statutory maternity pay', from her employer, for up to 18 weeks (14 weeks if she returns to work at the end of the maternity leave period described above as the first period). Six weeks are at 90 per cent of normal weekly earnings, the balance at a modest statutory rate reviewed each year (for 1997/8 £55.70 per week).

A woman who does not qualify for statutory maternity pay from her employer will generally qualify for a social security maternity allowance for 18 weeks, at the same modest rate as mentioned at the end of the last paragraph, if she has paid 26 weeks' national insurance contributions (ie regarding *any* employment) in the 66 weeks up to childbirth. This is not paid by the employer and is not to be confused with the statutory maternity pay described above and, as stated below, referred to in the SSA 1989.

6.3 Social Security Act 1989

Introduction

Schedule 5 to the Social Security Act 1989, and SI 1994 No 1661, are mentioned in para 6.1 above. The delay in bringing Sched 5 into force arose while the equality requirements of European law with regard to pensions were clarified (Chapter 22). As the purpose, stated in s 23, was to give effect to the equal treatment directive (the Second Directive referred to in Chapter 22 para 2.7), Sched 5 has a wider ambit than just pensions. Paragraph 7 therefore defines an 'employment-related benefit scheme.' While the whole of para 7, except for (d) relating to the public sector, is in force, the SI has only brought parts of the rest of Sched 5 into force, principally because other parts (such as the defined 'permitted age-related difference') have been superseded by firstly the *Barber* and *Birds Eye Walls* cases and secondly the equal treatment provisions of the Pensions Act 1995 (Chapter 22, para 2.8).

'Employment-related benefit scheme' is one that provides 'service-related benefits'. Para 7(e) defines the latter as benefits 'in the form of pensions or otherwise', lists these, including accident and unemployment benefits, and sweeps up with 'any other benefit. . . . in consequence of his employment'. However, for present purposes it is sufficient that the list includes retirement pensions, since the relevant questions are whether contributions are payable to, and whether benefits accrue under, a pension scheme in respect of maternity leave.

Schedule 5 clearly applies to periods of *paid* maternity absence, whether paid under contract or as the above statutory maternity pay—para 5(3). It might appear that it could also apply to unpaid periods (if the contract of employment subsisted eg the 14 weeks' statutory maternity leave where there had not been the 26-week qualification for statutory maternity pay) by reason of the general requirement to comply with the principle of equal treatment in para 3. However, this difficult question of compliance does not yet arise (under the 1989 Act) as SI 1994 No 1661 only brings into force para 3 for the *limited* purpose of giving effect to paras 5 and 6.

Unfair maternity provisions

Paragraph 5 is entitled (and defines) 'Unfair maternity provisions'. The effect of para 5 is fairly clear for a defined benefit scheme, but less clear for defined contributions (Chapter 8). Paragraph 5(1) declares 'unfair' any breach of the 'normal employment requirement' set out in para 5(3)(b). The latter (when taken together with the provisions mentioned below) requires that:

> any period of paid maternity absence [defined in (3)(a) to include a period after the employment when still in receipt of statutory maternity pay] shall be treated [for pension purposes] as if it were a period throughout which the woman in question works normally and receives the remuneration likely to be paid for doing so.

In effect an 'unfair maternity provision' is deemed to discriminate (for pension, and indeed other benefit, purposes) against a woman on paid maternity absence, when compared with a woman working normally, and is overridden by para 3, as applied by 5(2). Paragraph 5(1)(a), together with 5(2), applies the above to continuing membership of, or (meaning here 'and also') the accrual of rights under, the pension scheme. Paragraph 5(1)(b) applies similarly to the 'amount of any benefit payable' under the scheme, and is quoted in full towards the end of para 6.4 below.

Contributions

Although the contractual pay may (and the statutory pay will) be less than the para 5(3) 'likely' remuneration (applied to the pension benefit by the effect of the passage set out above and paras 5(1) and (2)), the woman (if it is a contributory scheme) need only *contribute* on the pay actually received—para 5(2) at the end. This raises an uncertainty regarding benefit accrual in defined contribution schemes—see para 6.4 below.

The SI does not bring into force para 3(2) or 5(2)(b) which specifically refers to 3(2). As 3(2) would have required the woman to contribute 'at a level appropriate to the treatment . . . accorded [by para 5]' or to elect for the less favourable treatment and to contribute accordingly, it is plain that the express omission of 3(2) gives the woman a pensionable salary based on the 'likely remuneration' as if she had been working normally, while requiring only the contributions based on actual remuneration or maternity pay.

Unfair family leave provisions

Schedule 5 also applies to 'Unfair family leave provisions' (para 6) brought in to force by the same SI (apart from para 6(3)(b) and (c)).

This relates to periods of paid family leave and in most respects contains identical provisions to the above, but raises no difficulty (assuming 'family leave' can be identified, and ignoring the minor drafting question mentioned below) as:

(*a*) The period of leave is only the period when contractual remuneration is paid.
(*b*) The requirement of para 6(4)(b) that corresponds to para 5(3)(b) in the quoted passage above differs in its essential feature, viz that while the period in para 6 is treated as normal work the member is to be treated as in receipt of 'only . . . the remuneration in fact paid to him' (ie no reference to remuneration 'likely to be paid [for normal work]'). The provision is unfair if the actual remuneration is not pensionable.

'Family leave' will normally be a father's absence during his wife's childbirth but could cover absence by either sex for family reasons. The question arises whether para 6 has any effect where the sexes are treated the same way, bearing in mind that, unlike para 5, there is an opening sub-para 6(1) that specifically refers to the principle of equal treatment (set out in para 2 and given effect in para 3). As 6(1) uses the words 'irrespective of any differences on the basis of sex', the answer appears to be 'yes' although the drafting would have been clearer if it had been 'irrespective *whether or not* there are any differences . . .'. However, as para 6 refers to *actual* remuneration, in practice few schemes, if any, will contravene it anyway.

6.4 Effect on pension accrual

Defined Benefit: non-contributory

For a defined benefit scheme, the period of 18 weeks statutory maternity pay (SMP) (and any longer period of contractual pay) will be pensionable service and will be treated as if full pensionable salary had been received (SSA 1989, Sched 5, per para 6.3 above) eg for life cover purposes and any pension calculation.

It seems probable that in the pension calculation pensionable salary should include any bonus or pay rise that would have applied if the woman had been working normally eg as paid to corresponding persons in the employment. (DSS, soon after SI 1994 No 1661 came in to force, expressed the contrary view viz that pay should be taken at the rate when maternity leave started).

For an employee not entitled to SMP (because recently engaged), nor (for the purpose of this example) to contractual pay, the 14 weeks maternity leave may still be pensionable. While the 1989 Act affords her no rights, the ERA, s 71, affords her the benefit of the terms and conditions of employment that would have been applicable if she had not been absent notwithstanding that, by s 71(2), no entitlement to 'remuneration' is thereby conferred. Some commentators have cited, fairly confidently, a number of reasons why the exclusion of remuneration does not serve to exclude pension terms. The arguments are persuasive, particularly (it appears) that in the passage of the earlier legislation (Trade Union Reform and Employment Rights Act 1993, in this respect consolidated in the ERA 1996) the word 'remuneration' was substituted for 'pay' as it was thought that 'pay', in the EU context, would include (ie have extended the exclusion to) pension contributions and benefits in kind. This assumes that pension benefits are a term of employment, even though provided under a separate scheme. On the EU approach that assumption would be strong, and even on the traditional UK approach *eligibility* for the scheme would be a term of employment.

It would therefore appear that, for a non-contributory defined benefits scheme, even where there is no SMP, life cover may well continue during the 14 weeks, crucially during the expected week of childbirth. Pensionable service may not give rise to a pension for such a short period but in at least two circumstances, if s 71 applies to pension rights, the scheme would be obliged by preservation (SI 1991 No 167, reg 21) to recognise the period:

(1) The first circumstance is if there is a preserved pension from an earlier period of pensionable service in the same scheme (reg 21(5)) or arising from a transfer from a personal pension scheme or from linked qualifying service with an occupational scheme (if in the latter case there is at least two years' aggregated qualifying service)—PSA 1993, s 71(1) and (7).

(2) The second circumstance is if the woman returns to pensionable service within a month after the expiry of the 14 weeks—reg 21(3)(a); in this second case, the 14-week period (and the immediately preceding short period of employment) would count towards the two years needed to qualify for preserva-

tion—but not necessarily towards the pension itself (the implication of reg 21(2), albeit the combined effect of preservation and the ERA 1996, s 71, may be to include the period for pension too if the two years is actually attained).

The position during the (unpaid) balance of the 29 weeks within the 'second period' mentioned in para 6.1 above seems to be that in the absence of a contractual term (or scheme rule) to the contrary, the period will not be pensionable nor will life cover apply. It is difficult to see how it could be otherwise (since the woman would not be working, let alone performing like work as a comparator) save pursuant to an extended judicial interpretation of Article 119 or UK legislation. The equality cases cited in Chapter 22 do not seem relevant.

Defined benefit: contributory

The period of 18 weeks SMP (and any longer period of contractual pay) is treated by the SSA 1989 uniformly for benefit purposes regardless of whether the (defined benefit) scheme is contributory or non-contributory, ie Sched 5 does not refer to the distinction (except regarding the contributions).

The first two paragraphs under the heading above '. . . *non-contributory*', regarding SMP (and/or other pay), therefore apply likewise to contributory schemes (and see para 6.3 above for a fuller treatment of Sched 5).

The position (while there is SMP or other pay) regarding the woman's own contributions is clear if the scheme is silent, but could lead to a curious anomaly if the scheme were specific:

(1) If the scheme is silent, ie makes no provision to accrue pension during paid maternity absence, Sched 5, by paras 3(1) and 5(2) excluding (b) and (c) which are not in force, provides that benefits are to be as if the woman receives normal remuneration but that her contributions are only 'required on the amount of contractual remuneration or statutory maternity pay actually paid to [her]'. Plainly the overriding effect of Sched 5 is to give her full benefits without requiring full contributions.
(2) In the second circumstance, however, if the scheme rules already provide the full benefits there is no 'unfair maternity provision', and Sched 5 has no effect; it could be argued that a rule requiring contribution based on the same full deemed

> pensionable salary as the benefits was valid. The contrary argument would be that the rule was a condition for the benefits, that a woman could refuse to pay and that she would then obtain the benefit of Sched 5 if she tendered contribution on the basis of actual maternity pay. In practice it seems unlikely that a defined benefit scheme would endeavour to require contributions on an amount above actual pay.

The next three paragraphs under the heading above '. . . non-contributory', regarding the 14 weeks maternity leave, are relevant where the employee is *not* entitled to SMP or other pay. They indicate the likely argument that the ERA 1996, s 71 confers pension benefits. For a contributory (defined benefit) scheme the same argument could apply even though the woman paid no contribution as the obligation to contribute would be based on remuneration of zero. The contrary argument would be to cite the European cases that require arrears of contributions to be paid where past pensionable service is claimed (Chapter 22) but these cases relate to denied access and not to deemed terms of employment. For the time being the position is uncertain. Either way, the employer may wish to make the intended position clear to members, as the risk of dispute over lump sum life cover may be considerable; alternatively the employer may prefer not to disclose a position while the law is uncertain, although in the event of a dispute, eg if the woman dies during the 14 weeks, her potential beneficiaries may claim a breach of the disclosure regs (Chapter 16, para 6).

The position during the (unpaid) balance of the 29 weeks within the 'second period' will plainly be the same as set out above for non-contributory schemes, unless the equal treatment legislation is extended (in which case it could be that contributory (defined benefit) schemes would differ unless the woman made special contributions but such differentiation would seem unlikely).

Defined contribution

Most modern defined contribution schemes are contributory ie require contributions from members as well as employers. It will be plain, however, that most of what is said below will apply equally to non-contributory schemes.

For a defined contribution scheme, even the period to which the 1989 SSA applies (the period of 18 weeks SMP and any longer period of contractual pay—see the beginning of para 6.4 above) has its uncertainty, viz whether the employer is obliged to contribute the difference between the *member's* actual contribution (based on actual pay, whether contractual or SMP—para 6.3 above) and the contribution based on the full pay that would have been applicable if she had been working normally (needed to be invested if the money purchase *benefits* are truly to be as if she had worked normally). DSS think not, but concede that the point may have to be resolved by the court.

The difficulty arises from para 5(1)(b) of Sched 5, which classifies as unfair:

> (b) [any provision] which requires the amount of any benefit payable under the scheme to or in respect of any such woman, to the extent that it falls to be determined by reference to her earnings during a period which included a period of paid maternity absence, to be determined otherwise than in accordance with the normal employment requirement [viz the requirement in para 5(3)(b) set out in the quoted passage in the fourth paragraph of para 6.3 above to the effect that the woman be treated as if in receipt of likely full normal remuneration].'

The words 'any benefit . . . determined by reference to her earnings' would seem to include the money-purchase benefit arising from the woman's contributions as much as from the employer's, as both are almost always a percentage of her earnings. Most commentators, and certainly DSS, seem to consider as a matter of course that Sched 5 applies to require the employer to contribute its own standard percentage (of the full notional earnings). That is also the author's view. From there one proceeds to consider the woman's own contributions. By para 5(2) she need only contribute on her actual pay. Therefore, if para 5(1) were viewed in isolation, the employer should have to make up the difference, just as it funds the balance of cost of defined benefit schemes. If para 3(2) were in force, it could be argued to the contrary that the woman can elect to pay at the lower rate and receive the less favourable benefit. However, the SI specifically did not bring 3(2) into force.

The contrary argument, to relieve the employer of the extra contribution, is that the *benefit* derives from the employer's standard contribution, and that the woman purchases the balance herself, and does not receive it as a benefit of employment. However, it seems more likely that the benefit derives from the total (indivisible) contribution, and that the employer must make up the balance. Nonetheless the point is sufficiently uncertain to justify an employer taking a policy decision and awaiting developments.

A COMP scheme (Chapter 20) treats part of the benefit (all of it if a minimum contributions scheme) as 'protected rights' (non commutable etc). DSS consider that only the part derived from actual pay falls into this category.

For a period of unpaid maternity leave (the 14 weeks, assuming the woman is not entitled to SMP or contractual remuneration) a defined contribution scheme seems only to qualify its member for benefits, if at all, in the same way as a defined benefit scheme, relying on ERA 1996, s 71. This suggests that the employer must pay its standard contributions as if the woman were in receipt of full pay. As the SSA 1989 does not apply it seems likely that there is no obligation to pay *her* contributions too. The position regarding both aspects, and life cover, must, however, remain uncertain until resolved by the court or by legislation.

For the position during the (unpaid) balance of the 29 weeks within the 'second period', see the end of each of the two sections above.

6.5 Other aspects

National insurance contributions

National insurance contributions in respect of maternity pay are (at least for the initial six weeks—see below) at the rate applicable before maternity leave started. In the case of a member of a contracted-out scheme, this is the reduced (contracted-out) rate—see PSA 1993, ss 41(2) and 42A(6).

A helpful guide is to be found in a booklet published by the Department of Social Security, CA 14 (printed as 'Effective from 6 April 1997' but in fact available some months earlier and therefore containing references to the pre-consolidation, ie pre-ERA 1996, legislation). Paragraphs 4.40 to 4.50 state the position regarding national insurance contributions during the 'second period' mentioned in para 6.1 above (assuming she is still in receipt of pay or SMP during the 'second period'), both when the woman has a right to return to work and when she does not intend to do so if her 'contracted-out employment is treated as having terminated' (4.48)—although regarding the critical question of *when* the employment terminates it simply states 'determined by her employer' (4.43). It barely mentions the 'first period' (ie the 14 weeks), possibly because that period is assumed to be within the contract for the reasons stated in para 6.1 above—para 3.10.

Paragraph 4.48 states that if contracted-out employment is treated as terminated, and payment is continued no more than six weeks, the period is treated as contracted-out; national insurance contributions are at the reduced rate—no doubt by reason of PSA, ss 41(2)(*b*) and 42A(6)(*b*). Ambiguously it states that if payment is more than six weeks after the termination date, contributions are at the full rate but from the previous edition this appears to mean that the contributions change at the six-week point.

By contrast, para 4.41 states that if the woman has the right to return under the 1978 Act (now the ERA 1996 ie, regarding the 'second period', if she has given statutory notice) and subsequently returns to work by the end of that period, contracted-out employment is not treated as having terminated.

The trigger, in practical terms, is the notification given to the Contributions Agency, and in practical terms this will be in accordance with the booklet, which also makes provision for cancellation (by notificationn to the Contribution Agency) of a termination notice where an employee returns to work (presumably by the end of the 'second period') having said that she did not intend to do so—para 4.45.

Preservation: avoidance of duplication or complexity

As stated in para 6.1 above, the balance of the second period (after the expiry of the first period) may be outside the contract of employment or may implicitly be brought within it—or there may be an express term that brings the period within it. Cessation of the contract will generally trigger the vesting of deferred pension and other rights under the rules of the pension scheme. Since a return to work on the expiry of the second period has to be treated as continuous with the previous period of employment for pension purposes—s 79(2)(*b*) cited in para 6.1 above—it is important to draft the rules of the scheme so that a woman who has given statutory notice of her intention to return to work does not become entitled to vested benefits until immediately after the expiry of the second period. Further, such provision will, it appears, avoid the vesting of benefits to which the revaluation or transfer/buyout provisions mentioned in paras 1.2 above and 10.2 below might attach. While this is not altogether clear, particularly in the case of transfers/buyouts, in practice the woman could always obtain these rights by opting out of the pension scheme, assuming she did not envisage returning to deemed *continuous* pensionable service and was not losing life cover.

It is not clear whether such provision in the rules can prevent the disclosure requirement that the rights and options available to a member 'whose pensionable service terminates before he attains normal pension age' be furnished automatically as soon as practicable after the member or employer has notified the trustees that the pensionable service has terminated (SI 1991 No 167, reg 27A as inserted by SI 1996 No 2131) but in practice no problem need arise as normally the member will have a right anyway to the information on request under reg 27A(1)(b).

The effect of preservation outlined in para 1.1 above, is to remove the right to a refund of contributions after two years' qualifying service. The two years, however, will usually coincide with the qualifying period (under ERA 1996, s 79) for the right to return to work by the end of the 'second period' mentioned in para 6.1 above. This removes any perceived disadvantage from the loss to pregnant women (deemed by most rules not to have ceased to be in service, by reason of their notice of intention to return to work) of the refund option.

7 Broken service: effect of preservation

If a member leaves service (or opts out of the pension scheme) entitled to short service benefit ie the preserved benefits that a scheme is obliged to provide after two years' pensionable or transferred-in service, and subsequently returns to pensionable service in the same scheme, he becomes entitled to further preserved benefits on subsequently leaving, even if the second period is less than two years (SI 1991 No 167, reg 21). This means that care must be taken to ensure that the application forms for membership include the question as to whether the person has previously been a member of the scheme (whether under the same or another name).

The requirement does not apply if the earlier period's entitlement has in effect been extinguished by a transfer, buyout, purchase back into the State scheme or lump sum payment (reg 21(5)).

Regulation 21(2) provides that pensionable service before a break must, in three other circumstances, be added to the later period in counting towards the two years required for preservation, whether or not the earlier period counts towards the qualification for normal retirement pension, *viz*:

(*a*) where the break does not exceed one month;
(*b*) where the break comprised maternity absence, and the member returns to work in exercise of her right under ERA 1996, s 79 (see para 6.1 above), rejoining pensionable service within a month after that return;
(*c*) where the break is caused by a trade dispute (as defined).

8 Dismissal

The following comments relate firstly to unfair dismissal and then briefly to unlawful termination (breach of contract).

Unfair dismissal is now re-enacted in the ERA 1996. Sections 112 and 113 enable a tribunal which finds a person to have been unfairly dismissed to require reinstatement (or comparable re-engagement) or to order compensation. Where compensation is ordered, the tribunal will try to value the claim for loss of pension rights (see s 74(2) and *Copson v Eversure Accessories Ltd* [1974] IRLR 247; [1974] ITR 406; [1974] ICR 636). Such assessment has frequently proved a matter of great difficulty although a straightforward starting point is the 1991 booklet mentioned below.

Tribunals take into account the possibility of finding new employment with similar or better pension arrangements. On the whole, however, a substantial increase in compensation seems to be awarded where the dismissed employee has achieved middle age and would have gone on to receive a considerable pension. The burden of proving the loss and its extent is placed on the claimant, even though most of the evidence (for example, the trust deed, rules, and details of employer's contribution rates) will be in the possession of or more readily available to the employer.

In many cases the loss in respect of future service has been calculated by reference to the employer's rate of contribution to the scheme over a future period, subject to reduction to take account of the possibility of premature death or of obtaining some other pensionable employment. The amount may be as low as two or three years' contributions.

Where the employee has received a refund of his contributions, or remains entitled to a prospective pension under the scheme, the tribunal, in valuing the loss in respect of past service, will give credit for this. The method of giving credit is normally rough and ready, rather than actuarial, and this approach has been approved by the court. Frequently the loss, formulated in one of the established ways, plainly exceeds the £11,300 limit for the compensatory part of the award (but should still be calculated as any excess reduces the liability to repay unemployment benefit under the Recoupment regulations).

The questions to be looked into should therefore include the following:

(*a*) the age of the employee;
(*b*) the normal retirement age under the scheme;
(*c*) whether employments in that field are generally pensionable;
(*d*) the duration of the employee's scheme service;
(*e*) the difference between the deferred pension entitlement based on salary at dismissal (plus revaluation under the pension scheme's rules and/or statute) and such entitlement based on the salary that might be reasonably expected at normal retirement age, capitalised and discounted;
(*f*) the percentage contribution rate of the employer, to assist in valuing both the past service loss and (at a discount, having regard to (*c*) above) the future service loss.

There are numerous reported cases relating to tribunal awards of compensation in respect of pension rights. Apart from the *Copson* case cited above, the practitioner is particularly referred to *Gill v Harold Andrews Sheepbridge Ltd* [1974] IRLR 109; [1974] ICR 294 (particularly pp 111–14 of the IRLR report), *Bingham v Hobourn Engineering Ltd* [1992] IRLR 298, EAT (an unusual case where new employment was obtained at a higher salary and with better future pension accrual) and *Manpower Ltd v Hearne* [1983] ICR 567.

The Government Actuary's Department (GAD) published in 1980 a suggested method of valuing the loss of pension rights ([1980] IRLR 216) but see below regarding the 1991 booklet. While some tribunals have adopted those guidelines, they remain free to avoid actuarial calculations if they wish (*Willmont Bros Ltd v Oliver* [1979] ICR 378, EAT). In *TBA Industrial Products Ltd v Locke* [1984] IRLR 48 the Employment Appeal Tribunal upheld an order based on the GAD guidelines but reduced by a 70 per cent withdrawal factor because the employee's poor record established a:

> 'very high degree of probability that [he] would have left the respondent's employment in any event either due to a continuation of his unsatisfactory work or to overall redundancy . . . [it was] plainly right to consider that he might have been fairly dismissed'.

The GAD guideline has been superseded by a booklet 'Industrial Tribunals—Compensation for loss of pension rights' prepared by a committee of chairmen of Industrial Tribunals and incorporating a new GAD paper, published by HMSO (2nd edition 1991). The booklet is essential reading. However, it states that other methods may be canvassed where appropriate (para 11.2, cited in the above *Bingham* case at para 26). Transfers were also cited in *Bingham*, albeit the evidence was too late to affect the award; for comment on transfer calculations see para 10.1 below.

Apart from tribunal awards for unfair dismissal, there are few examples of compensation for loss of pension rights on termination of employment (apart from those settled publicly and without judicial comment). However, provided the pension arrangements are adequately imported into the contract of employment, there is every reason to include them in the damages claimed in an action for breach of contract.

The old reported cases show the importance of distinguishing between pension rights gratuitously conferred by the employer and those to which the employee is entitled under his contract—see, for example, *Beach v Reed Corrugated Cases Ltd* [1956] 2 All ER 652, QBD. Since the enactment of the Contracts of Employment Acts (consolidated in the above ERA 1996), it is unlikely that there would now be doubt as to this question. It is probable that damages would be measured on similar lines to those described above in relation to statutory rights (see particularly the industrial injuries case of *Auty v National Coal Board* [1985] 1 All ER 930 CA for the court's disinterest in actuarial evidence regarding likely future salary inflation). In the *Beach* case (cited above) the court placed no value on the future service rights as the scheme was capable of being wound up at the discretion of the employer; however, the plaintiff had been the managing director and the scheme may well have been limited to a small number of persons (although the report is silent as to this); normally, it would be perverse to place much weight on this possibility as the likelihood of an employer, whose business continued successfully, invoking the power of discontinuance without replacing the scheme must, in the context of modern industrial relations, be remote. Indeed to do so might be unlawful (unless the economic affairs of the employer necessitated the termination) being destructive of the relationship of trust and confidence with the employees (*Imperial Tobacco*—see Chapter 24, para 10.6). See also Chapter 12.

9 Acting for the employee

You may be asked to advise an employee as to his rights under a scheme. Apart from the rules, you should obtain a copy of such announcements as have been published to employees (Chapter 3, para 11), including informal letters, since there may be promises binding upon the employer which have not been incorporated in the scheme. Occasionally, the question will be whether or not a discretion should have been exercised in favour of the employee. Unless you can establish that the trustees have acted without bona fides, there is little that can be done.

Despite the *Auty* case cited in para 8 above, an experienced actuary, given the case reports and 1991 booklet also there cited, may well be of great assistance in formulating a claim.

In industrial injury cases any disablement *pension* is regarded as insurance paid for by the employee and thus not to reduce the employer's liability (*Parry v Cleaver* [1969] 1 All ER 555, HL, affirmed by *Smoker v London Fire Authority* [1991] 2 All ER 449, HL). The same principle would appear to exclude an offset for early retirement pension where a long notice period has been ignored and a claim is made for loss of salary. Contrast *Hussain v New Taplow Mills Ltd* [1988] 1 All ER 541, HL, where payments under a 'permanent health' scheme (see Chapter 2, para 8) were payable as a continuation of the contract of employment and were deductible from the loss of earnings award (p 546j). *Hussain* was cited in *Smoker* but without comment save to note that there the contract of employment continued. The author is not aware of a move away from ill-health pensions towards 'permanent health' schemes as a result of these decisions but this must remain a possibility.

10 Individual transferring to another scheme

10.1 General

The preservation requirements (see para 1 above) allow a transfer to another scheme to be a valid alternative to the provision of a deferred pension within the scheme (PSA 1993, s 73(2)). They do not, however, confer a right to transfer. That right was introduced in 1985 (now PSA 1993, s 95) for members who satisfy certain requirements (see para 10.2 below). The entitlement ceases when the pension begins (and sometimes earlier).

Where the statutory right is not exercised, the rules of the scheme (or else the trust deed to which they are annexed) frequently provide discretionary power for the trustees to effect a transfer of members or pensioners. The power rarely prescribes the benefits which are to be obtained from the transferee scheme. Considerable controversy can be engendered by the terms of transfer.

Apart from any other factor, it is clear that if the two schemes assume different investment yields when calculating their liabilities, a given sum of money paid by the trustees of one to the trustees of the other will produce a promise of a smaller or larger benefit from the second trustees.

There is the further difficulty relating to members in service, that a final salary scheme provides a benefit according to salary immediately before retirement, so that if a member transfers to a scheme having had ten years' past service in his old scheme, and that ten years is fully recognised in the new scheme, it will probably produce a larger benefit (because the benefit will be based on his salary at retirement) than if a deferred pension had been paid from the old scheme on the basis of his salary when he left that scheme, even allowing for the statutory revaluation of the deferred pension. The cost of providing that larger benefit will be greater than the cost of the deferred pension in the old scheme.

The transferor trustees have a choice of method of calculating the transfer value for members in service (who may or may not be moving to a new employer). The most common methods include the following:

(*a*) the capital value of the deferred pension to which the member is entitled on leaving service (including any provision for increases); this will also usually be the statutory basis (see para 10.2 below);

(*b*) the above capital value, but allowing for future salary increases at the rate assumed by the scheme's actuary for those who remain in service.

The value may, if the fund is in deficit, be limited to the member's 'share of the fund' (the proportion of the fund equal to the proportion of liabilities represented by his pension or deferred pension) and, if the fund is in surplus, may be increased (although this is not likely on individual transfers, but may arise on bulk transfers—see para 11 below). Either way, where preservation applies, a transfer without the member's consent must comply with SI 1991 No 167, reg 12, which requires a connection (or financial transaction) between the employers and an actuary's certificate of equivalence for the transfer credits under the receiving scheme.

In practice, for individual transfers, method (*a*) is likely to be applied, albeit the transferring trustees can always choose to be more generous. See also the mandatory professional basis for the actuary (*Guidance Note 11* issued by the Institute and Faculty of Actuaries, updated February 1997).

It follows that only rarely will the receiving trustees offer the same length of back service as had arisen in the previous scheme (for that would require a transferred salary reserve) and that normally they can do so only where the additional cost is underwritten by one of the two employers concerned. This can create acrimony. The difference in cost is greater if the salary is higher with the new employer. In the public sector a 'transfer club' avoids this difficulty.

It also follows that even if the investment and other assumptions (salary increases etc) were the same, the back service in the transferee scheme would be shorter if its scale of benefit was more generous than that of the transferor scheme, for a given sum will produce a given benefit and if the scale per year is greater, the benefit would be represented by a shorter number of years. This is often misunderstood and, again, may cause acrimony.

Some schemes will therefore only grant, for transfer credits, deferred pensions of stated amount (which may or may not participate in annual increases) rather than added years of notional service.

The transferee scheme may well not include the same range of dependants' benefits as the transferor scheme. In practice there has been little consideration devoted to this question when the transferor trustees exercise their discretion to make the transfer. The effect of s 95 is to remove the discretion where a member exercises the right to a transfer, while giving a statutory discharge, so that the question will not arise in such cases, now the overwhelming majority (other than bulk transfers)—see para 10.2 below.

10.2 Member's right to transfer a cash equivalent

Apart from bulk transfers as mentioned in para 11 below, the majority of cases will now involve individuals exercising their statutory right to a transfer to another pension scheme meeting prescribed requirements. The statutory right, now PSA 1993, ss 93, 95, was introduced in 1985 but only for members whose pensionable service terminated on or after 1 January 1986. That limitation has now been removed, with one exception. The removal, effected by the Pensions Act 1995, s 152, enables persons who so wish to consolidate past rights into a current occupational or personal pension scheme, although the question whether this is of financial advantage will vary for each case. The exception (those pre-1986 leavers who are still unable unilaterally to transfer) applies to persons mainly in the public sector who have inflation-proofed pensions (SI 1996 No 1847, reg 2).

The observations in paras 12.2–12.4 below regarding cessation of pensionable service, and the requirements of s 99 are equally apt to transfers. However, the main question will be to establish whether the receiving scheme satisfies the requirements prescribed under s 95(2). These are set out in reg 12 of SI 1996 No 1847. The regulation does not expressly cover receiving schemes whose application for approval under ICTA 1988 is still under consideration but there is sufficient scope in the concluding words of reg 12(1)(d) '. . . or otherwise satisfies requirements of the Inland Revenue'. These words may also avoid the technical difficulty that a current amendment to the receiving scheme may cause approval to be lost, by reason of s 591B(2) of ICTA 1988, until the alteration has itself been approved by the Revenue.

A practical difficulty facing the transferor trustees is to establish that the receiving scheme is currently approved under ICTA 1988, or at least approved for the receipt of transfers. The letter conferring ICTA 1988 approval, of which a copy may be supplied, will probably bear a date many years earlier. If the scheme is well known, it may be considered sufficient to accept an assurance from the receiving trustees that it retains Revenue approval. In other cases, it may be prudent to enquire of the Revenue; since the Revenue may not reveal information to a third party, the traditional enquiry has been whether a transfer to such a scheme would prejudice the approval of the transferring scheme. This is more appropriate to a discretionary transfer. A corresponding enquiry for a statutory transfer would be whether it would fall within reg 12(1)(*d*) of SI 1996 No 1847. It remains to be established whether the Revenue will respond to such an enquiry without an authority from the scheme's administrator. In practice the administrator will obtain and pass on the Revenue's confirmation. Either way, the question arises whether a scheme can be adequately identified by its name alone.

These questions assume practical importance where the receiving scheme is not large, particularly in the light of the system operated by the promoters of the *Kestrel Pension Scheme* (Chapter 16, para 7).

If the transferring scheme is contracted-out, the requirements of reg 12(1)(*a*)–(*c*) are relevant. If the receiving scheme is an overseas arrangement, reg 12(5) and 12(6)(*b*) apply.

A transfer (or buy-out) payment made in response to a member's request under the statutory entitlement is to be calculated in the manner specified in reg 7 which, except where 7(5) applies, refers to the *Guidance Note GN 11* (see para 10.1 above). Regulation 8(2), which is particularly important, is set out below:

> '8(2) Where it is the established custom for additional benefits to be awarded from the scheme at the discretion of the trustees or the employer, the cash equivalent shall, unless the trustees have given a direction that cash equivalents shall not take account of such benefits, take account of any such additional benefits as will accrue to the member in question if the custom continues unaltered.'

It is important to ensure that each scheme's trustees have considered the above question if they award discretionary benefits, for example annual inflation awards or enhanced early retirement factors. They may not ignore the value of discretionary increases for the purpose of transfer payments without actuarial advice—reg 8(3).

Although reg 8(3) is drafted in the singular, it seems unlikely that there could be a proper reason for differentiating between one transfer payment and another, so that ordinarily a resolution to ignore discretionary benefits would relate to all intended transfers (until the policy is next considered). If the trustees direct that cash equivalents are not to take account of established discretionary increases, this direction must be published to members as part of the basic information about the scheme (ie in the Members' booklet or wherever)—SI 1996 No 1655 Sched 1, para 21.

Cash equivalents from salary-related schemes must now be guaranteed for three months—PSA 1993, ss 93A, 94, as amended by the Pensions Act 1995.

After a transfer without consent (eg a bulk transfer—para 11 below) the member's right to take the cash equivalent elsewhere springs up in the new scheme—reg 16.

11 Bulk transfers

Transfers of large numbers of members usually arise only on a takeover (see Chapter 11) or a group reconstruction.

On an agreed takeover (an acquisition) the receiving pension trustees will often be assured by one or other employer that if particular benefits can be granted, any shortfall in moneys will be made up by that employer. The extent to which there is such an assurance depends upon the wishes of the respective employers and their bargaining powers in the commercial transaction. It is, however, far more likely that year-for-year back service will be granted in a situation of bulk transfer than in the case of individuals—unless the individuals are 'key people'.

Bulk transfers frequently include pensioners and deferred pensioners, in which case it is rarely practical to seek consents. If both schemes are contracted out SI 1996 No 1462 (plus SI 1991 No 167, reg 12 as amended) provides the authority to transfer salary-related statutory benefits. There is an ambiguity in that para (a) of the definition 'connected employer transfer' refers to both schemes applying to employment with the same employer, which may not be the case in respect of pensioners who had left service some years earlier (but for the alternative para (b) see below). Nonetheless, the stated intention regarding the predecessor reg (SI 1985 No 1323, reg 2) was that it suffices for the transferor scheme to have related to some employer that then participates in the transferee scheme, and it is assumed that if the court were to find otherwise, the matter would be put right retrospectively.

Paragraph (*b*) of the definition (which also does not require the member's consent) applies to a change of employer where there is a bulk pensions transfer as a consequence of a financial transaction or in respect of connected employers.

The preservation regulations contain similar provisions for transfers without consent (SI 1991 No 167, reg 12) subject to the additional requirement for an actuary's certificate of equivalence for the transfer credits arising in the receiving scheme.

The above relates to the statutory requirements. It is still necessary that the scheme rules authorise a transfer without consent (the usual provision being 'save as may be required under the contracting-out or preservation requirements').

12 Buy-outs

12.1 Section 32

The term 'buy-out' is generally used to refer to an insurance policy chosen by a member who has left service, in place of both his rights to a deferred pension and contingent dependants' benefits.

Buyouts have become widespread by reason of s 32 of the Finance Act 1981 which introduced a new s 20(2)(*g*) to the Finance Act 1970 (now s 591(2)(*g*) of ICTA 1988) whereby a scheme could provide an annuity contract of the member's choice. They are still sometimes colloquially referred to as s 32 buyouts.

It is often assumed that since 1985 all deferred pensioners have had a statutory right to a buyout. That was not the case. For those who had left service before 1986 no such right arose unless an appropriate rule had been inserted. The right has now been conferred by PSA 1993, ss 93, 95, as amended by the Pensions Act 1995, except as mentioned in para 10.2 above. However, the position of dependants in respect of earlier buyouts may still give rise to dispute—para 12.3 below.

12.2 General

The entitlement of leavers to a buyout (or transfer) arises without any rule amendment, having been conferred by the Social Security Act 1985, now PSA 1993, Pt IV, Chap IV and s 129. This does not prevent the trustees from writing the provisions into the rules of the scheme but if they do so the question arises whether the statutory discharge remains applicable—see para 12.4 below.

The entitlement to a buy-out comprises the option to apply the 'cash equivalent' of the accrued rights 'to or in respect of [the member]' (s 94) to an annuity contract chosen by the member and meeting prescribed requirements (s 95(2)(*c*)). The buyout can be to a single premium policy or effected as a single (perhaps sole) premium to a personal pension scheme.

The right to a buy-out arises whenever a member leaves *pensionable* service at least a year before 'normal pension age' (s 93(1)(*a*)) so that on the cessation of participation in a scheme by an employer (eg on the sale of a company—see Chapter 11) or merger of two pension schemes within a group (see para 12.6 below) the right will normally arise.

The right is lost a year before 'normal pension age' (or, if later, six months after pensionable service terminates—s 95(8)). Normal pension age is defined in s 180, but the effect of s 180(2) is unclear if the scheme's rules permit an early leaver (a person retiring from the employment) to require an immediate pension (albeit reduced) at, say, age 50. Where a scheme imposes a requirement to obtain the employer's or trustee's consent to early commencement the ambiguity does not arise. The right to a buy-out is also lost if the scheme benefit in fact becomes payable before normal pension age or the scheme 'is wound up' (an imprecise phrase)—s 98(6) and (7). The right can, in effect, be postponed on application by the trustees to OPRA on various grounds including that the scheme is being or is about to be wound up (SI 1996 No 1847, reg 13). The combined effect *may* be to enable buy-outs to be excluded, rather than postponed, on a winding-up.

The statutory discharge to the trustees depends upon them having done what is required. The possibility of fraud is reduced if their cheque is drawn in favour of the insurance company (not the broker) and crossed 'a/c payee only'.

12.3 Position of dependants

The question arises whether a buy-out can replace the rights under the pension scheme of contingent beneficiaries.

So far as post-1 January 1986 leavers exercising their right to the cash equivalent are concerned, the matter is governed principally by the words of s 94 referred to in para 12.2 above, 'benefits which have accrued to or in respect of [the member]', the words 'or in respect of' having been added during the passage in 1985 of the Social Security Bill through Parliament. It is assumed that the added words refer to the rights of contingent beneficiaries, in which case the buy-out replaces those rights (and as to the trustees' discharge, see para 12.4 below). A buyout rule can, and an exercise of the statutory right will, fall within the permitted preservation requirements (SI 1991 No 167, reg 9).

The remaining question relates to pre-1986 leavers who chose a buyout before 6 April 1997, and whether trustees properly adopted a rule permitting (or exercised their discretion under a wide enabling rule to permit in any individual case) contingent beneficiaries to be disentitled. Frequently, they could not know whether a buy-out policy would provide for such beneficiaries since the majority of such policies specify that the option will be exercised by the member when his own annuity commences. The alternatives open to the trustees were firstly to refuse to adopt a buy-out rule for pre-1986 leavers; secondly, to adopt such a rule but permit only those policies that specifically provided for dependants, perhaps specifying choice from half a dozen insurers with whom a form of policy has been agreed; and, thirdly, to treat pre-1986 leavers on the same basis as those with the statutory entitlement on the assumption that the general climate had moved in that direction. In the latter case, some trustees required the current spouse to sign a consent form although this does not appear to have been a widespread requirement.

A disentitled spouse could well pursue a claim against trustees who introduced a rule. The likelihood, however, is reduced by the subsequent statutory entitlement.

12.4 Trustees' discharge

Again, a distinction arises between pre-1986 leavers (unless exercising the new statutory right to a cash equivalent) and current leavers.

So far as the former are concerned, the only statutory discharge was to be found in s 52C of the Social Security Pensions Act 1975, as amended substantially by the Social Security Act 1986, and later by the 1990 Act—now PSA 1993, s 19. The intention of the 1986 amendments was threefold. Firstly, to ensure that the section did not conflict with the discharge applicable to post 1 January 1986 leavers; secondly, to ensure that the buy-out did not have to mirror the benefits provided by the scheme; and, thirdly, to ensure that the discharge applied only to the statutory liability to meet the preservation requirements or, in the case of a contracted-out scheme, the contracting-out requirements (ie to avoid the inference that the discharge related to the trustees' liability to their beneficiaries under the scheme's rules). The amended section was a substantial improvement on the original, but still retained ambiguities. Nonetheless, it is reasonable to assume that it effected the intentions. If the third intention was effected it follows that the section was silent as to the question raised in para 12.3 above regarding contingent beneficiaries, and the trustees must rely (so far as pre-1986 leavers opting prior to the Pensions Act 1995, are concerned) upon the provision in the scheme's rules of a satisfactory enabling power or discharge.

So far as post-1 January 1986 leavers (and pre-1986 leavers now exercising the new statutory rights) are concerned, there is an unequivocal discharge in what is now PSA 1993, s 99, in relation to 'benefits to which the cash equivalent related' (and we have seen in para 2.3 above that the cash equivalent relates to benefits which have 'accrued to or in respect of' the member). There are only two requirements: firstly, that the member has, under s 95, made an application in writing to the trustees or managers of the scheme; and, secondly, that the insurance company is at the relevant time authorised under the Insurance Companies Act 1982 (which in case of doubt can be confirmed by the Department of Trade and Industry) and provides for the cash equivalent one or more annuities which satisfy prescribed requirements.

The cash equivalent regulations (and s 19 where guaranteed minimum pensions are secured) contain relevant provisions regarding authorisation of UK and EU insurance companies, and the annuities. These include conditions on which the policies may be assigned, surrendered or commuted, and the way in which the insurance company assumes obligations to the recipients—SI 1996 No 1847, reg 12(2) (as amended by SI 1997 No 786) and SI 1997 No 784.

A package of standard forms relating to requests for buyouts has been agreed between (inter alia) the Association of British Insurers and the National Association of Pensions funds, but while their use is widespread it is not universal.

12.5 Insurance company documents

The regulations relating to 'cash equivalent' buy-outs provide that the annuity must satisfy the requirements of the Inland Revenue—SI 1996 No 1847, reg 12(2)(b).

The questions arising, for all leavers, are therefore to establish that the insurance company is an approved insurer and that its form of policy meets the Revenue's requirements. Regarding the first point, in the case of uncertainty, it may in some cases be necessary to check with the Department of Trade and Industry that the insurer is genuine.

The insurers will be required by the Inland Revenue to endorse on the policy itself certain information regarding the member's former entitlement under the pension scheme. For this purpose the insurers may require a certificate from the scheme's trustees.

12.6 Scheme mergers: effect on buy-outs

The right to a buy-out may be exercised by a former member up to a year before his normal pension age (or, if later, six months after his pensionable service has terminated)—PSA 1993, s 95(8). It follows that there will be many cases of compulsory transfer of deferred pensioners, resulting from scheme mergers, where the transferees until the merger still had the right to call for a buy-out from the transferring scheme. That right will then arise in the receiving scheme in respect of the pensionable service under the transferring scheme—SI 1996 No 1847, reg 16.

The same position applies to employees in service at the time of the transfer, for the effect of the merger will be to terminate their pensionable service under the old scheme and thus to give them an entitlement to a cash equivalent. On a transfer they will then, after the merger, be able to call at any time for a buy-out in respect of their pre-merger service, although it is unlikely that it would be in their interest, if they were in a final salary scheme, to do so unless they expected to leave service shortly thereafter.

12.7 Other types of buy-out

Section 95 of the PSA 1993 permits the cash equivalent to be applied to other types of pension arrangements if prescribed. Regulation 12(5) of SI 1996 No 1847 prescribes 'an overseas arrangement or a self-employed pension arrangement'. The latter is defined in reg 12(6) and appears to be simply a personal pension scheme which is not limited to employed earners.

An overseas arrangement is defined in SI 1996 No 1462, reg 1, and is a scheme capable of providing benefits on termination of employment, death or retirement, which is administered wholly or primarily outside the United Kingdom.

Chapter 11

Takeovers

1 Is there a scheme?

If your client is taking over another company, it is essential to establish before terms are agreed whether or not that company operates a pension scheme. In assessing the cost of a scheme, it is not sufficient to look simply at the contribution liability, if any, shown in the accounts, as there is no standard actuarial basis for linking it to future liabilities. The accounting standard SSAP 24 requires the disclosure of certain information which should be discussed with your client's actuary or broker (see para 10 below).

Since the employees will (subject to redundancies) continue to be employed by that company, the purchase of the company does not alter the continuing pension liabilities. It is not acceptable to have a certificate by the reporting accountants showing the scheme to be solvent on a discontinuance basis (see para 4 below).

Where the company participates in a group or industry scheme, additional considerations apply (see para 5 below).

2 Insured?

If the scheme is insured, it is essential to obtain copies of all quotations, policies and other documents recording the arrangement with the insurer. This is analogous to an investigation of the company's title to its properties. However, remember that the insured risk usually goes beyond these assets (Chapter 8, para 2).

3 Bulk transfers?

If a business is being, or is to be, transferred out of another company to your client's company, a decision has to be taken as to whether or not past pensionable service is to be honoured year for year (Chapter 10, paras 10 and 11). The nature of the pension scheme is also relevant because of the risk that the employees may claim that they are constructively dismissed (Chapter 10, para 3).

The matters described in para 5 below will also usually arise. However, if the whole of a company's undertaking is being purchased it may be possible to substitute the purchaser as principal employer of the vendor's pension scheme (Chapter 13, para 3.16). Whether this is desirable may depend on the trusts of the scheme, the purchaser's intentions regarding its continuation, the funding level (for a weak basis may lead to a negotiated price reduction), the timing of changes in the employees' conditions of service and other such matters.

4 Solvency?

The accounts of the pension fund will not indicate its future liabilities. They will merely indicate the cash received, investment income and pension outgo. Although the notes to the employer's accounts (under accounting standard SSAP 24) will be helpful their scope will be limited and their basis will be only briefly described. Ask for a sight of the last actuarial report and for any changes in membership and salaries since then. These should then be submitted to actuaries engaged by your client (see para 10 below).

It may come as a surprise to both parties that the purchaser's actuary expresses concern about the funding basis of the acquired company's scheme. Such concern may arise if the purchaser habitually awards pay rises at a rate close to the investment yield of its own fund, and thus values the liabilities on that assumption, while the vendor had assumed a larger yield/salary gap. If it is intended to merge the acquired company's scheme into the purchaser's own scheme in due course, or to adopt the same funding approach, it will be necessary to compare the two bases. It is not the purpose of this book to offer actuarial advice. It will, however, assist in assessing that advice to be aware of six major aspects:

(1) The assumed gap between expected investment yield and expected salary rises. It may, for example, be assumed that the investment yield will be at least 4 per cent per annum more than the rate of price inflation and that salaries will increase by at

least 1 per cent per annum more than the rate of inflation. This produces a yield/salary difference of 3 per cent per annum. If salaries rise faster, more funds will be required—see Chapter 8, para 2 for an example. An assumed gap of 2 per cent (particularly if allowance is also made for promotional increases) is generally considered conservative, and requires substantial funding.

(2) The fund will be invested partly (probably mainly) in equities. Most actuaries include an assumption that the dividend yield from this part of the fund will increase at an annual rate, possibly at ½ per cent per annum less than the assumed rate of inflation, or possibly faster. The rate has a key effect on the valuation result.

(3) Some funds make an allowance for discretionary pension increases (either to pensions in payment or those of the early leaver while in deferment, or both) whereas others make no such allowance (apart from inclusion of the statutory liability) and have correspondingly smaller assets.

(4) Some valuations adjust the market value of the assets to allow for stock exchange fluctuations, or even value the assets exclusively on the basis of their yield, while others do not, producing differences which require actuarial advice.

(5) Some funds assume that a substantial number of members will leave service well before normal retirement age (a 'withdrawal allowance') and thus reduce the required funding for salary increases.

(6) The scheme may be solvent on its actuary's basis while still needing additional contributions under the statutory minimum funding requirement (see Chapter 16, para 17).

See also paras 12 and 13 below.

5 Agreement for part of fund

Where the company being purchased provides a salary related pension and participates in a pension scheme with several other companies, generally if it is in a group scheme, or if part of the business of a company is being purchased, and if pensionable service is to be 'continuous' so that past pensionable service continues to give rise to pensions based on salary near retirement, a transfer of part of the vendor's pension fund will be required.

This may be left for technical consideration after the sale, but more frequently the purchaser will be anxious to ensure that there is an obligation to transfer, and that the amount will provide, on his own scheme's funding basis, sufficient to enable the past service to be honoured in the manner stated; the purchase and sale agreement will then include specific provisions to cover the transfer.

In addition, the vendor or his trustees may require the purchaser to establish, or provide a special section within an existing scheme offering, mirror image benefits to those of the vendor's fund (ie substantially identical benefits). This requirement may arise for industrial relations reasons where the vendor is anxious to demonstrate to the remaining workforce that in a sale situation employees' rights are fully considered. Equally, it may not be possible to forecast trustee reaction to a proposed transfer if the nature of the purchaser's scheme is very different. A mid-way course is for the past service rights to be on a mirror-image basis (uplifted by future salary rises) but for future service to accrue on the purchaser's standard basis.

The commercial agreement will generally cover four, possibly five, aspects: firstly, the warranties regarding the vendor's scheme; secondly, the pension benefits to be provided by the purchaser; thirdly, the calculation of the transfer amount; and, fourthly, any interim period of continued participation in the vendor's scheme (Chapter 5, para 2). A fifth may be an indemnity either from the purchaser to the vendor regarding claims of constructive dismissal by reason of reduced or different future service benefits, or from the vendor to the purchaser regarding potential equal treatment or other claims. If it is expected that the purchaser will dismiss a substantial part of the workforce, it may be agreed that the transfer calculation will make allowance for this. Alternatively, the vendor may suggest that an interim period of continued participation is sufficiently long to cover the period when redundancies are made, so that the salary reserve for employees who will not remain in service will fall into profit in his, rather than the purchaser's, scheme.

The provision for calculating the transfer amount will generally refer to a separate letter or note from the vendor's actuaries to the purchaser's actuaries. Alternatively, the detail may be set out in the main commercial agreement. The vendor may insist that its obligation be to use its 'best endeavours' to procure the transfer payment, for there may be no certainty as to the trustees' agreement. The purchaser may respond that any shortfall between the intended amount and the actual amount must be made up directly by the vendor.

The transfer amount will also depend upon the number of members transferring. The formula for calculation will therefore need to be independent of the number. Some agreements may provide that members have an option whether or not to transfer. In others, the past service transfer may be compulsory (for those members still in service on the expiry of the interim period) although clearly an employee cannot be compelled to contribute for future service to a new pension scheme. Generally, there is greater industrial relations advantage to both sides in offering an *option* to transfer, but in some cases the option of future pension rights may be linked to a transfer of past rights. As to consents, see Chapter 10, para 11.

Members will also have the right to individual buyouts (Chapter 10, para 12). The new disclosure and transfer regulations (SI 1996 Nos 1655 and 1847) are in this respect less stringent than the old (SI 1986 No 1046) but at the very least the member will have a right to cash equivalent information on request. The statutory disclosure requirements continue to require that automatically the leaver is informed of his rights and options (if any). Until 6 April 1997 this requirement was set out in the old disclosure regulations. It is not to be found in their direct replacement (SI 1996 No 1655) but instead, and confusingly, it has been inserted in the preservation regulations SI 1991 No 167 by a new reg 27A, effective from 6 April 1997 and inserted by SI 1996 No 2131.

There is no established view whether the trustees are under a fiduciary obligation to enhance the cash equivalent to the same basis as the member's share of any bulk transfer that may be on offer. The probability is that they need not, since a bulk transfer is often calculated on a more generous basis than individual transfers to recognise the effect of the continuity of pensionable service that will have been arranged. The trustees would need to consider the propriety of the difference in calculation; it may seem to them entirely proper since a transferring member will not necessarily thereby obtain larger benefits in the new scheme, for this will depend upon the date that he leaves the new employer's service; by contrast, if the cash equivalent were enhanced, it would give a priority to the member who chose a buy-out.

See also Chapter 5, para 2 and Chapter 14, para 12.

6 Information you must have

At the outset of the transaction, before there are draft documents or formal disclosure, the purchaser and his solicitor will need a picture of the existing provisions for pension. To avoid delay in obtaining the broad picture it may be helpful to divide a request for documents into the following three parts, indicating that the information described in para 6.1 below is expected forthwith.

6.1 The vendor's main scheme

The most recent booklet or announcement issued to members and the current annual report from the trustees are required at this stage. The booklet gives an immediate picture of the scheme. The information will have had to be prepared for members under the statutory disclosure requirements (Chapter 3, para 11) and will normally be in booklet form; alternatively it will be in an announcement issued on establishment or last updating of the scheme—SI 1996 No 1655, reg 4(2).

The annual report is also a statutory requirement under the disclosure regulations. It should have scheme accounts and an actuarial certificate annexed to it—reg 6(1).

As a follow up within stage 1 the latest full actuarial report should be obtained (see para 10 below); conversely a vendor's trustees will want to be sure that they are not making a transfer to a thinly funded scheme that will dilute their members' security.

A copy of the Inland Revenue's letter of approval (or their confirmation) is needed if your client is taking over the whole scheme or if making a transfer to a scheme.

6.2 The scheme documents

The trust deed and rules are needed for a number of reasons. Nonetheless the request for them may bring a slow response (because they are not so readily located as members' booklets). Request a 'consolidated copy if it is readily available' and afterwards decide whether merely to inspect the underlying documents (perhaps even to rely on a warranty if you are not fishing for interesting amendments) or seek copies, albeit if your client is purchasing the principal company you will want to borrow (and your client will ultimately retain) all the original documents.

On an agreement for part of the fund the trust deed is needed:

(*a*) to check there is power to transfer (to avoid potential embroilment in a tracing action or some other claim); similarly if a vendor's trustees are making a discretionary transfer to a scheme they will need to check its powers to receive and apply transfers;
(*b*) to see whether the transfer might include a share of any surplus;
(*c*) to check that any participation by your client for an interim period is limited to a stated contribution liability (which should then be agreed in monetary figures).

6.3 Separate pension arrangements

While your initial enquiry should ask if there are additional individual or historical arrangements still in force it can make clear that the first stage above should not be delayed on that account. It is, however, important to return to the question as it is a part of disclosure that is often overlooked, leading to argument over cost at a later stage.

7 Guaranteed benefits?

The purchase and sale agreement should state (with a suitable warranty) whether any guarantees or representations have been given to employees as to the continuation of the pension scheme, the enhancement of its benefits or any benefits under separate arrangements (contractual, moral or otherwise).

The warranties should also include disclosure of any special terms of membership within the pension scheme—key persons may have been offered enhanced benefits.

8 Past service liability

For an initial idea of the scale of a likely transfer, it may be helpful to glance down the list of membership and the length of past service. If employees change rapidly in that particular employment, the past service liability may be so short in each case that a transfer is likely to be small. There is, however, considerable danger in forming more than a very provisional conclusion ahead of actuarial advice.

9 Former schemes

Frequently there have been old schemes that have been wound up, so that some members have greater rights than would appear from the booklets relating to the scheme. Disclosure of all former schemes which contain liabilities relating to current employees should be required, with any announcement explaining the effect on overall pension.

10 Actuaries

The importance of the last actuarial valuation to the scheme has been mentioned in para 4 above. It is essential to obtain actuarial advice on the matters disclosed by the investigations recommended in this chapter, and on the prospective result of the first valuation under the minimum funding requirement (Chapter 16, para 17).

The most difficult position for the solicitor to the purchaser is where neither party has an actuary and the scale of the transaction appears too small to justify the time and expense of finding and instructing one. Nonetheless, someone has to be sure that the pension liabilities are as immaterial as first appears. Three possibilities arise:

(1) Assistance from the client's broker; while he may not be familiar with actuarial detail he may be able to assess whether the liabilities are likely to be material; discussion with him should give the client an understanding whether to have confidence in his assessment; clearly there cannot be full professional comfort and this itself is a risk to be discussed with the client.
(2) Assistance from the actuary to the insurance company of one or both parties; this is workable only if telephone contact can be obtained; the purchaser's insurer may be willing to help as there is the prospect of new business; the vendor's insurer should be willing to supply information but cannot of course be one's client's adviser, and response time may be slow.
(3) A list from the Institute of Actuaries in London (the Faculty in Edinburgh) of nearby consultants; the list may include the

secretary of the Association of Consulting Actuaries; clearly the appointment of an actuary is the only secure route although the cost may be relatively high for a small transaction.

The fee basis will vary substantially between these approaches. For a sizable transaction there is no doubt that (3) is the best solution, partly for the obvious reasons and partly because the transfer may be sufficiently large to justify, when aggregated with one's client's own insured arrangement, a new overall form of investment such as a managed or segregated fund.

Experience also suggests that (1) and (2) increase the solicitor's time considerably, so that (3) has a lower net cost than might first appear.

Enquiry should be made as to the insurer's expenses and commission associated with any surrender or transfer, and particularly the differences between single and recurring premiums; some insurers levy the major cost on the first of recurring premiums so that care is needed to allocate transfer payments as single premiums.

Vendors and their trustees will benefit from the services of an actuary in a number of ways. They will wish to be sure that the funding basis of the purchaser's scheme will not weaken the security of their transferring members' benefits; they will also reduce the risk of action for breach of trust (possibly via the Pensions Ombudsman) if the purchaser's scheme subsequently becomes insolvent. They will also want to be sure that any warranties they give as to the solvency of their own scheme are on a basis that is not misunderstood by either party.

In the case of transfers without consent, in respect of members entitled to short service benefit under 'preservation', the vendor's actuary will be required to give a certificate as to the value of the transfer credits to be acquired in the receiving scheme (Chapter 10, paras 1 and 11).

11 Trustees' reports

Under the Disclosure Regulations referred to in Chapter 16, para 6 the trustees of the acquired company's scheme will have made available to members annual reports comprising prescribed information. It is likely that the trustees or the employer will take the opportunity to include in the report a section indicating the particular advantages of their scheme. It would be helpful to the purchaser to request a sight of the last such annual report, in order to assess the industrial relations aspect of any alternative approach to pensions that may be mentioned in the announcement to employees at the time of the takeover.

While the degree of members' interest in such reports at the time of their issue is usually minimal, the transfer arrangements need only interest one member for a vocal lobby to be initiated.

12 Litigation

The purpose of drawing a precise pensions provision in the commercial agreement (para 5 above) is to avoid subsequent disputes. Defined benefit schemes (Chapter 8, para 7) may have a surplus or a deficit. Where the vendor's scheme is substantially in surplus, the purchaser may have sought a 'share of the fund' (which includes a proportion of the surplus) (para 13 below). If the amount of the transfer payment has been left to the actuary appointed by the trustees of the vendor's fund, on the assumption that there will be adequate assets, and a later valuation reveals a substantial surplus, there may well be a dispute; a precise commercial agreement would avoid this.

In the case of *The Imperial Foods Ltd's Pension Scheme* [1986] 2 All ER 802 Ch D the court held that, as a matter of construction under the trust deed of the vendor's scheme, the calculation was to be made by the actuary. It was demonstrated that the particular method chosen by the actuary was one of a number that *could* competently have been used, so that the court (on established principles) was not prepared, as the ratio of the decision, to consider the matter further. However, the judgment went on to consider, obiter dictum, how the court might have assessed the transfer value if the discretion had been vested in it, and stated that in an ongoing pension scheme where the employer is paying the balance of costs, surplus does not belong to members. It is up to the employer, paying the balance of contributions needed by the fund, whether or not to choose a cautious funding rate, and the employer benefits or suffers from fluctuating investment experience (see Chapter 24, para 10 for a fuller commentary on this case).

The importance of following the transferor's trust deed is illustrated by *Stannard* v *Fisons Pension Trust Ltd* [1992] IRLR 27, CA relating to a sale agreement made in 1982 and properly implemented which nonetheless did not follow the procedures laid down in the pension deed. A transferred member claimed that a larger transfer might have been assessed under the deed. The 1990 case was adjourned for that assessment to be made. The actual transfer had been made in 1983, the enquiry arose in 1985, the writ was issued in 1987 and the case heard in 1990 (and again, on appeal, in 1991).

13 Funding glossary

The 'share of the fund' mentioned in para 12 above (for defined benefit schemes) is a term generally used to describe the same proportion of the assets of the fund as the proportion of the liabilities represented by the liability to the intended transferees. The liabilities are usually calculated as if all current employees left service at the date of transfer, although this approach might be modified if the winding-up provisions of the scheme conferred particular rights between classes of member or particular enhancements; alternatively, the proportion of liabilities could include an allowance for salary and pension increases.

The Institute and Faculty of Actuaries issued in 1986 (and updated in 1988) a document entitled 'Pension Fund Terminology: Specimen Descriptions of Commonly Used Valuation Methods'. It is not a function of this book to describe valuation methods (save briefly in the Glossary) but the legal adviser should be aware of the terms listed in the Report, as follows:

(*a*) entry age method;
(*b*) attained age method;
(*c*) projected unit method;
(*d*) current unit method;
(*e*) aggregate method;
(*f*) projected accrued benefit method.

The document refers to an earlier Working Party Report. The earlier Report is particularly useful in its descriptions of the characteristics of each method. It described methods (*a*)–(*e*) above and indicated that, with the exception of (*e*), these methods carry with them a 'standard fund' (described in the Report) which could be implied as the required assets to date.

Method (*f*) was added to dovetail with the surplus regulations (SI 1987 No 412, reg 5(1)) referred to in Chapter 17, para 10).

Mention has been made in para 5 above that a critical matter is that the transfer payment includes a reserve for the effect of future salary increases on the past service liability. It appears that the 'standard fund' under method (*d*) does not include such a reserve. Clearly the legal adviser can do no more than point to the apparent need for a salary reserve (for final salary-defined benefit schemes) and for an understanding of the effect of staff turnover, and ensure that the views of the actuary are obtained as early in the transaction as possible.

14 Defensive measures

14.1 Trust deed

A public company may be concerned that, if its pension fund is heavily in surplus, a predator who acquires the company might obtain a substantial refund from the scheme, perhaps by winding it up. There are numerous methods, generally known as 'poison pills', that may be employed to impede such a step. These are all triggered in the event of a takeover (a 'change of control') and include altering the power of appointment of new trustees, providing pension increases as an entitlement and the like.

It is unlikely that, in the ordinary course of preparing for a company a trust deed, one would advise the inclusion of poison pill provisions. Their inclusion, then or subsequently, would have to be in the interests of the company. Their adoption when a takeover is imminent might be in breach of Stock Exchange and Takeover Panel requirements, and it is possible that the former's listing requirements will extend in due course to any provision in the trust deed of a quoted company's pension scheme that will be triggered by a takeover. Note 8 to rule 21 of the Takeover Code requires prior consultation with the Panel before effecting constitutional changes to a pension scheme when a bid is in progress or if the board of a potential target has reason to believe that a bona fide offer might be imminent unless the change is pursuant to a prior contract. Rule 21 requires shareholders' approval, in general meeting, to the matters to which it relates. The Code is under revision at the time of writing but it is understood that there are no proposals to change the substance of the above, although the rule numbering may alter.

In the author's experience proposals for poison pills rarely survive the test of whether they could be in the best interests of the company. Prima facie it is unlikely that it can be in those interests to fetter the power of future management. However, each case will depend on its facts, particularly where the purpose is to safeguard the possibility of the continued exercise by trustees of an existing policy which is of importance to the workforce and thus to the company. If, however, the purpose is simply to frustrate a takeover, 'predator protection' as such, the proposal is likely to be unlawful.

A preferable form of defensive measure is to discuss with the client and the actuary the circumstances in which a surplus may arise. Increases to pensions in payment or deferment that have for many years been granted at discretion, say of three-quarters (or whatever) the rate of inflation may be written into the rules (perhaps subject to a cap at 8 per cent, or whatever, to protect the company, retaining discretion at higher rates of inflation) so that the formal liabilities of the scheme are increased and the surplus correspondingly reduced. Consideration may also be given to the winding-up clause either by removing the control of the company over application of surplus or by providing that particular increases shall be awarded before distribution of surplus, eg increases in the deferred pensions of employees then or recently in service in line with the reserve for their salary increases (subject to Inland Revenue limits although these may leave considerable scope except in the case of young entrants). The company may feel that the inclusion of these changes in the members' booklet will assist in the recruitment, management or retention of some or all the workforce.

It should be remembered that improvements of this nature cannot easily be reversed, both by reason of the fiduciary nature of the trustees' power to make or consent to amendments, and by reason of the industrial relations effect of any subsequent changes. Further, the drafting must avoid creation of a debt on the employer if the surplus on winding-up turns out to be insufficient to support the full increases—Pensions Act 1995, s 75(6).

Unless the company is prepared to write into the trust deed an objective standard of funding, there is no safeguard against the running down of a surplus by reduction in the future contribution rate. It would rarely be advisable to write in an objective funding provision, for all final salary pension schemes depend upon economic forecasts that are reviewed at each actuarial valuation. An inflexible provision will result either in accumulating surpluses without a power to reduce the future contribution rate or a deficit which, if not made good, would necessitate the discontinuance of the scheme or an application to the court by the trustees for directions (but possibly the minimum funding requirement might alleviate the problem by restoring the contribution rate—Chapter 16, para 17).

The essence of these measures is to preserve the pension fund for the purpose for which it was established. That may, but not necessarily will, involve an increase in the trustees' powers at the expense of the company (see Chapter 3, para 21, regarding the balance of these powers). Most commentators regard any benefit to employees at the expense of the company as unlawful unless it thereby benefits the company, being of the view that s 309 of the Companies Act 1985 does not change the law in this respect. It is therefore essential that the company's Board is advised of these matters when considering any proposal to reduce or fetter the company's powers. The greater awareness of the vulnerability of pension funds, following the 'Maxwell' scandal revealed in December 1991 (the apparent loss of funds in a secret share support operation), makes it more likely that employees will press for measures such as are described here, and thus assists a Board in adopting them.

A measure which may give comfort at a minimum risk of unlawfulness is the appointment of additional trustees from outside the company. It would be difficult to challenge the motive in such an appointment, and the expectation would be that they would resist bullying by a new Board. However, inhibitions to an existing power of removal would require more specific consideration of the interests of the company.

14.2 Sale agreement

The sale agreement may provide a defence mechanism for the pension fund either by direct covenant from the purchaser or by an agreement as to the form of announcement to employees. The first may take a number of forms. There may be an agreed funding basis applicable for the first five years (or whatever) after the purchase. During that period, buy-outs may be valued having regard to the transfer payment, or the trustees may be required to consult the actuary whether it is equitable, having regard to the number of transferees who leave service, to increase the value of deferred pensions. A number of similar covenants can be sought, although the purchaser will have to consider with his actuary the practicality of compliance with the proposals.

Where the purchaser is expected to retain the bulk of the acquired workforce, the sale agreement may provide that the announcement to employees states that the transfer payment includes an allowance for the continuation of the past policy regarding discretionary increases, and that the ability of the fund to meet such increases will be considered at each valuation. The trustees might agree to include a reference in each year's annual report, including a chart of progress.

None of these mechanisms is a complete answer. It is always possible that a reconstruction of the purchaser's business may result in a drop in the pension liabilities, or the inclusion in the fund of a number of other employees with less strongly funded past service benefits. Nonetheless, the foregoing may be a useful sample from which to generate discussion. It should also be remembered that an agreement requires a willing purchaser, and that the approach may differ according to the perceived bona fides of the purchaser.

15 Warranties, indemnities

The usual warranties regarding full disclosure should be sought by a purchaser.

It is also common to require a vendor to procure that the trustees of its pension scheme will make the intended transfer. (The vendor may then convene a meeting of the trustees, but alternatively may rely on an established and agreed course of conduct on their part, particularly if there has been a series of similar transfers).

A purchaser may well seek indemnity from the vendor regarding compliance with equal treatment and other requirements of the law. Such indemnity should also cover potential liability to persons denied membership of a scheme who might claim indirect discrimination. This could be a liability of a company (and thus relevant if shares are being purchased) regarding past as well as present employees. If a business is being purchased, there could be a liability under TUPE in respect of transferred employees who have not been admitted to the pension scheme (Chapters 10 and 22).

Chapter 12

The service contract

1 Acting for the employer

The statement of particulars of employment required under the Employment Rights Act 1996, s 1 (consolidating previous legislation) must include or refer to any applicable pension or pension scheme.

There is nothing, however, that requires an employer to provide pension arrangements. If he does so, it is not essential to include them (apart from the above-mentioned brief reference) in any service contract that may be drawn up (but see below regarding the disclosure regulations). Nonetheless, frequently they are included, particularly where the employer undertakes that special terms will apply to the employee, eg that he will be given an enhanced length of service (within Inland Revenue limits).

Occasionally, the benefits will be described in full in the service contract itself, particularly if there is additionally an unapproved top-up arrangement (Chapter 2, para 10).

The disclosure regulations (SI 1996 No 1655, reg 4) require the trustees of any scheme to provide basic information to prospective members and also, on request, to members and certain other beneficiaries—see Chapter 16, para 6.

Where the contract of itself confers the entitlement to pension benefits (as opposed to membership of an approved pension scheme) the terms will comprise a retirement benefits scheme requiring revenue approval if, inter alia, the tax advantages of such schemes are to be obtained (eg certain lump sum benefits to be tax-free) and the possible tax penalty on the employee (if the scheme is funded) is to be avoided. The wide definition of retirement benefits scheme and the requirements for notification to the Revenue are of great importance and are referred to (together with the definition of relevant benefits) in Chapter 17, para 1.3. The benefits must not exceed Revenue limits if approval is to be sought. For unfunded arrangements see Chapter 1, para 6 and Chapter 17, para 4.

If a surviving spouse's pension arises under the contract, consideration must be given to the definition (ie present spouse or spouse at death), enforceability and potential need to vary (ie any trust should include provision for alteration). A spouse could ordinarily enforce payment if he/she were the deceased's testator, but could also be given enforceable rights in a number of ways, including the following:

(*a*) he/she can be made a party to the contract;
(*b*) the employee could declare on behalf of himself and his personal representatives that he is a trustee for the spouse of the benefit of the covenant (with provision for alteration);
(*c*) the employer could declare himself a trustee for the spouse, in which case the scheme (so far as it relates to the spouse) can be exempt approved. There may be little advantage, by comparison with (*b*) above, and some practical disadvantages in this course. Again there should be provision for alteration.

Any of these courses would give rise to serious problems if the employee and his spouse were to be divorced although, in a sense, the new divorce legislation may help to unscramble them (Chapter 23). It follows that an undertaking by the employer to procure membership of a pension scheme (or the establishment of such a scheme) on special terms is generally preferred. The scheme would contain its own definition of surviving spouse.

2 Acting for the employee

The obvious provisions to look for are those mentioned in para 1 above.

It is likely that the employee consulting you will be leaving service. The first thing to ask for is a copy of both the members' booklet and the trust deed/rules. It has become usual for readily comprehensible explanatory booklets to be issued and the rules themselves to be merely 'available for inspection'. It may therefore prove difficult to obtain a spare copy of the rules at short notice. Much valuable information will usually be obtained from the booklet and rules, and the disclosure regulations give the employee a right to these (for a reasonable charge in the case of the rules—SI 1996 No 1655, reg 3(2) and see Chapter 16, para 6). The booklet will also be helpful in directing you to the broad terms of the rules. Any additional announcements to employees relating to pension matters will be essential since they may confer a contractual right outside the terms of the scheme.

The employee may not be aware of the general provisions applicable on leaving service. If it is a scheme with enhanced benefit for long-service employees, he may require guidance as to how an employee who leaves early is affected, eg whether the enhancement is granted proportionately. Where entitlement to preservation has arisen (see Chapter 10, para 1) there may be a statutory requirement of uniform accrual of the enhancement—PSA 1993, s 74(6). If the employee has not yet left service, he may not be aware of the matters of which the trustees would be bound to inform him once he leaves service, and it may not be politic to exercise his right to advance information. He may also require broad guidance on transfers and buy-outs (Chapter 10, paras 10 and 12).

If there is an allegation of dishonesty, set-off against pension (or forfeiture to the extent of moneys owed) may be permitted by the scheme rules, but cannot apply to transfer credits brought from the scheme of a previous (unconnected) employer (except where a bankrupt member has paid excessive voluntary contributions to defraud creditors—subject to the Commencement Order mentioned below). Further, such set-off or forfeiture can apply only in respect of monetary obligations arising out of a criminal, negligent or fraudulent act or omission by the member, and only to the extent certified by the employer (there being statutory provision for arbitration as to the amount)—Pensions Act 1995, ss 91–95. However, if the scheme does not include a rule permitting set-off, then set-off cannot be enforced, since the obligation is to the employer and not to the trustees of the scheme. Two of the bankruptcy provisions await Commencement Orders (see Chapter 13, para 3.26).

The employee may wish to retire through ill health. Apart from the question of construing the service contract, it may be necessary to construe the scheme rules. They will normally provide that special ill-health provisions (if any) apply only in cases of serious ill health. There is a variety of definitions ranging from inability to carry out one's normal job to incapacity to carry on any gainful employment, and sometimes a variety of enhancements to the accrued pension, dependent upon the degree of incapacity. It is essential to obtain a copy of the actual rule.

3 Insurance policy as a collateral or pension out of current revenue

If the employee is being offered a service contract containing considerable pension benefits, it is always right to enquire whether the employer is or will be funding these benefits and/or insuring any death-in-service benefits. If he is not funding them, or if the fund is not being invested prudently, there may be no security at all for the employee in the event of the employer collapsing. The absence of insurance can result in undue strain on a fund in the event of the early death of a number of employees.

4 Hancock

Occasionally, special pension arrangements are funded at or after retirement by payment of a single insurance premium. Such an arrangement is known as a Hancock payment (the reference arising from the transaction considered in *Hancock v General Reversionary and Investment Co Ltd* [1919] 1 KB 25; 7 TC 358). If arranged appropriately, it obtains all the normal tax advantages. The broker or insurer should be asked to confirm that it is being so arranged.

5 Deferred life cover; normal premium rates

Sometimes the employer will provide that the eligibility for death-in-service benefits (whether lump sum and/or spouse's pension) does not come into force for a period of, say, 30 days to enable a medical examination to take place. This will not be necessary if there is an automatic arrangement under which an insurer is on risk. However, if the benefit arises outside an existing pension scheme (see para 1 above) this will normally be an essential provision of the contract if the employer is to avoid the possibility of an uninsured risk. The employer may also require that these benefits be subject to an insurer accepting the employee at normal rates of premium.

5.1 Disability Discrimination Act 1995

The Disability Discrimination Act 1995 is unlikely to create a problem regarding excluded life cover, but the question may arise. The relevant provisions of the Act and regulations (SI 1996 No 1456) came into force on 2 December 1996.

Section 4 renders unlawful (among other things) terms of employment that 'discriminate' against a 'disabled person', but s 5 excludes from discrimination matters that are 'justified'.

Disability

Disability is defined by reference to 'substantial and long-term adverse effect on [the person's] ability to carry out normal day-to-day activities'—s 1. Schedule 1 amplifies these terms. Of its provisions, paragraph 8 is the most likely to be relevant to adverse premium rates for life cover, and provides that where a person has a progressive condition (eg cancer, multiple sclerosis etc) that has, or has had, an adverse effect which is not substantial, he is nonetheless taken to have a relevant impairment if the condition is likely to result (presumably in the longer term) in such an impairment. Refusal of life cover relates to longevity, but the latter is not necessarily relevant to work impairment. Plainly death would prevent the job being carried out, but that is not an impairment (which connotes a living person sustaining a difficulty). Conversely, there will be many examples of disability that impair the performance of the job but do not result in refusal of life cover or increased premium rates. Therefore, it will not often be necessary for trustees to consider a life cover problem in respect of a 'disabled person' as defined in the Act.

Section 17 deems every occupational pension scheme to contain a 'non-discrimination rule' in effect incorporating the Act where the trustees' actions or omissions would be unlawful if done by an employer.

The Act, however, contains express exemptions for justification—see below.

Justification

Where life cover is refused, or would only be available at significant extra cost, the Act (if it applies, ie if the applicant is a 'disabled person') provides that the less favourable treatment is justified if the reason for it is 'both material to the circumstances of the particular case and substantial'—s 5(3).

Section 5(6) and (7) provides that regulations may amplify 'justification' and may do so by reference to 'the cost of affording any benefit; and, in relation to benefits under *occupational pension schemes*, may make provision with a view to enabling uniform rates of contributions to be maintained' (emphasis supplied).

SI 1996 No 1456, reg 4, provides that special eligibility conditions can be set, or benefits adjusted, if the disability (including any clinical prognosis) would result in substantially greater 'cost of providing any benefit' than for a normal person. This relates to retirement, death and invalidity benefits (and various others). Regulation 5 provides that an employer (and thus the trustees too) may require the standard contribution rate from a disabled person even though a benefit has been excluded by reason of the disability.

It seems unlikely that at the time a new employee is engaged his disability would affect longevity. If it did, and after an appropriate medical examination, full life cover was not available from an insurance company, the exclusion would seem permissible under reg 4, and the maintenance of the full (member's) contribution rate permissible under reg 6.

Self-insured schemes

Where the pension scheme carries, ie does not insure, the risk (eg a very large scheme), there is uncertainty whether meaning can be given to the word 'cost' in the above-quoted exemption in reg 4. Regarding the employer's potential breach of the Act, its contribution rate to the scheme is unlikely to be affected by one potential death. Nonetheless there is a parallel in any defined benefit scheme where the cost of individual pay increases is a real cost even if there is no immediate impact on the contribution rate, and it is submitted that the same is true in assessing life cover.

Regarding the trustees, it would be strange if a particular potential liability were not treated as a cost when, for active members, *all* the liabilities are potential. This seems to be so even if in the out-turn there is no death, just as pension has a potential cost even if premature death prevents payment of the benefit.

In the light of the express reference to occupational pension schemes in both s 5 and reg 4 it seems likely that the court would treat an exclusion (following an adverse medical report) as justified.

6 Controlling directors

Controlling directors have, since 1973, been permitted to be members of approved schemes (Finance Act 1973, s 15 repealing s 19(2)(*f*) of the Finance Act 1970). However, the Inland Revenue under its discretionary powers introduced a new type of restriction, that a director who, alone or together with his spouse and minor children, is or becomes a beneficial owner of shares which, when added to any shares held by the trustees of any settlement to which he or his spouse has transferred assets, carry more than 20 per cent of the voting rights in the company (or in a company which controls that company) may only have his pension based in effect on the annual average of his remuneration during a period of three years (see the definition 'final remuneration' in the practice notes IR 12 referred to in Chapter 17, para 3). As to late retirement, see Chapter 17, para 7. These matters should be taken into account when preparing a service contract for such a director. Reference should be made to the Revenue's current practice before finalising any such agreement. A definition 'controlling director', only slightly different from the foregoing '20 per cent' definition is now applicable under s 417(5)(*b*) of ICTA 1988 (see Chapter 17, para 7).

7 Contractual effect of pension scheme

It is essential to be clear as to the contractual effect of the pension scheme where:

(*a*) the scheme fails to provide the expected benefits; or
(*b*) there is duplication between the service contract and the pension announcement; or
(*c*) the pension scheme states (or changes) the normal retiring age.

The question of the employer's contractual liability is of considerable importance. The employer will normally wish to ensure that his liability is limited to the establishment of the pension scheme and such contributions as he may make to it from time to time (albeit there are certain statutory obligations—see Chapter 3, para 16). The scheme itself will usually contain a power of alteration, albeit now constrained in respect of acquired entitlements, or accrued rights, by the Pensions Act 1995, s 67. If that power is exercised to alter benefits eg the future accrual, and the employee has a recourse to the employer, considerable difficulty will arise; occasionally a package of benefit changes will disadvantage a particular individual (say a bachelor where spouses' benefits are being improved but the basic definition of pensionable salary is being altered in a way which happens to be to his detriment); the question may well arise if a scheme is modified or wound up in the light of legislative changes, say the introduction in 1988 of personal pension schemes (Chapter 2, para 9). The question may also arise if the pension scheme becomes insolvent (see the reference above to Chapter 3, para 16), for the statutory debt due from the employer will rarely enable full deferred annuities to be purchased for active members.

The employer will therefore wish that the service contract states that membership of the pension scheme is subject to the terms of the trust deed and rules. It is a matter of judgment whether to add 'including the powers of alteration and discontinuance'; such addition would normally be found in the pension scheme booklet where there is room to expand it by reference to the benefits that would then be provided. If, however, all reference to these points is omitted from the service contract there is a danger of a subsequent claim that the employer has in effect warranted that the benefits will be provided in precisely the form applicable at the time the contract was made.

Question (*b*) above, duplication of benefits, may seem unlikely, but frequently arises where a senior executive receives a letter of engagement specifying some of, but not all, the particular benefits that he is to obtain, the balance being standard pension scheme benefits. He may assume that the specified benefits (eg particular lump sum life cover) are additional to the standard scheme benefits. The contract should therefore state clearly that it refers to the benefits provided under the pension scheme. It is also essential to specify whether additional benefits accrue immediately on entering employment or uniformly over the period of employment (so that only a proportion is received in the event of early leaving) or otherwise, and here the preservation requirements are relevant (Chapter 10, para 1.1, where the principle of uniform accrual is mentioned towards the end of the section).

Question (*c*) above, normal retirement age, can lead to considerable misunderstanding. It is essential that an employee should not assume that his contract of employment will necessarily continue until normal retirement age. Where there is any room for misunderstanding, the relevant document should include a phrase such as 'subject to earlier termination by notice from either party'. Some schemes designate the relevant age as 'pension date' rather than 'normal retirement age' to avoid this confusion, notwithstanding that the scheme will probably contain provision enabling pension to be taken earlier or later. Equally, care is needed where the normal retirement age in the pension scheme is altered, usually reduced to enable a full pension to be payable from an earlier age; the question then arises whether contracts of employment automatically come to an end at that age if not already terminated by notice. Although it is easy to clarify this point, there may be an industrial relations difficulty in spelling out either that the contract does come to an end or, where it does not automatically terminate, that individuals will not necessarily continue in employment beyond that date. An actual change to the contractual employment termination date may be more difficult to achieve.

Two further complexities are, firstly, the Inland Revenue requirement that a pension scheme specify an age (within certain limits) at which standard benefits are payable and that this be the age at which the relevant employees do in fact normally retire (any age from 60–75 being acceptable without special reference) and, secondly, that compensation for unfair dismissal does not apply after the individual (while remaining in service) has reached his normal retiring age in that job. Although the latter is a question of fact, the pension scheme terms may be evidential.

Chapter 13

The definitive deed

1 Changes since the interim deed?

The definitive deed (or definitive rules adopted by resolution, as the case may be) should always recite the establishment of the scheme by the interim document. It is essential to ascertain whether any changes have been intended or announced since that interim document. If so, it may be necessary to record their effective dates in the definitive deed to avoid an unintended retrospection to the date of establishment of the scheme.

2 Insurance company draft

If the scheme is insured, the insurance company should present a draft. It will usually be exceedingly long. There are two main reasons for this length. In the first place, the draft will be based on a standard document intended to be adapted readily to different types of benefit. It may have lengthy general provisions and separate special provisions which can be altered for each scheme. Secondly, there have been many changes in legislation affecting pension schemes since the new tax code in 1970. In order to avoid excessive delay in introducing definitive documents, many insurance companies have added extra sections to cover these provisions, rather than integrate them into the body of the text.

The question whether or not to adopt the draft is much more difficult than the equivalent question relating to the interim document when the scheme was established. In the case of the interim document, there may have been little time for discussion, making it essential that a suitable document be executed by the time the first contribution to the scheme was paid. The question now is whether to adopt a document which may be so long, and contain so many cross-references, that persons unfamiliar with it would find it almost impossible to establish what benefit is payable in a given circumstance, or to go to the expense of drafting a tailor-made deed that would then involve lengthy correspondence with the insurance company.

There is no simple answer to this question. It depends upon the quality of the draft submitted, the interest taken by the client, and the likelihood of subsequent changes to the benefit structure (such changes being difficult to discuss when the existing structure is not easily understood).

If it is decided to adopt the draft, particular items should be considered. Some of these are discussed in para 4 below.

3 General comments

It is beyond the scope of this book to include a precedent for a definitive deed. Reference should be made to an appropriate legal encyclopaedia. It is common for the powers of the trustees, and all powers relating to matters that do not affect normal benefits, to be included in the deed, but for the rules as to benefits (para 4.7 below) to be annexed or scheduled separately. There is no legal requirement for this, however, and occasionally all the provisions are in one document that is adopted by simple resolution.

The powers of the trustees can be subdivided into a large number of headings. It is impossible to be exhaustive. One can only mention the headings that one might include in a particular precedent. It is always possible that an alternative form might be more suitable. The following are commonly found to be essential or useful, including some that repeat, though generally enlarge, powers set out in the Trustee Act 1925.

3.1 Declaration of trust

The assets of the scheme must be declared to be held on the trusts of the deed (or rules, as the case may be).

3.2 Obligations of employer

The employer must covenant with the trustees to perform the obligations relating to it that are set out in the trust instrument. This may, on analysis, be (for the principal employer) no more than a covenant to contribute at such rate as it decides and until it gives notices of cessation. Nonetheless, the covenant is important for two reasons. Firstly, it creates a peg on which the trustees can apply to the court for directions if uncertain whether, apart from any statutory minimum funding requirement (Chapter 16, para 17), the contributions suffice to maintain the scheme (in which case they may obtain an order to wind up). Secondly, the Revenue requires to see a covenant from each participating company before allowing tax relief on its contributions (ie relief under s 592(4) of ICTA 1988, rather than by demonstrating that the contributions are wholly and necessarily incurred—see Chapter 17, para 1.1).

Many draft deeds include a covenant to contribute at such rate as the actuary may recommend, which, if not subject to a power to terminate, may amount to a guarantee of solvency (see para 3.13 below). The form of covenant should be discussed with the client.

3.3 Investments

As in a family settlement, the usual wide power of investment, including power to invest in land, should be included (The Pensions Act 1995, s 34, now provides such a power but statute could alter it). If there is any doubt as to whether the particular form of policy offered by an insurer is an 'investment' as traditionally understood, power to contribute to a policy for the provision of benefits (as well as for normal insurance) should be included. Power to retain or deposit cash balances is essential. It is useful to be able to invest in non-income-producing assets, to borrow and to charge trust assets. It is essential to include power to appoint a nominee or nominees to hold investments.

Increasingly trustees are being advised to consider dealing in financial futures or traded options. Clearly any such dealings require strict control, but if embarked upon should be generally authorised (unless *perhaps* their use is likely to be limited to the protection of permitted investments)—see also Chapter 16, para 14.5. For the tax position, see Chapter 17, para 1.1(4).

3.4 Appointment of professional advisers

The trustees should be empowered to appoint an actuary or obtain equivalent advice and should be protected if relying on such advice (which may be of wider scope than the duties of the required actuary under the Pensions Act 1995, s 47). They should be required to appoint an accountant (qualified to audit under s 389 of the Companies Act 1985) who should be obliged to prepare accounts annually. This is distinct from the audit function under s 47.

The trustees should also be empowered to appoint a solicitor or generally obtain legal advice and to rely on such advice: similarly to obtain and rely on medical advice.

Where legal advice is obtained, it must be from the trustees' appointee—s 47(3).

It is for discussion whether there is to be a custodian of the investments (not a custodian trustee as understood by the Public Trustee Act 1906, but a commercial keeper of the assets whose duties include collection of dividends, maintenance of investment records etc).

3.5 Power to delegate

The trustees should be given the widest possible powers of delegation and sub-delegation (Chapter 24, para 4). Some employers require that the appointment of an investment manager be subject to their consent.

3.6 Books and records

Books, minutes and other records as to decisions and membership should be required to be kept, although if a short definitive deed is desired, this can be omitted and reliance placed on SI 1996 No 1715, reg 12, which has this effect.

3.7 Determination of questions by trustees

Determinations by the trustees should be expressed to be conclusive so far as the law permits. The trustees should be empowered to rely on information from the employer as to employees or persons claiming under them.

3.8 Decisions by majority

It is for consideration in each case whether or not decisions of the trustees should be by majority. A specific provision, rather than reliance on the Pensions Act 1995, s 32, has the advantage that it focuses consideration of the question. Certainly, unanimity should not be required (Chapter 24, para 3). There should also be provision for a quorum of a majority or perhaps a two-thirds majority of the trustees.

A sole corporate trustee would fall outside these provisions (but in effect they would be considered under its articles of association (Chapter 24, para 8).

3.9 Appointment of trustees

It is normal for the power of appointment and removal of trustees to be vested in the principal employer, although occasionally the trustees are self-perpetuating (Chapter 24, para 7). The deed may also provide for a minimum and maximum number of trustees.

There may be provision for the trustees to be elected. In such event, certainty should be achieved by providing that existing trustees continue in office until the conclusion of an election.

It is preferable to include at the outset provision for a corporate trustee to receive such remuneration if any (out of the fund) as the principal employer from time to time may agree.

The provisions for appointment and removal of trustees are subject to the statutory requirements for member-nominated trustees or a member-approved alternative (Chapter 24, para 7).

3.10 Trustees as beneficiaries

To avoid doubt, it used to be provided in the deed that any trustee can benefit under the rules by virtue of membership and can benefit from the exercise of trustees' discretion.

The former is now implied, and the latter is stated, by the Pensions Act 1995, s 39. It is a matter of choice whether nonetheless to spell them out.

3.11 Safeguards for trustees

The trustees should have the benefit of the usual provision to be found in family settlements that they are protected from claims except in respect of conscious bad faith or fraud on their own part (Chapter 24, para 2). This is now of restricted effect regarding investments—Pensions Act 1995, s 33.

There could well be a disadvantage to an employer in extending this to a general indemnity from the employer, although some deeds do so provide. Clearly such provision would require specific instructions. Where trustees are directors of the employer, consideration is needed whether the Companies Acts permit such indemnity.

The deed may authorise insurance against loss to the fund, which could, perhaps incidentally, include cover for the trustees against liability for breach of trust (Chapter 24, para 11). Directors of a corporate trustee that is a subsidiary of the employer may be covered by the employer's Directors and Officers liability insurance.

3.12 Augmentation of benefits

It is normal for a general power of augmentation and a power to pay benefits to employees, former employees, or spouses or dependants of either, who have not been members of the scheme to be included in the trust deed. Having regard to the heavy fiduciary burden that such a power imposes upon the trustees, and the fact that at the end of the day the employer will bear or has borne the major part of (if not all) the costs, this power is normally only exercisable by the trustees with the consent (and in some cases at the request) of the employer.

The power of augmentation should not normally be exercised without the advice of the actuary as to the financial consequences. For this reason, some trust deeds include words such as 'with the approval of the actuary'. Such words may place a burden of fiduciary duty unfairly on the actuary, whose role should rather be that of professional adviser. If it is desired to protect the trustees from pressure to favour individual members, it can be provided that the exercise of the discretion should be on the payment into the fund by the employer of such sum (or allocation of such part of a surplus declared on a valuation or estimated) as the actuary may advise. A simpler provision is just to require that the trustees obtain the prior advice of the actuary. None of these provisions should preclude the control by the employer mentioned above.

3.13 Guarantee of solvency

As will have been seen (Chapter 3, para 16), guarantees of solvency should generally be avoided. If they are to be given, they are normally found in the trust deed, rather than any scheduled rules, and should be specific in their terms: solvency is a word of many meanings.

3.14 Termination

There should be provision for winding up the scheme.

Under SI 1990 No 1143 as amended by SI 1996 No 2131 (replacing SI 1973 No 1431, as amended by SI 1975 No 957), made pursuant to the Social Security Act 1973, s 69, now PSA 1993 s 163, the rule against perpetuities does not apply to approved pension schemes. Nonetheless, some drafts still include a perpetuity provision, perhaps in case a scheme ceases to be approved and is not wound up within the permitted period under the regulations. The existence of a perpetuity period can create great difficulty (eg on a merger of schemes with different perpetuity periods) and can usefully be omitted although the effect in other common law jurisdictions which do not have a 'wait and see' rule may require consideration.

In any scheme, and particularly if there is a guarantee of solvency, there must be provision enabling the employer to discontinue contributions and the trustees to wind up the scheme either in the event of such discontinuance or on the employer going into liquidation, perhaps with discretionary powers to postpone such winding-up and to continue the fund as a closed fund.

The termination provisions should set out the order of priority of application of assets in the event of an overall deficiency.

Salary-related schemes, with prescribed exceptions, must comply with the requirements of the Pensions Act 1995, s 73 (and transitional winding-up regulations), but there remains considerable freedom for discussion with the clients, particularly with regard to surplus. Section 73 follows tradition in according priority to benefits derived from members' voluntary contributions and to pensions in payment (but not to future increases to such pensions—a departure from tradition).

In a final salary scheme, there is likely to be a 'surplus' since the funding basis will usually make provision for the effect of future salary increases on accrued past service, and this reserve will fall into surplus on a winding-up. The Inland Revenue require that benefits may not be increased beyond published limits (Chapter 17, para 3) and that thereafter the surplus must be returned to the employers, but not all schemes include the latter provision. Nonetheless, there is usually considerable scope for improving benefits or for providing purchased annual increases. Index-linked annuities are available, at a price that generally doubles the financial liabilities of the fund. It is therefore necessary to include in the deed provision for disposal of the surplus. Otherwise, until the Pensions Act 1995, it would have passed to the Crown as *bona vacantia* (or to the employers and members on resulting trust if the relevant proportions could be established to the satisfaction of the court). Section 77(4) now provides that after maximising benefits, the surplus may be distributed to the employer anyway.

These are crucial matters which have been discussed briefly in Chapter 3, para 20.

Many deeds provide that the trustees may increase benefits at discretion but subject to the consent of the employer. That consent is not normally a fiduciary power (although it may be in the particular circumstances) and therefore will not be given by a receiver or liquidator having an eye to the ultimate return of surplus to the company. It is possible to exclude the provision in the event of receivership or liquidation. Other deeds provide only for 'consultation' with the employer, but, in view of the ambiguity of this phrase, it is better omitted.

It is possible for the trustees to be given, subject to Inland Revenue limitations, unfettered discretion to increase benefits. It is uncertain whether, in such case, they are obliged to consider the interest of the employer in the possible return of surplus. Nonetheless, trustee discretion may prove the most acceptable provision.

The deed may require the trustees to apply surplus up to Inland Revenue limits before returning the balance to the employers; in this case, it is necessary to include discretion to omit beneficiaries who cannot easily be traced and to omit calculations which cannot easily be made (for the Revenue will permit indexation of past salary records which may not be easily or cheaply obtainable). See also Chapter 11, para 14, regarding predator protection.

Before surplus can be paid to the employer, the Pensions Act 1995 has requirements, primarily at ss 37 and 76, and regulations made under those sections eg SI 1996 No 2156.

3.15 Disposal etc of a subsidiary

It is essential to provide for partial closure of the scheme, that is for cessation of contributions in respect of employees of a participating company that either desires, or is required, to cease to participate. Among other considerations is that, after the disposal of such a company to an unrelated purchaser, there may be a transfer payment to the purchaser's fund. Chapter 11 illustrates the importance of this provision. Large public companies generally provide for restricted transfer payments save with their consent, so as to have a suitable bargaining position in a commercial sale agreement. Smaller companies sometimes prefer an unfettered trustee discretion (up to a past service reserve or occasionally a share of the fund) to avoid a predator benefiting from subsequent disposals.

The Inland Revenue permit continued participation in the scheme by a sold subsidiary for a limited period of time, usually not later than the end of the fiscal year following that in which the disposal takes place (see para 21.6 of the practice notes IR 12 referred to in Chapter 17, para 3). It is often helpful to provide that participation ceases automatically on a disposal but that the trustees can, with the consent (or perhaps shall at the direction) of the principal employer, and with the agreement of the subsidiary concerned, permit continued participation for a limited period. The clause should provide that the period either is or is not pensionable and does or does not continue the death-in-service benefits, as the case may be, with power for the opposite to be agreed. See also Chapter 5.

3.16 Substitution of principal employer

There should be provision to substitute a new principal employer (with the powers and obligations of the original party) on liquidation, takeover, reconstruction or perhaps even on the sale of a subsidiary (but see Chapter 24, para 10.3). The drafting of such provision requires special care in the case of an employer that is a partnership or an unincorporated association.

3.17 Transfers in and out

There should be power to accept transfer payments from, and make such payments to, other exempt approved schemes, or other schemes approved for the purpose by the Commissioners of Inland Revenue. The statutory power for members to require transfer of cash equivalents (Chapter 10, para 10) is no substitute as, inter alia, (*a*) it is not a unilateral power of the trustees and (*b*) it does not apply to pensioners.

3.18 Special terms of membership

There should be power to admit persons on special terms of membership and also to admit persons who would not otherwise be eligible (the power being expressed to be subject to Revenue requirements).

3.19 Power of alteration

It is essential to include a power of alteration. The reasons for this, and the types of power, are discussed in Chapter 3, para 15. It suffices to say that without such power a scheme is permanently inflexible. The beneficiaries are usually far too numerous to envisage an application to the court to vary the trusts, and the powers of modification conferred on OPRA by the Pensions Act 1995, are very limited (Chapter 18).

3.20 Preservation

All schemes must comply with the preservation requirements which protect the pensions of early leavers (see Chapter 10, para 1). It is likely that the outline of benefits issued on the establishment of the scheme (Chapter 3, para 10) will comply with those requirements so far as the particular benefits mentioned in it are concerned. However, it is far less certain that the detailed provisions set out in the definitive trust deed and rules will meet those requirements. For example, in calculating whether the member has at least 'two years' qualifying service', broken periods are to be included in a number of circumstances (Chapter 10, paras 6 and 7).

The statutory references for preservation are set out in Chapter 10, para 1 and are amplified by SI 1991 No 167, which in reg 27 requires that a pension scheme contains express rules to provide for the particular listed preservation provisions. Although the Occupational Pensions Board (OPB) has been dissolved, their Memorandum 78 (May 1992 edition) remains a useful description of the detailed requirements, and contains in App 3 a checklist of drafting points.

Schemes established before 6 April 1997 containing rules relating to lien and forfeiture will usually restrict their application in accordance with the preservation requirements. The relevant statutory provisions have, however, now been widened to confer protection on all beneficiaries (and significantly altered in their details)—see para 3.26 below.

If there were pressure to execute a definitive deed rapidly (not only from the Pensions Schemes Office (PSO), who are usually prepared to wait, but from employers or members who for particular reasons may be anxious to see the detailed rules) it would be wise to include a provision similar to that mentioned in Chapter 10, para 1.8 in respect of the interim document enabling further amendments to be made retrospectively.

3.21 Further retrospective powers to meet Inland Revenue requirements

It may also be wise to include a further power, similar to the power mentioned above relating to preservation, to enable the deed to be altered retrospectively to meet Inland Revenue requirements. This can be a double-edged sword. If the draft has been submitted to the Revenue and meets their approval, and the deed is executed promptly thereafter one has achieved the certainty that the scheme will be approved, whereas if the deed contains the power to make further changes, one may be inviting further comments. Nonetheless the power is recommended.

3.22 Equal treatment

The scheme must comply with the equal treatment requirements, albeit if not, an equal treatment rule is deemed to be included. (Chapter 22, para 2.8). The requirements may appear relatively straightforward. However, the effect of an eligibility rule that appears to be uniform as between male and female employees, may be to discriminate indirectly by reason of the different proportions of one sex that can comply with it. The most general example is that of part-timers who are frequently mainly female. Since the effect will depend upon the composition of the employer's workforce, which may vary from time to time, it is not considered appropriate to address this question within the rules.

3.23 Contracting out

It suffices to refer the reader to Chapter 3, para 12.

3.24 Execution beyond the 24-month period

The interim document will have specified (Chapter 3, para 3) the period within which the definitive deed or rules must be adopted. This is normally 24 months. Sometimes, the draft definitive deed cannot be agreed within that period. The Inland Revenue (who must be satisfied under s 592(1)(*a*) of ICTA 1988, that there is an irrevocable trust in existence, if the scheme is to receive exempt approval—see Chapter 17, para 1) used to be willing to permit an extension beyond that period for successive periods of additional 12 months. However, following a consultation letter issued by the Revenue in August 1992 the practice has been significantly tightened. If the approval of the scheme is not to be prejudiced, the Revenue should be consulted well before the expiry of the first 24 months. If necessary, they should be offered the adoption of a standard 'limits' rule and a winding-up rule, with the current booklet annexed as a specification of benefits. This will usually be sufficient to obtain agreement to an extension and may even be sufficient to obtain approval.

The normal way in which the interim document will have been drafted will be that the requirement to execute the definitive deed within 24 months is an agreement between the company and the trustees, so that it is open to them to extend that period by subsequent agreement (although the beneficiaries might well bring pressure to bear in the event of excessive delay).

The recital to a delayed definitive deed should record that the parties thereto have agreed that it shall be the definitive deed referred to in the interim document (notwithstanding that the latter had specified a deed to be executed within the 24-month period).

3.25 Balance of power/refunds to the employer etc

The reader is referred to the very important comments in Chapter 3, para 21 on the balance of power between the employer and the trustees. It is essential to obtain instructions, before finalising the definitive deed, on the issue. Paragraphs 18–20 of Chapter 3 should also be considered and in particular whether to provide for refund of surplus to the employer from an ongoing scheme and the extent of trustee control over surplus on a winding up.

3.26 Lien, forfeiture and bankruptcy

Lien and forfeiture generally relate to monetary obligations owed by the member to the employer. Forfeiture also relates to attempts by a member to assign his rights under the scheme, for example to secure a debt.

Bankruptcy, where mentioned in pension scheme rules, is generally a disentitling event (to prevent the moneys simply passing to creditors) but may be coupled with a protective trust for the member and/or his dependants.

All these provisions are now regulated by the Pensions Act 1995, ss 91–95. Additionally, the Inland Revenue require that approved schemes contain a prohibition on assignment (but see Chapter 8, para 9 regarding both the Pensions Act and Revenue exemptions).

The possibility of lien or forfeiture for the benefit of the employer is subject to important restrictions, for the benefit of the member, contained in ss 91–93. These protections, which have direct effect by reason of s 117, replace similar (but not identical) provisions of the preservation legislation formerly consolidated in the PSA 1993 ss 77–80, now repealed. As preservation did not have direct effect, existing schemes, and most standard drafts still available, set out in full the protections, the basic provision being that both lien and forfeiture, so far as they benefit the employer, must be restricted to a monetary obligation due to the employer and arising out of a criminal, negligent or fraudulent act or omission by the member—Pensions Act 1995, s 91(5)(d) and 93(1). The lien or forfeiture is limited to the amount of the monetary obligation, with provisions for certification by the trustees, and for a dispute as to the certified amount to suspend the effect until settled by an Order of the Court or arbitration award. Lien in favour of the *employer* may only extend to transfer credits if derived from another scheme of the same or an associated employer which could also have placed such a lien (SI 1997 No 785, reg 3). This restriction does not apply to a permissible lien in favour of the *scheme* (s 91(5)(*e*)) nor, it appears, to a permissible forfeiture under ss 92 and 93.

A lien, unless accompanied by a provision for a capital payment by the trustees to the employer, will have no practical effect until a pension comes into payment. Older schemes often contain a prohibition on an alteration which would result in a payment to the employer, and therefore (if they do not contain from the outset such a provision) cannot be amended. Section 93 may afford a practical route since forfeiture can be followed, under 93(5), by a payment to the employer; it is not clear but seems probable that 93(5) is a direct authority for such a payment without the need for specific provision in the rules, but 93(1) is not an enabling provision so that the forfeiture itself would require an appropriate rule.

The prohibition on assignment is often incorporated in a single clause which refers also to bankruptcy, and often contains protective trusts to enable the benefit to be paid to the member or his dependants. Section 92(2) permits a scheme rule that forfeits pension on bankruptcy or attempted assignment. Section 92(3) confers a discretionary power to make payments to the member or dependants, following a permissible forfeiture. However, by s 91(3) (still to be brought into force—see below) a bankrupt's pension is excluded from his estate for the purpose of the Insolvency Act 1986. (Section 91(2) prevents any other court order, save regarding unapproved schemes outside the public sector—SI 1997 No 785—and save for matrimonial orders (s 166(5)).

It is permissible for scheme rules to provide for forfeiture of a dependant's (etc) pension where the beneficiary is convicted of the unlawful killing of the member or of aiding or procurring such offence (SI 1997 No 785, reg 6(1), (2)).

The exclusion of a bankrupt's pension will probably be brought into force simultaneously with s 95 which will enable a court to include excessive voluntary contributions paid, eg to defraud creditors. The latter awaits regulations to value the accumulated sum, at present under consultation between the DTI (being responsible for the Insolvency Act 1986) and the actuarial profession. The outcome is expected in Autumn 1997. Section 95 will then introduce to the IA 1986 new ss 342A–342C, the latter specifying that s 91 does not apply to prevent the above court order.

3.27 Members' voluntary contributions

With effect from 6 April 1988 it became mandatory for approved schemes to include provision for the acceptance of members' voluntary contributions—now PSA 1993, s 111. Lower and upper limits on these contributions are permissible under SI 1987 No 1108, as amended in 1994. Trustees are obliged by PSA 1993, s 132 to bring scheme rules into conformity with these provisions. OPB Memorandum 78 (May 1992 edition) contains a useful checklist at App 4. For the tax position, see Chapter 17 para 11.

4 Insurance company standard—what to look for

The fact that most life office drafts are of great length has already been mentioned in para 2 above. ('Life office' is the term still often used in Revenue correspondence. It distinguishes insurance companies having a life fund from those conducting general insurance business). The facts also that there is good reason for this (from the point of view of their administration) and that amendments may result in lengthy correspondence have also been mentioned. There is the further point that the drafts will undoubtedly follow a standard approved by the PSO or submitted to them for approval. If substantial amendments are made, the insurer may require those who have made them to correspond with the Revenue. This would be particularly unfortunate, since the Revenue may well raise comments on parts of the deed which have not been altered, and the party corresponding with them would have no knowledge as to the basis on which the Revenue had agreed the standard with the life office.

There is also the problem of the cost effectiveness of making amendments (para 5 below).

Although it will be essential for any particular draft to be perused from beginning to end—and it is not possible to forecast the form which such drafts will take since each life office has its own draft and is constantly amending it—it may be helpful to point to particular aspects, including some mentioned in 3 above, which merit special consideration. The outstanding ones are:

(*a*) PSO/OPB approval;
(*b*) trusteeship;
(*c*) alteration;
(*d*) solvency;
(*e*) closure and partial closure;
(*f*) balance of power, refunds to the employer etc;
(*g*) benefits and contributions;
(*h*) 'correspondence'.

4.1 PSO approval

A written question should be put to the life office as to whether the draft has been approved by the PSO as suitable for an exempt approved scheme whether it has been designed to conform with preservation and, if the scheme is contracted out on a money-purchase basis (a COMP scheme—see Chapter 20), whether it contains model rules regarding protected rights.

4.2 Trusteeship

It is of course necessary to check that the draft provides for the trustees of the interim document to be the trustees of the definitive document, unless there has been a change of trusteeship in between.

Frequently, an employer will say that a particular trustee has resigned, but one will find that the resignation is not effective. If the individual is no longer connected in any way with the employer or the scheme it may be appropriate to produce a short deed formally removing him. It is wise to recite the reasons for such removal since it is always a serious matter to remove a trustee and the existence of good reason is an indication that the power has not been exercised wantonly. Similar powers of appointment and removal (and possible remuneration) will be required to those advised for the interim document (see Chapter 3, para 7) and in para 3.9 above (which also mentions statutory requirements for member–nominated trustees or a member–approved alternative arrangement).

Such powers should never be casually exercised. It is therefore as well to provide that they be exercisable by deed. The trustees should be relieved of liability in respect of all acts other than fraud or conscious bad faith (see para 3.11 above). They should be given power to delegate and where appropriate to act by majority. All these powers are mentioned in para 3 above, together with requirements as to records, minutes etc (and the alternative, regarding records, of reliance on the overriding requirements of the Pensions Act 1995).

4.3 Alteration

As mentioned in Chapter 3, para 15, a life office draft will usually incorporate fetters to the exercise of a power of alteration. The reasons for their removal in Chapter 3, para 15 are equally valid in connection with the definitive deed. It should be remembered that a wide power of alteration can always be narrowed but it is probably ineffective to purport to widen such a power.

The final observation of Chapter 3, para 15 regarding substitution is equally valid as respects the definitive deed. The absence of a power of substitution from the interim deed should not prevent its inclusion in the later deed even if the effect of a substitution on the subsequent exercise of the power of alteration is uncertain. See also para 3.16 above.

4.4 Solvency

The comments in para 3.13 above as to a guarantee of solvency apply equally to the life office draft. The point is particularly serious because many clients assume that the payment of the recommended contributions to the insurance company will necessarily mean that they have met all their obligations under the scheme (Chapter 8, para 2).

4.5 Closure and partial closure

These provisions are crucial and have been described in para 3.14 and 3.15 above. It is essential that they are discussed with the client as they may well not be reviewed until the relevant events occur.

4.6 Balance of power, refunds to the employer etc

The detailed points made in Chapter 3, para 21 regarding balance of power and the specific question of refunds to employer (Chapter 3, para 19) should be considered, even though this will entail studying in detail a number of provisions in the draft.

4.7 Benefits and contributions

The rules will set out the benefits in detail. They will provide for the precise calculation of benefits and also for their destinations, eg to an unmarried dependant, as of right or at discretion, where a married couple have parted but not divorced (subject to contracting-out requirements where applicable).

The rules relating to normal benefits will depend upon the intention of the employer (Chapter 8). The usual rules of construction apply so that the task of checking the document often becomes one of achieving certainty. The question of cost effectiveness becomes important (para 5 below).

There are, however, a number of refinements that can usefully be added. Two that should particularly be considered are tax points, relating to inheritance tax and income tax respectively. The first is to provide that any lump sum death benefit is held on trust for beneficiaries, selected by the trustees at the time from a defined class (or on a *restricted* basis by the member), so as to avoid inclusion in the member's estate for inheritance tax purposes. The second is to ensure that there is power for the trustees to deduct from any refund of contributions an amount equal to the tax (at present 20 per cent) borne by them. As to the first, the discretionary trust relating to lump sums arising on death should include the usual enlargements of the trustees' powers under ss 31 and 32 of the Trustee Act 1925. It is also useful if provision is included for the appointment of separate trustees under s 37 of that Act and for the power of appointment of subsequent trustees of the lump sum to be vested in such separate trustees or the personal representatives of the survivor of them so that, if a separate trust is created, the main pension fund trustees will not subsequently be bothered to appoint a new trustee of the sub-trust on the death or retirement of an individual trustee of it.

It is always necessary to be precise as to the nature of a spouse's or dependant's benefit—see Chapter 22, para 4 and Chapter 23.

The benefits may include children's allowances. These usually continue until the child attains a specified age or else ceases (at a later age) to attend a course of full-time education. It is wise to provide that the course must be a type approved by the trustees and that they have an absolute discretion to decide whether or not the child is in such education (although the precise wording must take account of Inland Revenue requirements as set out in part 11 of (and the definition 'dependant' in) the practice notes IR 12 referred to in Chapter 17, para 3). It is also useful to provide that no one child has an entitlement to the benefit, and that although the amount of benefit depends upon the number of children, it can be paid to somebody to be applied for all or any of the children—partly to meet unforeseen circumstances, and partly to avoid reduction in education grants or welfare benefits applicable to some children but not others in a family.

In the case of a contributory scheme, the rules must provide for members to contribute at the relevant rate. They usually include provision for the employer to deduct the contributions from pay and for contributions to be suspended, on terms or otherwise, during periods of hardship or for some other stated reason. The deduction from pay must have been contractually notified in writing or agreed in writing by the employee (ERA 1996, s 13).

A major point to look for in the rules is the provision relating to absence from service, including strikes, or leave of absence (through maternity or otherwise). There should be precise provision (or clear discretion) as to the requirement to contribute and the accrual of pensionable service during such absence. There should also be precise provision (or discretion) as to whether or not death-in-service benefits apply during any such period.

4.8 'Correspondence'

It is essential to ensure that all benefits that may arise under the policy issued by the life office are included in the rules of the scheme. For the

Inland Revenue's requirements for statutory 'correspondence', see para 17.14 et seq of their practice notes IR 12 (1991). This correspondence between the rules and the policy need not amount to the provision of identical benefits so long as:

(*a*) from the Revenue point of view, the policy benefits are covered by the rules, to permit all the premiums to be placed by the life office in its 'pension business' fund; and
(*b*) from the client's point of view, it is understood that some benefits may not be fully underwritten.

In practice, the practitioner should inquire in writing of the life office whether the benefits described in the rules accord precisely with those provided under the policy, ie whether there is a balance of benefit which must be met out of uninsured resources. This question may not be completely appropriate in the case of a managed fund (Chapter 2, para 4) but even then will be applicable to death-in-service benefits if specifically insured.

5 Cost-effectiveness of solicitor

The question of cost-effectiveness applies as much to the company secretary or accountant as it does to the solicitor. His time may not be specifically recorded as a chargeable item, but if a great deal of it is taken up, it will prevent him attending to other matters.

The question therefore arises as to the extent to which a draft submitted by a life office should be dissected. It is clearly essential to look for the items referred to in para 4 above. These are matters which may not be capable of being put right if not correct at the outset.

The question of benefits is, however, a difficult one. To the member, they are the reality of the scheme. It is essential that somebody takes the responsibility for ensuring that the benefits described in the outline (Chapter 3, para 10) are incorporated in the rules. For a scheme with more than a couple of dozen members where the company secretary or some similar person may be expected to answer members' questions without bringing in the broker, the person doing this checking should be within the company. For a smaller scheme, it would still be prudent for somebody within the company or one of its professional advisers to check these specific items. Undoubtedly, he will have a substantial number of questions which should be resolved by a session with the broker or a representative of the life office.

The conclusion is, therefore, that the solicitor must check the matters that affect the relationship of the employer and the trustees but should establish his client's preference as to whether this is to extend to the benefits to be granted to the members. There is no doubt that, if his duty is to be fully performed, he should take responsibility for the benefit rules too. However, the length and possible unfamiliarity of the document means that the cost of doing so will be considerable. It is therefore essential to point out to the client the distinction between the relationships of company to trustee and trustees to members, and ensure that instructions extend to the whole task before embarking upon it. If they do not so extend, the fact that the client is taking responsibility for the benefit rules should be made clear in writing.

If the instructions do extend to the rules, it would be wise not to alter the drafting framework adopted by the life office. As stated in para 2 above, the life office draft is likely to be unusually long for the very good reason that it has to be capable of adaptation to a large number of permutations of benefit. Frequently, the method chosen is to employ a large, seemingly excessive, number of definitions so that to understand a given benefit one has to cross-refer to several of these definitions. Although one or more of the definitions may be used in only one place in the particular set of rules that is being examined, they may be used in several places in other sets. Therefore, although the elimination of some of the definitions (by use of each intended meaning directly in the one place that it occurs) would simplify the rules, it would also make the checking of the rules in the life office and the Inland Revenue that much more difficult. A decision therefore has to be taken whether the checking of the rules extends also to the simplification of them. If it does, the length of time involved, including correspondence, will be extended considerably. If it does not, then the task is that of following the text to ensure that it is correct.

In some cases, it will be found that there are additional options, or even additional benefits, of which the client was not aware. These are usually provided without additional charge by the life office because they have been taken into account in the costing or in the standard bases on which the insurer uplifts cash from the fund to provide, for example, dependants' benefits.

Finally, the life office must be asked at the outset, usually via the broker, to confirm that the draft follows a standard approved by the

Inland Revenue, and after execution of the document should be asked to confirm that it is being submitted to the Revenue, and that a copy of the Revenue letter of approval, when eventually received, will be forwarded to the solicitor as well as to the client.

6 Benefits

The approach of the draftsman to the rules of the scheme will depend upon the client's instructions. Some alternatives are considered under paras 4 and 5 above.

It is outside the scope of this book to lead the practitioner to prepare his own draft rules. If this is required there is little alternative but to dissect a precedent with a view to understanding the approach that it illustrates. The points mentioned in this chapter will assist in working through the precedent. Since the scheme will have already been established (by an interim document), there will normally be ample time to submit the final draft to the PSO for comment. Much correspondence will be saved, however, if the practitioner first tests each rule against the requirements relating to Inland Revenue limits (as referred to in Chapter 17, para 3 and the practice notes IR 12 there mentioned), preservation, contracting out and, including eligibility, equal treatment. Revenue limits are now best dealt with by adoption of a standard appendix, governed by a provision that all benefits are subject to the appendix 'or such greater amounts as may be agreed by the Inland Revenue in any particular case or with regard to any particular category'.

7 Buy-outs for Pre-1986 Leavers

There was considerable controversy in 1986 whether or not to provide power for pre-1986 leavers to exchange their deferred pensions, and their dependants' contingent rights, for insurance buy-outs (Chapter 10, para 12).

Some standards may therefore still contain such a provision. Broadly, now that the statutory rights have been extended, it is better to rely on the statutory discharge than a specific provision in the deed, but if the practitioner has any doubt about the scope of the proposed deletion, the point should be checked with the life office that supplied the standard.

Chapter 14

Forms and types of documents

The following is not an exhaustive list of all the types of documents that can relate to pension schemes. It is intended to be a useful reference guide to those most commonly met. Where the type of document is described more fully elsewhere in this book, there is merely a cross-reference. In other cases, a short explanation is included.

1 Interim document

See Chapter 3, para 3.

2 Supplemental interim document

Occasionally it is necessary to make specific provision for a matter that is not covered in the interim document, at a time when the definitive document is not yet available. Provided that there is power to do this in the interim document, or power can be inferred, a further document can be executed expressed to be supplemental to the interim document. Frequently, it recites that it is still the intention of the parties to execute the definitive document in due course, which will then supersede both interim documents (save as may be otherwise provided).

An alternative approach is an agreement between the parties (usually the principal employer and the trustees) that the definitive rules, when adopted, will include the provisions set out in the agreement. Such agreement may in effect constitute a variation of the document that established the scheme, by following the form of a power of alteration contained in it. See also para 4 below.

3 Deed of adherence or participation

Where several companies (usually subsidiaries of the same holding company, but occasionally merely associated with one another in business to an extent that enables them to adhere to the same scheme without prejudicing its Revenue approval) participate in a scheme, each should covenant with the trustees (and perhaps also with the principal employer) that it will accept the provisions of the scheme that relate to it. Each may do this by joining in the interim or definitive deed or by separate deed of participation (to which the trustees may or may not be a requisite party) sometimes known as a deed of adherence or deed of accession. See Chapter 5.

4 Deed of extension

Although the above name is sometimes given to a document as described in para 3 above, it is also used for a deed under which the company and the trustees agree to extend the initial period (of 24 months or whatever), agreed by them in the interim document, within which the definitive document is to be executed. Such a deed is often not necessary, but useful to record their agreement. It is frequently the simplest method of meeting a Revenue requirement as to an indication of timetable. However, see Chapter 13, para 3.24 regarding the tightening of the Revenue's requirements and the possible need for a substantive document.

5 Definitive deed or rules

See Chapter 13.

6 Document of alteration

All well-drawn schemes will include a power of alteration (Chapter 3, para 15 and Chapter 13, para 3). This power will usually be exercisable by deed, generally known as a deed of alteration or variation.

7 Appointment and removal of trustees

See Chapter 3, para 7 and Chapter 13 para 3.

8 Deed of closure

Such a deed (or, if authorised, resolution) may close the scheme to:

(*a*) further contributions (and/or accrual of pensionable service) by employees;
(*b*) further contributions by employers;
(*c*) new members (or classes of member);
(*d*) new members (or classes) if employed by a particular company;

or may simply be the label given to a deed under para 9 below.

9 Winding up (resolution or deed etc)

The method of winding up a scheme will depend upon its existing documents (which may or may not preserve a power of alteration). Similarly, the matters to be considered in the winding-up will depend upon such documents, and also upon the reasons for winding up. The most commonly dealt with matters are:

(*a*) purchase of annuities for beneficiaries or prospective beneficiaries;
(*b*) deficiency—rights against employers, liquidator (if any) to be preserved (Chapter 3, para 16)—see also PSA 1993, s 124;
(*c*) contracted-out scheme—Contributions Agency requirement to be met regarding surrender of certificate;
(*d*) where no definitive deed yet—benefits to be scheduled:
(*e*) where all employees have left service—as (*d*) above;
(*f*) transfer to another scheme—recital of power;
(*g*) augumentation—as (*f*) above, plus schedule;
(*h*) alteration—power may (dependent on text of winding-up rule) disappear unless reserved by the trust deed;
(*i*) ultimate surplus—destination (employer, receiver, liquidator etc) to be set out, subject to compliance with the Pensions Act 1995, and necessary indemnities given;
(*j*) Inland Revenue limits to be specifically retained.

The trustees' minutes will record that these matters have been dealt with. It is a matter of choice whether they make a declaration (by deed or resolution) that the assets have been applied and the scheme thereby wound up.

10 Undertakings

It is a regrettable fact that pension schemes are frequently governed by undertakings given by the company or the trustees either to one another or to the PSO. Occasionally, they are even governed by undertakings given to the trustees of other schemes. Such undertakings all form part of the documentation of the scheme and should not be overlooked.

It should also be ascertained whether the documents establishing the trusts of the scheme, as varied from time to time, authorise the giving of such undertakings.

A number of purposes may be served by undertakings, viz the maintenance of tax approval, the avoidance of hasty amendments, the requirements for contracting out, the exercise of powers under transfer agreements and generally in connection with the administration of the scheme.

11 Death benefit trusts

Lump sums arising on death are frequently held on trust (see Chapter 13, para 4.7). Occasionally, the precise trusts are set out in the definitive deed. More likely, that deed contains a wide power for the trustees to exercise, with provision to take effect in default of such exercise within a two-year period. The exercise of that discretion is usually recorded in a resolution setting out the trusts relating to that particular death benefit.

There may be power to appoint separate trustees. If there is such a power, and if it is exercised, there may be a deed between the trustees of the scheme and the intended trustees of the death benefit reciting the circumstances in which the benefit arose, and the trusts on which it is to be held.

12 Transfer agreement

Where assets in respect of a member are transferred to another scheme, the terms of the transfer should be recorded. This may be done simply by letter. If, however, there is a bulk transfer (Chapter 10, para 11 and Chapter 11, paras 3 and 5) it will normally be appropriate to have a formal agreement between the two sets of trustees recording which one will pay out benefits that arise before the transfer of assets has taken place, and other allied matters. It may even be necessary to delay the transfer until one scheme obtains necessary Revenue approval, in which case the provisions may be of considerable length.

Where the agreement follows a commercial sale whereby the parties undertake to procure (or use their best endeavours to procure) that a transfer takes place, the vendor and purchaser can usefully be parties to the trustees' agreement which can then include an acknowledgment that the obligation has been fulfilled (or can include a release if the transfer has been carried out in a manner different from that contemplated in the sale agreement).

Alternatively, if the commercial sale agreement had set out precise pension transfer terms, it may be sufficient for the transferring trustee to obtain a receipt for the assets stating also that they were accepted on the terms of the sale agreement (whether or not the trustees were a party to it).

13 Application form for membership

The application form can be simple but should include the necessary details for life cover, authority to deduct contributions (Chapter 4, para 4, and Chapter 13, para 4) and an acknowledgement that the member will be bound by the trust deed and rules. Some forms include a declaration that the individual has not formerly been a member of the scheme (whether under his present or a former name) as this may affect the consolidation of benefits and/or entitlement to preservation after less than two years (Chapter 10, para 7).

14 Consent to transfer or variation of benefits

Although there may be power under the trust deed to transfer benefits to another scheme without the member's consent, such consent is often prudently obtained and is required if the member leaves service and qualifies for preservation (save as mentioned in Chapter 10, para 11).

Occasionally it will be desirable to vary a benefit even though there is no power in the deed. Provided that the consent of the member and any other (adult) prospective beneficiary is obtained, this can usually be done. An indemnity may be required by the trustees (see para 15 below). A problem will arise if the class of beneficiaries is open. This will always be the case if a widow's benefit is to be affected under a contracted-out scheme.

In both cases it should be 'informed' consent, if it is to be effective. It is therefore helpful to include reference to the announcement or other documents which the individual has seen. Equally, it is important that these documents will have presented a fair picture.

15 Indemnity

Occasionally the trustees will be asked by the employer to do something which it is possible may not be totally within their powers. They may be asked to vary a benefit, which they can properly do if all beneficiaries affected concur, but whereas it may be possible to obtain the concurrence of those likely to receive the benefit, it may be argued that the giving of that benefit reduces the assets available in the general fund so that all members are affected. In such and other cases trustees may nonetheless feel it right to concur with the employer's request but on terms that they be given an indemnity.

16 Employee announcement

See Chapter 3, para 10.

17 Contracting-out notices

A notice of intention to elect to contract out of the State scheme must be issued at least one month in advance to those affected thereby (three months if there is a recognised trade union unless it consents to a one-month notice)—Chapter 20, and SI 1996 No 1172, reg 4.

The regulations also provide for a notice to employees where there is an election to vary a contracting-out certificate (reg 9). In some cases, an example being where a subsidiary is sold but continues to participate for a limited period in the scheme and requires a separate certificate, a simple notice of explanation under reg 10(3) will suffice, the reference to the Secretary of State meaning the Contributions Agency.

18 Reports etc under disclosure regulations

Since 1986, disclosure regulations have required annual reports to be available to members and others, and certain other information in particular form (see Chapter 16, para 6).

19 Investment management agreement

The rules under the Financial Services Act 1986 require an investment manager to provide to his customer an agreement relating to his services. If there is a commercial custodian, there should be a separate agreement (which may, in tripartite form, be part of the management agreement).

These documents tend to contain exclusions of liability on the part of the manager and custodian, and therefore require the most careful consideration (see Chapter 16, para 14).

The Pensions Act 1995, s 47 requires there to be a fund manager appointed by or on behalf of the trustees (with certain prescribed exceptions, eg wholly insured schemes) and SI 1996 No 1715 sets out certain formal requirements for the agreement, including that for the custodian where there is one (by inclusion in reg 2(c)).

Chapter 15

Employee and trade union consultation and participation

1 Mutual funds: history

Many of the older pension funds began life as mutual provident funds (frequently registered as friendly societies). Such funds were initially under the complete control of their members. However, the enormous strain on their finances brought about by the 1914–18 war caused many employers to inject subventions. In due course the majority of such funds have become absorbed into conventional, often non-contributory, pension schemes and the interest of their members in their administration has died away.

2 Schemes established by employers: history

The term 'pension' was used from the seventeenth to the nineteenth centuries to refer to an ex gratia regular income provided for an individual by another, often in gratitude for services rendered but usually as a matter of family or regal honour. The recipient was not necessarily old; the pension often ceased (unexpectedly) through a change in the circumstances of one of the parties or the desire of the giver.

Employers, particularly the great charter trading companies, adopted a similar approach at the end of the eighteenth century. The concept of a pension as of right did not become widespread until the regular establishment of contributory schemes following the tax legislation of 1921 (similar to the more recent, but now defunct, Income and Corporation Taxes Act 1970, s 208, referred to in Chapter 17, para 5). Even then, members rarely showed interest in the manner in which funds were administered (save for the occasional fund whose trustees included some appointed by the members through election). Trade unions, concentrating on actual pay, seldom attempted before 1978 to negotiate pension rights.

These attitudes on the part of members and unions have changed substantially since 1978. Members have frequently been involved through consultative committees; the Pensions Act 1995, arising out of the 'Maxwell' affair, has increased member interest and concern substantially (see para 6 below).

Trade union interest was strongly awakened by the obligation in 1977–78 to consult on the question of contracting out (see para 4 below). The growth of surpluses in the 1980s resulted in a number of highly publicised suspensions of employer contributions or repayments to employers (Chapter 3, para 19), sometimes creating demands for a negotiated allocation of surplus to increased benefits.

3 Revenue requirements

It will be seen from Chapter 17 that all approved schemes for current employees now come within the new code established by the Finance Act 1970 and consolidated in ICTA 1988. Section 590(2)(*b*), which relates to mandatory approval (Chapter 17, para 2), sets out as one of the conditions for approval that 'every employee who is, or has a right to be, a member of the scheme has been given written particulars of all essential features of the scheme which concern him'. The Revenue adhered to this condition when granting discretionary approval (Chapter 17, para 3), albeit the matter is now more comprehensively covered by the disclosure regulations (Chapter 16, para 6).

This requirement, and the desirability of demonstrating the care that has been taken to provide a good scheme, have led to the almost universal use of clear explanatory booklets describing the main benefit structures of schemes. These either constitute the initial announcement (Chapter 3, para 10) or follow it soon afterwards, leaving the trust deed and rules in the background as being available for inspection.

Nonetheless, neither the Revenue nor the disclosure requirement makes mention of consultation or participation and, save for the slightly increased interest that resulted from the improved communication, did not bring either in its wake. See, however, para 6 below.

4 Contracting out: requirement to consult

The introduction of the present State pension scheme (Chapter 20) brought trade unions into the area of consultation. Some schemes are contracted out (Chapter 20, para 4) but, whether an employer chose to contract out or not in respect of its scheme, a duty was imposed to consult (as to the question of whether or not to contract out) with an independent trade union recognised to any extent for the purposes of collective bargaining in relation to the relevant employees. The current requirement empowered by the PSA 1993 s 11, and contained in SI 1996 No 1172, reg 4, relates only to contracting out.

It was thought by many practitioners that the consultations would widen into negotiations. This rarely happened, partly because so many of the larger schemes presented contracting out as requiring little change (because the scheme benefits greatly exceeded those required for that purpose) but offering substantial savings, to employees as well as employers, in national insurance contributions. In subsequent years the larger trade unions become more actively concerned to negotiate improved pension schemes or to extend the definitions of eligibility (particularly regarding part-time employees) or pensionable salary where it excluded overtime or shift allowances (although these could present difficulties in a final salary scheme where fluctuations in overtime or shift allowances were considerable).

The Act does not impose any duty to consult non-unionised members, but there is a requirement to give all employees notice of the intention to elect to contract out. During the year 1997 schemes that are, and are to remain, contracted out on a salary-related basis (Chapter 20) must be the subject of new notices (and, where relevant, fresh consultation with trade unions). This does not apply to schemes already contracted out on a money-purchase basis (COMPs). The contrast occurs as COMP benefit structures are unchanged, whereas COSRs have had to change from GMP accrual to the reference scheme test.

As to changes to contracted-out schemes, see Chapter 21.

5 General provisions of equity

Almost all UK pension funds are held on trust (Chapter 17, para 1). It follows that a member's right to information is at least as great as that of any beneficiary under a settlement. The right undoubtedly extends to full information about his own interest and the terms of the trust deed and rules. It almost certainly extends to the accounts and perhaps to any actuarial report obtained pursuant to the provisions of the trust deed. These rights were enlarged in 1986 by disclosure regulations now replaced by SI 1996 No 1655.

A beneficiary cannot, however, dictate the manner in which the trustees exercise their discretion, unless (which is unlikely) the trust instrument provides otherwise, nor, until the Pensions Act 1995 (para 6 below) the choice of trustee. The member's role is, therefore, in the absence of statutory provision to the contrary, a passive one. This need not prevent the benefit structure of a scheme being improved through negotiation, but the negotiators would be employers and employees (or trade unions) rather than trustees and beneficiaries.

Any agreed improvements could be implemented if the trustees (assuming that the power of alteration is, as is normal, exercisable only by or with the consent of the trustees) were satisfied that the improvements were, or would be, properly funded or would not jeopardise the interests of a particular class of beneficiaries.

So long as the scheme is administered in accordance with the trust instrument, a beneficiary cannot question the manner of that administration. On the other hand, where there is maladministration a member can apply to the Pensions Ombudsman (Chapter 18) or to the court. While applications by single individuals to the court are rare they are of great importance in illustrating the need to consult the trust instrument for authority, the classic case being *Evans v London Co-Operative Society* (1976) *The Times*, 6 July.

The courts now recognise the importance of actions by pension fund beneficiaries on behalf of the trust fund as a whole, and in a prima facie case of breach of trust may make a preliminary order for their costs to be paid out of the fund, possibly until the appointment of an independent judicial trustee if that can be agreed (*McDonald v Horn* [1995] 1 All ER 961, CA at 973c, 975d).

6 Member trusteeship: history

When the first edition of this book was written, it seemed fairly certain that there would be some enactment in the near future requiring the appointment of trade union representatives to the trusteeship of pension schemes. A White Paper incorporating this suggestion was issued in 1976 and it seemed that, as soon as sufficient time had elapsed for representative organisations to put forward their views, legislation would follow. The change of government in May 1979 altered this course, but the change in May 1997 may raise it again.

The pressure for such representation has always been variable, for a trustee's function is fiduciary and onerous (Chapter 24). On the other hand, most schemes contain a discretionary power to enhance (with the consent of the employer) a member's pension, and it is assumed that the manner in which such power is exercised is of interest to negotiating bodies. Following the statutory provisions for disclosure (Chapter 16, para 6) the question of trusteeship became less controversial. The task of being a trustee requires considerable training, as many employees have discovered. An advantage of trade union representation was thought to be that a body of experience would build up within the trade union movement. In practice employers have tended to insist that representative trustees be members of the scheme, but frequently they have maintained active trade union links.

The (now dissolved) Occupational Pensions Board (OPB) reported in 1982 on the Rights and Expectations of Members (Cmnd 8649) and questioned both the retention of trust law as a framework for pension schemes and the ability of employers to appoint trustees. The report, in para 8.23, noted that voluntary action had increased the proportion of schemes with member trustees, and left for consideration by the Secretary of State whether there should be a statutory obligation.

The report was followed by a DHSS consultative document dated 29 February 1984 announcing the retention of trust law (para 60) albeit with clarifications. Member participation was left to voluntary action, and views were invited as to whether some schemes might need legislative assistance to modify their trusts to permit participation (para 61.1.7).

The question of balancing the interests of employers and members was again referred to the OPB in 1988; their report 'Protecting Pensions' was delivered at the end of the year and published by the DSS in February 1989 (Cm 573). It made numerous recommendations. On the foregoing points it recommended:

(*a*) trust law should continue as the legal basis of pension schemes;
(*b*) as a matter of good practice some trustees should be drawn from the employee membership of a scheme;
(*c*) as a matter of good practice the role of the employer as sole trustee should be discouraged.

These recommendations were accepted by the Government. Unlike other accepted recommendations of the report they did not require legislation. However, the 'Maxwell' scandal (Chapter 24, para 12) led to a wide-ranging review of occupational pension schemes, followed by the Pensions Act 1995 which requires member-nominated trustees or a member-approved alternative (Chapter 24, para 7).

The OPB report of 1988 recommended that upon the insolvency of an employer, the insolvency practitioner should be required to appoint an independent trustee of the pension scheme, unless there was at least one independent trustee already. This recommendation was implemented by the Social Security Act 1990, now the Pensions Act 1995, ss 22–26 (see Chapter 16, para 10.2).

Chapter 16

Administering the scheme

1 Death benefits

One of the areas where a discretionary power is regularly exercised is that of lump sums arising on death (either in service or within five years after commencement of pension). The principal reasons for incorporating into the rules this discretion are:

(*a*) the wide variety of family or dependants' requirements, according to the age and circumstances of the deceased;
(*b*) the fact that many members have no experience of making a Will and, when they do, rarely recall that their assets potentially include an occupational death benefit (which anyway will change in amount as salary changes, scheme rules are altered or a new employment is taken up with different lump sum benefits);
(*c*) the fact that for many older beneficiaries it would be unwise to swell the estate of the surviving spouse since this would increase the charge to inheritance tax on that spouse's subsequent death;
(*d*) to avoid necessarily benefiting a member's creditors, trustee in bankruptcy or successful dependant under the Inheritance (Provision for Family and Dependants) Act 1975;
(*e*) to avoid the necessity for a grant of probate or administration;
(*f*) to avoid removal of a local authority's financial obligations to an orphan in care.

Some or all these objectives can be achieved by a *limited* power of nomination exercisable by the member. In practice such powers are not common, perhaps because:

(*a*) a restriction is needed to ensure that the benefit is not included in the member's estate for inheritance tax;
(*b*) members may forget to update their nominations when circumstances change;
(*c*) unless there are strict rules as to the lodging of the nomination the trustees cannot be sure that they hold the latest version.

By contrast discretionary powers are usually accompanied by 'expression of wish' forms whereby members can make their wishes known to (albeit not binding on) the trustees.

It should be remembered that the State benefits cover pensions or allowances for widows and dependants but do not include substantial lump sums, whereas an approved scheme (Chapter 17, para 3) can provide on death-in-service up to four times salary plus the member's contributions and accumulated interest.

Frequently, the surviving spouse (if any) will have little experience of administering a sizeable fund, and the children may still be at school. Increasingly, it is found that the member was not living with the spouse.

The trustees are under a fiduciary duty to ascertain the objects of their discretion, although in practice they may limit their initial enquiries to ascertaining a narrow range of beneficiaries within the class. There are three standard procedures that most schemes adopt:

(*a*) the member's record card if up to date may indicate his marital status and the extent of his immediate family;
(*b*) members may be given the opportunity to indicate their wishes in the event of their death; such indication is expressed not to be binding (to avoid inclusion of the sums in the member's estate); but is often of great assistance;
(*c*) the pension fund officer is asked to inquire (either directly or through the unit personnel manager) as to any change of circumstances since (*a*) and (*b*) were completed; in practice this inquiry is exceedingly important.

The pension fund officer will then usually put a recommendation to the trustees (or an authorised sub-committee). This may involve setting up a separate trust for some of or all the moneys for infant beneficiaries. Generally, the pension scheme trustees should try to avoid taking on the trusteeship of such a separate fund since they will gradually lose touch with the beneficiaries and could find the expense of administration considerable. Nonetheless, occasionally it is right to retain this trusteeship, for example when the only beneficiary is an orphan without near relatives and in the care of a local authority; the local authority will have power to act as custodian trustee but will rarely have an officer capable of providing the continuity necessary for a managing trustee, and will rarely keep in touch with the orphan after attaining adulthood.

Frequently the pensions officer will have received delegated discretion to pay a small proportion of the lump sum to meet immediate funeral or family expenses.

The above recommended inquiries will occasionally lead to a decision (where the rules are sufficiently flexible) to pay the surviving spouse's pension to some other person, for example a person who has for many years been living with the member (save for the spouse's contracted-out or protected pension, where applicable (Chapter 20). This may happen when a couple parted (without maintenance arrangements) soon after their marriage but are not divorced.

2 Special contributions

The question of an employer's obligation to contribute is complex. It is discussed at some length in Chapter 3, para 16; Chapter 8, para 2; Chapter 13, para 3.2 and para 17 below. The trust deed (and now statutory regulations) will usually provide that there shall be an actuarial report every, say, three years. The question arises as to what action should be taken in respect of matters occurring between such reports. The trustees may be aware that from time to time they will be asked to enhance certain benefits under a discretionary power, in which case they may require the actuary to make allowance for this in recommending a contribution rate. Alternatively, they may consult the actuary when asked to exercise the power in a particular case, and may call for a special contribution from the employer. The Revenue have their own requirements in such an event since the contribution would not be an 'ordinary annual contribution' (as to ordinary annual contributions, see Chapter 17, para 1.1).

Occasionally, however, the employer will seek to make a special contribution either to avoid being compelled to distribute profits or to reduce tax in a particular year. The trustees are hardly likely to object to an addition to the trust fund, but are under a duty to be satisfied that its acceptance is unlikely to prejudice the Revenue's approval of the scheme. It is important, therefore, for the pension fund officer to be familiar with Revenue practice in this area—PSO Memorandum 115.

3 Increases—statutory and discretionary

There are numerous statutory provisions for increases to pensions both in deferment and once the pension has come into payment, intended to provide some protection against price inflation.

3.1 In deferment—statutory increases

Persons leaving service before normal retirement date will usually be entitled to a pension beginning at the latter date ie a *deferred* pension (Chapter 10, para 1).

Increases are required during the period of deferment (PSA 1993, s 83), and are generally referred to in the statutes as *revaluation* eg ss 83(1), 84(1), 85 etc. Separate provisions apply to the following:

(*a*) Final salary schemes (Chapter 8, para 1) *other than* the part protected under (*b*) below;
(*b*) Guaranteed minimum pensions (GMP) applicable to salary-related schemes contracted-out before 6 April 1997 (Chapter 20);
(*c*) Money purchase pensions (Chapter 8, para 6), albeit the requirement is simply that the underlying capital must, before pension begins, share in the appropriate investment yield—PSA 1993, Sched 3, para 5.

The above 'revaluation' is described in Chapter 10, para 1.2.

3.2 In payment—statutory increases

Post-6 April 1997 accrual

Pensions in payment (from a tax exempt occupational scheme) accrued *since* 6 April 1997, other than those derived from voluntary contributions, must include annual limited protection against price inflation—Pensions Act 1995, s 51(2), (6). The increases are to be at least the 'appropriate percentage' which is defined in s 54(3) as increases for a reference period to the preceding 30 September (*but see below*) by the revaluation percentage set out in PSA 1993, Sched 3, para 2—the same provision as applies in deferment to final salary schemes (see para 3.1 above) viz retail prices indexation subject to a cut-off of 5 per cent per annum compound, referred to in official reports as 'limited price indexation' or LPI.

A scheme can avoid the 30 September reference date by writing a provision into its rules for LPI at least every 12 months—s 51(3).

Sections 52 and 53 provide:

(*a*) that no increase is required to pensions in payment for members who have not yet attained age 55 unless incapacitated (see below); however, at age 55 the amount of pension has to 'catch up' to the rate that includes LPI—s 52(4);

(*b*) for crediting excess increases against the statutory requirement for the following year.

The incapacity provisions under (*a*) above are set out in s 52(2). They award the increase to a member under age 55 if either he is permanently incapacitated from engaging in regular full-time employment or he had retired from the particular job on account of mental or physical infirmity. There are provisions in sub-sections (3) and (4) relating to a member where infirmity has ceased, and also where it reappears.

Transfer credits are brought in, where appropriate, by SI 1996 No 1679.

Unlike the revaluation in deferment, LPI in payment applies to money purchase schemes too (but not to public service schemes, albeit these usually receive full indexation anyway). For money purchase pensions, LPI applies to the part attributable to contributions in respect of employment on or after the appointed day (6 April 1997). This poses a practical problem as schemes wishing to retain flexibility will need to keep for each member two accounts; a simple matter where the investment is in units, but potentially complicated in other cases. The purpose of flexibility would be to leave the member the option of a larger initial (flat rate) annuity in respect of the earlier period, without the need to achieve that result by uplifting a statutory cash equivalent before pension date.

Pre-6 April 1997 accrual

In one circumstance LPI is also required for pre-6 April 1997 accrual of *salary-related* benefits (other than certain 'small' or 'simplified' schemes), viz if there is to be a refund (strictly, a payment to the employer) from a tax-exempt 'trust scheme', whether the scheme is ongoing or in winding-up—Pensions Act 1995, ss 37, 76 and 77—with, apparently, a 30 September annual reference date.

'Trust scheme' is simply an occupational scheme established under a trust (s 124). (For other requirements before making the refund, see SI 1996 No 2156). LPI is not applied to any guaranteed minimum pension element (Chapter 20), no doubt as its equivalent is increased by the State (but see *GMPs* below regarding post-6 April 1988)—ss 37(6)(*b*), 76(5) and 77(3).

GMPs

Guaranteed minimum pensions accrued in salary-related contracted out schemes until 5 April 1997. When introduced in 1978, there was no obligation upon the scheme to increase them in payment as the terms for contracting out provided for the State to increase the equivalent amount in line with prices indexation. The element accrued from 6 April 1988 is partly increased by the scheme, partly by the State. Scheme increases are limited to 3 per cent per annum—PSA 1993, s 109(3)—and can be offset by excess increases paid the previous year (Pensions Act 1995, s 53). The new subsection (3A) to PSA 1993, s 109, refers in effect to the termination of the accrual period at 5 April 1997.

COMPs

Money purchase benefits accrued before 6 April 1997 are not subject to statutory requirements except for the 'protected rights' element of contracted out COMP schemes (Chapter 20). These, like GMPs, must provide prices indexation limited to 3 per cent per annum—SI 1996 No 1537, reg 4(3). For post-6 April 1997, see above.

3.3 Discretionary increases or awards

Augmentation usually refers to the discretionary award of increases in benefits.

The disclosure regulations require the scheme booklet to state whether there is a discretionary power to increase pensions once in payment, and also, by the transfer value regs, to mention where cash equivalents for transfers-out (prior to retirement) do not give credit for this prospect (para 6 below, particularly the reference to SI 1996 No 1847).

If increases are regularly granted, it is prudent to take them into account when instructing the actuary to assess the funding rate, or else special contributions should be sought from the employers (see para 2 above). During periods of high inflation, it was quite common for a funding rate to allow for, say, 3 per cent per annum pension increases and for each company within a group to be asked annually to pay a lump sum to meet the cost of the balance of discretionary increases awarded to its former employees. Such awards were usually 'across the board' and had regard to the general level of inflation.

A similar approach is sometimes taken to ill-health pensions ie immediate pensions on early retirement, usually unreduced despite early commencement, and often enhanced to include some or all notional future pensionable service. Where these are not paid from separate insured 'permanent health' arrangements (Chapter 2, para 8) they add to scheme liabilities. Where the augmentation is discretionary, it may be debited to the employing company. More commonly an allowance is made in the funding rate.

4 Reports/notifications to Inland Revenue and contributions agency

The lawyer is unlikely to be asked to prepare returns to the Revenue or the Contributions Agency. He should know, however, that apart from the regular supply of information (which is usually requested in routine correspondence) the Revenue must receive notification of any change in the terms of a scheme and confirmation must be requested that approval is not affected (ICTA 1988, 591B(2)). The wiser course is often to check in advance.

Returns and notifications to the Contributions Agency are required only in the case of contracted-out schemes (Chapter 20, para 4). The pension fund officer will deal with these on a regular basis; it is therefore not considered necessary to enlarge upon them here.

5 Members' right to opt out

Some employers establish voluntary schemes and others require all eligible employees to join. The latter requirement would appear to be no longer possible by reason of the Social Security Act 1986, now PSA 1993, s 160. However, the DSS regard automatic inclusion as lawful provided the member has a right to opt out (no doubt because s 160 prohibits a rule to the effect that an employee *must* be a member)—but for contributory schemes there must be adequate authority under the Employment Rights Act 1996 (and contractually) to deduct contributions from pay.

Typically a scheme will require one or two months' notice to opt out, but where this is given at the beginning of the employment it must, to give effect to s 160, be capable of retrospective effect to the commencement date.

The prohibition does not apply to a non-contributory death benefit scheme (SI 1987 No 1108, reg 3).

6 Disclosure requirements, registration

6.1 General

There are three areas where legislation gives rise to heavy disclosure administration, apart from the obvious need for booklets and (for defined contribution schemes) benefit statements.

Firstly, the entitlement for those leaving pensionable service, to seek a quotation for a cash equivalent transfer to another approved scheme or a buy-out policy (Chapter 10, para 12); as well as responses to these enquiries, the regulation necessitates a standard statement to new members whether the scheme will receive such transfers (and, if so, the corresponding provision of quotations). Secondly, compliance with the growing regulatory detail (para 6.2 below). Thirdly, the requirement of PSA 1993, s 111 that every scheme must (within prescribed limits) be prepared to accept members' voluntary contributions entails the illustration of potential benefits and the checking for Inland Revenue maxima.

See also Chapter 15, para 5 regarding a member's general equitable right to information.

6.2 Disclosure: information to members

The regulatory regime places great emphasis on disclosure, for three purposes:

(*a*) the structure it brings to administration; the annual Report and Accounts is the prime example;
(*b*) the necessary information for the individual when his benefits crystallise, as well as advance forecasts on request;
(*c*) the hinge for enforcement; a breach is easily shown and often reveals other problems.

Pension schemes differ from traditional trusts in two key respects. Firstly that the member has paid for his interest, whether directly or as a term of his employment. Secondly that the basic entitlement is a right, not a discretion—as if the trust had numerous tenants for life. But in another respect, a member is more closely akin to a trust beneficiary than to an owner, viz that decisions are taken by trustees which, if there is no dishonesty, are intended to be on the members' behalf—and thus many members are content to await their pension without enquiry.

The effect, before 1986, was that some schemes provided their members with very full information and others provided almost none (apart from the benefit structure on admission). Equity had always given the right to information on request, but too often members were unaware that there was reason to enquire. The purpose of statutory disclosure, introduced that year, was to remove that ignorance. It successfully did so without overlegislating. Members' attention had to be drawn to the availability of the annual report, without distributing it to all. After initial experimentation, many schemes took to issuing 'popular' reports, stating the availability of the full version. Very few are requested.

The 1986 regime lasted ten years. Some additional requirements were grafted on but, except for benefit statements for money purchase schemes, few points of major principle.

The 1996 regulations (para 6.3 below) replace the earlier regulations but adopt the same principles (but note that it now suffices to include in the booklet a general statement that a scheme Annual Report is available on request; there is no longer a requirement to draw specific attention to it). In one respect study of the new regs is more difficult for the practitioner, viz that some requirements have deliberately been placed in the preservation or transfer regulations, no doubt because they deal with leavers, but it is unhelpful that no longer are all the main requirements in one place.

6.3 Current requirements

The new regime is mainly in SI 1996 No 1655, authorised by PSA 1993, s 113 and Pensions Act 1995, s 41 (replacing, with little alteration, PSA 1993 s 114). Amending regs (SI 1997 No 786) add numerous detailed provisions, primarily regarding contracted-out mixed benefit schemes (see Chapter 20, para 4.8). Failure to comply is now subject to penalties under reg 11.

As before, the regime is directed at the trustees (or, where there is no trust, the managers) rather than the employer, and (apart from the *exclusions* mentioned below) applies to tax-approved (or pending) schemes and public service schemes (reg 2)—plus, for limited disclosure, unapproved schemes (reg 8), albeit many will be one-member schemes excluded by reg 2(2).

It appears that a spouse (even while the member is alive), or any dependent pensioner, is still entitled on request eg to the scheme booklet or the annual report—see regs 4(3) and 6(6).

The following is not a summary of the regulations, but rather a set of pointers.

Exclusions

Reg 2(1) excludes schemes which are not tax-approved (or pending), save for reg 8 which requires even these schemes to provide a certain minimum of information. Reg 2(2) sets out the other principal exclusions (single-member schemes, death-benefit only schemes, non-UK schemes with no UK-resident trustee). Note reg 2(4) that excludes any duty to any *member* if all members are trustees eg most small self-administered schemes (Chapter 17, para 8).

Definitions

The definitions are numerous but a quick glance will show that they are helpful and, with one interesting exception, sufficiently obvious for the regulations to be read with ease—reg 1. The exception is 'excluded person'—a deferred pensioner whose mail is returned, and who (for example) therefore cannot complain at non-receipt of benefit statements—reg 5(5).

Structure

The regulations divide into:

(*a*) formal (but important) information, available on request—reg 3 regarding the trust documents, and also all participating employers, but note 3(5) that excludes information regarding other classes of beneficiary;
(*b*) basic information about the scheme, to be given automatically—as normally found in the Members' Booklet—reg 4;
(*c*) individual benefit information, some to be automatic, some on request—reg 5;
(*d*) financial and actuarial information, available on request—regs 6 and 7. The basic information must mention the availability (Sched 1, para 23).

Regulation 8 relates to unapproved schemes (but presumably subject to 2(2) which excludes one-man schemes) and, curiously, the Salvation Army scheme.

Apart from the individual benefit information, the above is available to members and prospective members, their spouses and trade unions recognised for collective bargaining 'to any extent' (ie not necessarily regarding pensions); also, except for the booklet, beneficiaries (defined as non-members entitled to payment of benefits eg dependent pensioners or life cover beneficiaries).

Content

The 'basic information' (reg 4) will usually be available in a Members' Booklet. Where practicable, it will be supplied in advance, but at the latest within two months of joining—reg 4(2).

Importantly, members and beneficiaries must be notified, in advance where 'practicable', of material changes—and in any event not later than three months after the effective date. 'Member' is widely defined to include deferreds and pensioners, but *presumably* the effect of 4(4), which excludes in relation to a member non-relevant information, is that a change relating to current actives need not be notified to individuals who have ceased to be actives.

Schedule 1 lists 29 items of 'basic information', mainly about the benefit structure but including internal dispute procedures, and statements that OPAS is available, that the Ombudsman may determine complaints and that OPRA can intervene—Chapter 18.

For pre-6 April 1997 members (other than deferreds—SI 1997 No 819, reg 4), the additional information must be notified by 5 April 1998, but this is not a practical delay for drafting since new members must have it already.

Schedule 2 lists the information to be made available to individuals, but can only be understood alongside reg 5 which specifies the respective events to which certain paragraphs relate. Most specify automatic provision (the words are 'as of course') but 5(4) and 5(9) are 'on request'. However, the automatic information for a leaver, previously in reg 6(6) of the 1986 regs, is now (strangely) to be found in the preservation regs—see the new reg 27A of SI 1991 No 167 as inserted by SI 1996 No 2131. There is no change in the information ('the rights and options (if any) available to [the] member') and only a trivial change regarding the circumstances.

The leaver's (and indeed any active member's) entitlement to information, on request, regarding his cash equivalent transfer value is conferred by yet a different set of regs SI 1996 No 1847, reg 11. This includes, where discretionary benefits are not valued, the right to call for a copy of the actuary's report relating to their exclusion, even though the booklet will have mentioned the exclusion (para 3.3 above).

Members of money purchase schemes (generally 'Defined Contribution' schemes—see Chapter 8, para 7) are to receive automatically annual benefit statements—reg 5(5) of the Disclosure Regs. This includes deferred members (except where mail is returned—see *Definitions* above). The statements are to comply with paras 5 and 6 of Sched 2, showing contributions paid and the value of accrued rights. Where the cash equivalent transfer value is not equal to the latter, it too must be stated.

The Annual Report and Accounts (including an actuarial certificate) must be available within seven months of the end of the scheme year—reg 6(1). Schedule 3 lists the information to be included in the Report (for the Accounts see para 11 below); para 3 requires the names of professional advisers who have acted for the trustees during the year, and para 15 requires publication of any statement made by a resigning auditor or actuary.

Detailed information is required regarding investment management, principles, performance and allocation, except where s 35 of the Pensions Act 1995 does not apply (unapproved schemes, 'small' schemes if qualifying, wholly insured schemes etc—SI 1996 No 3127, Reg 10).

6.4 Registration

There is a minor administrative involvement in registration of a scheme with the Registrar (now OPRA)—see Chapter 18.

While the associated levy is at present modest, the principle could lend itself to the raising of funds for new purposes, if statute so provided, and already it appears that the OPRA budget (to be funded from the levy) will be significant.

7 Transfers generally

The statutory right to a cash equivalent (ie a transfer or buyout) (as detailed in Chapter 10, paras 10–12) will of itself generate considerable correspondence with other administrators and with brokers and insurance companies. However, there are the additional dangers that if the receiving scheme or insurer does not meet the prescribed requirements, the transferring trustees will not obtain the statutory discharge (Chapter 10, para 12.4) and, even if a member may sometimes be estopped from obtaining reinstatement of his own benefits in the transferring scheme, a spouse or other dependant, who may not receive equally good benefits under the other arrangement (or in some cases may receive no benefits at all), may obtain a declaration for reinstatement or an order for damages.

The difficulty is compounded by the suggestion that the statutory discharge is lost if the transfer is made under an enabling provision in the scheme's rules rather than in reliance on the statutory overriding power. Even if that is not so, few trustees would wish to study the benefits offered by the receiving scheme or insurer, particularly when the member could exercise his statutory right and thus terminate all further enquiry.

It follows that a standard procedure is required to ensure that the receiving scheme or insurer is authorised under the regulations. Suggestions in this respect are made in Chapter 10, paras 10–12. The importance of following these procedures is demonstrated by the action taken in the High Court by the OPB (see below) in 1985 in a particular matter (in *Re Kestrel Pension Scheme*, Ch D (unreported) where the transferee was a pension scheme rather than an insurance company but which well illustrates the principle). The scheme was established by Hill-Kestrel Consultancy, a firm of insurance brokers. The purpose was to attract those who were early leavers from other pension schemes and wished to purchase buy-out policies but could not do so because their own schemes had not adopted an enabling power—this being before the 1985 legislation. The promoters offered to receive the transfer payments in their own pension scheme which would then make a buy-out facility available.

(1) The overwhelming majority of the Kestrel scheme's assets (£1m out of £1.4m) were placed with an individual for investment or lent to others unsecured. The two individual borrowers or investors absconded with the funds, and both corporate borrowers entered into liquidation with little prospect of recovery.
(2) The Kestrel Pension Scheme had been submitted to the Inland Revenue for approval but the trustees had failed to include the normal administrative information essential to approval. Therefore although the managers had received a Revenue reference number, usual on submission of initial documents, and accordingly claimed to have 'provisional approval' (a colloquial term for the situation where the Revenue do not pursue members for tax on their contributions until it can be certain whether or not the scheme becomes approved) they never received actual approval.

The effect of (2) was that many transfers were not authorised by the transferors' trust deeds, although no doubt the usual procedures could have been followed to obtain Revenue approval to specific transfers. A suggested form of enquiry to the Revenue is mentioned in Chapter 10, para 10.2.

The Occupational Pensions Board (OPB) was dissolved as at 6

April 1997 (Pensions Act 1995 s 150) but OPRA, established by s 1 of the Act, has stronger powers to wind up (s 11)—Chapter 18.

8 Data protection act 1984

The purpose of the Data Protection Act 1984 was to meet a European Community requirement relating to the privacy of the individual in relation to computerised information. No doubt the greatest mischief related to data held for the purpose of credit control. However, the Act covers all personal data regarding living individuals held on computers, word processors or other automatic machinery. Save where specifically exempted, the data user is obliged to register the classes of persons and information held by him and the types of disclosure for which it will be used. Any unauthorised disclosure outside the registered purposes comprises a criminal offence.

Most pension scheme details are held on computer. The data user is a person who alone or jointly with others controls the use of the data, whether or not he operates the equipment. It follows that the trustees of all large schemes are data users and that the trustees of smaller schemes may be, although some of the latter will keep manual records. In relation to insured schemes, the question arises whether the storage of information on computer by the insurance company is 'controlled' by the trustees. Clearly they are under an obligation to keep records. However, if they keep manual records and it is irrelevant to them whether or not the insurer chooses to computerise its information, the probability is that they are not data users. The Data Protection Registrar issued guidance notes regarding pension schemes in 1986 in which, strangely, he suggested that once the annuity comes into payment for any scheme member, the trustees become data users even if they were not previously. The argument (which is based on life office administrative procedures rather than an inference of law) is not compelling but at the time of writing has not (it is believed) been tested. Recent correspondence with the Registrar indicates his preferred view that the trustees are data users throughout, and that the insurer is a bureau or a joint user. The guidance notes are currently (1997) being reviewed.

Section 32 of the Act contains an exemption in respect of pension accounting records. Unfortunately, the permitted disclosures would not enable details of individual members to be submitted to OPRA or the Contributions Agency when making enquiries. It follows that few administrators of any sophistication will rely on the exemption.

Registration itself is a simple procedure. The Registrar has recently introduced, as a preferred method, a telephone dialogue. Previously there were daunting application forms, but the requirement was only to tick the relevant boxes of multiple-choice questions. A recommended response could be obtained by members of the National Association of Pension funds from the Association's office at 12–18 Grosvenor Gardens, London SW1W 0DH.

If registering, the main choice will be whether the employer as well as the trustees should register. Frequently, the computer will be owned or operated by the employer so that it too will be a user and should register. There is also uncertainty whether, if it does not register, the trustees can make available to it information for its management analysis purposes. Some practitioners have agreed with the Registrar a form of registration for use by trustees that appears to overcome this last problem.

Where the employer operates the computer, it is likely that it will register as a Data Bureau as well as a user, and it may in any event be a Bureau even if not a user.

Where trustees operate their own equipment and intend to rely on the s 32 exemption, it was in 1986 and remains (in 1997) the view of the Data Protection Registrar that any disclosure of personal data to outside service engineers, in the absence of registration, comprises a breach of the statute unless members' prior consent has been obtained. This slightly surprising view has not, so far as the author is aware, been tested.

The holding on computer of details regarding tenants of property owned by the pension fund (assuming that not all the tenants or guarantors are companies) would entail registration.

The guidance notes (GN 10—Pension scheme data) and a comprehensive Guidelines booklet (November 1994, 130 pages) are available from:

Office of the Data Protection Registrar
Wycliffe House
Water Lane
Wilmslow
Cheshire
SK9 5AF
Tel: (01625) 545700

9 Financial Services Act 1986

9.1 Trustees

Investment managers, trustees and intermediaries will be concerned not to commit an offence under the Financial Services Act 1986 (or a breach of the Pensions Act 1995—para 16 below). Section 4 of the Financial Services Act 1986 makes it a criminal offence to carry on 'investment business' unless 'authorised' or exempted (and the exemptions will not generally be relevant in this connection). Apart from pension trustees, there is a general exemption for trustees unless they hold themselves out as offering investment management services or are specifically remunerated in connection with investment advice or management (Sched 1, para 22).

For pension trustees this exemption will not, by reason of s 191(5), apply to the specific provision in s 191(1) relating to the management of assets of a pension scheme—but see the reference below to s 191(2) which offers an exemption to that specific provision where there is appropriate delegation (at least of day to day investment decisions).

Apart from s 191, it appears that an element of commerciality would be necessary before a person carrying on a relevant activity is caught under s 4 by the definition in s 1(2) of 'investment business'. The text is not totally unambiguous but the generally accepted interpretation is given. It is also argued by the sponsoring Department that a salaried employee engaged as investment manager does not carry on a commercial activity for this purpose although his employer, if charging a fee, may do so. The legal distinction is said to lie between the person engaged under a contract of service and the person or company carrying on the activity under a contract for services.

Section 191 deems all persons (whether trustees or not—191(5)) who manage pension scheme assets to be treated as carrying on investment business, ie there does not have to be an actual 'business' element. However, s 191(2) provides that this is not to apply where 'all decisions, or all day-to-day decisions' are taken on behalf of the person concerned by an authorised or exempted person. The intention regarding the quoted words, as stated on the Lords' amendment, was to exempt trustees to whom decisions are referred by the investment manager in occasional circumstances, eg where the manager has a conflict of interest or the transaction is particularly large.

The phrase 'day-to-day [control]' is also used in s 75(2) which, although not relevant to pension schemes, may assist in interpretation. Clearly there will be grey areas where trustees, or investment committees, may commit an offence through closer than intended involvement with investment decisions. The Securities and Investments Board issued a guidance note (updated in March 1988 and still current in 1997) giving examples. Paragraph 17 suggests that strategic decisions about asset allocation are not 'day-to-day decisions', but para 18 warns that the frequency of referral has a bearing on the analysis.

Paragraph 15 of the guidance note states that the initial decision to invest in insurance policies is unlikely in itself to be investment management but para 20 warns that frequent switching between the different underlying unit funds *may* constitute 'day-to-day decisions'.

Since prosecutions require the consent of the Secretary of State or the Director of Public Prosecutions, or (by reason of the general law) the Lord Advocate in Scotland, it is to be hoped that they would accept the guidance note as an indication of their own intended exercise of discretion. It would remain necessary to consider the effect of s 5 which might render certain agreements unenforceable and give rise to rights of compensation.

For exemptions under s 191(3) see para 9.2 below.

For investment management agreements between the trustees and authorised persons (investment managers) see para 14 below.

Before the Pensions Act 1995, a few scheme trustees may have retained an active role in investment management and thus required authorisation by reason of the Financial Services Act 1986, s 191, even though not commercially in investment business. Where their activity was not undertaken with a view to profit they might have qualified for simplified application to the Investment Management Regulatory Organisation Limited (IMRO—see para 9.4 below). The effect of the Pensions Act 1995, s 47(2), is to render it necessary, save for exemptions under s 47(5), for such trustees to be appointed as fund managers, in a separate capacity (and probably as officers or employees of a separate body), leading to complex questions of conflict, or for other persons to be appointed as fund managers (para 16 below).

In practice, for tax-approved pension schemes, the requirement for separate fund managers will almost always exclude the trustees entirely, even in a separate capacity. In such case the need for trustees to be authorised will be limited to specialist areas such as regular referral back or day-to-day asset allocation between multiple managers.

9.2 Small schemes and other exceptions

An exemption from the effect of s 191, under subs (3), has been made for:

(*a*) certain small pension schemes, described below;
(*b*) schemes for 50 or fewer members who choose their own annuity contracts, a rare form of grouped occupational pensions scheme that has, for new schemes, probably been totally superseded by Group personal pension schemes (Chapter 2, para 9.5).

The exemption is made by the Financial Services Act 1986 (Occupational Pension Schemes) (No 2) Order 1988 SI 1988 No 724, the same order that, by reference from SI 1996 No 1715 reg 3(3), now also exempts the schemes falling within (*a*) above from the Pensions Act 1995 requirement to appoint a fund manager (see para 16.2 below).

The main exemption under the Order will apply to (*a*) above. It relates (in effect) to small self-administered schemes (Chapter 17, para 8) where all members or former members (if still prospectively entitled), unless incapacitated, are trustees and a majority of them participate in the investment decisions. The beneficiary trustees are fully exempted from s 191 and any other (eg a professional) trustee is exempted, notwithstanding the absence of an authorised manager, if he takes no day-to-day investment management decisions.

A trustee of an exempted class will still be committing an offence if he is carrying on investment business as such, as the above exemption relates only, in effect, to s 191.

9.3 Employer

Investment business includes advice on investments (Sched 1, para 15) if the adviser is carrying on 'the business of engaging in' that activity (s 1(2)). Paragraphs 1 to 11 of Sched 1 define 'investments'. Paragraph 11 of the Schedule contains, in the note, provision that was stated, on amendment, to enable an employer to promote his own occupational pension scheme to his employees or to advise them as to their rights under it without himself having to be authorised.

The note excludes interests under the trusts of an occupational pension scheme from being investments under para 11. A unitised money purchase scheme cannot fall within para 6 (collective investment schemes) by reason of the exclusion in s 75(6)(*k*)—but a common investment fund can (see para 15.1 below). Membership of an insured scheme (Chapter 8, para 2) could perhaps fall within para 10 (rights under certain insurance contracts) and thus comprise an investment, but it is more likely that only the trustees have (for this purpose) rights under the insurance contract, members having an interest in those rights which would thus fall within the exempting note to para 11; the latter is the intended result, according to the sponsoring department.

The main concern of the employer will arise when his staff provide the investment management and thus may, by reason of s 191, require authorisation whether or not they are commercially in business (see para 9.1 above). They will generally become employees of a subsidiary that applies to IMRO for authorisation. As the investment activity is limited to in-house funds, a simplified application procedure is available involving relatively few requirements as to the capital base of the adviser (see para 9.4 below).

Where the employer's staff also answer, on behalf of the trustees, questions referred back by an external investment manager the same considerations will apply in relation to s 191(2) as mentioned in para 9.1 above. Since the staff will generally not be authorised, they should (unless, it is argued, their employer is authorised) ensure that their involvement does not amount to 'day-to-day' decision-taking.

9.4 IMRO

Authorisation under the Act can be directly by the Securities and Investments Board or by self-regulating organisations (SROs) recognised under s 10. The Investment Management Regulatory Organisation Limited (IMRO) a company limited by guarantee is the SRO for both in-house and external fund managers (albeit some of the latter may additionally, or occasionally, alternatively, join another SRO, eg in the insurance industry).

IMRO was of the view from the outset of the Financial Services Act 1986 regime that, for at least two reasons, special provisions would be needed for the authorisation of pension scheme trustees who were not in the 'business' of investment management (see para 9.1 above) but who would be in breach of s 191 unless authorised. The first reason was the absence of a 'customer' as the trustee would be investing for himself (see para 14.11 below regarding the members of the scheme). The second reason, driven by judgment rather than necessity, was the view that, if trustees were to be able to choose the authorisation route, the absence of capital should not create a hurdle in terms of IMRO's requirements. As a result, IMRO created special rules for its 'OPS Members' (the definition is now OPS Firm)—OPS being the abbreviation for Occupational Pension Scheme which is defined in identical terms to PSA 1993, s 1.

OPS Firm is defined in IMRO's rules to include, as well as trustees, an employer or related company if their 'permitted business' is limited to OPS activity (itself defined) and is not undertaken with a view to profit. A detailed membership application pack includes questionnaires relating to the individual trustees or executives.

Section 10 of Chap II of IMRO's rules relates to OPS Firms. Paragraph 10.1(2) applies the rules as if the pension scheme itself were the customer; it is deemed to be a 'Private Customer' for the purpose of section 10. The section lists the rules which do not apply to OPS Firms.

The full reasoning behind the special OPS rules is to be found in Pts I and II of a Consultation Document on the OPS regime issued by IMRO in May 1992. Paragraphs 5.10 and 5.12 of the document list the two enquiries that have been made into the interaction between trust law and Financial Services Act 1986 regulation, the first being the Hayton Report of 1990 and the second being the Law Commission study which resulted in a consultation paper issued in May 1992 (see para 14.8 below regarding both).

IMRO's Consultation Document was primarily a response to the 'Maxwell' affair (Chapter 24, para 12). Following the consultation, the definition 'OPS activity' was extended to include management of the assets of an OPS Collective Investment Scheme ie assets derived from occupational pension schemes. IMRO's current address is:

IMRO
Lloyds Chambers
1 Portsoken Street
London E1 8BT,
Tel: 0171 390 5000

9.5 Personal Investment Authority (PIA)

The PIA was established operationally in July 1994 as a new regulator for almost all firms dealing with the private investor. In particular, members include, at opposite ends of the range, insurance companies and independent financial advisers.

The genesis of the PIA was probably the concern over the ineffectiveness of the previous regulatory authorities to prevent the misselling of personal pensions, but there were numerous other reasons for a fresh start. It was also desired to create a single regulatory body dealing with the retail market so as to have a uniform standard across the industry. (Nonetheless, the PIA does not regulate bank deposits, mortgages, general insurance products eg motor and household insurance etc). PIA's current address is:

PIA
1 Canada Square
Canary Wharf
London E14 5AZ
Tel: (0171) 538 8860

10 Winding up the scheme

10.1 Trust deed

The winding-up of a trust will occur either pursuant to a court order (which is rare in the case of a pension scheme, but see para 7 above) or by order of OPRA (see Chapter 18) or under the terms of the trust deed. It is essential that the administrator refers to the trust deed and obtains instructions from the trustees as to any matters requiring the exercise of their discretion (but note para 10.2 below). All tax-approved pension scheme deeds require that the liabilities be purchased in the UK from insurance companies (which can now include certain EU companies operating in the UK) or settled by transfer to another approved scheme, apart from liability to members of contracted-out schemes with less than two years' pensionable service, which can be purchased back from the State.

10.2 Independent trustee (on winding up etc)

Where an insolvency practitioner (or the Official Receiver) commences to act in relation to an employer to which a pension scheme (constituted by trust deed—a curious limitation) relates, the practitioner or Official Receiver is obliged to appoint an independent trustee if there is not one already—the new provision introduced in 1990 and now in the Pensions Act 1995, s 23. The section, together with the Occupational Pension Schemes (Independent Trustee) Regulations 1997 SI 1997 No 252, sets out the requirements for independence. Where there are no members reg 6 applies.

Regulation 2 excludes a person from acting as independent trustee who within three years before the relevant date has provided services to the trustees or the employer, in relation to the scheme, or has an interest in the scheme or the employer (or is connected with a person having such an interest).

Regulation 5 excludes from the requirement money-purchase schemes, death-in-service schemes, allocated annuity schemes, unapproved (non-statutory) schemes, and schemes where all members (as defined) are trustees.

Under s 23 in effect the appointment may be additional to the existing trustees; s 25(6) provides for remuneration out of the trust fund.

Under s 25(2) any discretionary power is exercisable only by the independent trustee; this applies also to a fiduciary power vested in the employer. Where there is more than one independent trustee (ie where several were in office when the practitioner or Official Receiver commenced to act) both these powers 'may also be exercised with the consent of at least half of those trustees by any person who could exercise it apart from [s 25(2)]'.

Where a s 23 trustee is required (whether or not already in place), within a month of commencement of winding up a scheme the trustees must give notice to members and beneficiaries—SI 1996 No 1655, reg 5(10).

10.3 Data and assets

It is essential to establish rapidly whether all the data is available. If there were members in service at the commencement of the winding-up, it will be necessary, while there is still satisfactory contact with the employer to update details of their pensionable salary and addresses, and to endeavour to trace deferred pensioners. The trust deed frequently gives discretion to assume that present spouses and dependants will continue to be married to or dependent upon members at the time of their eventual death, subject to the need to provide a pension to the actual surviving spouse of a contracted-out member, but details of all these will be needed.

The market value of the assets will be required so that an actuarial valuation can be undertaken (see para 10.4 below). Ordinarily, the assets will be converted into cash at the earliest opportunity but the trustees will require advice on:

(*a*) whether there is particular disadvantage in immediate liquidation of the assets;
(*b*) the short-term investment prior to purchase of annuities, generally aiming to match movements in annuity prices;
(*c*) in the case of a large scheme whether it will be necessary, or advantageous, to run it for a limited period as a closed fund (having regard to the availability or otherwise of bulk annuities), and in such event must within one month inform the scheme members, and failure to do so may give rise to a penalty—SI 1996 No 3126, reg 11.

Insurance policies will rarely be surrendered until the terms on which the insurer will provide annuities have been obtained.

Approximate accounts are vital at an early stage, and often it is found that the final month's contributions are still with the employer.

There are two statutory provisions regarding the recovery of arrears of contributions. One of these affords a preference in the indebtedness of the employer, and the other establishes a claim on the National Insurance Fund.

Firstly, the Companies Act 1985, by s 196(2) in respect of a floating charge and the Insolvency Act 1986, s 175, in a winding-up, confer a preference on the debts mentioned in Sched 6 to the latter, para 8, ie those specified (inter alia) in the PSA 1993, Sched 4. Schedule 4 refers in para 1 to employees' contributions (to an occupational pension scheme) deducted from earnings during the preceding *four* months, and in para 2 to employers' contributions to a contracted-out scheme (in respect of GMPs or minimum payments—see Chapter 20) payable in the preceding 12 months. Where the GMP contribution or minimum payment cannot be identified it is deemed to be (in effect) the contracting out national insurance contribution rebate (including, where the employees do not contribute to the scheme, the share of the rebate relevant to them). A slight amendment would appear to be needed to para 2 to take account of the cessation of accrual of GMPs on 5 April 1997.

Secondly, the PSA 1993, ss 124 and 177 provide that on the insolvency of an employer the following unpaid contributions shall be paid to the scheme from the National Insurance Fund, viz employees' contributions deducted from pay during the preceding 12 months; and employers' contributions limited to the smallest of:

(*a*) unpaid contributions due for the preceding 12 months;
(*b*) the amount needed to meet the scheme's dissolution liabilities to or in respect of the employees of that employer;
(*c*) 10 per cent of the remuneration paid or payable to these employees during the preceding 12 months.

10.4 Valuation

It is unlikely that for a defined benefit scheme the assets will precisely meet expenses and the scheme liabilities. It is essential to ascertain whether there is a surplus or a deficiency—the latter might entail cutting back on benefits currently being paid out for even though the Pensions Act 1995, s 75 (see Chapter 3, para 16) creates a debt due from the employer to the trustees of the scheme, the employer too may be insolvent.

10.5 Meetings and documents

As soon as a trustee or the pensions officer is aware of a prospective winding-up, a meeting of the trustees should be convened. There may be power in the trust deed to defer the winding-up and run the scheme as a closed scheme, ie closed to new members and further contributions, or perhaps accepting members' but not employers' contributions. There are several possible reasons for deferring the winding-up. There may be the prospect of a purchaser of the business who would be willing to continue the scheme and accept substitution as the principal employer (Chapter 13, para 3.16). Secondly, in the case of a planned winding-up, the employer may be establishing another scheme with the intention of making a transfer available. Thirdly, it may not, as a matter of construction, be possible to exercise the power of alteration once the winding-up has commenced, and there may be advantage in clarifying some matters (*Re ABC Television* 22 May

1973, unreported, Ch D, Foster J; *Re Thrells Limited* (1974) *Pension Scheme* [1992] OPLR 21, Ch D).

Save in the case of an original corporate trustee, it is essential to establish that the supposed present trustees have all been properly appointed, and to establish how new trustees are appointed during the course of the winding-up should that prove necessary by reason of death or incapacity. The duty of the insolvency practitioner to appoint an independent trustee (see para 10.2 above) extends to a subsequent appointment if at any time there should no longer be an independent trustee (eg by reason of death)—s 23(1)(*a*).

If the trustees were accustomed to granting annual pension increases, and if the assets are sufficient, the timing of the first meeting may render it appropriate to pass a similar resolution. There will also be routine discretions to exercise in respect of recent cases of ill-health and death. A summary of any disputed claims will be required and the question of insurance against claims arising after completion of the winding-up will need to be considered (see para 10.6 below).

10.6 Insurance and indemnity

Unless insurance can be obtained, or there remains a substantial employer able and willing to indemnify the trustees, a reserve will need to be set aside to cover claims from unrecorded beneficiaries or those for whom the data may have been incorrect. If the scheme's assets have been invested with an insurer, it may be possible to obtain this cover from the insurer, but normally a specialist policy will be required. A single premium quotation should be obtained to cover a considerable period of years ahead. In the case of a substantial employer, such insurance is often paralleled by an indemnity from the employer (but care must be taken to ensure that the terms of one do not negate the indemnity of the other).

11 Accounts

11.1 Regulatory requirements

Under general principles of equity, trustees are obliged to maintain adequate records and accounts. The first statutory requirements were introduced in 1986, as a by-product of the then new requirements for disclosure. While the 1996 disclosure requirements continue this principle, the Pensions Act 1995 has also introduced a specific requirement for an auditor (s 47) and regulations specifically requiring, within seven months of the scheme year end, accounts containing listed contents, to be audited by that auditor (SI 1996 No 1975). The disclosure regs (para 6 above) require the annual report by the trustees to contain a copy of the audited accounts—SI 1996 No 1655, reg 6(1).

The requirement for an auditor is subject to the exemptions in SI 1996 no 1715, reg 3, which exclude schemes which are not tax-approved nor relevant statutory schemes, and also exclude unfunded schemes, one-member arrangements, 'small schemes' in which all the members are trustees and effectively no other trustees make day-to-day decisions, as well as a number of other specific exceptions. These exceptions automatically exempt the schemes from SI 1996 No 1975 as reg 2 of the latter states that it is applicable where s 47 applies. Although the disclosure regs require a certain minimum of information to be given to members of non-approved schemes, under SI 1996 No 1655, reg 8, this does *not* include the provision of accounts. The accountancy profession is given scope whether, for schemes outside the regulations, accounts should be prepared in accordance with the Statement of Recommended Practice (SORP) mentioned in para 11.2 below. Paragraph 2.1 of the SORP encourages them to do so, but much will depend upon their instructions, and indeed whether accounts are prepared at all.

The practitioner should note the clear distinction between preparation of the accounts and their audit. In the case of an 'earmarked scheme' defined as a money purchase scheme under which a policy or policies are specifically allocated to individual members, reg 2(2) of SI 1996 No 1975 removes the requirement for accounts conforming with the detail of the regulations, while retaining the auditor's statement under reg 4—see below.

For all schemes to which the regs apply, reg 4 of No 1975 requires an auditor's statement whether contributions have been paid 'in accordance with the schedule of contributions or payment schedule'. Apart, therefore, from the requirements of the Act regarding the schedule of contributions, any intervaluation change in the contribution basis of a defined benefit scheme should, regardless of any clear improvement in the solvency of the fund, be formalised to avoid the question of whistle-blowing arising with the auditor.

The audited accounts must contain the information specified in the Schedule to No 1975 (Audited accounts regs) which is almost identical with the corresponding schedule to the 1986 disclosure regs. It is easily readable and lists thirteen sectors of investment that, if held, must be separately identified including a sub-division of each for non-UK investments. Any investment (other than UK gilts) exceeding 5 per cent of the net assets of the scheme, must be identified. Any employer-related investments must be noted (see para 13 below) and any breach of the limit on such holdings must also be noted. Total purchases and sales of investments, and various other matters, must also be listed, and a statement must be included whether the accounts have been prepared in accordance with the SORP mentioned below.

11.2 SORP (pension schemes accounts)

Paragraph 8 of the Schedule to No 1975 (see para 11.1 above) requires the accounts to state whether they have been prepared in accordance with the 'Statement of Recommended Practice (SORP), the guidelines ('Financial Reports of Pension Schemes') published by the Pensions Research Accountants Group or another organisation approved for this purpose by the Accounting Standards Board [itself prescribed under the Companies Act 1989], current at the end of the scheme year to which the accounts relate and, if not, an indication of where there are any material departures from those guidelines'.

The current SORP was published in July 1996. Copies can be obtained from the Accountancy profession, Milton Keynes (Tel: 01908 248000). The published document goes significantly beyond the narrow production of accounts; the 'standard' is comprised in section 2, being just 19 of the 68 pages. The document as a whole offers clear and helpful guidance on the production of the annual report itself, much additional accountancy guidance relating to special situations such as common investment funds, derivatives etc. Paragraph 1.5 encourages the use of plain English and clear layout, and in particular suggests consigning to a separate compliance statement the less significant required information, in order that the more important disclosures should be given greater prominence. Page 50 illustrates matters that might be relegated to the compliance statement, and while some advisers would disagree with this relegation for discretionary pension increases, it is helpful to see examples of the other more obvious items for relegation. Pages 37 and 38 comment on, and produce a checklist for, the popular type of summary report that many schemes issue to their members.

Accounts

The key requirement, in para 2.6 of the SORP is for:

(*a*) A *Fund Account*, confusingly not a balance sheet, but an income/outgo account—see below;
(*b*) A *Net Assets Statement* which is equivalent to a balance sheet.

The above titles may be adapted, but are likely to be used. The *Fund Account* is to be in two parts, the first showing contributions and benefits, and the second showing investment returns (both income and gains/losses). Illustrations are on pages 44 and 55.

The *Net Assets Statement* is self-explanatory, and is illustrated on pages 45 and 56, the latter being for a defined contribution scheme and thus including some assets designated to members.

Paragraph 2.33 of the SORP is a reminder that for a defined benefit scheme the accounts do not provide any relevant information as to the solvency of the scheme. Para 2.35 advises trustees to consider disclosing information if they are aware that the sponsoring companies are in financial difficulties and may be unable to continue with the recommended funding levels. (If they have confidential information they should, in the author's opinion, seek prior advice regarding their potential conflict of duties).

Appendices 3 and 4 contain useful summaries of the disclosure requirements in the UK and Ireland respectively.

Simultaneously with the publication of the SORP, the Accounting Standards Board issued a discussion paper regarding the accountancy treatment of derivatives and expects in due course an accounting standard that will introduce mandatory requirements.

11.3 Auditing Guideline

An Auditing Guideline for pension scheme accounts, designed for use under the regime introduced by SORP 1 (see para 11.2 above) was issued in November 1988 by the Auditing Practices Committee, now the Auditing Practices Board (APB). The APB offices are in the London building of the Institute of Chartered Accountants

(Tel: 0171 920 8100) and their publications are available from the same Milton Keynes number as above (Tel: 01908 248000).

A consultation draft of a new auditing guideline, to be known as a Practice Note, was published in April 1997. It comments on the auditor's whistle-blowing function under the Pensions Act 1995, s 48.

The 1988 Guideline sets out in valuable detail the key audit areas and the planning that must take place for the audit. In the light of the 'Maxwell' affair (Chapter 24, para 12) it is interesting to note that para 49 states that procedures and controls for assets include:

- (*a*) agreement of asset records maintained by the trustees to those of custodians;
- (*b*) holding of assets in safe custody under the control of persons other than those responsible for the keeping of records;
- (*c*) fidelity insurance for staff of various parties;
- (*d*) prompt banking
- (*e*) adequate mandate arrangements to banks and investment institutions.

The importance of the mandate arrangements is mentioned in paras 11.9 and 14.3 below. While some of the provisions of the Guideline seemed, when it was published, too ambitious, it has become apparent that fraud at the expense of a pension scheme is all too easy. The consultation draft states, in para 3, that practitioners should not undertake the audit unless they have or can obtain the necessary competence. Paragraph 28 refers to the scope of the audit, focusing on the financial statements but also compliance with the requirements of trust law and for the maintenance of Revenue approval. Paragraphs 36 and 40 require the auditors to consider the trustees' controls over service providers, eg custodians. Helpful appendices describe the regulatory framework and give examples of letters of appointment.

Detailed discussion with auditors of the implementation of the Guideline, and a report to the trustees, would therefore now seem to be an essential part of the administrator's role. It is the author's view that the trustees should interview the accountants from time to time to learn whether changes in procedures are recommended, and generally whether the requisite controls appear to be operating smoothly. Trustees and associates are not eligible to be auditors—Pension Act 1995, s 27—unless excepted by SI 1996 No 1715, reg 7 (as amended).

11.4 SSAP 24 (employer's accounts)

SSAP 24 is the Statement of Accounting Practice No 24 issued by the ASC in May 1988 and relating to the treatment of pension costs in the *employer's* accounts. The successor body, the ASB, issued a discussion booklet in June 1995 with a view to preparation of a new SSAP 24 for three main reasons, set out below, but the difficulty over (*c*) has prevented the issue of a new SSAP. The three driving considerations were:

(*a*) the existing SSAP 24 contains so many options that consistency in accounting practice has not been achieved, particularly by reason of the flexibility available to employers to adjust results;
(*b*) the disclosure requirements do not necessarily ensure that the pension cost and related amounts in the balance sheet are clearly explained in the accounts;
(*c*) a desire for harmonisation with overseas standards, some of which are used internationally.

The following analysis of the existing SSAP 24 will still be applicable for at least a year, and possibly several years. For defined benefit schemes, it appears that the ASB remains inclined towards the existing actuarial basis of measurement (but with less flexibility) whereas international standards have tended to adopt a market basis which recognises in the employer's balance sheet a surplus or deficiency dependent upon market value of the assets (and if relevant liabilities) at the reporting date.

SSAP 24 has two main objectives:

(*a*) to charge in the accounts the accruing cost of future pension during the period of employment, which may be different from the contributions paid (or suspended if there is a surplus) but taking credit for the surplus (generally spread over the same period)—paras 16 and 23;
(*b*) disclosure in the employer's accounts of sufficient information to give their user an understanding of the method of accounting and, if different, funding—paras 45–49.

The accounting objective is attained by application of an actuarial method and assumptions. It came as a surprise to many finance directors, on the introduction of SSAP 24, to learn that the method and assumptions could well differ from those used in the last actuarial valuation of the pension scheme and that the disclosed cost could vary substantially from the actual contribution rate. Paragraph 18 requires that the method should 'lead to the actuary's best estimate of the cost of providing the pension benefits promised'. The paragraph states that the selection of the actuarial method and assumptions, for a defined benefit scheme (ie a final salary scheme as described in Chapter 8, para 1) is 'a matter of judgment for the actuary in consultation with his client, taking account of the circumstances of the specific company and its workforce'.

The method should provide for a level percentage of current and expected future payroll (para 79).

The key to understanding SSAP 24 is the treatment of surplus and deficits. Save for exceptional circumstances, these variations should ordinarily be spread over the expected remaining *service* lives of the current employees after allowing for withdrawals (paras 23 and 80). This might lead, where there is a surplus, to just a small disclosed drop in the annual contribution rate whereas the scheme might take a short contribution holiday. During that period the accounts would show a charge which would build up as a creditor in the balance sheet, gradually being reduced when contributions re-start.

A transitional option, on the introduction of SSAP 24, was to take an accumulated surplus onto the employer's balance sheet (para 53). Only a relatively small number of public companies took this option because:

(*a*) the balance sheet would suggest that assets were available to the company, whereas a repayment from the scheme (even if within the trustees' powers) might entail improvements in benefits which would reduce the cash available;

(*b*) the balance sheet item would alter significantly on subsequent valuations, unless the requirement were to spread subsequent fluctuations across the future contribution cost while, oddly, leaving the balance sheet enhancement unchanged.

The disclosure provisions are set out in paras 87 and 88 and Appendix 1. (The draft of SSAP 24 had contained accounts examples in Appendix 2 but no Appendix 2 appeared in the final version).

It is essential to appreciate that an unfunded pension arrangement

(Chapter 2, para 9) is recognised as an annual cost on the same basis as a funded scheme (para 73) so that effectively a book reserve (usually unsecured) is built up during the working life of the employee.

SSAP 24 has been both praised and criticised for incorporating the flexibility mentioned in the above quotation from para 18. By comparison the system adopted in the USA, known as FAS 87, specified the actuarial method and the amortisation of surplus or deficit, albeit the assumptions could at the time still incorporate estimates.

A US company with subsidiaries in the UK and Germany (which has a standard known as BiRiLiG), making an acquisition or disposal in one of those countries, may value the pension arrangements differently from the other party to the transaction. The US company will be accustomed to having local accounts produced on the basis of the local accounting standard while US consolidated accounts are on the basis of FAS 87. An early assessment of the differences will generally be required.

SSAP 24 pre-dates the Social Security Act 1990 which introduced a potential liability of the employer relating to the winding up of the pension scheme (Chapter 3, para 16). If a scheme were underfunded presumably the employer's accountants would need to consider the likelihood of the scheme being wound up in the foreseeable future, ie before the MFR contribution Schedule would run off the deficit, with the possibility of disclosure (or provision) of the contingent liability in or in a note to the accounts.

Copies of SSAP 24 can be obtained from the Institute of Chartered Accountants (Tel: 01908 248000). Enquiries about updating should be addressed to the Accounting Standards Board (Tel: 0171 404 8818).

11.5 Disclosure of Directors' Pension Emoluments (*Greenbury* Report)

Following the *Greenbury* Report of 1995 on Directors' Remuneration, the Company Accounts (Disclosure of Directors' Emoluments) Regulations 1997 (SI 1997 No 570) were adopted and a new listing rule has been issued by the London Stock Exchange (effective for accounting periods ending on or after 1 July 1997).

The regs relate to financial years ending on or after 31 March 1997. They treat defined benefit schemes differently from money purchase. Contributions to the latter must be disclosed, as must membership of either—reg 2, substituting a new para 1(1) into Sched 6 to the Companies Act 1985 (and see the new para 1(5) for definitions, and 1(7) for treatment of hybrid schemes).

Where the threshold for disclosure of highest-paid director's emoluments is attained (now £200,000 in aggregate for the Board), money-purchase contributions must be shown for that director or, for defined benefits, the *accrued pension* at the year end—the new para 2(2) as amplified by 2(5). The accrued pension at the previous year end need not be shown until the first anniversary of the regs—reg 3(2).

Increases to pensions *in payment* to directors and past directors must be shown (except for small companies—reg 6) unless the increases are both pre-funded and paid on the same basis to all pensioners in the scheme—the new para 7, substituted by reg 4.

The listing rule, 12.43(x) and (xi), applicable to UK listed companies, is straightforward for money purchase schemes. For defined benefit schemes it adds a requirement to show for each director the increase, over the accounting period, in:

(a) the leaving service pension, excluding inflation; and
(b) the transfer value (less the director's own required contributions), or specified information which in effect would enable it to be estimated. Published Amendment No 10 gives examples.

12 Value added tax

There are three questions which will interest the administrator of a pension scheme in relation to value added tax:

(*a*) whether the trustees can recover VAT charged to them;
(*b*) whether the employer can recover VAT relating to the pension scheme;
(*c*) whether the trustees should register.

12.1 Trustees' registration

No recovery by the trustees is possible unless they are registered (but see below regarding the adverse effect of partial exemption, and see para 12.2 below regarding certain input that can only be recovered by the employer). They will normally register only if their annual taxable output exceeds £48,000 pa the registration figure as at 1 January 1997 (but they may be 'grouped'—see para 12.4 below). It is unlikely that an insured scheme will have any taxable output. A self-administered scheme may have taxable output in relation to underwriting or certain property activities. Further, its sale of shares outside the European Union, while now being outside the scope of VAT nonetheless attract an input tax credit, described by Customs & Excise as 'equivalent to the UK zero rate before 1 January 1993'—Leaflet 701/44/94 at para 6. Whether directly or through the voluntary option, this will be relevant to registration.

UK share sales will ordinarily be exempt (ie not taxable). The above treatment, equivalent to zero rating, of overseas share sales depends upon the place of belonging of the purchaser which must be outside the EU. The key to this treatment is the apparent interpretation of para 5 of Sched 5 to the Value Added Tax Act 1994 which relates (among others) to financial services. Notice 741 at para 9.15 lists the sale of securities, as principal, as an example falling within para 5 of the Schedule, and at 9.8 squarely illustrates this. The authority then runs through SI 1992 No 3123, reg 3 and SI 1992 No 3121, reg 16.

Customs and Excise accept that where the identity of the purchaser cannot be established, the place of belonging will usually be the location of the Stock Exchange where the deal is made—Notice 741, para 9.8. The brokers or bankers will usually have made specific arrangements with Customs and Excise for that purpose.

Property activities may be taxable or they may be exempt. The construction of a new building is taxable, being either zero-rated (residential dwellings, charity buildings and associated categories) or standard rated. Rent will normally be exempt but an election can be made to waive the exemption (ie an option to tax)—now 1994 Act, Sched 10, paras 2 and 3. The election will be made if there is an opportunity to recover associated input tax. It may also be made, at the property owner's option, where the tenant requests it (because, for example, a service charge passes on input which, if the VAT were identified, could lead to recovery by the tenant). However, there are potential disadvantages in an election, since VAT on a sale will have marketing implications, so that pension funds may make the election in respect of some properties but not others. The relevant provisions are explained in Customs and Excise Notices No 708 and 742 (the former relating only to the construction of buildings).

12.2 Recovery of VAT by trustees

A significant proportion of VAT should be invoiced to the employer and not to the trustees—see para 12.3 below. Recovery of VAT properly invoiced to registered trustees depends upon whether all, or only a proportion of, their output is taxable. Ordinarily, the majority of output (sale of stocks and shares within the UK) will be exempt rather than the equivalent to zero-rated, mentioned in para 12.1 above, so that only a proportion of input tax will be recovered. The main item of input tax paid by the trustees usually comprises investment management charges, for advice and execution (but not stockbrokers' commission which is now exempt for UK transactions).

Input tax for supplies that Customs regard as the responsibility of the employer is not recoverable by trustees unless the employer has ceased to be in business, and either way the VAT invoice must be addressed correctly—see para 12.3 below and paras 11 and 13 of Customs Notice 700/17/96 dated April 1996 and entitled 'Funded Pension Schemes'.

12.3 Recovery by the Employer

Following a number of cases where employers' claims to treat pension scheme expenses as input were, on the specific facts, upheld by the Court, Customs and Excise liberalised their opinion of the law in 1983. Their current Notice 700/17/96 (see para 12.2 above) maintains that revised practice and provides that the employer can recover VAT charged in connection with the setting up and administration of a pension scheme as these matters are treated as part of the employer's business. Clearly the employer must be registered for VAT in order to recover. It is also necessary that the suppliers address the VAT invoices to the employer. This can be done even if payment is by the trustees—paras 5 and 13 of the Notice which in effect clarify the slight ambiguity of para 6. The supplier could usefully be invited to endorse the VAT invoice with a statement that it is in accordance with Customs Notice 700/17/96, to avoid any suggestion of impropriety. The Notice sets out in paras 5 and 7 a number of useful examples of inputs to the employer and trustee respectively (and see Appendix B as referred to at the end of para 9).

Recovery by the employer does not extend to VAT on investment management services relating to the fund ie stock selection and/or custody (except where the employer is sole trustee—but then it may have a partial exemption problem arising from fund share sales). However, where the *administration* is carried out by a fund manager for a fee which includes investment advice Customs & Excise will generally have agreed with the fund manager a proportion of the fee attributable to administration (their standard approach being up to 30 per cent). The VAT on the latter can be invoiced to the employer.

12.4 Group registration

If a corporate trustee is a subsidiary of the employer they can be grouped for VAT purposes. The employer is then able to recover the input tax on all VAT charged to the trustee, including investment management. However, UK sales of securities by the trustees are exempt output which might bring the employer's partial exemption calculation above the threshold that can be ignored (unless a special method of attribution can be agreed with Customs). As a result, such groupings are still not common.

Customs and Excise used to claim that where grouping takes place the assets of the pension fund are available to them in the event of non-payment by the employer of VAT, eg on an insolvency. If this claim were correct, it would clearly not be right for trustees to put their assets at risk. In September 1990 Customs revised that view, and now state, in para 15 of Notice 700/17/96, that they are advised that the liability does not extend to the pension fund (except regarding VAT attributable to administration of the fund). It may be that the potential claim remains where the employer is also sole trustee of the pension fund, for the Notice, at para 8 indicates that such an employer can deduct input tax in respect of all supplies to himself as trustee (but any exempt supplies by the fund are then included in the employer's output and may lead to partial loss of input deduction). In practice, it is rare for larger funds outside the public sector to be under the trusteeship of the employer.

13 Restricted employer-related investments

13.1 Pensions Act 1995

Since 9 March 1992 there has been a restriction that not more than 5 per cent of a scheme's assets may be invested in employer-related investments, subject to certain exceptions.

The restriction was contained in The Occupational Pension Schemes (Investment of Scheme's Resources) Regulations 1992 (SI 1992 No 246), and although revoked and replaced by Pt II of SI 1996 No 3127 it is still necessary to refer to the 1992 regs as transitional provisions in the 1996 reg 7 continue to do so.

The regulations were made under an enabling power introduced by the Social Security Act 1990. By Sched 4 to the Act, a new s 57A was inserted in the Social Security Pensions Act 1975 which became PSA 1993, s 112, now replaced by the Pensions Act 1995, s 40 in almost identical terms (albeit the s 112 cross-reference to the Insolvency Act 1986 is now contained in the new regs, and differs in its detail). This in effect defines 'employer-related investments' as:

(*a*) shares or other securities issued by the employer or by an associate;
(*b*) land used by or leased to the above;
(*c*) other property used for the purpose of any business of the above;
(*d*) loans to the above;
(*e*) other prescribed investments (eg employer-related investments made via a collective investment scheme, an insurance policy etc—1996 reg 4).

By reg 2 of both the 1992 and 1996 regs, the restriction applies to tax-approved schemes which have a specified connection with the UK. An exemption is provided for 'small schemes' if all the members are trustees (a practical point to be watched) and if the scheme rules provide that each member shall agree in advance in writing to the making of an employer-related investment.

Regulation 4 of 1992, and reg 6 of 1996, disregard assets derived from members' voluntary contributions if the relevant members have agreed in writing to the investment. The regs also contain exemptions for banks, building societies and insurance companies as employers.

By reg 5 of 1996 the general restriction is that not more than 5 per cent of the current market value of the resources of a scheme may at any time be invested in employer-related investments, and (a new provision) employer-related *loans* are prohibited completely.

Important transitional provisions were contained in reg 5 of 1992, of which two remain in force by virtue of reg 7 of 1996. These permit certain investments held on 9 March 1992 to be retained, as follows:

(*a*) by reference to reg 5(2)(a) of 1992: employer-related loans which were in place on 17 February 1992, if still lawfully held on 18 December 1996; they may be retained until repayment can be enforced;

(*b*) by reference to reg 5(2)(d) of 1992: employer-related investments other than such loans and other than shares listed on, or traded in a second-tier market of, a recognised Stock Exchange, if held on 9 March 1992; the 1992 regs provided that any such investments might be retained indefinitely, but the 1996 regs divide them into three categories:
   (i) those that may be held until 6 April 2002;
   (ii) those that cannot be disinvested by 6 April 2002 by reason of contractual or other legal obligations, and which must be disinvested at the earliest date thereafter;
   (iii) those that may be retained indefinitely.

Items (i) and (ii) are both of the same type, viz securities as described in reg 5(3)(b) of 1996, being shares or other securities issued by the employer or an associate and falling within para 2 of Sched 1 to the Financial Services Act 1986; the latter narrows the category to debentures, loan stock and other such instruments.

Item (iii) relates to any investments lawfully retained under the 1992 regs other than the foregoing (and other than certain obscurely described employer-related loans that had also been retained on a transitional basis). The important category that can therefore be retained indefinitely is the ordinary share or shares issued by the employer and never listed (or second-tier traded) on a recognised Stock Exchange.

Regulation 12 of 1996 amends the minimum funding requirement (MFR) regs by excluding from the assets taken into account after 5 April 2002 the assets that could not lawfully be retained but for reg 7. Regulation 12(3) provides that, in testing *other* employer-related investments for the 5 per cent limit for MFR purposes, the value of the transitionally retained investments is excluded in finding the total value of the fund.

Regulation 7(4) of 1996 provides that there may be no new employer-related investment where more than 5 per cent (apart from the exempted AVC etc investments) has been retained lawfully under the transitional provisions; reg 7(3) applies if retained shares are 'floated', limiting the transitional period to six months from the listing date.

The disclosure regs (para 6 above) and the audit regs (para 11.2 above) respectively require details of the employer-related investments to be given in the annual report and the accounts (Sched 3 to each of the regs).

13.2 Draft EU directive

The Commission of the European Union issued on 12 November 1991 a proposal for a Council Directive relating to freedom of management and investment of pension funds.

Since the draft Directive also contained input from the Social Security Directorate of the Commission, the article prohibiting a requirement for local investments also contained a provision that the assets of a fund conform with the principle of prudence. The manner in which the principle was expressed caused no difficulty to the UK, and can be summarised as:

(*a*) investment appropriate to the liabilities, taking into account (in effect) the possible inflation-linked funding requirement;
(*b*) diversification to avoid major concentrations of risk;
(*c*) 'investment in the sponsoring undertaking or undertakings shall be restricted to a prudent level'.

The EC Commission received representations from interested UK bodies that the 'small schemes' exemption described in para 13.1 above should be reproduced and that there should be some recognition of the general transitional arrangements under the UK statutory instrument.

The draft Directive was withdrawn in 1994 but if resurrected its progress and content can be checked with the Department of Social Security.

A Green Paper from DG XV (Directorate for financial institutions) is expected during the summer of 1997, and may be followed by a new draft Directive.

14 Investment management agreements

14.1 General

Pension Fund trustees employing professional investment managers will typically receive a long specimen contract for consideration.

The effect of IMRO's rules (para 9.4 above) has been to require investment managers to disclose many practices of which previously their principal (the 'customer') had been unaware. The customer then has the option whether or not to agree the practices. On the other hand:

(*a*) the existence of a standard form agreement calls for strong determination by a customer to reject some parts of it;
(*b*) the customer frequently has no knowledge whether a particular practice is in effect a practical necessity for the portfolio management;
(*c*) the agreement may exclude the manager from liability, particularly in respect of his agents.

Nonetheless, the customer with a substantial portfolio has strong bargaining power. The manager will need to put an agreement in place in order to comply with IMRO rules albeit the trustees have a corresponding need under the Pensions Act 1995, s 47. The customer should never abandon straightforward critical faculties in analysing a draft agreement. Pension trustees have a particularly strong duty to consider three aspects of a draft:

(*a*) whether particular practices are prudent;
(*b*) whether certain practices are permitted to the agent of trustees (see para 14.8 below);
(*c*) whether all the terms of the draft agreement are within the trustees' powers as conferred by their own trust instrument and/or the general duties of trustees.

The task of the legal adviser to the trustees, when faced for the first time with an investment management agreement, is forbidding. Further, its terms will represent the best bargain that the manager expects to make whereas (by contrast) a pension scheme trust deed incorporates the unilateral wishes of a settlor who will usually be the client. The author is inclined to suggest that an inexperienced practitioner should not take on the task of negotiating the investment management agreement.

Notwithstanding this last important observation, some pointers can be given. Since the IMRO rules have in effect reduced much former custom to writing it is possible, given sufficient time, to check some aspects of (*a*) to (*c*) above. For example, it is a straightforward task to check whether the agreement provides for investment in financial futures and the like, and to advise whether the trust instrument permits this. (It is another question, if the instrument does permit such activity, whether the trustees should engage in it—see para 14.5 below).

Most management agreements include custody provisions. These are of the greatest importance—see para 14.9 below.

14.2 IMRO rules etc

When analysing a draft agreement, the practitioner will require a set of the IMRO rules and also a copy of the current form of agreement issued jointly by the IFMA and LIBA (Institutional Fund Managers Association and London Investment Banking Association) currently in its third edition IFMA/LIBA3 of November 1996 referred to below as IF/B3 (replacing BMBA2 of September 1991). While IF/B3, for which the separate explanatory notes should be requested, will not necessarily contain the right balance between manager and customer, in broad terms it is a fair balance, and comparison with the manager's own draft may be revealing.

The balance in IF/B3 needs the most careful consideration. For example the exclusion in para C5 of liability for non-associated sub-custodians may, dependent on the circumstances, be unacceptable (although the obligation upon the custodian in sub-paragraph (*a*), which may in some cases be tightened by amendment or representation, to act with due diligence in the selection, use and monitoring of sub-custodians, may be a sufficient compromise).

In the usual way, IF/B3 states, in para 1, that definitions set out in IMRO's rules have the same meaning, but helpfully it also labels, with a very brief description, the key IMRO definitions. Perhaps the most important is 'Best Execution' which is set out clearly but at length, with covering notes, in IMRO's r 3.8.

The central provision is that unless the customer's interests require otherwise, the investment manager must take reasonable care to find the best available price in the relevant market for the kind and size of transaction concerned, and deal at that price (or on a basis which is at least as advantageous to the customer, taking into account any compensating advantages obtained for him).

The manager may not contract-out of the duty of Best Execution for a private customer but may do so for a non-private customer. (For *in-house* managers, the pension scheme is deemed to be a private customer—see para 9.4). In either situation, even if only to ensure that there is no doubt, contractually, there should be added to the draft agreement (if not already there) an express provision that the manager shall conform with best execution at all times. IF/B3 contains such a provision at para 5(*a*), albeit the word 'principles' could usefully be changed to 'terms'.

If desired, the agreement might also expressly state that the manager will comply with the IMRO rules so far as they relate to the particular portfolio—in IF/B3 one might add this express statement to para 2.

The practitioner should consider an alteration to para 21 of IF/B3 so that amendments proposed by either party do not take effect until specifically accepted by the other. The existing provision, for automatic amendment on expiry of notice from the manager unless the customer responds, has obvious dangers. Automatic amendment may be thought practical for the implementation of technical changes; the contrary view would be that the changes would need approval anyway and that concern over delay should not remove the need for that approval, particularly as the person receiving the notification may not have authority to agree.

There are references throughout the specimen agreement to the Schedule. The latter is the place to add the pension trustees' guidelines for the limits on investment. The trustees may have a complete set of guidelines for adoption but if not the manager might be asked for a specimen with recommendations for consideration by the trustees. A typical example might be a limit for any single holding, firstly as a percentage of the pension fund and secondly as a percentage of the issued share capital of the relevant quoted company.

The general observations in para 14.1 above make it clear that it is beyond the scope of this book to advise on the full text of IF/B3. The practitioner's attention is particularly drawn to paras 14.4 and 14.8 below.

For the special IMRO rules that apply to an employer that, itself or through a subsidiary, provides investment management services to the pension trustees without a view to profit (OPS Firms), see para 9.4 above.

14.3 Mandate

It is vital that the pension trustees consider closely the authority that they give to directors or employees to instruct the investment manager. See also para 14.9 below regarding the custodian.

Whatever system is chosen, the trustees' auditors should be asked to advise on its establishment (including the security of any accompanying codes) and report regularly on its implementation in the light of developing practice in the industry (see 11.3 above). Regardless of intermediate checks, their annual report should include a statement that there has been compliance with the mandate throughout the period. They should also be asked to advise generally on appropriate security measures.

14.4 Exclusion clauses

Exclusion clauses, purporting to exempt the investment manager from potential liability to the pension trustees, should be considered with the same critical approach as would be applied to any contract.

The starting point should be to reject an exclusion clause unless it appears both that the manager will not otherwise make the agreement and that the risk to the pension trustees arising from the clause is commercially reasonable and proper in the circumstances. It may, for example, be reasonable and proper to accept the exclusion of the manager's liability for the misdeeds of his agents provided that there is an obligation on him to take care in their selection and to monitor them on a continuing basis.

The practitioner should not hesitate to insert obvious provisions of this sort and require the manager to justify their deletion. If, for example, the manager is unwilling to accept the above obligation because the customer wishes to invest in a distant and unsupervised market, there is good reason to question whether the scope of the investments should be so broad.

14.5 Unusual investments, stock lending etc

Trustees should not stray beyond traditional investments unless firstly they have the power and secondly they are satisfied that it is appropriate to exercise the power. The latter aspect may entail a paper from the investment manager indicating the advantages and disadvantages (eg risks) of a proposed course.

A few remarks are made in Chapter 13, para 3.3 regarding financial futures and traded options. Both are, for example, useful tools for acquiring investments ahead of an expected market rise and ahead of receipt of expected new moneys. It might be argued that when used in this way, with the intention of acquiring the underlying asset, they do not need specific authorisation but there are obvious dangers in operating without specific authority. The use of financial futures to increase the fund's exposure to trends in the market (which is their main purpose in the view of many dealers) would clearly constitute a breach of trust unless specifically authorised. A paper from the manager on the proposed use of financial futures should illustrate the proposed exposure and any other purpose, and explain the nature of the geared risk.

Similar considerations regarding the trustees' powers and the decision to exercise them apply to foreign exchange transactions. Large sums of money can be gained or lost in such translations. It is no part of a trustee's duty to deal in currency with a view to profit, unless specifically required to do so by the terms of his trust. On the other hand, dealings may constitute a proper hedge against fluctuations in the sterling value of the overseas part of the portfolio. More controversially it may be argued that the reality of a large pension fund is that professional managers are engaged with a view to maximising profit consistent with the degree of prudence that would be expected of a pension fund trustee. Where the employer is meeting, either by contract or in practice (or by statute under the minimum funding requirement—see para 17 below) the balance of cost, it is reasonable to consult him regarding the foregoing and investment policy generally. Indeed such consultation is now required for most large trust schemes—see para 16.4 below. It should always be remembered, however, that exposure to risk should not be disproportionate to the size of the fund and that the trustees have to exercise the usual principles of prudence, regardless of the views of the employer.

The draft agreement may state that investments may be bought which are subject to stabilisation. This is the practice whereby on a new issue the price is supported to avoid an excessive drop before demand is generated in the market place. Active stabilisation is unlikely to be a proper exercise of trustees' powers. By contrast the acquisition of a sizeable holding in a new issue at or below a particular price may entail purchase while the price is being stabilised. The client should discuss with the manager the question of general or specific authority regarding the latter.

Stock lending is the supply, generally to a dealer, of stock needed to complete his bargains, on the basis that it will be returned shortly thereafter. It may entail a swap of some other marketable stock that is held as security. The Central Gilts Office provides a secure market for lending of British Government stocks. Stock lending fees in general are modest and security is vital; unless trustees understand the mechanism and are satisfied with the security they should not seek powers to authorise these arrangements. In some overseas markets general procedures may already be in place requiring analysis. Market pressure to earn the fees will increase so that standard secure procedures for lending equities may emerge in the UK.

14.6 Parent company guarantee

A difficult question for the client may be whether to accept an agreement that is not guaranteed by the holding company in the manager's group. In practice, it is extremely difficult to obtain such a guarantee.

Few subsidiaries are capitalised to withstand substantial losses, so that the standing of the holding company, and the likelihood of it maintaining its reputation, is of paramount importance.

It remains probable that there will be a substantial disparity between the capitalisation of an investment manager and the funds of its larger clients.

14.7 Companies Act disclosure

Provision should be included that obliges the investment manager to notify the principal when a holding becomes subject to disclosure (Companies Act 1985, s 210). In view of the penal provisions of the section (which requires that the principal 'shall secure that the agent notifies him immediately of [relevant transactions]') its implementation should be discussed between the customer and the manager; a clause could be inserted to require the manager to make any requisite notification on behalf of the customer in conformity with Pt VI of the Act as amended from time to time.

The personal interests of trustees, where they are individuals, are aggregated but not those of pension beneficiaries (SI 1982 No 677).

Special arrangements are needed where a fund is divided between more than one manager. (The instructing trustees may employ an in-house executive to regulate multiple managers and he may need to take investment decisions and thus seek authorisation under the Financial Services Act 1986—see para 9.1 above regarding s 191).

14.8 Dual capacity

A major area of difficulty lies in the development of financial conglomerates offering a wide range of services (following the abolition of the Stock Exchange's single capacity requirement). The potential for conflict of interest between the investment manager and his customer, or conflicting loyalties between two customers, is considerable. This was the subject of a consultation paper issued by The Law Commission in May 1992 (No 124 completed on 3 April 1992). The paper was accompanied by a very useful Summary (itself 31 pages, but easy to read).

The Summary is a reminder that the investment manager himself has fiduciary obligations to his customer (para 1.3) and that in some respects these conflict irreconcilably with the new regulatory system introduced by the Financial Services Act 1986. For example para 2.4 refers to s 48(2)(*h*) of the Act which authorises rules enabling or requiring information obtained by an authorised person to be withheld from customers or from employees in another part of his business. This raises the possibility of conflict with a fiduciary's duty of undivided loyalty.

Interestingly, the same paragraph states that blanket consents in advance in customer agreements (eg to the capacity in which a broker-dealer may be acting) may not constitute adequate disclosure at law, because they do not disclose the full nature and extent of the manager's interest, and therefore (it may be argued) may not protect the manager. In para 4.7 the Commission consider that Chinese walls (organisational arrangements for restricting information flows in a firm) are sufficient protection against allegation of breach of the duty of undivided loyalty where the customer consents, but in para 4.8 they mention doubts whether, as a matter of private law, a Chinese wall protects a fiduciary in a conflict of interest situation. The Commission provisionally consider that the court should take some account of permissive regulatory rules of a public law nature, but that without legislation there is no certainty as to the extent that it would do so (para 5.9).

This issue of conflict between the Act (and rules made under it) and an investment manager's fiduciary duty to its customers is a problem for both the trustees (who may be in breach of trust in authorising a particular arrangement) and the manager (if the trustee as customer has a potential claim). At the drafting stage of the customer agreement the trustees' problem is whether to strike out provisions that permit the manager to deal with other parts of his organisation (and perhaps also permit him to make an undisclosed deal with the funds of another customer) albeit on the best terms available in the market (—for 'best execution' see para 14.2 above). The author was advised by leading counsel, soon after the Act came into force, that it was not possible for pension fund trustees to ignore the changes that had taken place in the financial market and that, provided the other party to a deal within the group were a separate company (a 'cousin'—see below), with predominantly separate management and executives, it would be in order for the trustees to make an agreement that permitted such deals (*on best execution*). The advice mentioned that this view was not universally held. A report by Professor D J Hayton commissioned by SIB and published in September 1990 offered a similar opinion (cautioning that the law remained uncertain). Both advised that the other party should not be a parent or subsidiary of the manager; ie the other party within the group should be a 'cousin' (para 6.39 and 6.40).

It would appear that such an arrangement can overcome the twin problems raised here of the fiduciary duty that any manager owes to his customer and the additional duty of a trustee when the manager is his agent, albeit the law is not certain (Hayton, para 6.39 and 6.43). Some investment managers who are aware of the dealing problem are so organised as to minimise it, and will therefore accept limitations (including the restriction to 'cousins' mentioned above).

Where this structure is not available, it may be possible for transactions by the manager itself or companies closely related to it, which would otherwise constitute a breach of duty, to be authorised by the trustees on an individual basis. The trustees would require sufficient information for informed consent so that they could be satisfied that the transaction was in the interests of their beneficiaries. The Hayton report cautions strongly against advance blanket consent in these circumstances (para 6.38).

The practitioner faced with these questions for the first time, and acting for trustees, would do well to discuss the relevant clauses (eg the disclosure provisions in para 14 of IF/B3—see para 14.2 above) generally with counsel, bearing in mind that there are now very few investment managers whose operations do not give rise to *some* potential conflicts of interest.

If a practitioner is willing to advise in principle in favour of authorising in the customer agreement some of the foregoing types of transaction, he may still wish to distinguish between ordinary market dealing and, for example, the acceptance of a placing or underwriting by a related company that is sponsoring an issue. The practitioner may advise that the latter should be accepted only with the customer's specific written consent in each case, although there may be contrary arguments.

14.9 Custody

Custody agreements constitute a specialist subject of their own. They may, particularly with the introduction of electronic title, relate to a range of functions to be carried out by the Custodian in addition to custody and settlement (including collection of income), each of which might otherwise be a function carried out by the manager or the customer. The following paragraphs do not attempt to cover the whole subject.

Liability

Ideally the pension fund trustees should simply require an unimpeachable covenant for safe keeping and secure receipt and delivery of stock. In practice, the resources of the covenantor cannot (generally) match the value of the funds under custody, so that the procedures of the custodian may be more important than its legal liability for a significant breach. Further, custodians have to deal with third parties, and therefore will state when they do and when they do not accept liability for the default of these parties. See para 14.4 above regarding exclusion clauses, and in particular the reference to agents; a custodian should be willing to accept liability for a sub-custodian that is within the same group of companies.

The client will need to discuss with the custodian procedures for reconciliation of stock. It is not the legal adviser's role to establish operating procedures; nonetheless, some reference to them may be found in the draft agreement.

Uninvested cash may be outside the custodian's control. Enquiry should be made and any such arrangement should be considered.

Custody arrangements should be vetted by the pension trustees' auditors (para 11.3 above).

Mandate: Fraud

The possibility of fraud, whether in the custodian's office or in the trustees', requires consideration—see Chapter 24, para 12 regarding the 'Maxwell' affair. A small pension fund might therefore be more secure in relying upon a custodian of standing, notwithstanding the apparent loss of control, than in itself keeping custody of its stock. However, a custodian is under a duty to act in accordance with the form of authorisation that has been agreed, so that the mandate to the custodian, as well as to the investment manager, is of critical importance. It is to be hoped that, after 'Maxwell', custodians will question unusual instructions, but in the event of fraud the legal adviser might find it difficult to establish that the custodian ought not, in the particular circumstances, to have acted in accordance with the mandate. Under many arrangements an external custodian will expect to operate on the basis of copy contract notes from the investment manager, but enquiry should be made as to the mandate for recalling part of or all the portfolio.

Liaison with manager

The investment manager's own policy may be to require a separate custodian (the question of such separation should be considered anyway). It is very common for an external custodian to be in the same group as the manager; the same considerations regarding substance and control should be applied as with a separate custodian. The client may require reconciliation of stock by the custodian, regardless of any reconciliation carried out by the related investment manager.

In-house custody by the pension trustees involves an internal mandate that is of the first importance, particularly as the fidelity bonding of in-house staff, to sufficient value, may not be practical.

Insurance

It is reasonable to enquire as to the extent of an external custodian's fidelity bonding. The custodian's own advice should be sought as to the risks that may arise in overseas markets.

Insurance by the pension trustees of stock against fire, theft, accidental loss and other risks (such as consequential loss from computer failure) should be considered by the client. An external custodian may carry insurance for the benefit of customers while the stock is in his hands (in which case any overlap of policies should be considered).

Sub-custodians

In many cases there will be sub-custodians (mainly in overseas markets). Where the investment manager or the custodian has the right to choose sub-custodians but does not accept liability for their actions, advance notification to the customer (the pension trustees) should be required of any intended appointment. A duty of care in choice and monitoring should be inserted. Where there is an unwillingness on the part of the appointor to accept liability for default by the sub-custodian, consideration should be given whether investment in that market is of sufficient importance to justify the risks. This will be a matter for discussion and practical input from the appointor.

Regulation

Custody as such may not require authorisation under the Financial Services Act if carried out by the trustees, although this may depend on the circumstances. IMRO's view is that custody does not comprise management of investments (paras 106(*b*) and 111(*b*) of their Note to Members dated March 1992). Interestingly Professor Hayton's report (cited at the fourth paragraph of para 14.8 above), at para 2.15, suggests that an active custodian who keeps records, holds investments, receives dividends, and exercises rights on rights issues but otherwise has no investment management role in the sense of discretion to buy or sell, could well be regarded as managing assets. On the other hand the para indicates why the draftsman probably intended mere administrative management to be excluded. The importance is that Financial Services Act 1986, s 191 (para 9 above) applies to management. The assumption, however, has to remain that custody does not *have* to be outsourced, regardless of whether the trustees are (exceptionally) authorised under the Financial Services Act 1986, for otherwise the Pensions Act 1995, s 47(2) could be expected to have included the provision. Instead, it is a prescribed function under s 47(3)(*a*) with the result that *if* it is outsourced the appointment of the custodian has to be made by the trustees themselves (SI 1996 No 1715, reg 2). By definition sub-custodians cannot be appointed by the trustees; it is understood that consideration is being given whether the function of custody needs to be defined for the purpose of the regs to exclude sub-custody. Meanwhile, by correspondence of 11 April 1997, formally copied to OPRA, the DSS have expressed the opinion that only the primary custodian need be appointed directly by the trustees (although in DSS's opinion it is essential that the trustees be aware of the terms of sub-custody and satisfied as to accountability down the chain).

Where a commercial custodian *is* appointed, the custodian will require authorisation for that function—a new provision in the Financial Services Act 1986 inserted by SI 1996 No 2958, with effect from 1 June 1997. A proposed guidance note issued by the Securities and Investments Board as a Consultative Paper (No 107) in March 1997 stresses that the mere activity of holding share certificates did not fall within the new requirement, as the SI refers to 'safeguarding *and administration*' (emphasis supplied). In practice all commercial custodians will require authorisation.

14.10 Counterparty risk

The investment manager should be asked to advise on the counterparty risks likely to arise in the intended markets.

Clause 12 of IF/B3 contains an example of a manager accepting the obligation of due diligence in the choice and use of counterparties.

14.11 Compensation

It was in 1987 the view of the Securities and Investments Board, that the customer of an investment manager is the pension fund trustee so that the compensation scheme available to private investors does not apply to the individual pension scheme members in the event of fraud by the manager. Even if this were not the case, the limit of £48,000 at the time of writing (of the Investors Compensation Scheme established pursuant to s 54 of the Financial Services Act 1986—helpline 0171 628 8820) would be wholly inadequate to compensate an individual for the complete loss of a full career pension.

IMRO's consultation document of May 1992, reviewing their pension scheme regime, states in para 3.2 that a pension scheme beneficiary is not a customer of the investment manager even where the trustees carried out the management themselves. The conclusion appears to follow from the statutory provisions cited in their para 3.1.

It follows that there is at present no protection under the IMRO compensation scheme for fund members against the loss of the fund assets from fraud or negligence by the manager. It may be possible for the trustees to insure against some of this potential loss—see Chapter 24, para 11.1. To the extent that the employer bears the ultimate cost of the scheme, the insurance is for its benefit. The employer therefore has an interest, particularly as the Pensions Act 1995, ss 75 and 89, impose a potential liability on an employer when a pension scheme winds up—see Chapter 3, para 16.

Where a scheme has suffered loss through fraud or theft, and the employer becomes insolvent, the new compensation scheme under the Pensions Act 1995 may make good some of the loss—Chapter 25.

14.12 Insurance policy

There are two ways in which an insurance company may (in effect) manage the assets of a pension scheme. The first is not relevant to this paragraph, *viz* the provision of a traditional insurance policy for which premiums are paid, and specified benefits are applied on the death, ill-health or retirement of the beneficiaries—see Chapter 4.

Many insurance companies, however, act just as asset managers. Nonetheless, they will issue a 'policy', and indeed are obliged to do so when offering units in a larger pooled fund. The 'policy' must then correspond with some liability of the pension scheme—see Chapter 13, para 4.8. In practice, where benefits are paid by the scheme administration, 'correspondence' is a nonsense. It is important therefore to ensure that the provisions retained in the policy for that purpose do not obscure the analysis of the relevant provisions applicable to the management of the assets. It is also important to advise the client that the assets belong to the insurer, and that on default the Policyholders Protection Act 1975 is unlikely to be of assistance. In practice the insurance industry is well regulated, but the point should not be overlooked.

15 Common investment fund: pension funds pooling scheme

15.1 Common Investment Fund

Where several exempt approved pension schemes are maintained within a single employing group of companies, there may be considerable advantage in pooling their investment funds in order to apply a single control over the investment principles and returns, and possibly to enable multiple fund managers to be appointed over assets of sufficient amount. Such arrangements are referred to by the Inland Revenue as 'common investment funds' (CIF) and are briefly described in para 17.11 of the Practice Notes IR12.

Agency or trust

The Revenue describe a CIF as 'merely an investment agency' so that the title to tax exemption of each of the participating schemes remains unimpaired. Nonetheless, while on the one hand a CIF may simply be a collection of assets, by contrast frequently it is held under a specific trust deed; in such event, the Revenue will require to be satisfied that the deed does not add any trusts in addition to those which govern the participating schemes ie that there is simply a bare trust. In practice, they do not regard provisions for unitising the funds as adding trusts, although in law they do so. In the first case the investment managers are simply agents for the participating schemes; in the second they are agents for the common trustee.

For either structure, the DSS is of the view that the investment managers are acting for the participating pension schemes. This has the advantage that there is compliance with the apparent *intention* of Pensions Act 1995, s 47(2), which uses the words (inserted in the Bill for that purpose) 'or on behalf of'. It does, however, imply in the case of a CIF held under trust that there is a direct relationship between the schemes and the managers, and in the case of the custodians (to whom the extra words do not apply) would require a joint direct appointment. On the coming into force of the section, on 6 April 1997, a number of CIF's have taken the practical course of a short joint supplemental agreement, but in the longer run this will have the inconvenience of novation if custodians are changed.

Common trustee

The advantage of imposing an umbrella trust over the CIF is that its trustee is then a single customer for the investment managers, and there is no need for individual fund management agreements with the participating schemes, or individual identification of their funds by the managers under the Financial Services Act 1986 regulatory regime. However, since the coming into force of the Pensions Act 1995, this advantage has lessened—see above.

The establishment of a CIF will not be a frequent occurrence. Where an umbrella trust is established, the practitioner should check at the time the position regarding income tax and capital gains tax in the event that the Revenue were wrong in regarding the funds as held on bare trust for the participating schemes (ie for their trustees). It will also be essential to check that neither stamp duty nor stamp duty reserve tax is payable on the transfer of funds to the trustees of the CIF; the author normally obtains specific confirmation of this from the Stamp Office.

Financial Services Act

The tax and stamp duty positions cannot be understood until it is determined whether the CIF is a collective investment scheme (CIS) for the purpose of the Financial Services Act 1986 (because the taxing statutes cross-refer). Ordinarily, it is essential to ensure that the CIF is not a CIS, or else the trustee will require authorisation under the FSA 1986, entailing initial and annual fees and significant record keeping for compliance purposes (whereas ordinarily the assets would be recorded exclusively by the fund managers and custodian). The simplest way to ensure that the CIF is not a CIS is to arrange for a corporate trustee which is a subsidiary within the same group as the trustees of all the participating schemes, for then the Financial Services Act 1986, s 75(6)(*c*) provides an exclusion. Where it is not possible to arrange for all the participating schemes to have such a corporate trustee s 75(6)(*a*) may offer an alternative, although the obscurity of the provision necessitates clearance from the Securities and Investments Board that the provision is applicable.

Inland Revenue

Paragraph 17.11 of the practice notes states that any proposal to establish a CIF should be submitted initially to the PSO. That office will then refer the matter to Claims Branch who in turn will seek confirmation that the arrangements can be terminated at short notice (to enable the Revenue to regard it as no more than a bare trust) and if there is an umbrella deed, will seek sight of it. The author invariably submits a draft in advance. Finally, when the arrangement has been established, the participating schemes will authorise the CIF manager or trustee to reclaim tax on their behalf, including authority to delegate this task to the fund managers. There is no standard form, and a very simple authority will be approved by Claims Branch, with a correspondingly simple delegation from the CIF trustee to the fund managers.

CIF trustee, accounts etc

The appointment to the Board of the CIF trustee is a matter for discussion with the participating trustees and possibly the sponsoring holding company. It is common to provide for two directors from each of the participating schemes.

Pensions Act 1995 accounting requirements apply to the participating schemes but not to the CIF. Nonetheless, the most practical approach is for the CIF accounts to be in identical form to those that would be required for the assets of an approved pension scheme, and for the participating schemes to annex these accounts to their own accounts which would state the number of units held, and provide the appropriate reference in the report. The new accounting standard for pension schemes mentioned in 11.2 above, the SORP published in 1996, provides, at paras 3.19–3.21 for such an arrangement (or for equivalent details of the CIF's portfolio to be reproduced within the participating scheme's accounts, but to the author this seems to have the disadvantage of requiring re-statement and of placing less clarity on the accounting arrangement for the CIF itself). The SORP rightly distinguishes a CIF from participation in open market unitised funds as the CIF is operated by connected parties who create or approve (and vary) the investment policy. It is therefore regarded as not sufficient simply to state the number of units and their value at the accounting date. Regarding employer–related investments, see para 13 above.

15.2 Pension funds pooling scheme

The purpose of a pension funds pooling scheme (PFPS) is to enable overseas pension funds to participate in exempt unit trusts which would ordinarily only be available to UK pension schemes. The concept is new, the regulations being made in 1996 as follows: SI 1996 Nos 1585 and 1583 regarding income and capital gains tax, and SI 1996 No 1584 regarding stamp duty. The concept arose from the needs of multi–national groups that wished to invest their worldwide pension funds through a single (untaxed) vehicle, and were obliged to use an overseas vehicle for the purpose. The UK Treasury was persuaded that a marketing opportunity existed for London fund managers, not simply for in-house pools but for fully marketed unit trusts governed by the Financial Services Act 1986.

The participants must be either UK-exempt approved pension schemes or s 615 funds (see Chapter 7, para 3.3) or overseas schemes accepted by the Inland Revenue as equivalent to a UK retirement benefits scheme—defined in SI 1996 No 1585, reg 2 and amplified in regs 4(3)(b) and 7(3) and (4). The schedule to the regs (and the Inland Revenue Press Release dated November 1996) list certain types of overseas scheme which are acceptable to the Revenue without the provision of further information, but this is not a closed list and other types of overseas scheme will be considered if the appropriate information is provided. The question whether such schemes are permitted by their own jurisdiction to invest in a UK unit trust is a matter for their domestic law.

The removal of potential stamp duty on transfers to the PFPS is said to be effected by SI 1996 No 1584, although the mechanism is not immediately obvious.

The analysis by the practitioner of the unit trust deed will not differ from that appropriate to any other investment to be effected by the UK pension scheme. The investment objectives, the question whether derivatives may or may not be used and other such issues will need consideration in the usual way. From the viewpoint of the pension scheme's own investment powers, the PFPS will simply be an investment in a unit trust, but the decision by the pension scheme trustees to enter into such an investment will be dependent (partly) on the investment powers and policy of the unit trust, and if the pension scheme is not prepared to use derivatives, it should be cautious investing in a unit trust that does so. On the other hand, if the unit trust does have such power, it can be expected to issue with its investment objectives a clear statement as to the manner in which the power will be exercised, and the extent to which it is limited by the trust deed or is a matter of policy adopted from time to time by the managers.

16 Investment compliance: pensions act

16.1 General

Sections 34 to 36 of the Pensions Act 1995 create a code of investment powers, restrictions and compliance requirements. For a large pension scheme, conventionally organised, these sections add very little to the practical security of beneficiaries. They do, however, require a new comprehensive statement, which is time-consuming to prepare and complex to understand, the statement of 'investment principles' (s 35). The statement is *not* required for a *trust* scheme if it is within one of the exemptions of SI 1996 No 3127, reg 10. The principal exemptions are unapproved schemes, publicly guaranteed schemes, those 'small' schemes that require *all* members' agreement to investments, and wholly insured schemes.

The exemption for wholly insured schemes extends even to schemes where the trustees can choose (and presumably switch between) different funds held by the insurer so long as the funds are not exclusive to those trustees—reg 10(6). However, the definition in reg 10(1) and the linked reference in reg 1(3) refer only to insurance business within Class I or III of the Insurance Companies Act 1982, Sched 1, whereas pension fund management comes under Class VII; it is understood that the option to take out annuities enables most (but not all) relevant policies to fall within Class I or III, but the question should be specifically asked of the insurer, to ensure that the exemption is available.

A similar question arises regarding a fund manager appointment—see the sub-heading 'Requirement' at the end of 16.2 below, where the differently worded exemption for wholly insured schemes is mentioned.

For schemes that may have been less than well organised, the sections should ensure that professional advisers and trustees jointly focus on the investment arrangements.

16.2 Delegation—requirements and restrictions

Pension trustees generally have wide powers of delegation, but these only arise where expressly conferred by the trust instrument or statute (Chapter 24, para 4).

The Pensions Act 1995 both confers a power (in fact three powers) and restricts other powers (s 34). It also contains a requirement—s 47(2). These are outlined in the paragraphs below.

The powers to delegate are conferred by s 34(2)(*a*) and (5), the restriction by s 34(2)(*b*). Section 34 relates only to a 'trust scheme' (ie a scheme established under trust—s 124) but in practice that qualification is immaterial as all relevant tax-exempt schemes will be trust schemes.

Main power

Section 34(2)(*a*) authorises delegation of any decision about investments (not necessarily Financial Services Act 1986 investments it appears—see for example s 34(5)(*b*)) to a Financial Services Act 1986 authorised or exempted person, but subject to exercise in accordance with s 36.

Section 34(4) exonerates trustees from liability for acts of fund managers if they have taken all such steps as are reasonable to satisfy themselves:

(*a*) that the fund manager has the appropriate knowledge and experience for managing the investments of the scheme; and
(*b*) that he is carrying out his work competently and complying with Section 36.

In effect the trustees, if they are to have the benefit of the exoneration, must take reasonable steps to monitor the performance by the manager of his duties.

The restriction

Para (*b*) of s 34(2) prohibits any other investment delegation except under the Trustee Act 1925, s 25 (delegation of trusts during absence abroad); or under s 34(5)—see below.

Two further powers

Section 34(5) confers the following two powers of delegation, subject to any restriction in the scheme (unlikely, except perhaps by implication):

(*a*) to a committee of two or more trustees;

(*b*) in the case of investments outside the Financial Services Act 1986 (eg land or cash) to a fund manager who is not authorised or exempt under the Financial Services Act 1986,

but in either case the trustees are potentially liable for the acts or defaults of the delegates—see the last three lines of s 34(5), but see the saving, by s 34(6), described in para 16.3 below.

The text of (*b*) begins 'any such discretion' which initially suggests that it must be exercised, if at all, by the committee in (*a*). However, the conclusion seems to be that the words are solely descriptive to avoid repetition, and the two powers are independent, for otherwise there could be no meaning in the words 'by . . . the trustees'. This conclusion also makes practical sense, for otherwise a committee would have to be established for the sole purpose of a delegation under (*b*). If there happens to be a committee, it too can delegate under (*b*) since the words 'or on behalf of the trustees' enable subdelegation.

Requirement

Any occupational pension scheme must, unless the exceptions apply, have a fund manager—s 47(2). The section applies where the assets are investments as defined in the Financial Services Act 1986 and there is no relevant exception under s 47(5) which provides for regs—see below.

It may therefore seem that for such a fund, with FSA 1986 investments, s 34(5)(*a*) is barely relevant. However, s 34 is not just about day-to-day investment decisions; it refers to any decision *about* investments. Section 34(5)(*a*) therefore authorises delegation by the trustees to an investment committee, to consider matters referred back by the fund manager. For non-Financial Services Act 1986 investments, it authorises delegation of investment decisions as such.

The exceptions under s 47(5) are prescribed in SI 1996 No 1715, reg 3(3). They include unapproved schemes, wholly insured schemes and, by paragraph (*a*) of the reg, the particular kind of 'small scheme' described in para 9.2 above that is already exempt from s 191 of the Financial Services Act 1986.

The exemption for 'wholly insured schemes' is only applicable if the definition in reg 1 applies, *viz* if 'all the benefits provided are secured by a policy or policies of insurance or an annuity contract or contracts'. This refers to deferred annuity policies, for which therefore no fund manager will be required. It is not clear whether it refers to unit-linked policies, although it would seem likely that the intention was to exempt trustees who invest in these if they are also exempted from the need for a statement of investment principles (see that sub-heading below, and para 16.1 above for the reference to the *different* definition). It is understood that the difference between the two sets of regulations is currently being considered.

Investment in a unit trust does not appear to exempt the trustees from a requirement to appoint a fund manager. The view of officials is that the unit trust manager is the obvious appointee as fund manager, that it is up to him to reject the appointment if the particular pension scheme's statement of investment principles conflicts with the investment objectives of the unit trust, and that he does not have to survey the market as long as he meets the requirements of his regulatory body to notify conflicts (under the administration regs SI 1996 No 1715 as amended by SI 1997 No 819).

These issues are of particular relevance to money-purchase schemes offering members a choice of units—see Chapter 8, para 6.

16.3 Powers and liabilities

Pension schemes need wide investment powers, or else the ability, by amendment, to create them. Even insured schemes may expand into wider investments. Section 34(1) of the Pensions Act 1995 confers the wide powers of an absolute owner, and s 35(4) prohibits a requirement for the consent of the employer to the making of investments. There are two key points:

(*a*) the new power is subject to any restriction imposed by the scheme; some schemes may for example be expressly limited to a particular insurance contract; where there is doubt whether a provision operates as a restriction, its removal should be considered before enlarging any investment activities;

(*b*) the power relates to an 'investment'; it is unlikely to extend to the use of derivatives, underwriting or the like.

Traditionally, pension trustees have been exempted by the trust instrument from all liability except wilful default (Chapter 24, para

2). By s 33, this will no longer be effective, for trustees or delegates, in relation to the 'investment functions' (subject to regs under s 33(3)—there being no DSS plans for any at the time of writing) but s 34 provides a partial substitute and a partial saving:

(i) by s 34(4), which is *not* dependent upon the trust instrument, trustees are not responsible for the acts of a fund manager in the case of a s 34(2) delegation, ie a manager who is authorised or exempt under the Financial Services Act 1986, if they have taken the reasonable steps to satisfy themselves as to (*a*) and (*b*) quoted under the heading *Main power* in para 16.2 above.

(ii) by s 34(6), *if* there is an exclusion from liability in the trust instrument for the benefit of the trustees in relation to the acts of a fund manager, it is not struck down by s 33 if it relates to a s 34(5)(*b*) delegation ie to the acts or defaults of a non-Financial Services Act 1986 authorised or exempt fund manager in relation to matters not comprising investment business within the Financial Services Act 1986 meaning (eg land, cash etc) and if the trustees, "or the person who made the delegation on their behalf, [have] taken all such steps as are reasonable to satisfy" themselves/himself in terms of the same (*a*) and (*b*) referred to in (i) above.

Regarding (ii) above, it may now become customary to express in the trust instrument an exclusion from liability so far as permitted by the Pensions Act 1995, lest the effect of s 33 be held to strike down the whole exclusion clause.

16.4 Exercise of powers (including Statement of Investment Principles)

Sections 35 and 36 are labelled 'Investment principles' and 'Choosing investments'. Section 35 obliges trustees to 'secure that there is prepared, maintained and from time to time revised a written statement of [investment] principles', but does *not* apply to the exempted trustees referred to in para 16.1 above.

The Act assumes that the trustees themselves are not experts. Section 35(5) requires them to obtain advice from a qualified person. The paragraphs below outline the two sections.

Consultation with the employer

Interestingly, s 35(5) requires the trustees to consult the employer. In a defined benefit scheme (Chapter 8, para 7) the employer bears the balance of cost and therefore has a keen financial interest in the investment policy pursued. During the passage of the Pensions Bill 1996 the Minister said that Leading Counsel had advised that this gave rise to a duty on the part of the trustees owed to the employer under trust law. In a long passage regarding that advice he said that while the trustees' prime duty was to members, in a balance of cost scheme they may owe a fiduciary duty to the employer because of this financial interest, the extent being possibly dependent upon the trust deed. There may be other duties (he said) in trust law, tort and contract or quasi-contract [Hansard 18 May 1995 col 232]. Note, however, that s 35(4) prohibits an employer's veto on the exercise of the power of investment.

Defined contribution schemes also fall within s 35(5). Presumably the employer has an interest in procuring appropriate investment returns for its employees—see the concluding paragraphs of Chapter 8, para 6.

Statement of investment principles

The statement must set out the trustees' policy for securing compliance with s 36 (see below) and s 56 (minimum funding requirement—para 17 below). It must also state policy regarding risk, return, the balance between different kinds of investments and other such matters—s 35(2), (3). See also the above sub-heading 'Consultation with the employer'.

Penalties are applicable for failure to comply—s 35(6).

For the main exemptions, including the question of insured schemes, see para 16.1 above.

Choosing investments

Section 36, entitled 'Choosing investments', is strangely drafted. Its leading statements are directed at *trustees* choosing investments. It refers to fund managers secondarily, and in s 36(4) not at all. The clue lies in s 36(3) where trustees are required, before investing in a broad manner, to obtain 'proper advice' regarding diversification and suitability.

The conclusion, governed partly by the requirement in s 47 (para 16.2 above—under *Requirement*), has to be that s 36 is really directed at the fund manager, but places a responsibility on the trustees which guides them in monitoring the fund manager's exercise of his duties. There will be some schemes within s 36 but exempt from ss 35 and 47(2), to whom s 36(3) applies, but for the generality it will not be relevant. Where it does apply, the trustees have to obtain and consider 'proper advice' as defined in s 36(6), given or confirmed in writing—subs (7). For UK investment business within the Financial Services Act 1986, this means advice from an authorised person or a specified alternative, and for other investments advice from a person 'reasonably believed by the trustees to be qualified and . . . [experienced in] the management of the investments of trust schemes'—s 36(6)(*b*).

Where s 36(3) applies, so will (4) requiring trustees retaining any investments to determine the timing of similar advice regarding its continued retention.

Penalties are applicable (to trustees) for failure to obtain and consider advice in accordance with the section—s 36(8).

17 Minimum funding requirement

17.1 Background

The Pensions Act 1995 has introduced, for the first time, a minimum funding requirement (MFR)—ss 56–61. It is primarily directed at defined benefit schemes (Chapter 8, para 7). By s 56(2) and SI 1996 No 1536, reg 28, it does not apply to money purchase schemes, unapproved schemes, publicly guaranteed schemes, and various others.

The MFR is a compromise, but nonetheless has raised the awareness of complexity and potential liability associated with defined benefit schemes, and may have increased the swing away from them in respect of new employees.

Originally entitled 'minimum *solvency* requirement' in the Pensions Bill it had been envisaged as a means to ensure that on discontinuance a scheme had sufficient funds to purchase annuities in respect of accrued rights. That was regarded as both impracticable (because the annuity market was not large enough to absorb the closure of a major pension scheme) and too expensive (because the investment portfolio of most large schemes is equity based whereas annuities are primarily gilts based). Numerous modifications have reduced its impact for large schemes and fairly young schemes, while nonetheless retaining a standard that still does *not* match the investment portfolio of most defined benefits schemes—see the references to reg 7 in para 17.6 below.

MFR is assessed under the above regs and GN27 (Guidance Note 27 issued by the Institute and Faculty of Actuaries and referred to throughout the regs). There is a buffer in that most ongoing (defined benefit) schemes contain a reserve to allow for the effect of future salary rises on accrued rights. Nonetheless, there is a mismatch inherent in the concept of equity based pension funds that provide fixed (or increasing) pensions rather than variable annuities. The MFR has not created the mismatch but has raised the awareness of it.

Future discretionary benefits appear to be excluded from the MFR liabilities, which offers a considerable buffer to schemes that have funded for, but not granted entitlement to, increases on the pre-6 April 1997 accrual of pension—see para 3.5 of GN27.

17.2 Purposes

The purposes of the MFR are:

(*a*) to ensure that on discontinuance a scheme will have assets to support, or that will come close to supporting, the benefit promise;
(*b*) to enable the level of that support to be disclosed to members—but see below;
(*c*) to provide a compensation target in the event of theft from a pension fund.

Item (*b*) above is now a reflection of the MFR itself rather than an indication of winding up solvency. Nonetheless it serves a healthy purpose and is the trigger for shortfall contributions from the employer (paras 17.4 and 17.5 below).

Item (*c*) plays a key part in the 'compensation provisions' (defined in s 81 of the Pensions Act 1995) introduced for trust schemes as a necessary response to the 'Maxwell' affair (Chapter 24, para 12 and Chapter 25). Section 81 provides for compensation in the case of theft where the employer is insolvent and, in the case of a salary related scheme, where the assets are valued at less than 90 per cent of the liabilities. These values are calculated on the MFR basis—s 81(7)—and compensation is limited to the restoration of the 90 per cent (which could mean nil compensation in the case of a well-funded scheme—s 83(3)(*b*).

17.3 Contributions schedule (and whistle-blowing)

The 'schedule of contributions' under s 58 is a key document in the new regulatory regime. Once the transitional period is over (see para 17.5 below) it will, for an adequately funded scheme, specify the required rate of members' and employers' contributions to meet MFR over the subsequent five years (albeit the rate will be revised following a valuation having an effective date normally within three years and made within a year thereafter)—SI 1996 No 1536, regs 10(3) (as amended) and 16(1).

Since the member's rate will be fixed by the rules of the scheme, s 58(4) gives the employer an opportunity to agree the overall rate (within 8 weeks of the signing of the relevant valuation—reg 15). Failing agreement, the schedule is determined by the trustees within the subsequent four weeks—s 58(3) and (4), and reg 15. Either way, it must be certified by the actuary. Penalties are applicable to trustees who fail to put the schedule in place—s 58(8).

Initial schedule

There is potentially a long run-in time from 6 April 1997, but for some schemes it will be longer than others. The schedule is required 12 weeks from the signing of the first MFR valuation—reg 15(1). For existing schemes which have already been the subject of a pre-MFR valuation, the first MFR valuation is to have an effective date by the third anniversary of the previous effective (pre-MFR) valuation date, and must be obtained within 12 months of its effective date—reg 10(2).

New schemes must obtain a MFR valuation with an effective date no later than 12 months after commencement, signed off within a year of that effective date—reg 10(1).

Regarding subsequent *annual* certificates under reg 18, see para 17.6 below.

Whistle blowing—Trustees' duty

Unpaid contributions (whether payable by the employer or not ie by the members) become a debt due from the employer—s 59(2). More importantly, the only *compulsory* 'whistle-blowing' required from the trustees relates to contributions delayed beyond the scheduled date—s 59(1) which provides for notice to OPRA (within 30 days—reg 23) and the members (within 90 days but not if payment is made within 60 days of the due date—reg 23). Penalties are applicable to trustees who do not report (s 59(4)) so that the most careful attention is needed to monitor compliance with the contributions schedule in good time. No doubt that is the purpose, to avoid the timing of contributions being dependent upon the employer's cash flow arrangements. (Members' contributions deducted from earnings must be paid over within 19 days of the end of the month, or if statutory payments to a COMPs, 14 days from the end of the income tax month (itself ending on the fifth day of a calendar month—SI 1996 No 1715, reg 16 as amended.)

17.4 'Serious underprovision'

The Act labels s 60 'serious underprovision', and this is the term by which it is referred in the regs. By reg 2, an MFR valuation that gives rise to a s 60 shortfall is a 'serious shortfall valuation'.

Section 60 applies where the scheme assets are less in value than 90 per cent of the liabilities, on an MFR basis. By s 60(2) the employer must pay the shortfall (ie restore the level, it appears, to the 90 per cent) within a year of the appropriate date or secure assets within 12 weeks of that date—reg 20(1), and, in the case of secured assets, reg 22. The one-year period is extended to 6 April 2003 in the case of an effective valuation date before 6 April 2002—reg 20(3).

Amending regs insert a new s 60(7A) to remove the above requirement if, by the time the actuary certifies the contribution schedule, he is of the opinion that there is no longer a shortfall below 90 per cent—SI 1997 No 786.

The 'appropriate date' is defined in reg 20(2) and means in effect the date of signing an MFR valuation revealing the shortfall or a certificate under s 57(2) that the contribution schedule is no longer adequate (which is to be followed within six months by a valuation). In the former case, signature may be up to a year after the effective date—reg 10(4)—but in general the trustees, and hence the actuary, will be under a duty to obtain a speedy valuation where a serious underprovision is expected.

17.5 Other underprovision

The basic period in which to restore a modest underprovision is five years ie to restore assets having a level of 90 per cent or more of liabilities, to 100 per cent. This derives from the five-year period of the contribution schedule (para 17.3 above).

Where the first MFR valuation, or indeed any MFR valuation before 6 April 2002, reveals a shortfall, the five-year period is extended to 6 April 2007—reg 16(2).

17.6 Other aspects

Regulation 6 has already been amended by reg 12 of SI 1996 No 3127. Apart from matters of detail, this excludes from reckonable assets after 5 April 2002 the value of excess employer-related assets which are retained only by virtue of the transitional permission of reg 7 of the latter regs.

Regulation 7 of the MFR regs provides in 7(3) that ordinarily pensioner liabilities will be valued by reference to gilt-edged securities but that for large schemes ie those having pensioner liabilities over the subsequent 12 years exceeding £100 million, by reg 7(4) the 12-year liabilities are valued by gilts and, save where the investment policy is in gilts, the balance of pensioner liabilities is assumed to be met from equities. By reg 7(5) where the 12 year liabilities are less than £100m, the excess over £100m of the total pensioner liabilities can be assumed to be met from equities.

For actives and deferreds, reg 7 assumes an equities policy until ten years before normal retirement age, subject to any gilts-investment policy regarding deferreds.

A schedule may be revised under s 58(3)(*b*) and, if not, the trustees are obliged after 5 April 2002 to obtain a new MFR valuation if, having consulted the actuary and obtained his opinion, it appears that an event or events have affected either the assets or the liabilities sufficiently to put the MFR at risk during the schedule period. Reg 11(1) imposes an obligation to obtain the valuation within six months of the date of the actuary's opinion (unless a revised contribution rate, certified by the actuary, is agreed with the employer within the six months—albeit, the effect of s 57(3) may be to require the full valuation anyway if the MFR level is below 90 per cent). The above reference to 2002 derives from the 'transitional period' mentioned in reg 11(2)(b).

Regulation 18 provides (as authorised by s 57) for annual certificates by the actuary during the schedule period that the contributions are adequate to meet MFR throughout the period (or at least by its end) or indicating any relevant change since the last valuation. Section 57(3) provides for a full valuation in certain circumstances (and always where MFR level has fallen below 90 per cent), subsection (6) provides for copying the valuation to the employer and (7) provides for penalties for non-compliance.

Regulation 21, entitled 'Failure reports', requires trustees to prepare a report stating the reasons for failure to meet MFR if there has been a deterioration since the previous valuation, and for the report to be available to members (and others) on request.

Theft, fraud or general economic collapse can be followed by an application to OPRA to extend the contribution schedule period, or the one-year period for restoration of 90 per cent MFR level, subject to certain safeguards—regs 25, 26, and (where bulk applications are likely by reason of economic collapse) reg 27.

Regulation 29 and Sched 5 apply to industry-wide schemes (referred to as multi-employer schemes), closed schemes, foreign (unapproved) sections of UK schemes and schemes with only a partial government guarantee.

Regulation 30 provides for an ongoing scheme valuation in accordance with GN9, and Sched 6 to the regs provides for the appropriate statement. It seems possible that the ongoing contribution rate may often exceed the MFR scheduled rate, leading to the possibility that the one could be treated as advance payment of the other (to avoid whistle-blowing in the event of inadvertent hiatus). OPRA may publish views on this.

Section 61 of the Act provides that regulations may modify ss 56 to 60.

18 Internal disputes resolution

Section 50 of the Pensions Act 1995 requires the trustees or managers of an occupational pension scheme to put in place internal disputes resolution procedures. Regulation 8 of SI 1996 No 1270 exempts one-member schemes and schemes in which all the members are trustees.

There has to be a two-stage procedure. by s 50(2) an individual is to give a decision at Stage 1, and the trustees, on appeal, at Stage 2. Failure to put this in place brings a penalty.

The regs add very little except that they provide the framework for applications and notices.

The key question is whether the dispute is limited to a matter of maladministration or whether it amounts to an appeal from a discretionary decision. The Act is unclear on the point. It refers to the 'resolution of disagreements between prescribed persons about matters in relation to the scheme'. By reg 2 the persons are beneficiaries under the scheme (more elaborately defined). By reg 3 an applicant can nominate a representative. Regulation 4(2)(d) gives a slight clue to the above question by requiring the applicant to make a statement 'as to the nature of the disagreement with sufficient details to show why the complainant is aggrieved'.

The safest course is to draft the procedure by using the same text ie the 'resolution of disagreements'. If, however, there is a complaint about the exercise of a discretion, which does not raise a question as to the procedure adopted for the exercise, but simply prefers that a different decision had been taken, the safer course is for the grievance officer, if he upholds the complaint, to refer the matter back to the trustees for reconsideration (which may or may not result in a different decision). This has the further merit that it avoids the uncertainty whether the Act confers upon the grievance officer an external power to take decisions under the trusts of the pension scheme.

On the other hand, matters of maladministration can be decided by the grievance officer.

In the author's view, if no procedural irregularity is shown, and the trustees took into account all appropriate matters when making the original decision, there would appear to be no grounds for the grievance officer to refer the matter back. However, others have expressed the view that a different discretionary decision can be substituted. In practice, it is probably sound policy to re-hear a matter if it has reached such a disputatious stage, for otherwise there is likely to be an application to OPAS or the Pensions Ombudsman, either of which would take up management time, however unmeritorious the complaint.

The disclosure regulations (para 6.3 in this chapter) require members to be informed of the procedures and of the person to be contacted for application forms. As this is a new requirement, reg 4(2) specifies that for active members and pensioners on 5 April 1997 (but not deferreds—SI 1997 No 819, reg 4), the information must be given by 5 April 1998. However, as it must be given to new members or prospective members as soon as practicable, and in any event within two months of joining, it is likely in practice also to be given to existing actives during 1997. Further, s 50 itself requires trustees to take all reasonable steps to implement the arrangements, which clearly includes the availability of information within a reasonable time. For actives this may possibly be sooner than for pensioners (for whom it might be given with the annual report or other convenient circular).

19 Legal aid for beneficiaries

Death benefit trustees may be asked to fund litigation on behalf of children, whether in respect of the cause of death or some unrelated matter.

Typically, the trustees will have a discretion whether to apply monies (capital or income) for the maintenance, education or benefit of the child. It is for them to consider the benefit, having regard to the nature of the litigation, its likely outcome and the prospective receipts, if successful. Where they refuse payments, and the advisers to the child apply for legal aid, the following (unpublished) procedure at present applies:

(1) The Legal Aid Board first writes to the trustees of the trust fund asking whether they are prepared to release income or capital from the fund to finance the litigation.
(2) If the trustees state that they are not prepared to exercise their discretion in this way then the Legal Aid Board will consider the reasonableness of the decision. If they consider the trustees to have acted unreasonably they can refuse to issue a legal aid certificate, but such refusal is rare.
(3) Normally, the Legal Aid board asks the Government Actuary's Department (GAD) to value the fund in question and apportion an amount to the child requesting legal aid.

(4) The notional value of the fund is then taken into account when the Legal Aid Board assesses the child's capital for the purposes of considering eligibility for legal aid.

Informal enquiry of the Legal Aid Assessment Office indicated uncertainty where trustees might wish to release a limited sum, but the probability that the GAD valuation (in (3) above) would still be sought.

Chapter 17

Powers of Inland Revenue

1 Part XIV of the taxes act

There are references throughout this book to the Inland Revenue. These arise because the overwhelming majority of occupational pension schemes in the United Kingdom are intended to be approved by the Revenue under their statutory power.

The current code for approval was originally set out in the Finance Act 1970. As amended from time to time it was consolidated in Chapter I of Pt XIV of ICTA 1988 (itself now amended and referred to throughout this chapter as the 1988 Act). Chapter I should be read together with Scheds 22 and 23 to the Act, s 76 and Sched 6 to the Finance Act 1989 and s 271 of the Taxation of Chargeable Gains Act 1992.

The tax code relating to personal pension schemes falls outside the scope of this book. It is primarily to be found in Chap IV of Pt XIV of the 1988 Act and Sched 7 to the 1989 Act.

For approvable occupational pension schemes, permissible benefit limits and pensionable remuneration were radically affected by the Finance (No 2) Act 1987 (now consolidated in the 1988 Act) and the Finance Act 1989. However, both statutes preserved (with one exception—see para 3.2 below) the rights of existing members of pension schemes, and regulations permit these rights to be retained on certain transfers within a group, so that most schemes now have three categories of member:

(*a*) pre-17 March 1987;
(*b*) pre-1 June 1989;
(*c*) current joiners.

The changes are described in para 3 below and principally affect augmented benefits and/or high pensionable earnings, thus severely restricting the voluntary job mobility of senior executives. Further, all joiners on or after 17 March 1987 are affected by new lump sum scales and certain other changes.

1.1 Tax advantages

The four tax advantages applicable to most schemes are as follows (with references to ICTA 1988):

(1) Full relief, as an expense, for the employer's ordinary annual contributions to the scheme, with further relief (which may, however, be spread over several years) on other (eg specially large) such contributions—s 592(4) and (6) and para 5.6 of the Revenue's practice notes IR 12 (1991). These reliefs relate to contributions in respect of employees in a trade or undertaking the profits of which are assessable (on the employer) to UK income or corporation tax—s 592(5). The reliefs might often be obtained, apart from the statute, by demonstrating that the contributions were a necessary expense of the trade, but this argument is rarely required as the other three advantages described here can only be obtained by seeking exempt approval, and thus the automatic relief under the statute for employers' contributions.

(2) Relief for the employee from assessment to tax under Schedule E in respect of the employer's contributions—s 596. This section actually confers relief only from the specific charging provisions of s 595, but the Revenue do not in practice claim that a charge arises in respect of such contributions or cost other than under that section, and probably could only do so if the benefit of those contributions was available for the employees' disposal.

(3) Full relief for the employee, by deduction as an expense, from income tax under Schedule E in respect of his contributions to the scheme—s 592(7) et seq. The Revenue require the rules of an exempt approved scheme submitted to them for approval under s 591 (see para 3 below) to include a limit on the contributions (including voluntary contributions) to all exempt approved schemes in any tax year of 15 per cent of the

member's remuneration, including director's fees. For members who joined the scheme on or after 1 June 1989 (14 March 1989 for new schemes) the relevant remuneration is normally limited for tax relief by s 592(8C), the figure being £60,000 per annum for the tax year 1989/90 and thereafter rising approximately in line with the retail price index (£84,000 for 1997/8). For the disapplication of the limit for other members (including transitional cases) see the Finance Act 1989, Sched 6, para 18(4) and SI 1990 No 586.

(4) Exemption from income or capital gains tax on investments held for the purposes of the scheme—s 592(2) and (3) and Taxation of Chargeable Gains Act 1992, s 271(1)(*g*), but see para 1.6 below regarding the tax credits available on dividend income. The exemption from income tax relates to income from investments or deposits but not trading income (but see below regarding financial futures and traded options). The importance of ensuring that receipts are not trading income is particularly great when the funds of a pension scheme are invested in agricultural land. Section 592(3) exempts underwriting commissions but only where they would otherwise be chargeable to Case VI of Schedule D, a limitation whose effect is the subject of current dispute between the Revenue and a number of pension scheme administrators.

The approval by the Revenue may be mandatory or discretionary (see paras 2 and 3 below) but becomes 'exempt approval' only if one of the conditions set out in s 592(1) is fulfilled, ie:

(*a*) that the scheme is shown to be established under irrevocable trust (see, however, Chapter 3, para 1); or

(*b*) the Revenue, having regard to any special circumstances, direct that the section shall apply. They will normally do this only in the case of an annuity policy purchased for a retiring employee under a 'Hancock' arrangement (Chapter 12, para 4) and belonging to the annuitant absolutely.

The importance of obtaining 'exempt approval' cannot be stressed too highly, for mere approval brings only the relief under s 596 mentioned in (2) above, following which it becomes necessary to demonstrate to the employer's inspector of taxes that its contributions are made 'wholly and exclusively for the purpose of its trade' etc if they are to be deductible from chargeable profits. The exemptions described in (3) and (4) above would not be obtained at all.

Futures contracts and options contracts are deemed to be 'investments'. Income derived from transactions relating to such contracts is in effect deemed to be income from investments, by s 659A of ICTA 1988. The section does not limit dealings in financial futures to particular market places, but it is probably as well to limit dealings to the 'recognised futures exchanges' referred to in the Taxation of Chargeable Gains Act 1992, s 143(2), and defined in s 288(6) and (7) of that Act.

A similar question arises regarding traded options. Section 143(2)(*b*) refers to traded and financial options as defined in s 144(8). The latter refers to certain recognised exchanges and/or defined dealers.

1.2 Irrevocable trust

The practical meaning of 'irrevocable trust' is enlarged upon in Chapter 3, para 4. It is of great significance since the Revenue interpret the exception mentioned in (*b*) above very restrictively. On the other hand, they may be content with informal evidence of a trust if it can be shown to be sufficiently certain and of binding intent. However, s 592(12) and s 271(1)(*g*) of the Taxation of Chargeable Gains Act 1992 make it clear that the exemptions and reliefs, apart from (2) above, apply only in respect of contributions paid, income arising or gains accruing at a time when the scheme is an exempt approved scheme, so that the trust must be established before the first contribution is paid if these reliefs are to apply. The Revenue are always concerned that the existence of a trust at such time be demonstrated to them. A possibly defunct further exception to this rule (an insured scheme for a single employee) is mentioned in Chapter 3, para 1, where the Revenue's less strict requirements are outlined.

As a matter of drafting, reference to exempt approval in a trust deed or rules is usually to 'approval by the Commissioners of Inland Revenue for the purposes of Chap I of Pt XIV of the Income and Corporation Taxes Act 1988' (the deed itself being the indication of the trust) or to the scheme being 'treated under Chapter 1 [etc] as an exempt approved scheme'. In recent years the Revenue have preferred the use of the word 'Board' in place of 'Commissioners'.

1.3 Retirement benefits scheme

Approval under ICTA 1988 relates to the 'retirement benefits scheme' rather than to its fund or any other particular aspect of it. Whereas all other relevant definitions are contained in the interpretation provisions of s 612 this particular term is defined in s 611. It includes a scheme relating to a single employee and whether made under a specific agreement or 'other arrangements providing for relevant benefits'. Thus a service contract which itself confers entitlement to relevant benefits will comprise a scheme but if unfunded no longer requires approval as the old provisions for taxation of the employee on the notional cost have been repealed. However, it must be notified to the Revenue under s 605(3) within three months of coming into operation (a date which should be checked with the local Inspector of Taxes).

Relevant benefits are defined widely (in s 612) but do not include benefits arising solely through the death by accident or disablement by accident of the member while in the employer's service. The definition is of importance partly because of the notification provision mentioned above but also because of the tax position of ex gratia lump sums (see Chapter 10, para 5). It is set out here in full:

> '"relevant benefits" means any pension, lump sum, gratuity or other like benefit given or to be given on retirement or on death, or in anticipation of retirement, or, in connection with past service, after retirement or death, or to be given on or in anticipation of or in connection with any change in the nature of the service of the employee in question, except that it does not include any benefit which is to be afforded solely by reason of the disablement by accident of a person occurring during his service or of his death by accident so occurring and for no other reason.'

Section 612(2) indicates the broad scope of 'retirement benefits scheme' by giving one example as to how relevant benefits may be provided, namely by contract with a third party, eg an insurance company. The subsection opens as follows:

> '(2) Any reference in this Chapter to the provision of relevant benefits, or of a pension, for employees of an employer includes a reference to the provision [thereof] by means of a contract between the administrator or the employer or the employee and a third person;. . . .'

Although the definition of 'retirement benefits scheme' includes an 'arrangement' for a pension, payment of which then starts immediately, it may not include a direct ex gratia pension terminable at any time or a direct payment to a retired employee without any pre-existing obligation or arrangement. This theoretical possibility has become of little practical significance in the light of a revised Revenue interpretation of 'arrangement' adopted in 1991 (see Chapter 10, para 5).

1.4 Administrator

Section 611AA(2) of ICTA 1988 provides that where a scheme has a UK-resident trustee, the trustee shall be the 'administrator'. (Until 1994 it was simply the person having the management of the scheme, who might be the employer).

The administrator is chargeable to tax under s 598 et seq in respect of certain payments. ICTA 1988 imposes (in s 604 et seq) certain duties upon the administrator (and, by s 606, in default upon the employer) but in practice these are fulfilled automatically during the correspondence with the Revenue leading to approval and during subsequent routine annual correspondence.

In practice the point is of little importance except where there is a foreign employer (see s 590(2)(*c*) and Chapter 7, para 2 above).

1.5 Effect of interim documents

Most schemes are established by interim documents (see Chapter 3, para 2). If the Revenue are satisfied that the scheme has been established under irrevocable trust, and thus is capable eventually of approval with effect from its establishment if the necessary definitive documents are executed, they will apply provisional tax relief to employees' contributions. They will also refrain from closing corporation tax assessments on the employer, ie in effect they will grant provisional tax relief also on the employer's contributions.

It is often said that a scheme at the interim stage has 'provisional approval'. The Revenue discourage use of the term since (unlike that term for personal pension schemes) it has no statutory basis and can be misleading for there is no guarantee that eventual approval will be obtained (although the practitioner who follows the established steps can be confident of the outcome).

The status of the scheme is of great importance where a transfer is being made to it from another scheme (see Chapter 10, para 10.2 and Chapter 16, para 7). Where the interim document contains specific power to receive transfers, the Revenue require a standard form of undertaking from the trustees that if approval is not eventually obtained, the moneys received will be applied in the purchase of annuities from an insurance company. If such an undertaking has been given, the Revenue will normally approve the scheme for the purpose of trustees who wish to make a transfer to it, this approval relating to the transfer and not to the tax status of the receiving scheme. The transferring trustees will usually rely upon a power in their deed whereby a transfer can be made to a scheme approved under the statute 'or approved for the purpose of transfer by the Commissioners of Inland Revenue'.

The question whether such approval applies also to the exercise by an individual member of his statutory right to transfer from another scheme (assuming willingness to receive him) depends upon the particular regulations in force (see Chapter 10, para 10.2). The distinction is of importance since the first-mentioned transfer relates to the exercise by trustees of a discretionary power (which brings with it a duty to make some enquiry as to the credit to be conferred upon the member by the receiving scheme) whereas the statutory transfer brings with it a statutory discharge to the trustees.

It is common for there to be considerable delay between the establishment of the scheme and the submission to the Revenue of definitive documents. The delay is rarely of practical importance where the funds are invested with an insurance company since it will have been permitted by the Revenue to place the moneys in its tax-exempt fund. However, a self-administered scheme (Chapter 2, para 5) will not obtain tax relief on its investment income (save in the case mentioned below) until approval is obtained. Once obtained, the approval dates back to the establishment of the scheme so that tax paid on the investment income and gains is recovered. The recovery brings with it a supplement (colloquially regarded as 'interest') but calculated only from 12 months after the relevant tax payments. It follows that a substantial loss of interest on the tax temporarily in the hands of the Revenue can be suffered if a scheme is established with a large transfer payment from another scheme that has been merged with it.

Where there is a reason for the delay, and a substantial likely loss of interest, the Revenue will usually accept an indemnity from the employer and the trustees to the effect that if approval is not obtained within a specified period, uncollected tax will be paid together with a supplement equivalent to interest. The text of the indemnity is in standard form and appears forbidding. In the past, the Revenue have often extended the time mentioned in the indemnity so long as steps were clearly being taken to finalise the definitive documents. However, the current practice notes refer to a period of up to two years—para 18.10 of IR12. See also Chapter 13, para 3.24, for the tightening of Revenue practice regarding this period of delay.

1.6 Tax credits on dividend income

Exempt approved pension schemes are not taxed on investment income—para 1.1 above. They obtain repayment of tax credits on dividend income—ICTA 1988, s 231(3).(Tax credits arise on qualifying distributions from UK resident companies, other than foreign income dividends which are excluded by s 246 C.)

The amount of the tax credit was, prior to 1 April 1993, equal to the basic rate of income tax (then 25 per cent) on the grossed-up dividend. From that date the tax credit dropped to the 'lower rate' (20 per cent)—Finance Act 1993, s 78(3). For a given distribution this reduced the value to an exempt pension scheme by 6.25 per cent eg a £75 dividend attracted a credit of £18.75, totalling £93.75, instead of a credit of £25, totalling £100, the reduction in gross receipt being £6.25.

Taken in isolation, this was said to be an attack on pension schemes' tax exemption, and undoubtedly it reduced the actuarial value (generally assessed on gross income flows) placed on the assets. The criticism seemed justified as basic rate taxpayers were relieved from charge to the 5 per cent difference (ICTA 1988, s 207A, now replaced by s 1A having, in this respect, the same effect) and the corresponding reduction (phased in over two years) in the rate of advance corporation tax (s 14) did not represent a fall in overall taxation as normally the actual payment is just an offset for 'mainstream' corporation tax. The subsequent reduction(for individuals) in tax to 20 per cent on certain other income from savings (Finance Act 1996, s 73) obscures the issue further and leads to the possibility of lower rates (for selected income) being used to set tax credits and thus to remove a significant part of the effect of the tax imputation system that has operated since 1973.

On the other hand, if basic rate income tax for *all* purposes were lowered to 20 per cent (without reducing the band) it would follow that tax credits could be expected at that rate. Presumably this would not be expected in a single year, and the climate would be conducive to lower rates of corporation tax (at present 33 per cent or for small companies 23 per cent) and increased dividend flows.

In the context, the 1993 change was an effective reduction in pension schemes' tax relief under the imputation system. The climate of the Budget was one of tax increase, eg the effective extra charge of 5 per cent on dividends receivable by higher-rate taxpayers. Equally importantly, the existence of a lower rate of tax, below basic rate, indicates the possibility of a *range* of lower rates and therefore a further reduction in the rate of tax credit. If taxpayers below the top rate were to continue to be relieved of the difference between the basic rate and the tax credit, the change would plainly be an effective targeting of pension funds (and other zero taxpayers); if such taxpayers were not so relieved, it would simply be a further departure from the tax imputation system affecting them as well as pension schemes.

For the different effects on defined benefit and defined contribution schemes, see Chapter 8, para 7.5.

2 Mandatory approval

The approval of the Revenue cannot be withheld if a retirement benefits scheme satisfies all the conditions referred to in s 590(3) of the ICTA 1988.

It is very rare for a scheme to be submitted for approval under s 590 as it is much more restrictive than s 591 as to the scope of permitted benefits. Whereas the scope may well be adequate for normal retirement pensions, it is not wide enough to cater for late entrants, early retirers or children's allowances or lump sums on the death of a member. Further, the section bases pension on a restricted definition of final remuneration (see below). The opening provisions of s 590(3) are set out here to facilitate understanding of the discretionary approval described in para 3 below.

'(3) Subject to subsection (1) above, the Board shall approve a retirement benefits scheme for the purposes of this Chapter if the scheme satisfies all of the conditions of this subsection, that is to say—

(*a*) that any benefit for an employee is a pension on retirement at a specified age not earlier than 60 and not later than 75 which does not exceed one-sixtieth of the employee's final remuneration for each year of service up to a maximum of 40,

(*b*) that any benefit for any widow or widower of an employee is a pension payable on his death after retirement such that the amount payable to the widow or widower by way of pension does not exceed two-thirds of any pension or pensions payable to the employee,
(*c*) that no other benefits are payable under the scheme.
(*d*) that no pension is capable in whole or in part of surrender, commutation or assignment, except in so far as the scheme allows an employee on retirement to obtain, by commutation of his pension, a lump sum or sums not exceeding in all three-eightieths of his final remuneration [see below] for each year of service up to a maximum of 40.'

The reference in (*a*) to final remuneration must be read together with the definition in s 612(1), under which it means 'the average annual remuneration of the last three years' service'. Under discretionary approval (para 3 below) the Revenue permit a number of alternative definitions, the most common being the last 12 months' remuneration (save where earnings exceed £100,000 pa).

For schemes approved before 27 July 1989 (the passing of the Finance Act 1989) para (*d*) (and Sched 23, para 6) contains a requirement, retained by the Finance Act 1989, Sched 6 paras 3 and 18(2), to disregard for commutation purposes remuneration above the permitted maximum (£100,000 per annum unless increased by Treasury Order, which is unlikely) save for pre-17 March 1987 members.

Paragraphs (*e*)–(*h*) require associated employments and associated (approved) schemes to be taken into account.

3 Discretionary approval

The provisions relating to discretionary approval and the manner in which it is granted form the pillar around which the benefit structure of almost every modern pension scheme is constructed. The provisions are set out in s 591, as follows:

'*591 Discretionary approval*

(1) The Board may, if they think fit, having regard to the facts of a particular case, and subject to such conditions, if any, as they think proper to attach to the approval, approve a retirement benefits scheme for the purposes of this Chapter notwithstanding that it dos not satisfy one or more of the prescribed conditions; but this subsection has effect subject to subsection (5) below.

(2) The Board may in particular approve by virtue of this section a

scheme—

(*a*) which exceeds the limits imposed by the prescribed conditions as respects benefits for less than forty years' service; or

(*b*) which provides pensions for the widows of employees on death in service, or for the children or dependants of employees; or

(*c*) which provides on death-in-service a lump sum of up to four times the employees' final remuneration (exclusive of any refunds of contributions); or

(*d*) which allows benefits to be payable on retirement within ten years of the specified age, or on earlier incapacity; or

(*e*) which provides for the return in certain contingencies of employees' contributions; or

(*f*) which relates to a trade or undertaking carried on only partly in the United Kingdom and by a person not resident in the United Kingdom; or

(*g*) which provides in certain contingencies for securing relevant benefits falling within subsection (2A) below (but no other benefits) by means of an annuity contract made with an insurance company of the employee's choice; or

(*h*) to which the employer is not a contributor and which provides benefits additional to those provided by a scheme to which he is a contributor.

(2A) Relevant benefits fall within this subsection if they correspond with benefits that could be provided by an approved scheme, and for this purpose:

(*a*) a hypothetical scheme (rather than any particular scheme) is to be taken, and

(*b*) benefits provided by a scheme directly (rather than by means of an annuity contract) are to be taken.

(3) In subsection (2)(*g*) above "insurance company" has the meaning given by section 659B.

(4) In applying this section to a scheme which was in existence on 6th April 1980, the Board shall exercise their discretion, in such cases as appear to them to be appropriate, so as to preserve—

(*a*) benefits earned or rights arising out of service before 6th April 1980; and

(*b*) any rights to death-in-service benefits conferred by rules of the scheme in force on 26th February 1970.

(5) The Board shall not approve a scheme by virtue of this section if to do so would be inconsistent with regulations made by the Board for the purposes of this section.

(6) Regulations made by the Board for the purposes of this section may restrict the Board's discretion to approve a scheme by reference to the benefits provided by the scheme, the investments held for the purposes of the scheme, the manner in which the scheme is administered or any other circumstances whatever.'

Subsection (1) confers on the Revenue power to approve a scheme bearing no resemblance to one which could be envisaged from s 590. Apart from subss (5) and (6) there appears to be no fetter on the degree of departure from that section. It might be thought that subs (2) indicates the boundaries of the discretion but whereas in general terms its influence can be seen in the Revenue's practice notes, they range beyond it in many respects. (For regs under subs (6) see para 8 below.)

Further, whereas the section refers to 'the facts of a particular case' the Revenue will normally (but are not obliged to) grant approval to any scheme falling outside the terms of s 590 but within those of the practice notes. These notes are published as a looseleaf booklet IR 12 (1991) available from the Pension Schemes Office (PSO) (Chapter 1, para 5). Guidance as to any question arising in a particular case, can be obtained from the PSO. While the current edition of IR 12 clearly sets out the major transitional rights of pre-1989 entrants there are some options available to them, and indeed to pre-1 October 1991 entrants, which are to be found only in the previous edition of IR 12. They are not there readily identified but, on enquiry, the author has not been notified of any of great significance (being limited to mortality tables and the like).

While it is outside the scope of this book (and quite unnecessary in view of the lucid presentation of IR 12) to take the reader through the practice notes, the following outlines certain major provisions.

3.1 Members' contributions

The most important provisions regarding members' contributions are mentioned in (3) under para 1.1 above, namely the limit of 15 per cent of remuneration and the application of the earnings cap to certain members. Under the normal rules of a scheme, the members' contributions rarely exceed 6 per cent, so that there is plenty of scope for additional voluntary contributions (a required facility under the PSA 1993, s 111). There has never been a Revenue requirement for members to contribute.

3.2 Final remuneration

As mentioned at the end of para 2 above, the Revenue permit under their discretion alternative definitions of final remuneration. Subject to a number of refinements (including certain provisions for index-linking) either of the following bases may be used:

(1) Remuneration for any one of the five years preceding the normal retirement date. For this purpose 'remuneration' means basic pay, eg wage or salary, for the year in question, plus the average over a suitable period (usually three or more years) ending on the last day of the basic pay year of any fluctuating emoluments such as commission or bonuses (but see below regarding certain excluded items). Director's fees may rank either as basic pay or as fluctuating emoluments according to the basis on which they are provided.

(2) The average of the total emoluments (save the excluded items mentioned below) for any three or more consecutive years ending not earlier than ten years before the normal retirement date.

Only the second basis may be used in the cases mentioned in (*a*) and (*b*) below.

Normally the 12 months' pay (plus three-year average of fluctuating emoluments) under (1) will be greater than the three-year average under (2) but occasionally the provisions for index-linking earlier years will favour (2). In two cases Sched 23, para 5(3) requires three-year averaging:

(*a*) '20 per cent' directors (para 5(5) and s 417, and see para 7 below);

(*b*) pensionable remunerations exceeding £100,000 per annum (see below).

The £100,000 provision was introduced by the Finance (No 2) Act 1987 and, unlike most of the restrictions under that Act, applies to all members, ie pre-1987 as well as subsequent joiners. It is to be found by following the reference now in Sched 23, para 5(3)(*b*) of the 1988 Act to the 'permitted maximum' through to its definition in s 612 and its description at the end of s 590(3)(*d*) *but* some reproductions of this section omit the description as, by reason of the Finance Act 1989, it applies only to schemes approved before 27 July 1989. The figure £100,000 can be varied by Treasury Order but to the time of writing no variation had been made and it is understood that none is at present contemplated. The figure, which for para 5 purposes relates only to averaging, should not be confused with the earnings cap described in para 3.3 below.

The excluded items mentioned in (1) and (2) are set out in the definition of 'remuneration' in s 612 of the 1988 Act and are:

(*a*) anything in respect of which tax is chargeable under Schedule E and which arises from the acquisition or disposal of shares or an interest in shares or from a right to acquire shares;
(*b*) anything in respect of which tax is chargeable by virtue of s 148 (golden handshakes);

but SI 1988 No 1436 (transitional provisions) reg 7 permits, and proviso (i) to the definition 'final remuneration' in the Revenue's practice notes confirms, the inclusion of (*a*) above where the shares or rights etc which give rise on or after 17 March 1987 to a Schedule E tax liability had been acquired before that date.

Subject to the above, benefits in kind assessed under Schedule E may be included in pensionable remuneration and will normally be regarded, under (1) above, as fluctuating emoluments.

3.3 Earnings cap

The description 'earnings cap' is to be found in the headnote to s 590C of ICTA 1988, the section having been inserted by the Finance Act 1989. It limits pensionable remuneration, in schemes to be approved, to £60,000 per annum (rising annually with the retail price index). The figure for 1997/8 is £84,000 per annum (SI 1996 No 2951).

For schemes approved before the Finance Act 1989 came into force, Sched 6, Pt II of that Act introduced a corresponding provision (paras 20 and 30) which has direct effect on the rules of the scheme, but where the scheme existed before 14 March 1989 the restriction does not apply to persons who became members before 1 June 1989. There are reliefs for new members transferred from existing schemes within a group (see para 3.9 below).

The 1989 Act also applies a direct limit on contributions by all members, being 15 per cent of remuneration with exceptional provision for a higher amount (Sched 6, para 21) and introduced the £60,000 (now £84,000) limit to remuneration for contribution purposes subject to the same exemption for pre-June 1989 members as applies to benefits (para 22). For tax relief see para 1.1(3) above.

The earnings cap has created a revolution in pension provision. With it was introduced a tax scheme for unfunded (usually contractual) unapproved schemes containing no limits, the intention being that employers could offer top-up arrangements so long as there was no associated tax-free fund and no tax-free lump sum benefit.

As before, unapproved funded schemes are permissible but are not attractive unless the employer is prepared to assist the employee to meet the tax charge on the contributions; they do have a place, however, in the provision of death benefits. The tax position of unapproved schemes is described briefly in para 4 below.

See para 3.9 below for a summary of the effect of the earnings cap on the job mobility of senior executives.

3.4 Uplifted sixtieths

Section 590(3)(*a*) of ICTA 1988 relating to approval (there is no limit for unapproved schemes—see para 4 below) permits pension to be calculated up to one-sixtieth of final remuneration for each year of service up to a maximum of 40 (ie a maximum pension of two-thirds final remuneration). Note the reference to service, not membership. The governing factor is the period with the employer, even if the scheme was established part-way through that period.

For late entrants the Revenue have always permitted an uplifted table. Since 1970 this table, subject to deduction for 'retained benefits' from earlier schemes or approved retirement annuity contracts, has enabled the full two-thirds pension at retirement age after ten years' service. The uplifted table is now available only to pre-17 March 1987 members of a scheme or transferees from within a group who had such rights in the previous scheme (see para 3.9 below). For eligible members who had in total potentially less than ten years to their normal retiring age the table was:

years	*fraction*
1–5	1/60th for each year
6	8/60ths
7	16/60ths
8	24/60ths
9	32/60ths
10 or more	40/60ths.

3.5 Thirtieths (post-16 March 1987 entrants)

New members and those who joined the (approved) scheme on or after 17 March 1987 have a (generally) less beneficial uplifted table. It comprises a straight accrual of two-sixtieths (ie one-thirtieth) of final remuneration per year (up to 20) of service with the employer (even if the service began before 17 March 1987). As with para 3.4 above, the maximum of two-thirds final remuneration must take into account 'retained benefits' (see para 7.4 of the Revenue's practice notes IR 12, subject to the relaxation in paras 7.4A and B).

For new schemes the Revenue will require, as a condition of approval, that this scale is written into the rules (assuming the rules permit accelerated accrual). The rules of existing schemes were altered by the Finance (No 2) Act 1987, the provision now being consolidated in the 1988 Act, Sched 23, para 2.

Note that for a member retiring after less than six and a half years, and for most members retiring early (on a salary below the cap), the table is more beneficial than that in para 3.4 above. It is now possible for pre-1987 members to opt for this table so long as the complete post-June 1989 package is applied (meaning principally the earnings cap—see para 3.3 above).

3.6 Commutation: uplifted eightieths

The provision of s 590(3)(*d*) permitting part of pension to be commuted for a lump sum not exceeding three-eightieths of final remuneration for each year of service up to a maximum of 40 is expanded by published Revenue discretion, with a 20-year requirement for the grant of the maximum. It applies fully only to the pre-17 March 1987 members and the class of transferees mentioned in para 3.4 above, and lump sum retained benefits must be taken into account where the maximum 120-eightieths applies. The table is:

years	*fraction (80ths)*
1 to 8	3 for each year
9	30
10	36
11	42
12	48
13	54
14	63
15	72
16	81
17	90
18	99
19	108
20 or more	120

Commutation must take place when (or, for a late retirer, on or before) the member's pension begins. For restrictions on lump sums derived from voluntary contributions see para 3.8 below. For commutation of the whole pension (triviality or ill-health) see Chapter, para 19.4.

3.7 Commutation (post-16 March 1987 entrants)

As for pensions (see para 3.5 above) new members and those who joined the scheme on or after 17 March 1987 have a less beneficial uplifted scale for commutation. The scale is different for pre- and post-June 1989 entrants; for the former a complicated adaptation of the uplifted 80ths scale was adopted while for the latter (which includes all members of a scheme which began on or after 14 March 1989) a simple formula applies (that may be more or less beneficial according to the underlying pension scale). For simplicity the two classes are referred to below as post-1987 and post-1989.

For post-1987 entrants the lump sum must not exceed three-eightieths (of final remuneration—but see the reference below to £100,000 per annum)—unless pension (before commutation) exceeded one-sixtieth per annum. The intention was to restrict access to a disproportionate tax-free lump sum. The new limit was three-eightieths per annum plus a percentage of the difference between that figure and the amount shown in the table at para 3.6 above. The effect is to permit the uplifted eightieths table where maximum pension had been awarded on the uplifted sixtieths table. The formula is to be found in paragraph 8.23 of the revenue's practice notes IR 12 and (in words) in ICTA 1988 Sched 23, para 3 which applies it to the rules of existing schemes.

For post-1987 (and post-1989) entrants final remuneration is limited in the lump sum calculation to £100,000 per annum (Sched 23, para 6), referring to the same permitted maximum as para 5(3)(*b*) cited in para 3.2 above relating to final remuneration (but in this case in relation only to post-1987 entrants). The figure is also in para 8.25 of the above practice notes (where the reference to pre-1989 rights means post-1987 as defined in the glossary to the notes).

Approved schemes can provide lump sum benefits without pension (the maxima being the same as stated in para 3.6 above). The effect of the 1987 change is that for post-1987 entrants if no pension is provided the lump sum is limited to three-eightieths per annum of service.

For post-1989 entrants (as more precisely described above) the maximum lump sum is the greater of three-eightieths (maximum 120) per annum (of final remuneration, as defined) and 2.25 times the first year's pension (as it would have been but for commutation and certain other factors). Post-1987 entrants can elect for this basis but then also adopt the earnings cap (para 3.3 above). The Finance Act 1989, Sched 6 para 23 (and para 29 for the election) applies the basis to existing approved schemes.

3.8 Voluntary contributions—lump sum restrictions; refunds

As part of the 1987 reduction in available tax-free lump sums it was provided that future pension derived from newly started voluntary contributions could not be commuted. The restriction applies to any (additional voluntary contribution) AVC arrangement begun by a member on or after 8 April 1987 even if scheme membership had begun earlier. (A switch between investment media within a scheme is not considered by the Revenue to be a new arrangement for this purpose). For subsequent applications for scheme approval the restriction became a rule requirement. For schemes approved before the Finance (No 2) Act 1987 the rules were altered by that Act, the provision now being consolidated in ICTA 1988, Sched 23, para 7.

In practice the restriction has not been of importance as the main pension usually suffices to provide the maximum lump sum, and for post-1989 members the 2.25 multiple may take into account the AVC pension (and even an FSAVC provision—SI 1990 No 2101, reg 7). However, for schemes that follow the public sector design in providing separate pension and lump sum, the ratio of these has to be altered when AVCs are applied under post-8 April 1987 arrangements to purchase 'added years'.

Until the Finance Act 1989 schemes could not refund excess AVCs. Schedule 6, para 33 alters scheme rules to require such refund where the member's benefit attains the maximum. Regulations set out a practical regime to establish the relevant circumstances—SI 1993 No 3016. The refund is taxed under s 599A of ICTA 1988 at 33 per cent but only a 23 per cent (or other basic rate) credit is given to the member (and is not reclaimable if by then he is a non-taxpayer). The credit is on the grossed-up payment which is then taxable on a higher-rate taxpayer.

Similar refund rules apply under para 33 where AVCs have been paid to a free-standing AVC scheme maintained by an external provider (a creation of the Finance (No 2) Act 1987 and now approvable by reason of s 591(2)(*h*) of the 1988 Act set out at the beginning of para 3 of this chapter).

3.9 Summary of 1987 and 1989 changes (and transitional regulations)

The most important changes affected highly paid employees and those likely to be awarded (or to pay voluntary contributions for) substantially increased pension. If a pre-17 March 1987 member changes jobs he could previously have negotiated a pension of two-thirds final remuneration (less retained benefits) if there were ten years to retirement. Now he needs 20 years and is restricted, perhaps severely, by the earnings cap (£84,000 per annum at 1997 prices). If the balance is provided by an unfunded arrangement he lacks security and if by a funded arrangement he faces a regular tax bill while contributions are paid. In the unfunded case the balance of the emerging lump sum benefit will no longer be tax-free.

If the same individual had changed jobs between 16 March 1987 and 1 June 1989 (exclusive) there would have been no earnings cap on the pension but the 20-year rule (in the new job) would still have applied and the proportion of pension commutable for a lump sum would have been restricted by the £100,000 per annum earnings limit which looks unlikely to alter.

In both cases, regardless of earnings, the maximum lump sum from the scheme is likely to be reduced if pension is not awarded at the maximum permissible level.

All classes of member are now subject to three-year averaging of final renumeration if earning over £100,000 per annum, and to the exclusion of golden handshake and (subject to transitional relief) share option income from any level of pensionable earnings.

There are improved early retirement rules which do not fall within the above headings of this chapter but which benefit only those caught by the other 1987 and 1989 changes. The overall effect is generous to those not materially affected by the other changes. A pre-1989 member can opt for the new regime to take advantage of these rules, but then is subject to the earnings cap and commutation rules.

There are detailed anti-avoidance provisions in both ICTA 1988 (ss 590A and 590B) and the Finance Act 1989 (Sched 6, paras 25 and

26) relating to associated employments and connected schemes to ensure that in such cases the earnings cap applies to the aggregate pension.

The transitional regulations relating respectively to the 1987 and 1989 changes are:

(*a*) The Occupational Pension Schemes (Transitional Provisions) Regulations 1988 (SI 1988 No 1436);
(*b*) Retirement Benefits Schemes (Continuation of Rights of Members of Approved Schemes) Regulations 1990 (SI 1990 No 2101).

Both sets of regulations contain numerous detailed provisions relating to full commutation of ill-health and trivial pensions, temporary cessation of membership (or of voluntary contributions) and the like, and the two basic provisions have similar purposes, viz:

(*a*) the continuation of the pre-1987 or pre-1989 status where the individual transfers to another scheme of the same or an associated employer (1988 reg 3(2)(*b*)(i) and 1990 reg 3(6) and (7);
(*b*) protection of benefits arising from transfer payments (1988 reg 5 and 1990 reg 5).

The detail of these provisions is not identical and should be studied if relevant. It is worth noting the effect of 1990 reg 2(4) on reg 3(7), ie specifically to cover a transfer to another scheme in which the relevant employer participated (rather than actually 'established'). While the 1988 regulations do not contain a similar provision it is understood that the distinction between a participating and principal employer was not intended. If relevant to a particular case an application can be made to the Revenue under 1988 reg 11 to treat a transferee as if the relief applied, and may well be successful.

3.10 Spouses etc and dependants

In addition to the prospective pension for a widow or widower payable on death after retirement permitted under s 590(3)(*b*), there may be a surviving spouse's pension on death-in-service of up to two-thirds of the member's maximum approvable prospective pension (at then current salary) as well as the lump sum suggested by s 591(2)(*c*).

A similar pension can be paid to any other person financially dependent on the member so long as the total such benefits do not exceed the member's maximum approvable prospective pension (based on his salary at death) or, in the case of a deceased pensioner, the maximum pension that he could have received. Children's allowances must cease when they attain age 18 or, if later, cease full-time educational or vocational training.

If the former employee died within five years after his pension began, a lump sum equal to the balance of five years' instalments may be paid (or greater life cover, subject to conditions that in practice make it rare—see para 7.26 of the Revenue's practice notes). Alternative amounts may be calculated on early retirement, in effect a continuation of life cover subject to various conditions (which are considerably more restrictive for members who had joined the pension scheme on or after 1 October 1991—see Chapter 10, para 2).

3.11 *Ex gratia* payments

Following legal advice, the Board of Inland Revenue announced in 1991 that in most situations a payment of an ex gratia lump sum on retirement would constitute a retirement benefits scheme, with generally adverse tax consequences (Chapter 10, para 5).

4 Unapproved schemes

Unapproved schemes were encouraged in the Budget statement of 1989 which announced the removal of two penal provisions (the old ss 590(7) and 595(2)) and stated that unapproved schemes would thereby be available as a mechanism for providing unrestricted pensions without subjecting the Revenue to a loss of tax. Their importance stems from the earnings cap on new members of approved pension schemes described in para 3.3 above.

They are colloquially known as FURBS (funded) and UURBS (unfunded).

Unapproved schemes have a number of drawbacks—see Chapter 2, para 10.3. The salient tax features are:

(*a*) FURBS entail an immediate tax charge on the employee (1988 Act, s 595—from which approved schemes and certain employment are exempted by s 596)—see the Inland Revenue publication cited in Chapter 2, para 10.2;

(*b*) UURBS may provide insured death benefits to avoid taxation on the receiving beneficiaries under s 596A (albeit at the cost of an immediate tax charge on the employee in respect of the premium). This will almost certainly entail:

   (i) a medical examination in each case;
   (ii) regular persual of new policy documents as the broker chooses the appropriate life office or a new employee brings non-medical cover from his previous job;
   (iii) Individual discussion of the trust provisions relating to the policy.

Notification to the Inspector has been mentioned in 1.3 above.

Since Government policy of limiting 'tax breaks' is unlikely to change, the main tax focus on unapproved schemes is likely to be on their impractical aspects. Of these, the most severe is the necessity to provide a lump sum, rather than a pension, from a FURBS, to avoid double tax. It would seem preferable for Government to remove the tax charge on contributions, and to tax emerging lump sums. Possibly this may become a matter for consultation in due course, as the earnings cap continues to spread its effect lower in to middle management.

A more general commentary on unapproved schemes is given in Chapter 2, para 10.

5 Old code

Earlier editions of the Revenue practice notes use the expression 'old code' to refer to earlier legislation relating to pension schemes consolidated in s 208 and other provisions of the Income and Corporation Taxes Act 1970 (itself a consolidating statute enacted, confusingly, just before the Finance Act 1970). Generally, however, the term is often used to refer both to s 208 and s 222 (and their respective predecessors, ss 379 and 388 of the Income Tax Act 1952, these being the references normally found in the documents relating to old code schemes) as well as occasionally to the numerous less well-known types of arrangement such as excepted provident funds (see para 6 below).

Section 208 conferred on an approved 'superannuation fund'

similar tax exemptions to those applicable to exempt approved schemes under the Finance Act 1970 (now ICTA 1988).

Section 222 enabled the Revenue to approve a retirement benefits scheme for the purpose of exempting employees from the charge to tax (under s 220) on the employer's contributions corresponding to that imposed by s 595 of ICTA 1988 (see (2) under para 1.1 above). It follows, from the absence of relief on members' contributions, that such schemes were rarely contributory. If members' contributions were desired, they were generally arranged in one of two ways:

(1) By 'salary sacrifice', that is by way of reduction in salary to enable the employer to pay the extra amount. The Revenue's attitude to such arrangements has varied from time to time, but was normally sympathetic so long as only the lower salary was legally enforceable.

(2) By 'three-quarter/quarter' arrangements, under which three-quarters of the eventual pension was to be provided from a s 208 contributory fund and one-quarter from a s 222 scheme. The proportions enabled, under the Revenue conditions of approval, the whole of the s 222 quarter to be commuted for a lump sum.

Both forms of approval ceased to have effect on 6 April 1980 save that paid up s 208 funds continue to receive tax relief under the Finance Act 1980, s 36, now re-enacted in s 608 of ICTA 1988 and s 271(2) of the Taxation of Chargeable Gains Act 1992.

The amending provisions of the Finance Act 1971 (s 21 and Sched 3) postponed the repeal of s 208, and extended the transitional arrangements for the introduction of the new code. However, s 208 did not apply to a scheme established after 5 April 1973 or to an existing scheme altered after that date. An existing scheme, comprising an approved fund, when altered, was therefore submitted for exempt approval under the new code.

6 1980—Schemes affected

As stated in para 5 above, s 208 of the Income and Corporation Taxes Act 1970 ceased to have effect on 6 April 1980. In order that the four tax advantages described in para 1.1 above (which, as indicated in para 5, applied to s 208 funds as well as new code schemes) should continue to apply, any scheme whose fund was approved under s 208 was normally altered to satisfy the new code with effect from 6 April 1980 or an earlier date.

Further, all other types of old code scheme had to satisfy the new code and be submitted for approval if the employees were not to be taxed under s 23 of the Finance Act 1970, now s 595, ICTA 1988 (see (2) under para 1.1 above). The Revenue, in the former practice notes, described these schemes (references being to sections of the Income and Corporation Taxes Act 1970) as follows:

(*a*) s 208 funds, ie superannuation funds approved or partly approved under s 208;
(*b*) s 222 schemes, ie funds or schemes approved under s 222;
(*c*) three-quarter/quarter arrangements, ie s 208 funds with a complementary fund or scheme approved under s 222 providing a lump sum benefit;
(*d*) excepted provident funds and staff assurance schemes (for employees earning not more than £2,000 a year, with employer's contributions not exceeding £100 per member per annum) which were defined in s 224(1) of the 1970 Act and did not require approval under the old code because they were exempted by s 221(1)(*b*) from the tax charge under s 220;
(*e*) pre-1944 schemes, ie schemes in operation before 6 April 1944 under which the main benefit was a pension for life and which did not require approval under the old code because they were exempted by s 221(2) from the tax charge under s 220;
(*f*) pre-1947 schemes, ie insured schemes in operation before 6 April 1947, not substantially confined to persons earning more than £2,000 a year, which did not require approval under the old code because they were exempted by s 221(1)(*c*) from the tax charge under s 220;
(*g*) schemes (not approved under s 208) established by employers who were individuals or individuals in partnership, which did not require approval under the old code because s 220 applied only to employees of bodies corporate; and
(*h*) schemes providing benefits solely by reason of the death or disability of a person occurring during service, which did not require approval under the old code because these benefits were not within the definition of 'retirement or other benefit' in s 224(3).

7 Controlling directors and 20 per cent directors

Until 1973 no controlling director could be admitted to an approved fund or scheme, and no benefits could continue to accrue once a member of such a fund or scheme became a controlling director. With effect from 6 April 1973 (the effective date of the repeal of the old s 19(2)(*f*) of the Finance Act 1970) this restriction was lifted for new code schemes, subject to the '20 per cent' provision mentioned below.

The definitions of 'controlling director' and 'director' are to be found in s 224(1) of the Income and Corporation Taxes Act 1970, and the prohibition on accrual of service in the old s 222 schemes is to be found in s 222(1)(*f*). Such directors frequently made other pension arrangements which may have to be taken into account on their admission to new code schemes. (The particularly restrictive requirement that these might have to be taken into account even where the approved scheme provided non-uplifted sixtieths and eightieths (paras 3.4 and 3.6 above) was dropped by the Revenue's Memorandum 108, para 21). Broadly, such a director controlled (directly or indirectly) more than 5 per cent of the ordinary shares of a director-controlled company. The two most common methods of providing for retirement or death were:

(*a*) by taking out retirement annuity contracts under the Finance Act 1956 or its successor, now Chap III of Pt XIV of ICTA 1988 (Chapter 2, para 7);
(*b*) by arranging for the company to take out a whole life policy, the proceeds of which were held on trust for the director's family.

The first of these is not permitted in respect of earnings from pensionable employment. If a director who has taken out such policies is subsequently admitted to an approved pension scheme, the prospective pension and lump sum rights under the policies may have to be taken into account in calculating his maximum permissible benefits. It is not easy to establish a general ruling on the subject. The Revenue do, however, require all such contracts to be notified to them and therefore still ask (in their standard questionnaire issued before the grant of approval) whether membership includes any controlling directors.

The second method is referred to in para (*h*) of the list of schemes in para 6 above. In June 1973 the Superannuation Funds Office (SFO) stated that the continued existence of a whole life policy, unless it can be surrendered, cancelled or altered to the current tax code for approval, would prevent the director from being admitted to an approved scheme. It may be that on application the PSO would now modify that view.

The concept of a '20 per cent' director was introduced by the Revenue as part of their practice for discretionary approval but now has a statutory basis consolidated in ICTA 1988, Sched 23, para 5(3) and (5). Paragraph 5(3) refers to a [scheme member] who 'at any time in the last ten years of his service is a controlling director of the company'. Regulation 8 of the transitional provisions SI 1988 No 1436 disapplies this where the employee ceased to be a controlling director before 17 March 1987.

Paragraph 5(5) refers to s417(5)(*b*) of the 1988 Act which provides as follows:

> '(*b*) [a director who] is, either on his own or with one or more associates, the beneficial owner of, or able, directly or through the medium of other companies or by any other indirect means, to control 20 per cent, or over of the ordinary share capital of the company.'

Section 417(3) defines 'associate' and is amplified by s417(6). The essential parts of the foregoing are also to be found in the definition 'Controlling director' in the appendix to the Revenue's practice notes IR 12 (1991).

There are three main provisions which affect the normal rules of the scheme so far as they relate to a 20 per cent director. The first restricts the definition of 'final remuneration'. The basic alternatives for that definition are set out in para 3.2 above. As there stated, there are a number of refinements to those alternatives. In respect of a 20 per cent director the scheme may not base pensionable remuneration on one year but must adopt alternative (*b*) there set out. Paragraph 5(3), cited above, has direct effect on the rules of then existing schemes.

Directors frequently have retirement annuity contracts from earlier periods. These may restrict the maximum approvable pension from the scheme.

The second main provision affecting 20 per cent directors relates to lump sum death benefits payable where retirement has been postponed (whether under the normal or late retirement rule) beyond age

75 (not possible for members who joined on or after 1 June 1989—see para 7.26 of the practice notes IR 12).

Any such lump sum paid on death after the 75th birthday, where pension has not begun, must be paid either to the member's personal representatives or to his surviving spouse. This provision also applies to non-20 per cent directors who have life appointments (on the basis that ultimately there will necessarily be a large death-in-service payment). There is no restriction on the distribution of a lump sum which is a reducing five-year guarantee.

The third main provision affecting 20 per cent directors (who joined the scheme before 1 June 1989) is that where the normal retirement age is less than 70, a late retirement pension must (as for post-1 June 1989 schemes) be calculated as at the date of actual retirement (when it may be based on then final remuneration, as defined) and not as at the normal age actuarially uplifted—see para 7.35 of IR 12. However, where retirement takes place after age 70, the calculation should be made as at that age and then actuarially uplifted. The practical effects of this provision are rarely severe, but the need to draft a suitable rule must be remembered.

Where the company is treated for tax purposes as an investment company, the Inland Revenue will not normally approve a scheme (and may consider withdrawing approval of an existing scheme) if membership is offered to 20 per cent directors or directors who, while not falling within the above 20 per cent definition, are members of a family who together control more than 50 per cent of the shares. See para 3.8 of the practice notes IR 12.

8 Privately invested schemes for fewer than 12 members (pensioneer trustee): SSAS

Since the introduction in 1973 of eligibility for controlling directors (see para 7 above), some employers have preferred to manage the investments of small schemes outside the traditional life office market, particularly where the beneficiaries have often been exclusively the directors and their families. Such beneficiaries have understood more readily the nature of the final salary risk, and have accepted money-purchase benefits and the risks of private investment. The preference has also arisen, in some cases, from a desire to build up out of a company's gross income a reserve to enable a particular investment (such as a factory) to be purchased, albeit see below regarding the sole purpose requirement that the scheme provides retirement benefits (for which liquid assets must be available at the relevant ages).

These schemes are commonly referred to as 'SSAS' (small self-administered schemes). The Revenue issued a Memorandum on the subject, No 58 of February 1979. This has been replaced by Pt 20 of the practice notes IR 12 (incorporating the provisions of Memorandum 109 issued in August 1991).

Although Memorandum 58 laid down a uniform set of rules for this type of scheme, in law the Revenue were obliged, by reason of s 591, to consider applications to vary these rules on an individual basis. To reduce this administrative burden regulations were made under s 591(6), *viz* The Retirement Benefits Schemes (Restriction on Discretion to Approve) (Small Self-administered Schemes) Regulations 1991 (SI 1991 No 1614). Regulation 2 defines small self-administered scheme and the type of special trustee required by reg 9 (and, previously, by Memorandum 58) as follows:

'"scheme" means a retirement benefits scheme as defined in section 611(1) of the Act;
"small self-administered scheme" means a scheme—
- (*a*) some or all of the income and other assets of which are invested otherwise than in insurance policies, and
- (*b*) which, if a scheme member is connected with—
  - (i) another scheme member,
  - (ii) a trustee of the scheme, or
  - (iii) a person who is an employer in relation to the scheme, has less than 12 members;

"scheme member" in relation to a scheme means a member of the scheme to whom benefit is currently accruing as a result of service as an employee;'

The words 'connected with' in (*b*) are amplified by reg 2(3). The Revenue may also require a larger scheme to be treated as a small scheme if the additional members are in effect a make-weight to avoid the regs (para 20.1 of IR 12).

'"pensioneer trustee" means a trustee of a scheme who—
- (*a*) is approved by the Board to act as such, and
- (*b*) is not connected with—
  - (i) a scheme member,
  - (ii) any other trustee of the scheme, or
  - (iii) a person who is an employer in relation to the scheme.'

Although the foregoing definition 'pensioneer trustee' refers merely to a 'scheme', reg 3 which applies it refers to approval of a 'small self-administered scheme'. Regulation 3(*b*) prohibits approval where, save for transitional relief, the scheme documents do not contain the provisions described in regs 4 to 10. Regulation 9 requires one of the trustees to be a pensioneer trustee and provides for notification to the Revenue after it has ceased to act.

Paragraph (*a*) of the foregoing definition refers to Revenue approval. Paragraphs 20.4, 20.6 and 20.7 of IR 12 state the Revenue's long-established requirements:

'20.4 . . . A pensioneer trustee is an individual or body recognised by the Inland Revenue as being widely involved with occupational pension schemes and having dealings with the Pension Schemes Office, who has given an undertaking to that Office that he or she will not consent to any termination of a scheme of which he or she is trustee otherwise than in accordance with the approved terms of the winding-up rule.'

'20.6 The object of the appointment of a pensioneer trustee is to block any proposal that the trust should be terminated and the funds distributed among the members. It is, however, accepted that trustees have no power to resist such a proposal if all the persons having an interest under the trust are agreed in requiring this action (*Saunders v Vautier*, 1841). Such a consensus is unlikely in the context of a typical pension scheme where, even if the number of members is small, the existence of further contingent beneficiaries can rarely be excluded.'

'20.7 The trust provisions of an approved small self-administered scheme must be framed to allow the pensioneer trustee to fulfil his or her function. Thus a provision which allows trustees to act on majority rather than unanimous decisions must be qualified so as not to apply in relation to the termination of the scheme. A scheme subject to Scottish law must expressly require the pensioneer trustee's concurrence in any decision about the scheme's termination.'

Part 20 of IR 12 sets out requirements as to funding and benefits. However, it is in the area of investments (and borrowing and lending) that interest has arisen over the years. These areas are controlled by SI 1991 No 1614 whose practical effect is set out in paras 20.23 to 20.43 of the practice notes IR 12. There are transitional provisions relating to certain investments of existing approved small schemes (para 20.24). The acquisition of certain types of investment must be reported to the Revenue within 90 days (para 20.25). There is a general warning regarding tax avoidance and also regarding the 'sole purpose requirement' viz the provision of retirement benefits (para 20.26).

As stated above, reg 3(b) imports regs 4–10. Consumer chattels and (with certain exceptions) residential property may not be purchased (reg 5).

Loans to members are forbidden, and loans to employers are limited to a specified basis (reg 6). Further, during the first two years of a scheme's existence the total amounts lent to the employer (and the market value of any shares in the employer held within the scheme's fund) must not exceed 25 per cent of the value of the scheme's assets excluding received transfer values (reg 7).

After the first two years the limitation on the above loans and investments increases to 50 per cent, without the exclusion of transfer values (reg 7). There are provisions in reg 7 and reg 2(9) to include loans to bodies associated with the employer, and a warning about connected persons in para 20.27 of IR 12. Generally a rate of interest at least 3 per cent above base rate must be charged (para 20.31).

It should be remembered that 'small' schemes are no different in principle from any other scheme submitted for approval under s 591 of ICTA 1988 (see para 3 above). The usual type of trust instrument will be required (Chapters 3 and 13) and the usual rules relating to limitations on benefits (see para 3 above), as well in most cases as the special rules for 20 per cent directors (see para 7 above). Part 20 of IR 12 indicates the few areas where special provisions are actually required by the Revenue in the trust documents (eg in relation to winding up, full commutation of ill-health pensions etc).

Care should be taken over the power of appointment of new trustees (which should not be vested in the employer if a takeover is likely) and the trustees' powers of investment and borrowing. See Chapter 24, para 7.2 for the exemption from the member-nominated trusteeship requirements.

9 Payments to employers

There has always been a charge to tax on payments from an exempt approved pension scheme to the employer (Finance Act 1970, Sched 5, para 4 and its predecessors, now s 601(5) of ICTA 1988). However, the charge would (until 1986—see below) be offset by any tax losses brought forward. If an employer paid contributions in profitable years, the tax charge in those years would be reduced, and if moneys were recovered from the fund on a winding-up at a time when trading losses had been incurred, there would be an overall tax loss to the Revenue.

With certain exceptions, this situation was changed by the Finance Act 1986, Sched 12, now consolidated in ss 601 to 603 and Sched 22 of ICTA 1988, which provides for a free-standing tax charge of 40 per cent of any payment (unless winding up had commenced on or before 18 March 1986 etc.).

For excluded payments see The Pension Scheme Surpluses (Administration) Regulations 1987 (SI 1987 No 352), eg commercial loans to the employer, payments under a lien rule etc. In the author's experience the Revenue have treated discretionary lien payments in like manner as those which the administrator is obliged to make.

The tax does not apply where the employer is a charity or otherwise exempt from income or corporation tax s 601(3) and (4) nor does the charge under s 601(5) apply in such cases (see the last para of that subsection).

Payment includes a transfer of assets s 601(6).

The Pensions Act 1995 ss 37 and 76 contain sophisticated provisions, formerly in much simpler form in section 11(3) of the Social Security Act 1990, which prevent a payment to the employer until provision has been made for annual increases to pensions in payment in respect of pre-1997 accrual (Chapter 16, para 3 above). In the *Thrells* case cited in Chapter 16, para 10.6 it was held that power to award the increases (which was not present in the rules except for *prospective* pensioners) was derived from a combination of s 11(3) and the scheme rule providing for return of surplus to the employer—judgment on this issue, 5 June 1992, stated:

> 'Section 11(3) of the 1990 Act precludes the liquidator, who is claiming payment, from objecting to this application of funds to which otherwise he would be entitled.'

10 Taxation of surplus

Schedule 22 of ICTA 1988, mentioned in para 9 above, provides for the reduction of surplus within the pension scheme and for the taxation of income or gain derived from that surplus valued in accordance with The Pension Scheme Surpluses (Valuation) Regulations 1987 (SI 1987 No 412).

By para 2(1) of Sched 22, the Board of Inland Revenue may require the administrator of a scheme to produce either a certificate stating whether or not there is a surplus beyond a prescribed amount or a valuation in accordance with the prescribed principles. Where a surplus of more than 5 per cent (on the prescribed basis) is disclosed, then, unless further information is requested by the Revenue under para 4 of Sched 22, the administrator of the scheme must submit to the Revenue proposals for reducing the surplus (para 5(3)). The proposals must comprise one or more of the following:

(*a*) payment to an employer;
(*b*) suspension or reduction for up to five years of the employer's obligation to contribute to the scheme;
(*c*) similar suspension or reduction of the employees' contributions;
(*d*) improvement of benefits;
(*e*) provision of new benefits;
(*f*) such other ways as may be prescribed.

It is important to note that item (*a*) must leave a surplus of *at least* a prescribed minimum (para 3(2)(*b*))—being 5 per cent (SI 1987 No 412, reg 10(3) referring to para 6(2)(b) of Sched 12 to the Finance Act 1986, now re-enacted as the foregoing para 3(2)(b)—curiously only parts of reg 10, and none of the rest of the regs, have been updated to refer to the re-enactment).

The Inland Revenue's Memoranda 82 and 86 set out their requirements regarding the above and associated matters such as scheme mergers. Memorandum 82 states that where a scheme is being replaced by another scheme of the same employer, there will be no objection to a payment to the employer if there is surplus in excess of 5 per cent, and that failure to observe this requirement (which presumably means a payment where the surplus, on an ongoing basis, is less than 5 per cent) will normally prejudice approval of the replacement scheme (para 19(i)). However, it is understood that no prejudice occurs (where a lesser surplus remains) if the new scheme does not provide continuity of pensionable service; clearly this should be checked with the Revenue in the particular circumstances before any commitment to a payment and new scheme is made.

Schedule 22 does not include an enabling power to authorise the trustees to make payments to an employer or reduce surplus in any of the other permitted ways. Where there is insufficient power in the trust deed, it may be possible to apply to OPRA under s 69 of the Pensions Act 1995.

Paragraphs 6 and 7 of Sched 22 provide that where the administrator fails to carry out the proposals within a prescribed period, the Revenue may specify a loss of income and capital gains tax exemption on a proportion of the fund representing their estimate of surplus.

The taxation provisions of para 7 in themselves appear reasonable. However, in practice, the fluctuations of investment experience may give rise to taxation during a period of substantial investment returns, without recovery during a subsequent period of poor experience. While in theory trustees may not have the option simply of allowing surplus to give rise to tax, since paras 3 and 5 require the administrator to submit to the Revenue proposals for reducing the surplus, the Revenue do not appear to object to the absence of proposals and the acceptance of the tax charge. It does not appear that any sanction applies beyond the taxation provisions of para 7.

The intention to withhold approval of a replacement scheme, mentioned in para 19(i) of Memorandum 82, repeats the policy announcements of 1984 and 1985. It is possible that the court would declare the withholding of approval from a bona fide scheme to be an improper exercise of discretion. In most circumstances, however, it would not be right to establish a new scheme without the assurance of Inland Revenue approval, so that the question is more likely to be put to the courts on a merger with an existing scheme. Where an employer wishes to recover surplus from a scheme, it is more likely that this will occur through the winding-up of the scheme, and its replacement, than by reason of payment by the trustees to the employer from an ongoing scheme. Unless there is a power in the original trust deed, or OPRA makes a modification order, trustees of an ongoing scheme could rarely properly deplete the capital in their hands by payment to an employer. However, where the surplus cannot be applied to members' benefits without the agreement of the employer, there may be a bargaining position that would enable the trustees to part with some of the surplus (see final para of Chapter 24, para 10.3). This is a matter that will turn on the construction of each trust deed, albeit the opportunities for a payment from an ongoing scheme will remain rare.

11 Refund of surplus voluntary contributions

11.1 AVCs

Until the Finance Act 1989 the Revenue would not (with one exception) approve a rule permitting a refund of voluntary contributions, even when circumstances prevented the full application of the contributions for the benefit of the member or his dependants. The exception was where all the member's other contributions were refunded and no other benefits arose apart from guaranteed minimum pensions; this exception became of no practical significance when the qualifying period for preservation was reduced to two years (Chapter 10, para 1).

With effect from 6 April 1988 it became mandatory for approved schemes to include provision for the acceptance of members' voluntary contributions (now PSA 1993, s 111). Further, the Finance (No 2) Act 1987 provided for members to contribute for additional benefits, if they wished, to free-standing schemes, typically offered by insurance companies or building societies—now consolidated in ICTA 1988, s 591(2)(*h*). It became inevitable that constant monitoring of contributions and their investment yield would become impracticable. The Revenue therefore introduced a new regime in the Finance Act 1989, Sched 6, Pt III whereby if a surplus arose it could (and should) be repaid.

The provisions were applied automatically to then existing approved schemes—see Sched 6 paras 31(1), 32(1) and 33(1). For schemes not approved before 27 July 1989 a rule requiring excess voluntary contributions to be repaid to the member became a condition of approval.

Paragraph 33(1) of Sched 6 refers to a payment of a prescribed amount. The relevant regulations are SI 1993 No 3016. The 1991 edition of IR 12 (as subsequently updated) refers in paras 16.13 to 16.17.

The practice notes set out the tax position regarding a repayment, in paras 17.31 and 17.32. These refer to s 599A of ICTA 1988. As varied by Treasury Order, this provides for tax at 33 per cent (unless varied by Treasury Order) but for the member to be given a smaller tax credit, viz a credit of basic rate tax (currently 23 per cent) on the payment grossed up as if basic rate had been deducted. The differential between 33 per cent and basic rate is a broad assessment of the tax advantage gained by the investment of the surplus contributions in a tax-exempt fund. The section relates to payments made 'in pursuance of a duty to return surplus funds'. Presumably the word 'duty' is the cause of the Revenue requirement that new schemes contain a rule *requiring* surplus funds to be repaid, for otherwise tax would be assessed at 20 per cent.

The 33 per cent tax is charged on the scheme administrator (s 599A(2)). The practitioner should ensure that scheme rules provide for an equivalent amount to be deducted from the payment to the member.

The responsibility for calculating surplus will be that of the scheme administrator. If, however, the member has also paid contributions to Free-standing Additional Voluntary Contribution Scheme (FSAVCSs) (see para 11.2 below), paras 16.10–16.12 of the practice notes should be consulted.

If a member has died, any excess would be paid to his personal representatives.

11.2 FSAVCSs (generally)

FSAVCS is a standard Revenue abbreviation for Free-standing Additional Voluntary Contribution Scheme. Provision for approval of schemes to which the employer does not contribute was introduced by the Finance (No 2) Act 1987. The provision is now consolidated in s 591(2)(*h*) of the 1988 Act which confers on the Revenue discretion to approve a scheme:

> '(*h*) to which the employer is not a contributor and which provides benefits additional to those provided by a scheme to which he is a contributor'.

The purpose was to enable members to invest their monies with a provider of their choice. The Inland Revenue have stated (see below) that approval to a FSAVCS can be given only if it is established by one of the following:

- (*a*) an insurance company or authorised unit trust manager;
- (*b*) a building society;
- (*c*) a bank (in effect);
- (*d*) the trustees of an approved centralised scheme for non-associated employers (ie an industry-wide scheme such as those

established for non-associated water companies and electricity supply companies).

The Revenue requirements are contained in paras 16.10 and subsequently in the practice notes IR 12. These set out detailed provisions for checks to be made on the aggregate benefits provided by the free-standing schemes and the employer's scheme. Tax on repayment of surplus is levied at 33 per cent under s 599A of ICTA 1988 as described in para 11.1 above. For schemes approved before 27 July 1989, Pt III of Sched 6 cited in para 11.1 above applies. Paragraph 31(2) states that para 32 applies to an FSAVCS. The latter refers to abatement of benefits. Paragraph 33(2) refers to repayment of excess contributions. The relevant regs are SI 1993 No 3016.

Chapter 18

OPRA, Ombudsman, OPAS, former Occupational Pensions Board

1 Statutory provisions

OPRA was established by s 1 of the Pensions Act 1995. Its full name is Occupational Pensions Regulatory Authority. It is defined in the Act as 'the Authority', ss 1 and 124. OPRA has three broad functions: firstly to regulate compliance by trustees with various requirements of the Pensions Act 1995—(para 2 below); secondly to act as Registrar of Occupational and Personal Pension Schemes in succession to the OPB under SI 1997 No 371 (para 3 below); and thirdly to exercise the power conferred on it by s 69 of the Pensions Act 1995 to make modification orders for specified limited purposes where a pension scheme cannot otherwise be modified without undue complexity, or to wind them up—para 4 below. Section 1 provides for six members of the OPRA board, in addition to the chairman, to be appointed by reason of specified backgrounds. Schedule 1 in effect sets out the constitution of OPRA and provides for regulation of its proceedings.

The Pensions Ombudsman was established by the Social Security Act 1990, now PSA 1993 s 145. His functions go beyond investigation of maladministration and include disputes of fact and law—s 146. See para 5 below.

OPAS is the Occupational Pensions Advisory Service funded under PSA 1993, s 174.

The Occupational Pensions Board (OPB) was established by the Social Security Act 1973. By regulations introduced under the Social Security Act 1990 it was appointed registrar of occupational and personal pension schemes with effect from 1 January 1991. It was dissolved by the Pensions Act 1995, s 150, the Commencement Order having effect from 6 April 1997. From that date its functions, so far as they are continued, are split between the Contributions Agency of the DSS and OPRA (see para 7 below).

2 OPRA as regulator

2.1 Powers

OPRA's main regulatory powers, conferred by the following sections of the Pensions Act 1995, are:

(*a*) to prohibit, suspend or remove a person as trustee, with discretion to appoint a substitute—ss 3–9; throughout the Act failure by a trustee to carry out provisions is stated to be subject to s 3 ie to prohibition from being a trustee (which has the effect, by s 3(3), of removing the person);

(*b*) to require a person to pay a civil penalty of up to £5,000 in the case of an individual and £50,000 in the case of a corporate body (these figures being subject to increase by statutory instrument)—s 10;

(*c*) to apply to the Court for an injunction where there seems reasonable likelihood of misappropriation of assets of an occupational pension scheme or OPRA satisfies the Court that a particular person who has misused or misappropriated assets will continue or repeat the act—s 13;

(*d*) to disclose to the Director of Public Prosecutions information which presumably might lead to a prosecution (s 108(3)) and, it would appear, itself act as a prosecuting authority in respect of the small number of matters which are specified to be an offence—but see below regarding the unclear position regarding criminal prosecution.

By s 155, a new provision is inserted into the PSA 1993 whereby regulations may provide for the above s 10 penalty to be specified in respect of any regulation under the PSA 1993. The same section also inserts into the PSA 1993 a provision that any person who knowingly or recklessly provides the Registrar with false or misleading information is guilty of an offence, on summary conviction being liable to a fine and on indictment to imprisonment or a fine or both.

The powers of OPRA relate only to a breach of the clear statutory code, primarily the Pensions Act 1995 (with two exceptions) but also certain specified provisions of the PSA 1993.

Section 96 of the Pensions Act 1995 provides that OPRA may review its own determinations, but subject thereto they are final save on a point of law (which can be appealed to the High Court—s 97). Section 99 authorises an OPRA inspector, carrying out an investigation, to enter premises (at a reasonable time) and make enquiries.

2.2 Main supervised provisions

There is no single statement of OPRA's functions or the provisions that it supervises. However, its own published material draws attention to the following supervised provisions (and this can be confirmed from the penal provisions within them):

- (*a*) Scheme trusteeship requirements; ss 27–39 and 49–51 are mentioned, but there are numerous other provisions such as member-nominated trustees (for one example of the many sanctions, see s 21(1)), appointment of professional advisers (several provisions in s 47), whistle-blowing (several provisions in s 48) etc;
- (*b*) Minimum funding requirements (ss 56–61);
- (*c*) Breaches of requirements regarding surplus or excess assets on winding-up (eg s 76(7));
- (*d*) The new cash equivalent quotation requirements—PSA 1993 s 93A(4);
- (*e*) Registration requirements—PSA 1993, s 168(4);
- (*f*) Breach of the obligation to pay the levy—PSA 1993, s 175 (as amended), SI 1997 No 666, regs 4 and 13.

The supervisory functions appear not to extend to questions relating to equal treatment or indexation of pensions in payment (unless in either case the breach has led to under-funding sufficient to affect the minimum funding requirement or in some other way is material to the exercise by OPRA of one of its functions). The exclusion of these two items is to be found in ss 3(2)(*a*)(i) and 99(2)(*a*) of the Pensions Act 1995. The matter was debated during the passage of the Pensions Bill and resulted in a letter from the Minister to a noble Lord dated 14 February 1995 stating that it would not be OPRA's task to enforce trust law but rather to enforce *statutory* obligations aimed at ensuring that pension schemes were secure and appropriately funded (author's emphasis). The Pensions Ombudsman was to continue the task of settling disputes between members and administrators. Specifically, indexation would only arise under the Act, the Minister wrote, where scheme rules did not already provide for it, so that the inclusion of it within OPRA's powers would lead to the anomalous situation that members of some schemes could go to OPRA while others would go elsewhere, described by the Minister as not an acceptable situation. After describing certain other provisions, he wrote that the position of equal treatment was much the same as that of indexation. The Government believed that the arrangements for industrial tribunals to handle disputes on equal treatment, and the fact that the Pensions Ombudsman might also investigate such disputes, provided adequate safeguards. (Nonetheless, see the concluding paragraph of 2.3).

OPRA has announced that it will have close working arrangements with the Ombudsman and OPAS.

2.3 Whistle-blowing

While OPRA is able to initiate an investigation, it will on the whole rely on information received. For that purpose, s 48 (labelled 'Blowing the whistle') of the Pensions Act 1995 requires the auditor or actuary of any occupational pension scheme to report 'immediately' to OPRA any matter where he has reasonable cause to believe that there has been a breach by the trustees, the employer, any professional adviser or any prescribed person, of any duty which is likely to be of material significance in the exercise by OPRA of any of its functions. There is also an option for any other professional adviser, any trustee or any other person involved in the administration of the scheme to report any such matter to OPRA; any duty of privilege is raised except in the case of the duty of confidentiality owed by a legal adviser to the extent that legal professional privilege would entitle him to refuse to produce a document to the court.

In Chapter 16, para 17.3 the trustees' whistle-blowing duty under s 59 has also been mentioned. Whereas the latter is an obligation to give notice within a prescribed period (30 days—SI 1996 No 1536, reg 23) the obligation upon the auditor and actuary under s 48 is to give notice immediately.

OPRA published its guidance on whistle-blowing on 25 March 1997, ref ON1, entitled 'Section 48: Reporting to OPRA'. It identified in its accompanying press release a number of key features, from which the following is a selection:

(1) OPRA would *always* (their emphasis) wish to be informed of rule breaches that carry a criminal penalty or which may threaten the security of pension fund assets.
(2) OPRA would not normally need to be told of isolated and inconsequential errors which have already been corrected, *unless* (their emphasis) in the professional judgment of the actuary or auditor such matters indicate that the trustees are not administering the scheme properly.
(3) OPRA does not want to be told about *suspicions*. The professional adviser should establish that there is *substance* to the matter (their emphases).
(4) It is for the pension scheme actuaries and auditors to use their professional judgment in assessing whether to report a particular matter. OPRA considers that these professional advisers are well placed to alert the regulator to those issues which need immediate attention.

It seems to the author that the advisers are better protected by looking at the Act and recording on their own file why they do not consider a breach to fall within s48(1)(b). However, paragraphs 6.7 and 6.8 of the guidance give helpful examples of both the general approach and matters that OPRA would not normally expect to be reported.

Section 13 and Appendix D of the guidance set out practical procedures for making reports, and also for obtaining from OPRA informal telephone advice.

2.4 Prosecuting authority

The Act does not specify many criminal offences but where it does, it simply indicates that a person in breach is 'guilty of an offence and liable on summary conviction . . . [and on conviction on indictment . . .]' or other similar text. Regulations on OPRA's' procedures for its own determinations are set out in SI 1997 No 794, but these do not relate to criminal prosecutions. It appears from background information that OPRA is to be the criminal prosecuting authority. Unlike other regulatory statutes, there appears to be no provision in the Pensions Act for the Secretary of State to prosecute or delegate.

Specimens of provisions in the Act providing for criminal prosecution are s 31(4) (a trustee, in breach of s 31, who reimburses himself out of the assets of the scheme in respect of a civil penalty imposed by OPRA), s 28 (a person acting as auditor or actuary when connected with a trustee) s 40(5) (a trustee or manager who agrees in a decision to make an employer-related investment in excess of the prescribed limits), s 49(8) (an employer who fails to pay over employees' contributions within a prescribed period), ss 98 and 101 (various provisions regarding withholding or destroying information etc). Other provisions are to be found in the Act (or in regulations eg regarding the withholding of information to the Registrar), and are listed in Appendix B to the note ON1 cited in 2.3 above.

Nonetheless, criminal prosecution is not a sanction for the probable inadvertent offences, nor is it likely to be OPRA's chosen course since the standard of proof would be higher.

OPRA can be contacted at the following address:

OPRA
Invicta House
Trafalgar Place
Brighton
East Sussex
BN1 4DW
Tel: (01273 627600)

3 OPRA as Registrar

OPRA has taken over the Registry from the OPB on the latter's dissolution—para 1 above. Its address as Registrar is:

Pension Schemes Registry
PO Box 1NN
Newcastle upon Tyne
NE99 1NN
Tel: (0191) 225 6393

The authority for the Registrar is delegated to the Secretary of State by what is now the PSA 1993, s 6. The original provisions SI 1990 No 2278 have been revoked and replaced by SI 1997 No 371. Indirectly, through the definition 'registrable scheme' the regs apply only to tax-approved (or pending) schemes (including personal pension schemes) established in the UK or having a representative akin to a trustee in the UK, or a public service pension scheme—and in either case excluding one-member and death benefit only schemes. The obscure type of scheme approved under s 591(2)(*g*) of the Taxes Act (ICTA 1988) (a form of occupational grouped annuity contract) is excluded.

The registrable information is very simple, comprising mainly the name and address of the scheme and its trustees and administrators, some basic details relating to it, any reference number assigned to it by the Inland Revenue, whether it is open, closed or frozen, whether money purchase or not and whether insured or not.

By reg 4, trustees must provide the Registrar with the above information within three months of the scheme becoming registrable, which for a new scheme is likely to mean within three months of application to the Inland Revenue for approval. The reg also provides for the Registrar to issue a notice requiring information.

Regulation 5 provides for notification to the Registrar of any change in the information already provided, within 12 months of the occurrence of that change. As the register existed before the current regulations, the alternative expiry date, if later, is 12 months from the coming into force of those regs. However, by reg 8, certain information has to be provided by 30 June 1997. Failure to comply with these duties is an offence liable to summary conviction, but separately OPRA may require a financial penalty if information supplied *by* the registrar to anyone is used for the purposes of marketing a product or service.

Regulation 6 enables access to the register by a number of interested parties, viz beneficiaries or prospective beneficiaries under a scheme (or any person acting on their behalf), the Pensions Ombudsman, an insolvency practitioner, the trustees themselves to check the information regarding their own scheme, the Pensions Compensation Board etc.

3.1 Costs—levy

The PSA 1993, s 175, provides for the imposition of levies on occupational and personal pension schemes. The provision commenced in 1990, and has been expanded by the Pensions Act 1995. Levies may be raised for the purpose of meeting expenditure by or for:

(*a*) the registrar;
(*b*) the Pensions Ombudsman;
(*c*) any body to whom OPRA makes grants under PSA 1993, s 174 (formerly grants by the OPB)—in practice to OPAS—para 6 below:
(*d*) OPRA, including the costs of its establishment;
(*e*) the Pensions Compensation Board, not necessarily at the same times and rates as the main levy.

Interestingly, by s 175(3), the levy is offset by moneys collected by OPRA under s 168(4) for breaches of the PSA 1993, and by penalties collected by OPRA under s 10 of the Pensions Act 1995.

The levy is set by SI 1997 No 666, on a sliding scale ranging from a maximum annual amount of approx £1 per member for small schemes (or a total of £8.75 for less than 12 members) to 30p per member for very large schemes. These figures relate to the general levy. A maximum annual compensation levy is set at 23p per member, although the actual rate will be set by the Pensions Compensation Board. Personal pension schemes do not pay the compensation levy as they are not in the compensation scheme, and have a lower general levy as they are not subject to OPRA jurisdiction (albeit they probably have a much higher internal FSA 1986 compliance cost).

4 OPRA's powers to wind up or to modify

4.1 General

The Pensions Act 1995 confers on OPRA a wide ranging power to wind up schemes, and fairly limited powers to modify them—ss 11 and 69.

With one exception, the powers do not relate to public service schemes (but in respect of these, identical powers are conferred on the appropriate Minister or government department—ss 12 and 72). The interesting exception is s 11(7) which provides that OPRA can wind up a public service scheme if it is necessary to protect the interests of members—by s 11(1)(*c*) this power applies to occupational schemes generally.

Apart from this provision of s 11(1)(*c*), the powers are all exercisable on the application of specified persons, primarily the trustees, and are intended to be of assistance where the scheme itself contains insufficient powers. They replace similar but—apart from s 11—rather more extensive powers of the former Occupational Pensions Board (see para 7 below). The powers are not needed where the scheme itself contains adequate powers to modify or wind up.

4.2 Winding-up order

Section 11 confers on OPRA an extensive power to direct or authorise an occupational pension scheme to be wound up if satisfied that:

> '(*a*) the scheme, or any part of it, ought to be replaced by a different scheme,
> (*b*) the scheme is no longer required, or
> (*c*) it is necessary in order to protect the interests of the generality of the members of the scheme that it be wound up.'

The powers in (*a*) and (*b*) are similar to those conferred on the former OPB in the now repealed PSA 1993, s 142 and its predecessor in the Social Security Act 1973, but in both those cases the power arose 'having regard to [the provisions of the Social Security legislation]' and was interpreted by the OPB to mean that it was 'desirable as a result of social security legislation' that the scheme be replaced or terminated.

In the author's view, s 11 will be construed without reference to the former legislation. The word 'ought' in s 11(1)(*a*) opens the door to a very wide power, particularly as it can apply to *part* of a scheme.

Para (*c*) above is a very wide power. Possibly it is designed to meet a situation such as the *Kestrel Pension Scheme* that has been described in Chapter 16, para 7. Interestingly, the writ issued by the OPB did not seek an order to wind up that scheme, but an inquiry as to whether trust property had been misappropriated. The court appointed a receiver of the trust assets and, with the consent of the OPB, substituted a beneficiary as plaintiff.

As before, (*a*) and (*b*) only arise if the winding-up cannot be achieved another way or only by unduly complex etc procedures, and where it is reasonable to make the order—s 11(2).

An order under (*a*) or (*b*) may only be made on the application of the trustees or managers, some other person that has the power of alteration or the employer—s 11(3). By contrast, para (c) can presumably arise if OPRA of its own accord considers it appropriate, or members apply.

Regarding public service schemes, see para 4.1 above.

4.3 Modification order

Section 69 confers on OPRA, on an *application* made to them, a power to modify an occupational pension scheme (but for a public service scheme see para 4.1 above) or authorise its modification for any of the following purposes:

(*a*) to reduce or eliminate surplus where an Inland Revenue requirement arises for a proposal—subject to meeting any requirements of s 37(4) and SI 1996 No 2156, reg 11, where payment to an employer is contemplated (these include provision for annual pension increases, for notice to members and for the trustees to be satisfied that the proposed payment is in the interests of the members);

(*b*) where a tax-approved scheme is being wound up, to enable payments to the employer, subject to similar safeguards to (*a*) above—reg 11(*b*);

(*c*) to enable the scheme to meet contracting out requirements during a prescribed period.

Application to OPRA for an order can be made by the trustees in any of the three cases, and in (*c*) also by the manager, the employer or anyone else having the power of alteration.

As before, (*a*) and (*b*) only arise if the winding up cannot be achieved another way or only by unduly complex etc procedures, and where it is reasonable to make the order—s 70.

An order may be retrospective—s 71. The order can, in theory, avoid consents needed by a scheme rule—ss 70(1)(*b*)(ii) and 71(3)(*b*)—but where a payment to the employer is contemplated SI 1996 No 2156 regs 4 and 7 require two notices to members (effectively a six month route) and, by reg 11, that the second notice advises the member (in effect) of the application to OPRA, presumably so that representations can be made.

In practice applications to OPRA are likely to be rare, and limited to cases where a large surplus has built up in a final salary pension scheme that still has a continuing purpose but can support both a payment to the employer and a significant improvement to benefits while retaining sufficient surplus to meet the possibility of purchasing annuities on winding up. Possibly other meritorious situations will arise but not with any frequency. The reference to purchase of annuities is speculative but it should be remembered that the statutory minimum funding requirement (Chapter 16, para 17) will not necessarily be sufficient to purchase annuities and that the possibility of a winding-up is likely to be a factor in OPRA's consideration of an application.

5 Pensions ombudsman

In para 1 above, it is mentioned that the Pensions Ombudsman was established in 1990 and that his functions go beyond the investigation of maladministration. The background is that a simple and cheap method for a scheme member to bring a complaint was required, and the Government of the day rejected the idea of a Pensions Tribunal. The Ombudsman is in effect a one-man tribunal, with just the one office. Nonetheless he has a certain number of staff and handles a considerable through-flow of cases. His report to 31 March 1996 indicated a staff of 20, and 401 complaints cleared in the preceding 12 months, a further 353 in progress and 300 more awaiting commencement. Since the Ombudsman's jurisdiction is exceedingly wide, trustees and employers may consider initiating proceedings in the courts where they apprehend that an individual is about to make an application to the Ombudsman, if they consider that the Courts will provide a more appropriate forum—see below.

By the PSA 1993, s 146, the Ombudsman may investigate and determine the following complaints and disputes:

(*a*) a complaint by an actual or potential beneficiary who alleges that he has sustained injustice in consequence of maladministration . . . [by] a person responsible for the management of the scheme;

(*b*) a complaint, by trustees or managers, in relation to the maladministration of another scheme;

(*c*) any dispute of fact or law arising in relation to an occupational or personal pension scheme between the administrators and an actual or potential beneficiary;

(*d*) any dispute of fact or law between the trustees or managers and *another* scheme.

The relevant regs are SI 1991 No 588 (as amended up to and including SI 1996 No 1271) SI 1995 No 1053 (as amended by SI 1996 No 2638) and SI 1993 No 1978. The latter enable a direction by the Pensions Ombudsman for the payment of money to be enforced by an applicant through the County Court.

SI 1991 No 588 comprises the following important provisions:

(*a*) an extension of the Ombudsman's jurisdiction (in relation to pension schemes) to complaints or disputes involving an employer or administrator—regs 2 and 2A;
(*b*) an exclusion from his jurisdiction of complaints that come under the aegis of other regulatory organisations eg under the Financial Services Act 1986;
(*c*) a provision for time limits subject to authority for the Ombudsman to extend the period (three years from the act or omission complained of or from the earliest date on which the complainant knew or ought reasonably to have known of it) if 'it was not reasonably practicable for a complaint or dispute to be made' within the period, and the Ombudsman considers the extension reasonable.

There is a complex but important relationship between ss 146(6) and 148. The former provides that the Ombudsman shall not investigate a complaint if before the complaint was made proceedings had been begun in any court in respect of the same subject matter. Section 148 deals with the opposite situation, viz where proceedings are begun in a court after a matter has been referred to the Ombudsman. The defendant may, after acknowledgment of service but *before* taking any substantive steps, apply for an order to stay the proceedings; the court may make the order (to stay the proceedings) if it is satisfied:

(*a*) that there is no sufficient reason why the matter should not be investigated by the Pensions Ombudsman; and
(*b*) that the person applying for the stay was at the time when the legal proceedings were commenced, and still remains, ready and willing to do all things necessary to the proper conduct of the investigation [by the Ombudsman].

The provision for applying for a stay before taking any substantive steps is of significant importance to the practitioner who will need to advise at the outset whether such application should be made.

Similarly, if a practitioner is informed that there are circumstances where in all likelihood an application will be made to the Ombudsman, he will need to advise whether the trustees or the employer should first apply to the court to determine a dispute of fact or law in order, under s 146(6), that the matter be heard in court rather than before the Ombudsman. This might be particularly important where the nature of the complaint relates to matters affecting numerous other members and is more appropriately argued under the full procedures of a court action. If it is decided to wait, it may later be appropriate to ask the Ombudsman himself (but it appears that the cannot be compelled) to refer a question of law to the High Court (or in Scotland the Court of Session) under s 150(7), which does not however include questions of fact. Similarly, under s 151 (3) and (4) a determination by the Ombudsman is binding save that an appeal on a point of law lies to the High Court.

The Ombudsman has power to order a remedy that is equally applicable to other scheme members who can thereby benefit—*Hillsdown Holdings v Pensions Ombudsman* [1997] 1 All ER 862 QBD. Regarding the extent of his jurisdiction in two other respects, *viz* redundancy payments that operate as additions to pension, and compensation for distress, see *Westminster City Council v Haywood* [1996] 2 All ER 467, albeit partly reversed on appeal (to be reported), and likely to be further appealed to the House of Lords.

The Ombudsman has determined many well-publicised cases relating to matters of law, the effect of which is probably to raise the awareness of pension scheme members of their right to take advantage of the very simple procedure for initiating a complaint.

The Pensions Ombudsman's address is:

11 Belgrave Road
London
SW1V 1RB
Tel: 0171 834 9144

6 OPAS

The Occupational Pensions Advisory Service (OPAS) is a necessary adjunct to the Ombudsman's function, notwithstanding that it is constitutionally entirely separate. It was originally a charity which brought together a number of nationwide voluntary advisers. In due course it came to be funded by grant from the OPB under powers introduced by statute in 1990. It is now funded by grant from OPRA under PSA 1993, s 174, as amended. The section authorises grants to any person or body of persons 'providing advice or assistance, or carrying out other prescribed functions, in connection with occupational or personal pensions'. OPAS receives over 30,000 applications a year, which rapidly reduce to 8,000 requiring investigation. It functions from the same address as the Pensions Ombudsman but on a separate telephone line 0171–233 8080.

The overwhelming majority of cases referred to OPAS arise by reason of inefficiency rather than malevolence. Pension schemes for small- and medium-sized companies are often run by executives with other primary functions. Calculations may be overlooked or appear too burdensome for initial reply. OPAS reports indicate that a letter from an OPAS adviser very often results in action and the provision of appropriate information for the applicant.

The Ombudsman refers applicants to OPAS for initial advice. OPAS also receives references from Citizens Advice Bureaux as well as directly from the public.

7 The former Occupational Pensions Board

As stated above, the OPB was established in 1973 and dissolved in 1997. Its functions, so far as they are continued, are split between the Contributions Agency of the DSS and OPRA.

Until its dissolution, the OPB had numerous statutory functions including the following:

(*a*) to advise on compliance with the 'preservation' and other regulations protecting early leavers (Chapter 10);

(*b*) to advise on compliance with the 'equal access' regulations regarding membership for men and women (repealed);

(*c*) where a scheme was to be contracted out of the State scheme, to grant the necessary certificate (Chapter 2, para 9.3; Chapter 3, para 12 and Chapter 20, para 4);

(*d*) to modify or enable the modification of schemes for any of the purposes specified in s 64 of the Social Security Act 1973 (compare OPRA's powers—para 4.1 above);

(*e*) to act as Registrar of Occupational and Personal Pensions Schemes;
(*f*) to report to the Secretary of State (Department of Social Security or 'DSS') on matters submitted to it and also in any event annually.

The OPB was always highly regarded. Its advisory function under (*a*) above was valuable, and its reports under (*f*) above were professionally highly competent. It was never intended, however, to be a regulator and was therefore deemed superfluous under the Pensions Act 1995.

Its powers of modification under (*d*) above were similar to those of OPRA (para 4 above) but additionally could enable a scheme to write in a number of provisions that were applicable under overriding legislation. These included transfer rights, equal treatment for eligibility purposes, compliance with the voluntary contribution requirements etc. Similar (but different) enabling powers are now conferred directly on the trustees of a scheme by the Pensions Act 1995, s 68 (see Chapter 21, para 4).

For a historical survey of the OPB's activities, see its final report, published March 1997.

Chapter 19

The old state graduated pension scheme

1 Origin

An earnings-related addition to the State flat-rate pension was introduced in 1961 (the consolidated provisions being subsequently set out in the National Insurance Act 1965—see ss 4, 36 and 37 of that Act). The arrangement was generally known as the Graduated Pension Scheme, although it had occasionally been referred to, after the Minister who sponsored it, as the Boyd-Carpenter scheme.

The method of assessing contribution and calculating benefits was similar to the 'average salary' type described in Chapter 8, para 5.

2 Termination

The level of contributions and the salary ceiling above which they did not increase were both low. The combined effect of the low contribution rates and inflation (Chapter 8, para 5) was to render the prospective benefits of little value.

The scheme was closed to further contributions on 5 April 1975 (Social Security Act 1973, Sched 28, Pt I).

It had been intended to replace the scheme with a new State earnings-related arrangement, as set out in the Social Security Act 1973, but on the change of government in 1974 it was decided to defer the introduction of the replacement until 1977 (later to become 1978) in order to improve its benefit structure—see Chapter 20).

3 Contracting out—EPBs

Where an occupational pension scheme guaranteed adequate benefits, known as 'equivalent pension benefits' (EPBs), employments of its members could be 'contracted out' (the same term as now used in connection with the current State scheme) of part of the graduated scheme (National Insurance Act 1965, ss 56 and 57). This enabled the employer and employees to pay lower national insurance contributions. Originally graduated contributions were not payable at all in respect of contracted-out employments but by the National Insurance Act 1966, s 1, they became so payable, but at a lower than standard rate. Since the majority of private schemes provided greater benefits than the required minimum, many introduced the necessary rule to enable a certificate of non-participation to be issued (by the Registrar of Non-Participating Employments—see 1965 Act, ss 56(5), 73(1) and 74(1)(*a*)).

The practitioner will therefore come across many schemes which contain an obscure rule, usually running to several paragraphs, referring to the above-mentioned expressions, to 'payment in lieu' (PIL) (a means of buying back into the State scheme—see 1965 Act, s 58) and to the National Insurance Act 1961 or 1965. Where payments in lieu were not made, individual certificates of assurance were issued by 5 April 1980 to each employee in respect of the equivalent pension benefits.

Bulk payment of a PIL was unattractive in many cases for two reasons:

(*a*) a substantial cash sum might be required;
(*b*) benefits might be duplicated.

Regarding (*b*), the effect of the preservation requirements (Chapter 10, para 1) is that most employees leaving service after 5 April 1980 who had been contracted out of the graduated arrangement (and thus in service before 6 April 1975) will be entitled to a deferred pension. If a PIL had been paid, unless the scheme rules provided that retirement pensions and deferred pensions were to be reduced by the amount of the benefit purchased by the PIL, the benefit would still have to be provided within the scheme. Any such reduction might well have been difficult and costly to explain as employees' recollection of the graduated arrangement became dimmer.

The PIL did have the advantage to the employee that the State would increase accrued rights in the graduated scheme in accordance with the retail prices index from April 1978. In absolute terms, however, the pension entitlement is likely to be very small.

4 Removal of restriction on commutation (and tax position)

During the currency of the graduated scheme, equivalent pension benefits had to be expressed to be non-commutable and non-assignable (National Insurance Act 1965, s 57(1)(*b*)). The latter requirement was already contained in rules approved by the Inland Revenue but the former became a nuisance in cases where the total pension was so small (ie below £39 per annum for old code schemes and £52 per annum, later increased in steps to £260 per annum, for new code schemes, as defined in Chapter 17) or the retiring member was in such serious ill-health that the Revenue would have permitted complete commutation, ie the discharge of liability by payment of a single lump sum.

There are a large number of such trivial pensions arising, for example, as a residue in respect of transfers to schemes not containing the necessary contracting-out rule (so that a small part of the fund, relating to the equivalent pension benefits, had to be retained by the transferor scheme). The official view (which is now generally accepted) is that such a pension can be commuted with the member's consent once a scheme has 'settled' its obligations by issue of 'certificates of assurance' (as mentioned in para 3 above) since s 57(1)(*b*) (referred to above) will have ceased to have effect.

If it is decided to commute such trivial pensions, ie assuming that no other pension arises in the scheme, no problem arises from the preservation requirements as these currently contain the same reference to £260 per annum. It may be necessary to change the rules of the scheme, as they will contain a prohibition on the commutation of the equivalent pension benefits. If the Revenue confirm that approval is not prejudiced, it may be possible (particularly on winding up a solvent scheme) to dispense with the introduction of an amending rule if the relevant members consent to the commutation.

A contracted-out scheme is likely to be an approved scheme, ie Revenue approved, whether under old or new code. It would normally follow that pensions already in payment may not be commuted (see Chapter 17, para 3.6). However, in Memorandum 53 of May 1978 the Revenue lifted this restriction in respect of trivial equivalent pension benefits provided that they did not exceed £52 per annum at date of commutation, subject to there being inserted a suitable power in the scheme rules and to the commutation being effected immediately after the change of rule. The Revenue practice notes, IR 12 (1991), provide in para 8.12 that a pension already in payment may be commuted for triviality in the following circumstances:

(*a*) on the occasion of any increase in the measure of a trivial pension [if within the new limit but not the old];
(*b*) in two circumstances where a scheme contracted out [of the current State scheme] pays pension of less than £260.

The normal provisions apply as to tax on the lump sum arising from commutation. Where the sum is within the normal rules of the scheme and the general Revenue limits (Chapter 17, para 3) no tax is payable (this being the general, and indeed the Revenue's interpretation of what is now s 599 of the Income and Corporation Taxes Act 1988). Where these limits are exceeded (and the whole pension is commuted on grounds of triviality or ill health) the excess is taxable—s 599(1)—but only, it appears, in respect of an employee's (interpreted as former employee's) pension and not that of a surviving dependant. The administrator (see Chapter 17, para 1.4) is chargeable to tax—s 599(3). The current rate of tax is 20 per cent under s 599(3) referring to s 598(2) and (3). However, if the rules of the scheme have not been altered to authorise the commutation the administrator will not be chargeable but the employee (or former employee), whether or not he is the recipient, will be chargeable under Schedule E for the year of assessment in which the payment is made—s 600. Commuted ill health pensions appear not to be taxable when a guaranteed minimum pension (GMP) is preserved (under the current State scheme)—para 17.25 and footnote of para 17.26 of IR 12 (1991).

5 Transfers between schemes

The normal 'transfer' situation arises when an employee leaves service (either voluntarily or, inter alia, on the sale of an undertaking) and joins the pension scheme of another employer. In that situation the former scheme will have 'assured' the benefits arising from contracted-out service under the graduated arrangement and issued the relevant certificate. Thereafter, there is no prohibition on transfer of the rights to which that certificate relates, although there was much discussion as to whether an effective transfer could be made.

The Minister of State commented on this (by letter of 14 January 1976 to the relevant committee chairman of the National Association of Pensions Funds) as follows:

> 'As to the status of the certificate of assurance, its legal significance has not changed. A valid certificate serves to remove the employer's liability for making a payment in lieu to the National Insurance Fund and is evidence of the employee's rights in the occupational scheme. But it does not itself confer those rights . . .; but once a valid certificate has been issued in relation to rights which the employee enjoys in a particular scheme, it is a matter between the employee and the respective scheme authorities whether those rights are transferred to another scheme.'

Clearly, it is essential to ensure that there is a valid power of transfer (with, where relevant, a record of the employee's consent). However, to ensure that the DSS were aware of the transfer and would not (as it then appeared) at a future date expect payment to be made by the transferor scheme, details were to be sent to DSS, NPE Group, Newcastle upon Tyne, NE98 1YX of the name of the employee, his national insurance number and the name and address of the transferee scheme. Currently practitioners have been informed by DSS that they no longer require or desire this information.

Chapter 20

Brief outline of present State pension scheme

The present structure of State pension benefits comprising a basic pension plus an additional pension known as SERPS (see para 2 below) derives from the Social Security Act 1975 and the Social Security Pensions Act 1975 (both now almost entirely re-enacted—see below) which introduced a new scheme that began on 6 April 1978. The Social Security Act 1986 altered the scheme substantially with effect from 6 April 1988, and other changes have subsequently been made.

There was previously a small graduated pension dependent on each individual's earnings, but this ceased to accrue in 1975 (see Chapter 19).

The following summary of the State scheme may be useful. A few notes are also included on some of the more common questions which are not easily answered from leaflets published by the Department of Social Security.

The Social Security Act 1975 as amended, together with other legislation, has been re-enacted in the Social Security Contributions and Benefits Act 1992, in this Chapter referred to as the 1992 Act. The Social Security Pensions Act 1975 was partly included in that consolidation but its provisions relating to occupational schemes are now to be found in the PSA 1993 (as amended by the Pensions Act 1995). Equalisation of State pension ages is to be introduced progressively—para 15 below).

1 Flat-rate pension (the basic pension)

A person who has a complete national insurance contributions record on attaining state pensionable age (65 for men, 60 for women, but shading in to 65 between the years 2010 and 2020—1992 Act s 122 and Pensions Act 1995, s 126) becomes entitled to a flat-rate pension (1992 Act, s 44). The amount in April 1997 was £62.45 per week for a single person without dependants. For a married male earner, where the wife does not have a contribution record of her own, and there are no other dependants, the amount was £99.80 per week.

Where the pensioner has an incomplete record, because of periods of unemployment, service overseas, full-time studies (for which credit is not always given) or other reasons, the pension may be reduced, according to the extent to which the record is incomplete (1992 Act, Sched 3, Pt 1, para 5). There are special arrangements under which persons whose domestic duties prevent them from taking up regular employment can receive up to 20 years' contribution credit (principal Act, Sched 3, para 5(7)).

The basic pension was originally called the basic component, the change of title being enacted by the Social Security Act 1986, s 18(1).

2 Additional pension (SERPS)

The State scheme provides an additional, earnings-related pension (1992 Act, s 44 (3)) colloquially known as SERPS. It depends upon remuneration earned after 5 April 1978 (ss 44(7) and 45). Earlier years do not count towards this additional pension.

The intention was that a person in receipt of a low income, who could barely subsist on that income, should continue to receive it in full in retirement. Hence, in effect, remuneration up to a lower earnings limit (in April 1997 £62 per week) is 100 per cent pensionable. The band of earnings above that level (to an upper earnings limit which is normally seven times that level) earns pension which, after 20 years of the new scheme, will equal 25 per cent (*but for later years see below*) of the average of that band, each year's band being revalued in line with the national average rise in wages. This is expressed as earning 1.25 per cent (or one-eightieth) of revalued upper band earnings for the best 20 years of a person's contribution record, starting on 6 April 1978. As a result of changes introduced in 1986 the accrual rate is reduced for persons attaining State pensionable age after 5 April 2000; the figures 25 per cent and 1.25 per cent (or one-eightieth) mentioned above are reduced to 20 per cent and 1 per cent (one-hundredth) respectively subject to phasing-in over the period to 5 April 2009 (1992 Act, s 45(3)).

For persons attaining State pensionable age after 5 April 1999 the SERPS pension will be based on the average lifetime earnings (revalued) rather than the average of the best 20 years (subject to special protection for women and others with breaks in their employment).

Some pension schemes which are not contracted out of the additional State scheme (see para 4 below) calculate pension in such a way as to offset or partially offset this additional component either by reducing their own pension fraction from, say, sixtieths to hundredths or introducing a deduction of eightieths of upper band earnings (or a smaller fraction for persons more than 20 years below State pension age in 1978). Such modifications relate only to service after 5 April 1978 so that pension based on service up to that date is not affected. The modification enables the scheme contribution rate to be reduced (to compensate for the additional national insurance contributions described in para 3 below).

The widow of a pensioner who had qualified for an additional pension (and who dies before 6 April 2000—*see below*) will receive from the State the full amount of that additional pension after his death (as well as her flat-rate widow's pension—see s 50(3) of the 1992 Act). There are a number of refinements (for death below pensionable age, or cessation of widow's pension in certain circumstances etc). Since these refinements affect the provision which must be made from a contracted-out scheme, some are mentioned in para 4 below.

Where a married person dies after 5 April 2000 a widow or widower will inherit only half the deceased's additional pension rather than the full amount (1992 Act, ss 50(5) and 51(3)).

3 Contributions

National Insurance contributions often appear baffling, principally for three reasons:

(1) The total amount raised each year is assessed in respect of current earners but depends upon actual benefits paid out in that year, ie it bears no relation to the accrual of future benefits for those earners—the system being known as Pay-As-You-Go.

(2) For earners whose employment is contracted out of the State scheme (see para 4 below) contributions are reduced by an amount that *is* assessed broadly on the reduction in accrual of their future State benefits.
(3) For budgetary reasons, quite unconnected with the pension scheme, a surcharge has from time to time been added to the employers' contributions.

Contributions by both employers and employees apply up to the upper earnings limit. Where the employment is contracted-out, the amount exceeding the lower earnings limit (confusingly known as 'upper band earnings') is reduced as mentioned in (2) above.

Since October 1985, employers have been required to pay contributions on earnings above the upper earnings limit, although employees do not do so and the earnings above that limit do not count towards State benefits. The employer's contributions above the upper earnings limit are at the full rate regardless of whether or not the earner is in contracted-out employment. The contributions above the upper earnings limit are in effect a tax and since no benefits accrue in respect of them it is not surprising that the rate is the same for both categories of employment.

The reduced rate applicable to upper band earnings in respect of contracted-out employment is shown in the table in para 4.3 below.

National Insurance contributions cease to be payable by an employed person (but not his employer) at pensionable age (see para 1 above)—s 6(2) of the 1992 Act.

4 Contracting out

4.1 Reasons for introduction

The 1974 White Paper that introduced the new scheme stated that by 1971 over 60 per cent of members of private schemes, as well as almost all members of schemes operated by nationalised industries, were covered by a final salary basis of pension (Chapter 8, para 1) and almost all of these were earning pensions of at least one-eightieth of pensionable salary (which may, of course be somewhat less than actual salary) for each year of pensionable service.

It was therefore decided (despite all the other complications that would thereby be introduced) to permit such schemes to contract out of part of the State scheme.

The correct reference should be to a scheme contracted out in relation to an earner's employment (PSA 1993, s 7(3)), but since most schemes provide that either all or none of their members shall be contracted out, it is convenient to refer to the scheme as being contracted out; the Act uses the term 'contracted out' as indicating the inclusion of the scheme in a contracting-out certificate relating to an employment, and refers throughout to a scheme being contracted out (eg, s 12).

The substantial changes to the State scheme outlined in para 2 above were introduced by the Social Security Act 1986. They did not alter the basic contracting-out procedures although the benefits to be provided by a contracted-out scheme (see para 4.2 below) have been substantially altered.

The Pensions Act 1995 radically altered the requirements for a Contracted-Out Salary Related scheme (COSR). The accrual of guaranteed minimum pensions (GMPs) was terminated as at 5 April 1997, subsequent accrual being measured against a 'reference' scheme. The reason was the need to meet European requirements for equal treatment; GMPs were payable from State pensionable age which will not be fully equalised until the year 2020. GMPs were therefore inherently unequal. (The Government has offered no legislative assistance regarding the pre-1997 inequality which may, as respects service from the date of the judgment is 17 May 1990 *Barber*, be unlawful, or may, adapting the *Birds Eye Walls* judgment, be lawful. See Chapter 22, para 2.4).

4.2 Benefits

Contracting out can be either salary-related (reference scheme test, formerly guaranteed minimum pension) or money purchase (protected rights). These are all specified in PSA 1993, s 9, being respectively under s 9(2B) for the new reference scheme, s 9(2A) for guaranteed minimum pensions and s 9(3) for money-purchase benefits (defined in s 8(1)(ii)).

Reference scheme test (COSR)

The 'reference scheme' is a final salary benchmark introduced by PSA 1993, s 12A(3), and described in s 12B as amplified by SI 1996 No

1172 regs 17–29. The description is very simple and in its essentials is in s 12B with just two additions from the regs, *viz* commutation or lump-sum benefits so far as ordinary Revenue rules permit (reg 19) and normal pension age, which need not be 65 so long as it is equal for men and women and permissible by the Revenue (reg 21).

Section 12B describes an eightieths scheme based on a three-year average final earnings—as indicated in Chapter 8, para 1, this is a conventional structure, less valuable than many and therefore easily attainable. The section requires qualifying earnings to be, in effect, at least 90 per cent of earnings, above the annualised lower earnings limit (up to the upper earnings limit); employers paying large overtime may therefore need to include it in the pension calculation if choosing the reference scheme test. A 50 per cent pension is required for a surviving spouse, with similar provision on death before retirement (intended to be clarified by SI 1997 no 819 although in one respect more obscure—but the DSS commentary on the draft states the policy intention which, like the original section, is to refer to *actual* periods of service). Regulation 26 permits the exclusion of post-retirement marriages, spouses cohabiting with another at the member's death and surviving spouses who subsequently remarry or cohabit—a reflection of the State benefit conditions that hopefully few schemes will adopt in their entirety.

There are three relevant *labels*. Numerous regs use the label 'satisfying section 9(2B)'. That section requires compliance with s 12A (labelled 'statutory standard'—a label not generally used) which itself requires the scheme, for members considered 'collectively . . . as a whole', to be 'broadly equivalent to, or better than, . . . a reference scheme'. The latter (*reference scheme*) is the heading to, and label within, s 12B. The test is to be certified by an actuary, s 12A(6), but may not be collectively certified if more than 10 per cent of the members' or spouses' pensions would not attain the standard (reg 23).

Guaranteed minimum pension (pre-1997 COSR)

A guaranteed minimum pension (commonly known as GMP) not applicable in respect of pensions after 5 April 1997, was normally equal to that part of the State pension which is given up by virtue of being contracted out. It is payable from State pension age. The member's guaranteed minimum is, like the additional State pension described in para 2 above, based on earnings between the lower and upper earnings limits revalued in line with the general UK rise in earnings to State pensionable age (or prior death). For a man aged 45 or more, or a woman aged 40 or more, on 6 April 1978, the guaranteed minimum was one-eightieth of these earnings arising from his years of pensionable service. From 6 April 1988 the fraction reduced to one-hundredth (but the corresponding change to the State additional pension is phased so as to apply only to persons attaining State pensionable age after 5 April 2000). For a younger person, the guaranteed minimum is less than these fractions, the reduction factor being the ratio of 20 to the number of years of working life, as statutorily defined, that could occur after 6 April 1978—see PSA 1993, s 14 and also s 8(2).

A member's GMP (and thus his prospective widow's) must increase if he leaves service before State pensionable age. There was a choice available for each scheme, being either linked to national average earnings, or a fixed rate (6.25 per cent pa for members leaving service after 5 April 1997) or the first of these capped at 5 per cent pa where the scheme paid to the State a 'limited revaluation premium' (no longer possible). The increase must be additional to the scheme's pension, even if the latter exceeds the GMP; this provision, known as anti-franking, is described in Chapter 10, para 1.3. See also para 14 below.

The guaranteed minimum of a member's widow is half his guaranteed minimum. A widow will be entitled to this (PSA 1993, s 17(2)) so long as she is entitled to the corresponding State benefit. In most cases that entitlement ceases on cohabitation or remarriage (1992 Act s 38(3); but see s 49). In some cases there is no relevant entitlement because of the widow's young age (and the absence of children). A wife in a potentially polygamous marriage will lose her prospective entitlement in most cases where there is a subsequent marriage (for normally neither wife will then qualify see Chapter 22, para 6). Suffice it to say that the contracted-out scheme must provide a widow's pension for any period 'for which a Category B retirement pension, widowed mother's allowance or widow's pension is payable to her [from the State] by virtue of the earner's contributions' or would be so payable but for duplicated entitlement (PSA 1993, s 17(5)).

There are a number of other refinements contained in the statute, but it is felt that the foregoing is sufficient for the practitioner as GMPs ceased to accrue at 5 April 1997.

Widowers' GMPs were introduced by s 9(3) of the Social Security Act 1986, amending what is now PSA 1993, s 17. The requirement did not apply on a member's death before 6 April 1989. By s 17(4) the widower's GMP (which is half the deceased member's) derives only from earnings after 5 April 1988.

GMPs must be given priority (with certain other benefits) on a winding-up of the scheme. This provision is required by PSA 1993, s 23 and Pensions Act 1995, s 73 as amended by SI 1996 No 3126, reg 3(5). The practitioner will have had to advise as to whether it could be included in an existing scheme which may have had a restricted power of alteration.

COMPs

The foregoing does not apply to a contracted-out money-purchase ('COMP') scheme established under the new provisions introduced by the Social Security Act 1986.

A COMP scheme contracts out on the basis of a guaranteed minimum level of *contributions* as an alternative to the provision of a GMP. Nonetheless, in respect of periods up to 5 April 1997 (see Pensions Act 1995, s 140(3)) an amount equivalent to a GMP is deducted from the State additional pension (SERPs) so that the benefit to the individual depends upon the investment performance of the occupational scheme. For periods of COMP membership after 5 April 1997, there is simply no SERPs accrual (PSA 1993, s 48A).

The governing provisions of COMP schemes were introduced by s 6 of the Social Security Act 1986 and are to be found in, or by reference to, PSA 1993, s 9(3).

A COMP scheme need not receive contributions above the minimum level. That level equals the reduction in National Insurance contributions applicable to all contracted-out schemes, so that in effect there is no cost to the member (or employer). Indeed there is a saving as the member obtains tax relief; unlike appropriate personal pension schemes (Chapter 2, para 9.3) this relief increases net pay rather than the scheme investment.

As with appropriate personal pension schemes, a COMP scheme receives age-related rebates although the timing is radically different (and thus the rebate is slightly different) by reason of the employer's participation—see Chapter 2, para 9.4.

The minimum payments to a COMP scheme earn *protected rights*—see para 4.7 below.

4.3 Reduced rate of National Insurance contribution

For members of a Contracted-Out Salary Related (COSR) scheme, national insurance contributions to the State are reduced. For a COMP scheme there is a mixture of reduced contributions and age related rebates (payable, with the reductions, to the COMPs). The following table sets out the contributions for a COSR member in the year 1997/8.

	1997/8 (% of lower band earnings)*	*1997/8 (% of upper band earnings*)*
Employer	*3–10%*	*3–10%*
Employee	*2%*	*10%*
Contracted-out reduction:		
Employer (COSR)	—	3%**
Employee (COSR or COMP)	—	1.6%

*There is no contracting-out reduction on the part of earnings falling below the lower earnings limit (in 1997/8 £62 per week), but where total earnings are below that limit no contributions are payable. Contribution rates subject to change of government.
**COMP employer's rebate 1.5% but age-related payments from DSS (see below).

The contracting-out reduction was set at 7 per cent of upper-band earnings (4.5 per cent for the employer and 2.5 per cent for the employee) for the introduction of the current State scheme in 1978 and was said to be likely to fall towards 4 per cent by the turn of the century as the scheme approached maturity. The changes occur every five years. It will be seen from the above table that the current rate for COSRs (aggregating employer and employee) is 4.6 per cent; this has been effective since 6 April 1997 (SI 1996 No 1054). For COMPs, the aggregate of 3.1 per cent is added after the tax year, the DSS payments ranging from nil for a 15 year old employee to 5.9 per cent for a 50 year old (SI 1996 No 1055).

Whereas a member's contributions to an employer's pension scheme are usually fully allowable as deductions for income tax purposes, National Insurance contributions are not so allowable. This distinction favours the contracted-out scheme.

4.4 Notice of intention to elect to contract out etc

In order that a scheme may be contracted out, procedures must be followed as set out in SI 1996 No 1172 as amended by SI 1996 No 1577 and SI 1997 No 786. Notice of intention must be given to the employees affected thereby, a certificate of solvency obtained from the actuary and certain other steps taken (Chapter 3, para 1 and para 12) with a view to obtaining a contracting-out certificate from the Contributions Agency. COMPs may still have certificates issued by the now dissolved OPB. A COSR having such certificate and intended to remain salary related (ie to contract out under the reference scheme test, PSA 1993, ss 12A and 12B) must re-elect by 31 January 1998, having issued notices to relevant employees and consulted any relevant trade unions—SI 1996 No 1172, regs 70 and 71 (which also provide for an extended deadline at the Secretary of State's discretion, but DSS have announced that this would not ordinarily be exercised).

Very clear manuals to the procedures, with specimen notices, are available from the Contributions Agency, labelled CA 14B–E (CA 14A relating to termination procedures for COMPs and mixed benefit schemes). The practitioner should avoid the task of listing and preparing these documents unless he is familiar with the questions involved.

Notices of intention to elect to contract out are normally of at least one month's duration but if there are any relevant trade unions the period is three months unless they have assented to the one-month period (not merely been consulted)—reg 3(4) and (5). In practice one month is commonly accepted. The notice itself can, apparently, be retrospective, ie once it has expired it can relate back to a specified earlier date (which may even precede the notice); this conclusion reflects the practice of the Contributions Agency (CA)—the texts of reg 3(2)(*b*) and reg 8(2)(*d*) are not specific but the latter particularly implies retrospection ('where the Secretary of State considers it appropriate'—clearly the CA must be consulted in advance in any such case). Since all notices must state that representations can be made to the Secretary of State, ie the CA (reg 3(2)(*f*)) there is ample opportunity for the CA to learn of dissent.

Similar provisions apply to the variation of a contracting-out certificate—see regs 9 and 10(1).

4.5 State scheme premiums

There are provisions for 'buying back' into the State scheme (from a COSR, or possibly a mixed benefit scheme) those members who leave service after a very short period of contracted-out employment (two years employment, or less if a transfer has been linked for presentation purposes)—PSA 1993, s 55 as amended. Earlier buy-back on terminating provisions for the whole arrangement for contracting-out the scheme have ceased to apply, this being the effect of the repeal by the Pensions Act 1995 of the remainder of s 55 of the PSA 1993. The remaining case requires a 'contributions equivalent premium', colloquially known as a CEP. See also regs 50–52.

4.6 Employer's decision

The decision whether or not to contract out is for the employer, notwithstanding the statutory provisions as to consultation and notice. Consultation with trade unions recognised for the purpose of general wage-bargaining is now only required if it is intended to contract out, but may occur after members have been given notice of intention (but before the election)—reg 4. In practice the unions do not disagree as the result for a COSR is lower National Insurance contributions, and the culture seems to apply to COMP elections even though the reasoning is different. At the last resort, consultation does not require agreement.

4.7 Contracted-out money purchase (COMP) schemes

COMP schemes were introduced by the Social Security Act 1986 with effect from 6 April 1988. The governing provisions are to be found in PSA 1993, ss 8(1), 9(3), 10 and ss 26–32. Throughout the PSA 1993, a COMP scheme is identified by a reference to s 9(3). As a result, members have 'protected rights' in respect of the type of benefit deriving from the minimum level of contributions.

Under PSA 1993, ss 48 and 48A the member of the money purchase contracted-out scheme is treated for the purpose of the offset to his State additional pension (SERPs) as if he accrued a GMP at a prescribed weekly rate, until GMPs ceased to accrue on 5 April 1997 and thereafter as if he accrued no SERPs. The effect will be that the reduction in the State additional pension will not be precisely matched by the protected rights accruing in the money-purchase scheme, the difference being positive or negative according to the investment experience of the scheme. In practice, some employers contribute substantially above the minimum to a contracted-out scheme established by themselves, by contrast with personal pensions chosen by the member where it is less likely that additional contributions will be paid. However, there are also many minimum-level COMP schemes.

The PSA 1993, s 8(2) provides that the minimum payment is to be the appropriate flat rate percentage (determined under ss 42A and 42B). Additionally the Secretary of State pays to the COMP an age-related rebate equal to the excess of the age-related percentage over the flat rate percentage that the employer has paid under s 8(1)—see para 4.3 above.

By s 10, protected rights derive from the aggregate of the minimum payments and the Secretary of State's payments (plus incentive payments from earlier years).

4.8 Mixed benefit schemes

It is possible for separate sections of a scheme to be contracted out on different bases—Pensions Act 1995, s 149 and SI 1996 No 1977. The effect for contracting-out purposes is to treat it as two separate schemes—reg 2(1). The rules must provide that at any one time a member's service may only qualify under one of the parts—reg 2(2). A COMPs in existence before 6 April 1998 may not become a mixed benefit scheme before that date—reg 5.

4.9 Switching—disallowed rebates

Paragraph 4.3 above indicates that COMPs receive a greater National Insurance rebate (the aggregate of 3.1 per cent and the age-related payments) than COSRs at older ages, and less at younger ages. The crossover age is 37, rising to 39 by the year 2001. However, if an employer operates two schemes (or a mixed benefit scheme) and requires members to move from the COSR at a certain age, of if a member's age is 'the only or main reason' for the move, the age-related payments will not be made—SI 1997 No 946, regs 5 and 6.

The matter must be disclosed to the member in advance, with penalties for non-disclosure—regs 8–10.

5 Married women still paying reduced contributions

Under the old national insurance scheme, married women were permitted to pay a reduced rate of contribution on the basis that their husband's married person's pension would be sufficient for them. The reduced rate is no longer available except for women who remain married or are entitled to a State widow's benefit and were paying contributions at such reduced rate in April 1978 or had been so paying before 6 April 1977 and do not, after 5 April 1978, have a break of more than two years from work. Employment abroad resulting in a two-year contribution gap (because the employment is sufficiently long and voluntary contributions are not paid—see para 11 below) may also extinguish the right to pay at the reduced rate.

6 Transfers

Transfer from one employment to another does not affect a person's contribution record in the State scheme.

Transfers of employment can have a number of alternative effects for members of occupational schemes (see Chapter 10, para 10). If a transfer is made between occupational pension schemes, it is not possible to transfer the whole of the benefit from a contracted-out scheme to a contracted-in scheme because the latter is not able to accept the GMP or protected rights (see para 4 above), and it is not possible to make such a transfer of any rights accrued in a COSR after 5 April 1997.

7 Subsidiary companies

A subsidiary that participates (Chapter 5) in a contracted-out scheme can be included in the principal employer's notice and thus on its certificate (SI 1996 No 1172, reg 12) or, if the subsidiary gives the appropriate notice and makes the appropriate election, it can have a separate certificate.

The convenience of a single contracting-out certificate has led most holding companies to give notice on behalf of all group companies. Nonetheless, reg 12(4) requires that each subsidiary take part in the trade union consultations unless the union has agreed that the holding company may consult for all. Consultation, however, is not onerous (see para 4.6 above).

The date of participation (in the scheme) of each subsidiary must be not later than that from which the contracting-out certificate is to take effect or the subsidiary is to be added to it. The OPB would generally accept a later covenant (usually a deed) of participation so long as it could be demonstrated that it effectively related back to the relevant date, but the absence of such covenant at the time of the election could delay the issue of the certificate. The approach of the CA to this question is not yet known.

8 Associated companies

In certain circumstances a company which is not a subsidiary may nonetheless participate in a contracted-out scheme (reg 12(1)(*b*)(iii)). It remains necessary to ensure that the Inland Revenue accept that there is an association in business between the two companies, for otherwise the tax approval of the scheme would be prejudiced.

9 Channel Islands

The Channel Islands do not participate in the additional State pension scheme and therefore employees in the Channel Islands are not in contracted-out employment even if they are members of a scheme whose mainland members are contracted out by reference to it. See also para 11 below.

Regarding transfers from the mainland, the CA should be consulted, particularly with respect to the liability for accrued GMPs, and the Inland Revenue should also be consulted.

10 Isle of Man

The Isle of Man has enacted a scheme that is similar to that of the mainland of the United Kingdom. It has also adopted the UK provisions relating to preservation (Chapter 10, para 1). The method of recording National Insurance contributions (for contracted-out as well as contracted-in schemes) is integrated with the mainland system.

11 Overseas service

The amount of pension payable under the UK State scheme depends on an individual's National Insurance contribution record during his working life. It follows that employment abroad will only count towards UK pension if UK National Insurance contributions are payable and paid.

The general position affecting a UK resident whose UK employer transfers him overseas (and remains his employer) is that National Insurance contributions continue to be payable on the normal (contracted-out if still covered by a contracted-out scheme, otherwise contracted-in) basis for the first year abroad. Thereafter they are payable on a voluntary basis (at a different rate). Voluntary contributions can be on alternative bases (according to whether it is desired to include cover for certain sickness, invalidity and other benefits immediately on return to the United Kingdom, and in certain circumstances also while abroad), both of which count towards flat-rate UK pension but neither of which count towards the additional pension (but as to the latter, see paras 12 and 14 below).

An exception to the one-year rule applies when the employee replaces a colleague whose term of duty in an EU country has ended, when contributions may not be payable at all. There are also special provisions applicable to mariners and cabin crews of civil aircraft.

The foregoing paragraphs also apply where the UK resident goes abroad to work for a different employer who nonetheless has a place of business in the United Kingdom. However, compulsory contributions are not payable in respect of employees recruited abroad, ie persons who were not living in the United Kingdom when recruited.

Reciprocal arrangements with several countries, as well as special regulations applicable to EU countries, produce variations in the above-mentioned general rules. However, it is almost always possible to pay voluntary contributions towards UK basic pension if there has been a continuous period of three years' UK residence at any time or (before departure abroad) a prescribed amount of contributions had been paid in the preceding three or more years.

Pensions are payable to persons living abroad, although they may be replaced by a local equivalent if certain EU or other reciprocal arrangements apply.

It is outside the scope of this book to describe in detail the provisions referred to above since they rarely, if ever, affect the intended benefits under a UK occupational pension scheme. Guides to the relevant regulations can be found in the leaflets published by the Contributions Agency and available from its International Services Branch at Newcastle upon Tyne, NE98 1YX (helpline 06451 54811), the three essential leaflets being NI 38, NI 132 and SA 29. The catalogue of leaflets lists the subsidiary leaflets relating to reciprocal arrangements with other countries (including Jersey and Guernsey), and most are listed in NI 38.

Although it is stated above that the UK National Insurance contribution requirements rarely, if ever, affect intended benefits under a UK occupational scheme, overseas service (assuming membership continued—see Chapter 7) may require special provisions for assessing the sterling equivalent of a foreign currency salary, or even the UK (lower) equivalent salary for a similar job. Where the scheme has an offset for the UK basic State pension (Chapter 8, para 4) the special provisions usually include a rule that the offset is not applicable in respect of overseas service, either to scheme employees' contributions, if any (for these are frequently suspended during overseas service to avoid local taxation complexities), or to benefits.

The question whether, in a contracted-out scheme, contracted-out employment ceases when a member serves abroad is usually a matter for consideration by the scheme administrator in each case, rather than the legal practitioner. As a general rule, so long as the UK contract of employment continues (and the employee is covered by the scheme's contracting-out certificate) the contracted-out employment is not regarded as terminated (so that, for example, a State scheme premium is not payable—see para 4.5 above). The administrator should note that when class 1 National Insurance contributions cease, a special form, RD 559, is required by the DSS.

12 Incomplete contributions record

As stated in para 1 above, a complete or almost complete contributions record is required to obtain the full flat-rate pension.

Since, for a person retiring before 6 April 1999, only the best 20 years of earnings count towards the State earnings-related pension (but all years are included for contributions purposes), there could be doubt as to the position of a person who was in employment for only 20 years of his career (after 5 April 1978), ie whether the incomplete contributions record gives rise to abatement as with the flat-rate pension. The original intention of the Government had been that such a person's additional component (see para 2 above) would be abated. It was announced early in 1977 that there had been a change of policy so that 20 actual years would suffice for the additional component. Regulations were subsequently introduced to give effect to this change (SI 1978 No 392, reg 6, later replaced by SI 1979 No 642, reg 6).

13 People with more than one job

Employees with two or more jobs normally have to pay National Insurance contributions for each one in which their earnings exceed the lower earnings limit (see para 2 above), but if their total earnings exceed or are likely to exceed the upper limit, application can be made for a refund or to defer payment in one or more jobs (see leaflet NP 28 available from any social security office).

Employees who are also self-employed have to pay both types of contribution. The self-employed type of contribution may be deferred until the end of the tax year (see leaflet NP 18).

14 Changes—Social Security Act 1986: Pensions Act 1995

Substantial changes to the present State earnings-relating pension scheme (colloquially referred to as SERPs) were made by the Social Security Act 1986, some of which came into force on 1 November 1986 but the majority of which (as respects pensions) came into force on 6 April 1988.

Demographic projections to the middle of the 21st century, made in the early 1980s, began to indicate particularly high levels of National Insurance contribution (because the scheme is funded on a Pay-As-You-Go system—see para 3 above).

Subject to transitional arrangements, the main changes are stated in para 2 above.

Additionally, occupational contracted-out schemes became responsible for inflation-proofing GMPs (accrued after 5 April 1988) once they come into payment, up to 3 per cent per annum, leaving only the balance above that figure to be borne out of current National Insurance contributions (PSA 1993, s 109). This additional liability was matched by a reduction in the accruing GMP while the member is in service (see para 4 above)—PSA 1993, s 14.

These changes remain politically controversial. It may therefore be that a change of Government would alter some or all of them, although this is now unlikely.

The 1986 Act effected three other changes designed to encourage contracting-out and thus reduce the future cost of SERPS:

(*a*) the authorisation of money purchase contracted-out occupational schemes (s 6)—see para 4 above;
(*b*) the introduction by s 1 of personal pension schemes which would receive the full contracting-out contribution rebate (Chapter 2, para 9);
(*c*) a financial incentive to encourage contracting-out during the first five years of the new arrangements, amounting to 2 per cent of upper band earnings (ss 3 and 7).

Additionally, the 1986 Act introduced a number of other changes affecting occupational schemes, principally the prohibition of compulsory membership (and thus additional encouragement for personal pension schemes as an alternative)—s 15; the requirement that occupational schemes make available a facility for the payment by members of additional voluntary contributions (s 12) and the control of information relating to occupational and personal schemes (s 13); the reduction from five to two years of the qualifying period for preservation of benefits, by s 10 (see Chapter 10, para 1.1 above) and the simplification of the requisite benefit test for contracted-out schemes, albeit combined with the introduction of widower's pensions (see para 4 of this chapter).

The financial incentive mentioned in (*c*) above proved particularly controversial. The incentive comprised a payment by the State to an occupational or personal pension scheme between 6 April 1988 and 5 April 1993 of 2 per cent of each member's earnings between the lower and upper earnings limits mentioned in para 4.3 above, subject to certain exceptions. In the case of occupational schemes, the incentive was provided under s 7(1) of the Act. The section applied only to a scheme which became contracted-out during the period beginning 1 January 1986 and ending on 5 April 1993, having not previously been contracted-out during any part of that period. The purpose of bringing forward to 1 January 1986 the commencement of the period was to prevent delay in the introduction of new schemes. The actual rebate applied only from 6 April 1988, and only to an earner who was in employment which had not previously been contracted-out employment by reference to any other scheme during any part of the period from 1 January 1986 to 5 April 1993; it was therefore advantageous not to merge a newly contracted-out scheme into another scheme (whether or not the second scheme is also newly contracted-out) during the stated period.

A similar incentive payment applied to 'appropriate' personal pension schemes (ss 1(1) and 3(1)). In effect, an appropriate scheme is equivalent to a money purchase contracted-out occupational scheme (see PSA 1993, ss 7, 9(3) and 9(5)). The incentive was modified where the individual was formerly a member of a satisfactory contracted-out occupational scheme. The purpose was to allay fears that members would be induced to leave good occupational schemes through lack of understanding of the other advantages conferred by them, and also concern that personal pension schemes would have an unfair advantage over new money purchase contracted-out schemes.

The Pensions Act 1995 made a number of changes to reduce still further the prospective liabilities of SERPS. The most significant was probably the provision that occupational schemes, and COSRs and COMPs in particular, must inflation-proof pensions in payment, up to a 5 per cent per annum maximum, in respect of accrual from 6 April 1997 (see Chapter 16, para 3.2). For past accrual the State bears the burden in respect of full inflation-proofing of accrual of SERPS rights accrued before 6 April 1988 and part of the inflation-proofing of SERPS rights accrued between 6 April 1988 and 5 April 1997.

15 Equalisation of state pension ages

State pension ages for men and women will be equalised 'progressively over a period of ten years beginning with 6 April

2010'—(Pensions Act 1995, s 126) ie equalisation will be complete by 2020.

The equalisation is upwards, to the men's age of 65, and therefore diminishes the current expectations of working women to a pension at 60. For that reason it is being phased in so as not to affect women aged 45 or more at the time the Pensions Act 1995 was passing through Parliament.

Schedule 4 to the Pensions Act 1995 sets out the phasing, in monthly steps ie for each month younger than age 45 (when the Act was made in 1995) the State pension age is increased by 1 month beyond age 60, for example:

Woman's age on 5 April 1995		*State pension age (next higher month)*		*State pension date (fixed date—see Sched 4)*
yrs	*mths*	*yrs*	*mths*	
45	—	60	—	6 April 2010
44	11	60	1	6 May 2010
44	10	60	2	6 July 2010
44	9	60	3	6 Sept 2010
44	—	61	—	6 March 2012
43	—	62	—	6 March 2014
42	—	63	—	6 March 2016
41	—	64	—	6 March 2018
40	—	65	—	6 March 2020

The reason for equalising at 65 rather than 60 (or say 63) is cost. In Chapter 8, para 7.4 the projected fall in the ratio of those below 65 to those aged 65 and over is shown dramatically.

The White Paper preceding the Pensions Act 1995, Cm 2594-1, at page 27, set out the figures based on women retiring at 60 (but men still at 65), projecting a fall in the support ratio from 3:3 in 1991 to 2:2 in 2030. By equalising at 65 the latter becomes 2:7 in 2030. As the State pension is unfunded, it is supported by the National Insurance contributions (and taxes when needed) paid by the working population. As the elderly are living longer, the burden on the working population increases. The projections depend on a number of variable estimates, but the trend is clear. It also explains the changes to SERPS, reducing its 'real' value, outlined in this chapter.

Equalisation at 65 does not directly affect occupational pension schemes, but indirectly it does as many offset their pension to allow (usually partially) for the State pension once it is in payment, or pay a supplement until it comes into payment. This is less likely to affect occupational schemes that have equalised at 65, but is significant for those that have created promotion opportunities by equalising at 60.

Chapter 21

Alterations to schemes

1 General

Most occupational pension schemes have a power of alteration—Chapter 3, para 15. Until the Pensions Act 1995, this power, if included when establishing the scheme, could be entirely unfettered (except regarding certain changes to contracted-out schemes—para 3 below). Section 67 of the Pensions Act 1995, now prevents alteration to the accrued rights of members without their consent—para 2 below.

For certain very limited purposes (but including the important payment to employers) OPRA has power to modify or authorise the modification of schemes—Chapter 18, para 4.

The Pensions Act 1995, confers powers on the trustees to modify schemes to achieve conformity with statutory provisions and for limited other purposes—para 4 below.

Modifications by the court remain a possibility, but (save for limited administrative purposes) remote on account of both the procedural difficulties and the likelihood that the court will regard the statutory powers as a statement of Parliament's delineation of the external power to modify—para 5 below.

2 Protection of accrued rights—s 67

Section 67 of the Pensions Act 1995, is a new and important provision intended to protect scheme members from an improper, or at least inappropriate, amendment to their accrued rights. Inevitably, it may limit flexibility in some cases, and may invite challenge to alterations on the basis of differing views as to whether particular rights are accrued.

The section applies to all occupational pension schemes other than public service schemes.

No alteration can be made which 'would or might affect any entitlement, or accrued right, of any member of the scheme acquired before the power is exercised'—unless members have consented or prescribed requirements for a certificate have been met—s 67 (2) and (3).

The section also introduces a control by the trustees where the power of alteration does not already provide for it, as sub-section (3)(*b*) requires the trustees to have approved the exercise of the power in the above circumstances.

Two aspects arise:

(*a*) the meaning of s 67(2);
(*b*) the requirements in s 67(3) for certification or consent. It will be seen below that the regs add very little in this respect.

Sub-section (5) exempts prescribed situations (but again, the regs add little) see below.

Sub-section (6) enables the regs to deem members to have consented— a practical provision.

2.1 Entitlement; accrued rights

The quoted passage above refers to the entitlement, or accrued right, of any member. Entitlement is generally used in the regulations to refer to a benefit in payment. Accrued rights are defined in s 124(2) as the rights which have accrued to or in respect of a member at a particular time to future benefits under the scheme. Where pensionable service is continuing, the accrued rights are to be determined as if the member had opted, immediately before the relevant time, to terminate that service. Plainly deferred pension and contingent spouse's pension, with increases if the rules so provide, are included in accrued rights. For a scheme that provides, but wishes to delete, enhanced early retirement rights, s 67 *might* add a requirement for consents from those who had already attained age 50 (the earliest age at which a pension can normally be paid from an occupational scheme, other than on ill-health) but not from younger members, albeit the trustees would still need to consider the propriety of the change. The question may arise whether the exercise of a discretionary power amounts to a modification of the scheme. In the author's view it does not, but even if it did there would be no pre-existing accrued right unless there had been a regular and consistent exercise of that discretion.

2.2 Certification; consent

Regarding (*b*) above, s 67(4) defines the 'certification requirements' as prescribed requirements for the purpose in effect of ensuring that no member is to be, in the opinion of an actuary, adversely affected without his consent (in respect of an entitlement or accrued right). SI 1996 No 2517, reg 3, provides that the actuary must certify that the proposed exercise 'would not adversely affect any member of the scheme (without his consent) in respect of his entitlement, or accrued rights, acquired before that power is exercised'—which adds nothing to the provision in s 67(4). Actuary is defined within the reg, and reg 2 extends member to include widow or widower or some other person with an entitlement to payment under the scheme in respect of the deceased member.

The other provision in (*b*) above is the requirement for consent, defined in s 67(4) as 'prescribed requirements for the purpose of obtaining the consent of members of a scheme to the exercise of a power to which this section applies'. Regulation 4 simply provides that the consent must be in writing. However reg 5 provides that consent may be treated as given where two notifications have been sent to the member's last known address, at least two months apart, and no response is received to either of them by the end of a month from the date of despatch of the second notification.

Regulation 6 contains a minor provision that where an occupational pension scheme is not established under trust, the restriction in s 67 does not apply where the alteration is made by the managers with the member's consent—which effectively restores s 67(2).

The section is restrictive rather than enabling. Therefore any restrictions on amendment affecting accrued rights contained in the occupational scheme documents will still require compliance, in addition to the provisions of s 67.

3 Changes to contracted-out schemes

3.1 Present position

The restriction on alteration of the rules of contracted-out schemes is to be found in the PSA, 1993 s 37 and SI 1996 No 1172, reg 42.

Except in prescribed circumstances, an alteration is only permissible if of a prescribed description. However, by s 37(2), regulations can provide for the validation with retrospective effect of alterations that would otherwise be void.

Regulation 42(1) and (2) have been slightly updated by SI 1997 No 786. The new (2) deals with a salary-related scheme while a new (2A) deals with a money-purchase scheme. The former requires the trustees to have informed the actuary in writing of the proposed alteration and to have obtained his written confirmation that the scheme will still continue to satisfy the 'reference scheme' requirement to which the PSA 1993, s 12A refers. The alteration must also not be one that would otherwise prevent the scheme from satisfying the contracting-out requirements. Similarly, in respect of guaranteed minimum pensions (GMPs) retained from the period before 6 April 1997, a new reg 42(2B) provides that the alteration must not prevent the scheme from satisfying the relevant requirements.

Regulation 42(2A) is far simpler and provides that for a money-purchase scheme (a COMP) the alteration must not, in respect of accrued rights, adversely affect any of the matters dealt with in Part III of the PSA 1993, or regulations made under those provisions which relate to protected rights, and again the alteration must not otherwise prevent the scheme from satisfying the requirements for a COMP.

For a salary-related scheme it may be thought that, for example, a reduction in future accrual from 60ths to 80ths of pensionable salary would not require the actuary's certificate as the individual would remain within the requirements for a reference scheme, unless the test of overall benefits for 90 per cent of the members were adversely affected. Nonetheless, the relevant rights are being altered, and it would appear necessary to obtain the actuary's confirmation in advance. Where time is short, the amendment could be expressed not to have effect until the actuary has confirmed but that it will then be retrospective to the date of the intended alteration.

3.2 Former provision

The former s 37, reproducing earlier legislation, provided that (with certain exceptions) an alteration that affected a whole list of matters was void unless made with the consent of the Occupational Pensions Board. The question used to arise as to what aspects of a scheme were capable of alteration without affecting its contracting-out provisions. Although the OPB's views were set out in their Memorandum 77, most practitioners checked in advance with the OPB, and occasionally alterations for the purpose of commercial transactions were held up by the need for this consent.

For this reason, flexibility was built into several of the rules, and in particular into the eligibility rule.

Regulation 76B, as inserted by SI 1997 No 786, provides that any requirement in the scheme rules for OPB consent under the old s 37 shall cease to have effect.

4 Trustees' additional powers (ss 65 and 68)

Both the above provisions are designed to assist the trustees of an occupational pension scheme (or managers in the case of s 65) to bring the scheme into conformity with overriding provisions of the statute ie to enable the constitutional documents to reflect the applicable law.

Section 65 refers to the equal treatment rule, and is applicable where the trustees do not have power to make the necessary alterations or can only do so by a procedure that is liable to be unduly complex or protracted, or involves the obtaining of consents which either cannot be obtained or can only be obtained with undue delay or difficulty.

Section 65 does not require the trustees or managers to consult with the employer. It may seem, therefore, that they have a clear path to equalising upwards. However, the opening words are permissive rather than obligatory ('the trustees or managers . . . may'); where the employer is meeting the balance of cost, and may be entitled to a share of surplus on winding up, the employer's interests should be borne in mind by the trustees, so it would seem that in practice they should consult the employer before exercising the power. On the other hand, if there is sufficient surplus for an indefinite contributory holiday, it would be very difficult for an employer to give trustees reason not to equalise upwards (for future as well as accrued service). If no action is taken, s 62(3) had overriding effect to introduce the more favourable term.

Section 68 relates to a trust scheme ie any tax-approved scheme and possibly a number of unapproved schemes. It enables the trustees by resolution to modify the scheme in a number of significant ways, as follows:

(*a*) with the consent of the employer, to extend the class of death benefit members;
(*b*) to enable the scheme to operate the member-nominated trustee arrangements required by ss 16 and 17 (but curiously not where there is a corporate trustee—presumably because the provisions for member-nominated directors require changes to the articles of association and are not affected by the provision within the trust deed for trusteeship);
(*c*) to enable the scheme to comply with terms imposed by the Compensation Board;
(*d*) to enable the scheme to conform with s 37(2) (refund of surplus from an ongoing scheme—if there is a power it is to be exercisable only by the trustees); s 76(2) (provision of limited price indexation to pensions in payment, and notices to members, where a scheme is being wound up and a payment to the employer is contemplated); ss 91 and 92 (restrictions on lien, forfeiture etc).

Section 68 can also include prescribed purposes although at the time of writing there were none. Interestingly, s 68(5) provides that alterations under (*d*) above are not to be treated as effecting an alteration for the purpose of Inland Revenue approval—an unusual provision to find in a non-taxing statute, but curious in its limitation just to (*d*) above.

SI 1996 No 2517, reg 7, excludes from s 68 trust schemes guaranteed by the State and trust schemes which are public service schemes.

5 Modification by the court

Before the enactment in 1973 of the now repealed power for the OPB to modify schemes, an application for modification of the trusts of a pension scheme could only be made to the court. Apart from a number of specialised provisions (such as s 53 of the Trustee Act 1925, relating to certain difficulties in connection with infant beneficiaries) the relevant authorities for such an application were:

(*a*) s 57 of the Trustee Act 1925;
(*b*) s 1 of the Variation of Trusts Act 1958;
(*c*) the inherent jurisdiction of the court.

The power of the court under (*a*) above relates to 'the management or administration of any property vested in trustees' and has been held to enable the court to authorise a particular transaction (or perhaps, type of transaction) falling within those opening words rather than to rewrite or vary the trusts generally. However, it was held in *Mason v Farbrother* [1983] 2 All ER 1078, Ch D, that the court had jurisdiction under s 57 to substitute a wider investment clause for the existing clause. The case related to the pension scheme of the Co-operative Society. (The Pensions Act 1995 now confers a wide power of investment, subject to any restriction imposed by the scheme—s 34.)

An application under (*b*) above is for the approval of the court on behalf of certain persons or classes of persons, being primarily infants, unascertained persons contingently entitled and unborn persons. Such an application would be impractical in the case of most pension schemes, where a large number of beneficiaries would be of full age and have vested or contingent rights (and thus have to assent) and the number of classes of other beneficiaries (who would have to be represented before the court) would be considerable. Further, each class (apart from contingent beneficiaries interested only on the failure of determination of protective trusts) must be shown to benefit from the proposal, this being a requirement under the proviso to s 1(1) of the Act. This proviso may create practical difficulties in view of the multiplicity of prospective benefits under a pension scheme. In the *Mason* case cited above, the application had proceeded in the alternative under the 1925 and 1958 Acts. Three of the defendants purported to represent particular classes of beneficiary. However, two of them had made no attempt to consult the persons whom they purported to represent. The judgment stated

> 'The matter of the Variation of Trusts Act 1958 has not been pursued, because perhaps of difficulties in connection with the representative parties. That leaves s 57 of the Trustee Act . . .'.

The jurisdiction referred to in (*c*) above may well enable an application to the court to succeed. However, the success of the application cannot be forecast. For example, although the inherent jurisdiction is specifically preserved by s 15 of the Trustee Investments Act 1961, the court was subsequently reluctant to confer wider investment powers than those set out in the Act except where there were special relevant circumstances.

It appears that the reluctance arose because the then recently enacted provision demonstrated Parliament's intention with regard to trustees' investment powers. The above-mentioned *Mason* case referred to the special circumstances of 'inflation since 1961. And also of course the fact that the trust is an unusual one in that it is not a private or family trust but a pension fund with perhaps something of a public element in it.' This aspect of the judgment was referred to in *Trustees of the British Museum v Attorney General* [1984] 1 All ER, Ch D, at p 343 where inflation was mentioned as a 'very general circumstance' and 'for the reasons that I have given I would prefer to say that the rule [preventing enlargement of powers] has gone, and with it any question of what circumstances are special'. The extension of s 57 was the subject of the following comment:

> 'Much of the [*Mason*] judgment is directed to questions of jurisdiction and the details of the revised investment clause there under consideration. Of these matters I need say nothing.'

Despite *British Museum* s 57 remains of limited application. The limited powers of OPRA (Chapter 18, para 4) may therefore be of more practical help although it is more likely that a reasonably modern pension scheme will contain a sufficient power of alteration.

Chapter 22

Sex discrimination

1 Introduction

The pensions world was rocked in 1990 by the *Barber* judgment in the European Court. The details are given in para 2.4 below but in essence the court held that pensions were a form of pay and therefore in all their details must be equalised.

If *Barber* had affected accrued rights, all schemes which followed the State retirement ages of 65 and 60 would have had to permit the male who leaves early to draw his pension at age 60. The capital cost to industry was variously estimated at £20–60 billion.

On the other hand if *Barber* were only to affect future accrual ie accrual after 17 May 1990 (the date of the judgment), there would be no capital cost albeit an important increase in the required future contribution rate if ages are equalised downwards.

The first possibility, the possible retrospective effect of *Barber*, was to have been excluded by a protocol to the Maastricht treaty agreed in December 1991 but the validity of that protocol was not universally agreed. The extent of the retrospective effect was therefore likely to be decided by the *Coloroll* judgment expected in early 1993. In the event *Coloroll* was delayed (albeit it decided several subsidiary points) but retrospection was excluded by the *Ten Oever* judgment—regarding both judgments, see 2.4 below.

2 European community law

2.1 Direct effect

The Treaty of Rome, made in 1957 to establish the European Economic Community, has direct effect within Member States and can be litigated without further national laws.

By contrast, Directives made under the Treaty are instructions to Member States to implement their provisions by national law. Until such laws are adopted (eg by the UK Parliament) they do not confer rights between individuals. However, where a Member State has failed to implement a Directive and itself would be affected, for example as an employer, individuals may have rights against the State.

The importance of *Barber* (para 2.4 below) is that, by confirming direct rights under the Treaty, it leapfrogs a long timetable for equalisation by Directives.

2.2 Areas affected

European law requires equal treatment in:

(*a*) eligibility—the *Bilka-Kaufhaus* case;
(*b*) benefits—*Barber* and *Coloroll*;
(*c*) retirement dates—*Marshall* and *Barber*.
(*d*) possibly part-timers—*Vroege*.

Each of these areas is capable of considerable enlargement, firstly by the doctrine of indirect discrimination (particularly regarding part-timers) and secondly by encroachment on the exemption regarding unequal actuarial factors. (See paras 2.3–2.5 below).

European law exempts pension schemes from the EC Business Transfer Directive (Directive 77/187) but see Chapter 10, para 3 regarding TUPE 1981.

2.3 Eligibility—effect of Art 119 ('equal pay')

Article 119 of the Treaty of Rome is as follows:

'Each member State shall during the first stage ensure and subsequently maintain the application of the principle that men and women should receive equal pay for equal work.

For the purpose of this Article, "pay" means the ordinary basic or minimum wage or salary and any other consideration, whether in cash or in kind, which the worker receives, directly or indirectly, in respect of his employment from his employer.

Equal pay without discrimination based on sex means:
(*a*) that pay for the same work at piece rates shall be calculated on the basis of the same unit of measurement;
(*b*) that pay for work at time rates shall be the same for the same job.'

Article 119 has direct effect on individuals (*Jenkins v Kingsgate (Clothing Productions) Ltd* [1981] IRLR 228 and the many earlier cases there cited). The article relates to equal 'pay' for equal work. Pay is defined as including 'any other consideration . . . received, directly or indirectly, in respect of his employment from his employer'. The question was whether it includes pension arrangements. In a very significant judgment, *Bilka-Kaufhaus GmbH v Weber von Hartz* [1986] IRLR 317, it was held that (1) a contractual pension arrangement did comprise pay and that (2) Art 119 is infringed where part-time employees are excluded from eligibility where that exclusion affects a far greater number of women than men, unless the employer shows that the exclusion is based on objectively justified factors unrelated to any discrimination on grounds of sex. For the various ways of finding the proportion of one sex that can be affected, see *Staffs v Black* IRLR [1995] 237. For treatment of a 4 per cent disparity as de minimis, see *R v Sec State, ex parte Unison* [1997] 1 CMLR 459 (QBD). The test for indirect discrimination has been referred to the ECJ in *Ex parte Seymour-Smith* [1997] 2 All ER 273 HL at p 281—for a succinct analysis see its High Court judgment [1994] IRLR 448 at para 28.

Bilka-Kaufhaus was part of a department store chain. The pension arrangements were regarded as an integral part of the contracts of employment. Regarding point (1) above, the court had no difficulty in holding that 'benefits paid to employees under the scheme therefore constitute consideration received by the worker from the employer . . . [per Art 119]'.

Barber reached the same conclusion regarding the applicability of Art 119 where a scheme is administered by trustees but established by the employer ie a typical UK pension scheme (see para 2.4 below).

Regarding point (2) above, *Bilka-Kaufhaus* illustrates the rapidly growing doctrine of indirect discrimination that is also applied by the court to areas such as statutory dependency benefits.

It is therefore clear that the exclusion of *part-timers* from eligibility for pension scheme membership may be difficult to justify in terms of Art 119 if, as is usually the case, the overwhelming majority of part-timers are female. The doctrine of indirect discrimination removes the defence that females are eligible under the rules if they qualify by virtue of full-time contracts of employment. On the other hand, if the administrative cost of admitting to membership persons working a very small number of hours, say below eight hours per week, is disproportionately high, that would be an objective reason for a minimum eligibility requirement that would probably be upheld by the court. It would be a matter of fact in each case whether a particular minimum level could be justified on objective economic grounds.

2.4 Benefits—*Barber*; *Coloroll*

On 17 May 1990 judgment was delivered in the European Court in *Barber v Guardian Royal Exchange* [1990] 2 All ER 660, with the possible consequences mentioned in para 1 above.

Barber was a male whose redundancy pension was payable at a later age than that of a comparable female member of the pension scheme. In typical fashion, there was a five-year difference in the normal retirement ages under the scheme, albeit unusually the ages were 62 for men and 57 for women rather than 65 and 60. The contract of employment provided that on redundancy members of the pension scheme were entitled to an immediate pension if they were aged 55 in the case of men or 50 in the case of women. Barber was made redundant at 52 and therefore, instead of an immediate pension he became entitled to a deferred pension payable from age 62. He complained of discrimination contrary to ss 1(1)(*a*) and 6(2)(*a*) and (*b*) of the Sex Discrimination Act 1975, Art 119 of the EEC Treaty, Directive 75/117 on equal pay and Directive 76/207 on equal treatment.

The Employment Appeal Tribunal rejected his claim as it related to access to pension benefits and therefore fell within the equal treatment Directive rather than equal pay. The Court of Appeal referred the case to the European Court of Justice under Art 177 of the Treaty for a preliminary ruling. The questions raised, in summary were:

(1) Are the benefits, being received in connection with redundancy, 'pay' within Art 119 and the Equal Pay Directive or do they fall within the Equal Treatment Directive, or neither?
(2) Was it material that one of the benefits was a pension paid from an occupational scheme operated by the employer?
(3) In effect, does one look at each benefit or the total value of the package?
(4) Were Art 119 and the Equal Pay Directive of direct effect in the circumstances of the case?

(5) In effect, was it material that entitlement to an immediate pension applied to both sexes within seven years of their respective normal retirement dates under the pension scheme?

The ECJ answered the five questions but added a number of further paragraphs limiting the retrospective effect of the judgment, mentioned in para (6) below. The respective answers, in summary were:

(1) The Court cited *Jenkins v Kingsgate* (mentioned in para 2.3 above) and held that Art 119 applied (and that accordingly there was no need to discuss whether or not the Equal Treatment Directive was applicable).
(2) A pension paid under a contracted-out private occupational scheme falls within the scope of Art 119. It appeared that the same reasoning would apply to a contracted-in scheme (p 701j) and this was confirmed in *Coloroll*—see *Overview* in 2.5 below. The economic nature of the pension scheme was held to be similar to that of the *Bilka-Kaufhaus* supplementary scheme (see para 2.3 above).
(3) The principle of equal pay applies to each of the elements of remuneration. This ensures 'transparency' ie the ability for the courts to verify compliance without the need for a complex assessment of the total package.
(4) Article 119 is of direct effect (citing the above *Jenkins* case). Since Art 119 applied, it was unnecessary to discuss the question whether the Equal Pay Directive had direct effect.
(5) Even if the difference in normal pension ages is based on the difference in the State scheme, it is contrary to Art 119. While expressed to apply to a contracted-out scheme, the reasoning appeared equally applicable to a contracted-in scheme.
(6) Paragraphs 40–45 of the judgment (pp 703–4) related to the retrospective effect. Paragraphs 40 and 41 mention the importance of the financial consequences and the precedent for taking these into account. Paragraphs 42 and 43 mention the reasonable understanding of Member States that Art 119 did not apply as the Second Social Security Equal Treatment Directive 86/378 had included an exception regarding pensionable age. The effect of the judgment, by reference to these observations, was not clear. Its possible meanings are mentioned in (1)-(4) below. Paragraphs 43 to 45 of the judgment are as follows:

'43. In the light of those provisions, the Member States and the parties concerned were reasonably entitled to consider that Art 119 did not apply to pensions paid under contracted-out schemes and that derogations from the principle of equality . . . were still permitted in that sphere.
44. In those circumstances, overriding considerations of legal certainty preclude legal situations which have exhausted all their effects in the past from being called in question where that might upset retroactively the financial balance of many contracted-out pension schemes . . . Finally, . . . no restriction on the effects of the aforesaid interpretation can be permitted as regards the acquisition of entitlement to a pension as from the date of this judgment.
45. It must therefore be held that the direct effect of Art 119 of the Treaty may not be relied on in order to claim entitlement to a pension with effect from a date prior to that of this judgment, except in the case of workers or those claiming under them who have before that date initiated legal proceedings or raised an equivalent claim under the applicable national law.'

The exemption from retrospective effect was capable of having a number of meanings. This was not explained to the court so that no further help was to be gained from analysis of the text. The main possible meanings were:

(1) The future instalments for existing pensioners, ie instalments paid after 17 May 1990, must be equalised (but without awarding an addition in respect of past instalments). This is the narrowest form of retrospective exemption and does not assist the employer in respect of deferred pensioners or active staff.
(2) An exemption from equalisation where, by 17 May 1990, a pension had already begun. This would have precluded equalisation for existing pensioners but again would not confer on the employer an exemption regarding deferred pensioners or actives.
(3) An exemption where, by 17 May 1990, the individual had left service. This would have excluded deferred pensioners from equalisation but would not have assisted the employer regarding the accrued rights of active employees.
(4) An exclusion from equalisation for all pension attributable to past pay periods, ie pensionable service prior to 17 May 1990. The effect would be to exclude pensioners and deferred pensioners from equalisation, and also to exclude the accrued pension of existing staff.

Item (4) was the interpretation which the UK Government promoted and which the Dutch Government incorporated in the proposed Maastricht protocol mentioned in para 1 above. The matter was expected next to come before the court again in the case of the *Coloroll Group Pension Schemes*, Case no C–200/91.

Coloroll raised a number of other issues for decision by the court. While some of the Coloroll schemes were in surplus, others were not. As the employer was in receivership, and had no funds, the court was asked whether Art 119 imposes a duty on *trustees* and, if so, how they are to implement it where there are no surplus funds, ie whether they are to reduce the benefits payable to females (or, under sequential priorities, some other class) in order to equalise other benefits.

Coloroll raised a number of actuarial questions. These included transfers in and out and commutation tables.

All five relevant *Coloroll* schemes were of the 'final salary' type (Chapter 8, para 1). Many of the above inequalities will only arise in this type of scheme. However, the question of unisex actuarial factors, raised in the *Coloroll* reference to the European Court, would also be relevant to money purchase schemes.

Where a pension scheme equalises retirement ages below 65, it may be desired to provide for men a supplement to their pension until they attain age 65 when the male State pension begins (females being able to receive it from age 60). The question whether such 'bridging pension' is unlawful, as the occupational pension scheme provides unequal benefits for that period, or lawful because the aggregate of State and occupational benefits is equalised, was raised in the case of *Birds Eye Walls v Roberts* which was referred in March 1992 to the European Court. The European Commission came out in favour of them as a means of implementing overall equality. However, they highlighted the present inequality in the State pensionable age (see para 3 below but also Chapter 20, para 15).

In *Birds Eye Walls v Roberts* [1994] IRLR 29, the ECJ held that during the period between ages 60 and 65 when only women received a State pension, a bridging pension intended to compensate the men could lawfully be greater than that paid to women.

The most burning issue, the question of retrospection expected to be decided by *Coloroll*, was in the end decided by an earlier judgment, in October 1993—*Ten Oever v Stichting BedriifsPensioenFonds* [1995] 2 CMLR 357, and see also *Moroni v Collo* decided two months later and set out in the same report. It was held that equal treatment is only required for service from 17 May 1990 (the date of the *Barber* judgment) or earlier where proceedings had been commenced before that date. (But contrast eligibility—see (7) in 2.5 below).

Another case that came before the ECJ in 1993, from the UK, was *Neath v Hugh Steeper* [1994] 1 All ER 929, which confirmed the *Ten Oever* judgment and additionally held that sex-based actuarial factors in funded *defined benefit* schemes are outside Article 119 and may therefore be used to calculate employer's contributions, transfer payments and lump sum options.

Eventually *Coloroll* and five other equal treatment cases were decided by the ECJ on 28 September 1994. They were the following, generally referred to by the abbreviated names shown on the left:

		ECJ Case No:
(1)	*Coloroll* (*Re Coloroll Pension Schemes*)	C–200/91
(2)	*Avdel* (*M/s Smith etc v Avdel Systems Ltd*)	C–408/92
(3)	*van den Akker or Shell* (*Mrs van den Akker v Shell PensioenFonds*)	C28/93
(4)	*Vroege* (*M/s Vroege v NCIV Institut etc*)	C–57/93
(5)	*Fisscher* (*Mrs Fisscher v Voorhuis Hengelo BV etc*)	C–128/93
(6)	*Beune* (*Mr Beune v Bestuur van het ABP*)	C7/93

These are all reported in the special All ER volume [1995] EC. The first two cases were referred from the UK, the remaining four from the Netherlands.

2.5 Brief Descriptions of the 28 September 1994 cases

(1) *Coloroll*: an application by trustees to resolve numerous issues where the employer was in receivership. Heard simultaneously with *Ten Oever*, *Moroni* and *Neath* which, however were decided earlier (in 1993) leaving principally trusteeship and AVC issues to *Coloroll*.

(2) *Avdel*: until 30 June 1991 retirement age was 65 for men, 60 for women. From 1 July 1991 it was equalised at 65 regarding past as well as future service.

(3) *Van den Akker/Shell*: in 1985 pension ages were equalised upwards, but with an option for existing female members to main-

tain the lower age. After *Barber* the pension fund thought it necessary to reverse that option. The females disputed that necessity.

(4) *Vroege*: until 1991 part-timers/married women were excluded from the pension scheme. Back service could only be purchased by the over-50s. The question was whether the *Barber* (and *Maastricht*) retrospective limitation regarding benefits applied also to excluded eligibility.

(5) *Fisscher*: until 1991 married women were excluded from the pension scheme. In addition to the above question (4), could back service be demanded without payment of the normal contributions, and did any time limits apply?

(6) *Beune*: a married male pensioner under the (funded) Dutch Civil Service scheme claimed discrimination because his pension would have been higher if he had been female. The Dutch and British Governments claimed that, notwithstanding its statutory basis, the scheme was an occupational (and not a social security) arrangement, and therefore entitled to the restrospective limitation of *Barber* and *Maastricht*.

Overview (including 1993 cases)

(1) Article 119 applies to all occupational schemes, whether contracted in or out *(Coloroll—and Moroni 1993)*, and to at least some **public service schemes** *(Beune)*.

(2) The direct effect of Article 119 can be relied on by members **and their dependants** *(Ten Oever 1993)* against both the employer and the **trustees** *(Coloroll, Fisscher)*.

(3) The employer **and the trustees** must do everything within their powers to ensure compliance with the principle of equal treatment *(Coloroll)*. Article 119 *may* not override scheme rules but trustees unable to amend may obtain powers from the national court *(Coloroll)*.

(4) It is for **national courts** to resolve problems of underfunding where the employer is in receivership, applying the principle of equal pay *(Coloroll)*.

(5) Equal treatment is only required for service from **17 May 1990** *(Ten Oever)* (or earlier where proceedings commenced before that date). Unequal pension ages from prior **transitional options** must be equalised for service from 17 May 1990 (*van den Akker)*.

(6) Benefits **unrelated** to actual service must be equal if caused after 17 May 1990 *(Coloroll)*.

(7) Equal access *(eligibility)* to occupational schemes (eg for **part-timers** suffering from *indirect* sex discrimination—see 2.3 above) is required from **8 April 1976**, subject to back payment of employee contributions where applicable and to **time limits** for claims *(Fisscher)*. Exclusion of part-timers *may* be justified on objective grounds *(Vroege)*. Time limits have particular relevance in the UK and are mentioned under their own heading below.

(8) Levelling **downwards** is not against Community law *(Avdel)* except for the period between 17 May 1990 and the equalising change *(Coloroll, Avdel)*, (albeit there may be other rights). **Phasing in** for one sex the lower benefits, post 17 May 1990, is not permitted *(Avdel)*. For periods of service prior to 17 May 1990 Community law is silent and does not of itself justify a retro-active reduction in value *(Coloroll, Avdel)*.

(9) Sex-based **actuarial factors** in funded *defined benefit* schemes are outside Article 119 and **may** therefore be used to calculate employer's contributions, transfer payments, lump sum options *(Neath 1993)*, and early retirement and allocated pensions *(Coloroll)*.

(10) It remains unknown whether **defined contribution** schemes must provide unisex benefits.

(11) Article 119 does **not** apply to:
- (i) **bridging pensions** *(Roberts/Birds Eye Walls 1993)*
- (ii) segregated **AVCs** *(Coloroll)*
- (iii) schemes which have at all times applied to work done by **one sex** only *(Coloroll)*.

(12) Schemes receiving **transfers** in respect of unequal post-17 May 1990 service must equalise as at retirement date the benefits attributable to that service *(Coloroll)*.

Part-timers: time limits in the UK

The *Vroege and Fisscher* judgment were given wide publicity in the UK and gave rise to trade-union sponsored multiple applications to the court, both by women still in service and those who had been excluded from former employers' pension schemes for which part-timers had not been eligible. In some cases women in service had only been admitted to the pension scheme part way through their career.

In most cases there was no doubt that indirect discrimination had occurred. (Exclusion from the pension scheme of part-timers as such is not discrimination under Article 119 if, for example, there are respectively equal numbers of men and women who have the opportunity and are admitted to, or are denied the opportunity and are excluded from, membership of the scheme). Although there might be a defence of objective justification, the preliminary issue in all cases was that of time limits.

Fisscher reiterated the long-established but imprecise ECJ ruling that national time limits may be relied on against claims, provided that the limits are not less favourable than the domestic time limits for similar actions and that they do not render the exercise of rights under community law impossible.

In the UK there was at the time no specific time limit set out in legislation in respect of such a claim. The Employment Appeal Tribunal (EAT) had held that time limits under Article 119 must be decided by analogy to time limits for similar claims under UK law, in one case suggesting that three to six months would be reasonable, in another referring to an analogous limit of one year in exceptional cases—but in both these cases the actual claim was within three months—*Rankin v British Coal* [1993] IRLR 69, EAT; *Cannon v Barnsley MBC* [1992] IRLR 474, EAT.

Analogies had been made to claims under the Equal Pay Act 1970 (time limit six months from leaving service) and the Sex Discrimination Act 1975 (time limit three months from the date of the discriminating act, subject to the Industrial Tribunal's discretion to extend this period). Other analogies involving considerably longer periods were also thought to be relevant. The critical question was the date from which the period runs. In the *Rankin* case the EAT took a view 'as to the equities involved'.

The multiple claims (some 40,000 applications) were held pending judgment in specific test cases that had been selected by the Industrial Tribunal. Judgment was rapidly given in order to promote referral to the Employment Appeals Tribunal ('EAT') which gave judgment on 24 June 1996 (as amplified by addendum—see 3(*c*) below)—in *Preston & others v Wolverhampton, Fletcher and others v Midland Bank* [1996] IRLR 484. In substance, the EAT upheld the Industrial Tribunal's rulings, deciding the following:

(1) *Time limit for bringing claims.* A part-time employee has to start proceedings in the Tribunal within six months after termination of the employment to which the complaint relates. In the EAT's view, this is not incompatible with European Law and it is not relevant that part-timers did not know until 1994 (when the European Court of Justice (ECJ) issued its decisions in *Fisscher and Vroege*) that they had a right under European Law to access to the pension scheme. That right had existed since 1976 (*Defrenne No 2*), and there had never been a bar on its enforcement—paras 112 and 115.

(2) *Successive employment contracts with the same employer.* If a part time employee is employed under a succession of part-time contracts, the basic position is that he/she is not entitled to bring a claim under any contract of employment which has expired more than six months before he/she starts proceedings in the tribunal. The answer may be different if the successive contracts follow each other without a break, or if there is an underlying continuing 'umbrella' contract—para 125.

(3) *Limit on the extent to which claims can be retrospective.*
   (*a*) No claim may be made for backdated membership of an occupational pension scheme in respect of a period earlier than two years before the claim is initiated.
   (*b*) The two-year retrospection limit is not inconsistent with European Law, and no reference to the European Court was needed. It is a limit on backdating, not an upper limit on the amount of the claim. (A limit on the *amount* of a claim was held by the ECJ to be inconsistent with European Law in *Marshall No 2.)*—para 133.
   (*c*) However, in the case of *Levez v TH Jennings (Harlow Pools) Ltd* [1996] IRLR 499—a case relating to equal pay but not pensions—a differently constituted EAT decided (the president dissenting) to refer this question to the ECJ. The EAT in the part-timers' cases in effect did not agree with the *Levez* decision and, in an addendum to the ruling of 24 June 1996, decided neither to make any reference to the ECJ nor to defer its final judgment until the result of the *Levez* reference is known, but gave leave to appeal—*Preston at* page 498..

(4) *Remedies for successful part-time claimants.* The only remedy is a declaration of the employee's right to join the pension scheme. There is no right to damages.

The EAT was upheld by the Court of Appeal on 13 February 1977—*Preston etc* [1997] IRLR 233. Leave was granted to appeal to the House of Lords (which may or may not refer questions to the ECJ). Progress reports are issued by the Birmingham Industrial Tribunal, the above information regarding the House of Lords being contained in a Bulletin dated February 1997 and issued mid-March.

A reference from the Northern Ireland Industrial Tribunal to the ECJ on 21 March 1995 on similar issues is apparently still pending (*Magorrian and others* IT ref 2632-6/92).

Regarding limitation on retrospection, see also *Steenhorst-Neerings v Bestuur* [1995] 3 CMLR 323 at pp 342–345. Generally for pre-1996 claims, see the Equal Access regs SI 1976 No 142 as amended by SI 1995 No 1215, effectively repealed with PSA 1993 s 118 by SI 1995 No 3104 with effect from 1 January 1996. For claims after that date, see SI 1995 No 3183 which is unlikely to be challenged regarding time limits but may, regarding limits on arrears, be affected by the outcome of either *Preston* or *Magorrian*; a footnote to reg 5 helpfully summarises the above earlier Equal Access regs.

2.6 Equal treatment in working conditions, retirement etc

Section 2 of the Sex Discrimination Act 1986 was enacted to give effect to the decision of the European Court in *Marshall v Southampton & SW Hants AHA* [1986] 2 All ER 584. There it was held that different dates for compulsory termination of the service of male and female employees were:

- (*a*) discriminatory in terms of the EC Directive 76/207 on equal treatment regarding access to employment and working conditions;
- (*b*) unlawful despite the exclusion permitted in the EC Directive 79/7 (on statutory social security) of pensionable age for the purpose of granting retirement pensions, this being different from the question of employment;
- (*c*) unlawful despite the exclusion of all matters relating to death of retirement from the general effect of the Sex Discrimination Act 1975 by s 6(4) of that Act, since it was the duty of a Member State to enact the provisions of a Directive and therefore the UK as employer could not plead a defence that relied upon its failure to carry out that duty (the Court of Appeal having stated that the Area Health Authority was a public

authority, and the Advocate General having argued that no distinction should be drawn between the State as employer and the State in some other capacity).

The case finally answered the question whether Directives are directly enforceable against a Member State in the absence of domestic legislation. The court observed, at p 600e of the report, that the same would not apply against a private individual.

The *Barber* case, outlined in para 2.4 above, held that each element of an occupational pension package must be tested separately for equality, and therefore rendered unlawful unequal pension ages.

2.7 Equal treatment in social security

In European terms 'social security' covers statutory benefits and occupational schemes (the latter being 'occupational social security'). There have been two Directives of the Council:

(1) EC Directive 79/7 of 19 December 1978, on the progressive implementation of the principle of equal treatment for men and women in matters of social security, which by Art 3 relates to *statutory* benefits.
(2) EC Directive 86/378 of 24 July 1986, colloquially known as 'the Second Directive' (on social security), on the implementation of the principle of equal treatment for men and women in *occupational* social security schemes which are defined by Art 2 as excluding schemes governed by EC 79/7 above. This has now been amended to bring it into line with the judgments outlined in paras 2.4 and 2.5 above—EU directive of 16 December 1996.

Article 12 of the Second Directive required Member States to introduce domestic legislation by 30 July 1989 requiring, by Art 8, scheme compliance by 1 January 1993. Accordingly the UK enacted s 23 of the Social Security Act 1989:

'23 Equal treatment for men and women 86/378 EEC
Schedule 5 to this Act shall have effect for the purpose of implementing the directive of the Council of the European Communities, dated 24th July 1986, relating to the principle of equal treatment for men and women in occupational social security schemes, and of making additional, supplemental and consequential provision.'

The intention was to bring Sched 5 into effect on 1 January 1993 but in the event the UK Government awaited the outcome of the *Coloroll* case (para 2.4 above). Meanwhile, in 1994 the unfair maternity leave provisions of the Schedule were brought into force (Chapter 10, para 6.3). The rest of the Schedule has been overtaken by the Pensions Act 1995, s 62—see para 2.8 below.

2.8 Equality under Pensions Act 1995—occupational schemes

Sections 62–66 of the Pensions Act 1995 and SI 1995 Nos 3104 and 3183 (see last section of para 2.5 above), write into UK statute law the effect of Article 119 on occupational pension schemes as from 1 January 1996. Section 62 writes into every such scheme, if needed, an 'equal treatment rule'. This applies, by subsection (2)(*a*), to eligibility, and by (2)(*b*) to benefit terms.

The equalisation of benefit terms is retrospective to 17 May 1990 (the date of the *Barber* judgment)—s 63(6). This is applicable to dependants' benefits too—s 63(1). It does not apply to difference 'genuinely due to a material factor which is not the difference of sex'—s 62(4). Nor does the equalisation apply to bridging pensions—actually the text of s 64(2) is wider, referring to State benefits and prescribed circumstances—nor to actuarial factors to the extent prescribed, nor other aspects that may be prescribed.

The equal treatment rule is, by s 63(4) enforceable under the Equal Pay Act 1970 which itself is amended by s 66 to exclude any wider ambit of the 1970 Act's 'equality clause'. Section 66(3) similarly amends the Sex Discrimination Act 1975.

Trustees are given, by s 65, a unilateral power to alter scheme rules to conform with the equal treatment rule. As s 65 came into force on 1 January 1996, employers equalising downwards had a harder negotiating task after that date.

3 Different retirement dates

3.1 General inequality

From 1986 to 1990 (the years of the *Marshall* and *Barber* judgments cited in para 2 above) it was necessary to distinguish between the normal retiring date for employment purposes and the date at which pension begins, ie the normal retiring date under the rules of an occupational pension scheme. It remains useful to bear the distinction in mind as discriminatory early retirement selection is unlawful under European law. Unequal pension ages are also unlawful under European law, but only in respect of post-17 May 1990 accrual—see paras 2.2–2.5 above.

Until the Pensions Act 1995 (para 2.8 above) there was no UK legislative requirement as to unequal normal retiring date under an occupational scheme. However, as soon as the *Coloroll* judgment was given (para 2.4 above) virtually all remaining schemes that had not equalised did so.

3.2 Early retirement

Where a scheme previously had unequal retirement ages, a man retiring early may still suffer a greater actuarial reduction than a woman, as *Ten Oever, Coloroll* etc (para 2.4 above) exclude pre-1990 service from compulsory equality. In most cases, therefore, where females had a special early retirement, males have only been given that entitlement in respect of post-17 May 1990 service.

4 Polygamous marriages

The only legislation (but as to the general position, see below) affecting the provision under occupational pension schemes for the spouses of polygamous marriages is to be found in the contracting-out requirements (Chapter 20, para 4). The effect of s 36(6) of the Social Security Pensions Act 1975, now PSA 1993 s 17(5), s 121 of the Social Security Contributions and Benefits Act 1992 and the regulations made under its predecessor (SI 1975 No 561) is that in certain circumstances a contracted-out pension scheme must provide a widow's pension to a person whose marriage to a scheme member had been celebrated under a law permitting polygamy. Such circumstances will only apply if in fact the member had no other spouse at the date of his death or throughout a day occurring after both of them had attained State pensionable age and retired from regular employment; in either such case, the widow will qualify for a pension if and so long as she qualifies for one of the benefits mentioned in s 17(5).

The effect of the regulations is that a potentially polygamous (but in fact monogamous) marriage is treated as monogamous and an actually polygamous marriage is also so treated in some circumstances but to the benefit only of the first wife. However, the first wife (who was a potential beneficiary while she was the only wife) is excluded from prospective entitlement if the husband marries a second wife (for example, while on vacation in his country of domicile) before the first wife attains State pensionable age and before she and the member retire from regular employment, unless the second wife predeceases the member or is divorced from him, and he does not in either case remarry.

The main questions arising for the practitioner are:

(*a*) whether, apart from the regulations, a widow of a potentially polygamous marriage is entitled to benefit under a pension scheme;
(*b*) if the answer to (*a*) is 'yes', whether several widows of an actually polygamous marriage could each successfully claim the benefit;
(*c*) whether, in a contracted-out scheme, it is right to limit the benefit to the circumstances stated in the regulations and disentitle the first wife if an employee marries again (polygamously);
(*d*) how to treat children's allowances.

The answer to the first question appears to be 'yes', subject to any specific provision to the contrary in the rules of the scheme. In *Re Sehota* [1978] 3 All ER 385 it was held that the first wife (who had been excluded under the deceased's will in favour of the second) was nonetheless a wife for the purpose of claiming under the Inheritance (Provision for Family and Dependants) Act 1975. The judgment quoted with approval from a speech in *Din v National Assistance Board* [1967] 1 All ER 750 in the Court of Appeal:

> 'When a question arises of recognising a foreign marriage or of construing the word "wife" in a statute, everything in my view depends on the purpose for which the marriage is to be recognised and the objects of the statute.'

There is no reason to doubt that the courts would adopt the same approach in construing a trust deed. The foregoing assumes, of course, that the marriage was celebrated under a law permitting polygamy.

The answer to the second question is more difficult. It would appear from *Re Sehota* that each widow could claim, but the amount of her entitlement would be uncertain. On the construction of some draft rules, each could claim the full pension. The practitioner should therefore seek instructions; if not intended, the rules might split the pension equally or confer discretion. The rules should also protect the trustees (and the fund) if payments are made in good faith on the basis of incorrect information.

The third question may fall into two parts. A scheme may incorporate contracting-out provisions by separate underpinning rules for protected rights (COMP schemes) or for pre-6 April 1997 GMPs (see Chapter 21). In that event it would be right to leave the obligatory widow's pension as the minimum required (and thus ensure that it is payable only when the corresponding State benefit is payable). However, in relation to the main rules, the answer will follow the decisions taken in respect of (*a*) and (*b*) above.

Children's allowances rarely present a difficulty. Almost all such allowances are limited, ie once the number of children increases above a particular figure, the allowance is unaffected. In practice, the trustees of a scheme are unlikely to wish to exclude dependent children (partly because a real need arises and partly because of the limitation on the amount of the benefit) including perhaps a discretion as to illegitimate children where in receipt of financial assistance from the deceased. In any event, in the case of rules adopted after 1969 the Family Law Reform Act 1969, s 15, provides that references to children (unless the rules provide otherwise) include illegitimate children, so that in the unlikely event that a polygamous marriage was held not to be a legitimate marriage (perhaps because of doubt as to where it was celebrated) the children would probably still qualify for benefit under the pension scheme. The practitioner is therefore well advised to include such children specifically (to avoid doubt) but to ensure that the totality of the benefits is limited and perhaps that the trustees have discretion as to the division of the benefit between the children.

Chapter 23

Divorce

1 General

Two major changes regarding pensions and divorce have just been enacted, and are outlined in paras 2 and 3 below. They are:

(1) 'Earmarking'—a court order directing that an ordinary scheme benefit, when it arises, be paid to another party—effective regarding lump sums since 1 July 1996, and regarding pensions since 6 April 1997, provided the divorce (or separation or nullity) proceedings had begun on or after 1 July 1996.
(2) 'Splitting'—a court order to split the member's pension entitlement, creating a pension also for the other party, possibly starting at a different date—not yet in force.

Divorce is therefore now relevant to pensions in a number of ways, eg:

(1) The question whether the member's pension, in whole or in part, and/or a lump sum arising on death, will be directed to the other party.
(2) If a lump sum is payable on the retirement or death of a member (or on his leaving service), and is not the subject of a court order, the question whether a former spouse can claim a share of it.
(3) If the rules provide for a pension to a member's surviving spouse the question whether a present spouse will lose that prospective benefit on divorce.
(4) The loss of a prospective widow/widower's pension and /or the prospect of a lump sum (either during a member's lifetime to

help him meet commitments to the respondent or on his death) may influence the financial provisions which the court may order.

(5) The question whether the loss of a prospective widow/widower's pension may still be a means to oppose a petition for divorce.
(6) The provision of information by scheme administrators.
(7) The administration of notices and transfers.

The practitioner who is acting for an employer or trustees will usually find that there is no desire to be involved in the matrimonial problems of members. However, items (6) and (7) above will inevitably involve administrators, under the new legislation. Further, it is the almost universal practice for pension scheme rules to favour a current spouse and not a divorced spouse (regardless of financial dependence) so that the questions raised in (2) and (3) will usually result in requests for information.

Under the Disclosure regs SI 1996 No 1655, reg 4(3), a spouse is entitled to obtain from the trustees basic information about the pension scheme eg the published booklet. Interestingly, the Divorce regs SI 1996 No 1676, regs 4 and 5, as amended by SI 1997 No 636, require the trustees to provide transfer value information to the member (not the spouse who must presumably seek it through the divorce proceedings).

2 Earmarking

2.1 New provisions: Pensions Act 1995

The Pensions Act 1995 introduces a new provision to enable the courts in respect of payments that would otherwise go to a member or would be distributed on his death, to direct pension trustees or administrators to pay these to the other party to the matrimonial proceedings. This does not create an extra liability for the pension scheme, but it does involve administration.

The provision, colloquially known as 'earmarking', is regarded as a half-way house towards 'splitting'—para 3 below. However, earmarking had the advantage that it could be implemented with a minimal impact on the State pension scheme or public sector schemes. It also addressed the key problem under English law (Scotland was more advanced) that in making financial provision and property adjustment orders the Court was to have regard to the income and other financial resources of the parties to the marriage that they had or were likely to have 'in the foreseeable future' which was generally interpreted as ignoring pension whose commmencement was more than ten years in the future—Matrimonial Causes Act 1973, s 25(2)(*a*). See for example *Roberts v Roberts* [1986] 2 All ER 483 where a lump sum was payable in the year 2003; it was held that the guesswork involved in forecasting the capital available in the year 2003, having regard to possible promotion and other factors, caused the question to fall outside the 'foreseeable future' mentioned in s 25(1)(*a*) (plainly a misprint for (2)(*a*) which is quoted at page 485j).

Secondly, the Pensions Act 1995 addressed the need for an order against the pension scheme itself (ie the trustees or managers) so that the divorced spouse was no longer dependent upon the agreement of the pension scheme member not to exercise options that could defeat the payment of benefits at an expected date, and was also not dependent upon the implementation by the *member* of an order for payment to be made out of those benefits.

Section 166 of the Pensions Act 1995 inserted the following new provisions in the 1973 Act (ignoring s 166(2)—(6) since they do not affect the principle to be derived from the main provisions, but note that they enable the court to override s 91 of the Pensions Act 1995 by ordering a diversion of pension). The provisions are numbered from 25B as there was an existing s 25A (which has no direct relevance to pensions).

25B Pensions

(1) The matters to which the court is to have regard [when exercising its powers to make financial provision orders] under section 25(2) above include—

(*a*) in the case of paragraph (*a*), any benefits under a pension scheme which a party to the marriage has or is likely to have, and

(*b*) in the case of paragraph (*h*), any benefits under a pension scheme which, by reason of the dissolution or annulment of the marriage, a party to the marriage will lose the chance of acquiring,

and, accordingly, in relation to benefits under a pension scheme, section 25(2)(*a*) above shall have effect as if 'in the foreseeable future' were omitted.

(2) In any proceedings for a financial provision order under section 23 above in a case where a party to the marriage has, or is likely to have, any benefit under a pension scheme, the court shall, in addition to considering any other matter which it is required to consider apart from this subsection, consider—

(*a*) whether, having regard to any matter to which it is required to have regard in the proceedings by virtue of subsection (1) above, such an order (whether deferred or not) should be made, and

(*b*) where the court determines to make such an order, how the terms of the order should be affected, having regard to any such matter.

(3) The following provisions apply where, having regard to any benefits under a pension scheme, the court determines to make an order under section 23 above.

(4) To the extent to which the order is made having regard to any benefits under a pension scheme, the order may require the trustees or managers of the pension scheme in question, if at any time any payment in respect of any benefits under the scheme becomes due to the party with pension rights, to make a payment for the benefit of the other party.

(5) The amount of any payment which, by virtue of subsection (4) above, the trustees or managers are required to make under the order at any time shall not exceed the amount of the payment which is due at that time to the party with pension rights.

(6) Any such payment by the trustees or managers—

(*a*) shall discharge so much of the trustees or managers liability to the party with pension rights as corresponds to the amount of the payment, and

(*b*) shall be treated for all purposes as a payment made by the party with pension rights in or towards the discharge of his liability under the order.

(7) Where the party with pension rights may require any benefits which he has or is likely to have under the scheme to be commuted, the order may require him to commute the whole or part of those benefits; and this section applies to the payment of any amount commuted in pursuance of the order as it applies to other payments in respect of benefits under the scheme.

25C Pensions: lump sums

(1) The power of the court under section 23 above to order a party to a marriage to pay a lump sum to the other party includes, where the benefits which the party with pension rights has or is likely to have under a pension scheme include any lump sum payable in respect of his death, power to make any of the following provision by the order.

(2) The court may—

(*a*) if the trustees or managers of the pension scheme in question have power to determine the person to whom the sum, or any part of it, is to be paid, require them to pay the whole or part of that sum, when it becomes due, to the other party,

(*b*) if the party with pension rights has power to nominate the person to whom the sum, or any part of it, is to be paid, require the party with pension rights to nominate the other party in respect of the whole or part of that sum,

(*c*) in any other case, require the trustees or managers of the pension scheme in question to pay the whole or part of that sum, when it becomes due, for the benefit of the other party instead of to the person to whom, apart from the order, it would be paid.

(3) Any payment by the trustees or managers under an order made under section 23 above by virtue of this section shall discharge so much of the trustees, or managers, liability in respect of the party with pension rights as corresponds to the amount of the payment.

25D Pensions: supplementary

(1) Where—

(*a*) an order made under section 23 above by virtue of section 25B or 25C above imposes any requirement on the trustees or managers of a pension scheme ("the first scheme") and the party with pension rights acquires transfer credits under another pension scheme ("the new scheme") which are derived (directly or indirectly) from a transfer from the first scheme of all his accrued rights under that scheme (including transfer credits allowed by that scheme), and

(*b*) the trustees or managers of the new scheme have been given notice in accordance with regulations,

the order shall have effect as if it has been made instead in respect of the trustees or managers of the new scheme; and in this subsection "transfer credits" has the same meaning as in the Pension Schemes Act 1993.

(2) Regulations may—

(*a*) in relation to any provision of sections 25B or 25C above which authorises the court making an order under section 23 above to require the trustees or managers of a pension scheme to make a payment for the benefit of the other party, make provision as to the person to whom, and the terms on which, the payment is to be made,

(*b*) require notices to be given in respect of changes of circumstances relevant to such orders which include provision made by virtue of sections 25B and 25C above.

(*c*) make provision for the trustees or managers of any pension scheme to provide, for the purposes of orders under section 23 above, information as to the value of any benefits under the scheme,

(*d*) make provision for the recovery of the administrative expenses of—

(i) complying with such orders, so far as they include provision made by virtue of sections 25B and 25C above, and

(ii) providing such information,

from the party with pension rights or the other party,

(*e*) make provision for the value of any benefits under a pension scheme to be calculated and verified, for the purposes of orders under section 23 above, in a prescribed manner,

and regulations made by virtue of paragraph (*e*) above may provide for that value to be calculated and verified in accordance with guidance which is prepared and from time to time revised by a prescribed person and approved by the Secretary of State.

(3) In this section and sections 25B and 25C above—

(*a*) references to a pension scheme include—

(i) a retirement annuity contract, or

(ii) an annuity, or insurance policy,

purchased or transferred for the purpose of giving effect to rights under a pension scheme,

(*b*) in relation to such a contract or annuity, references to the trustees or managers shall be read as references to the provider of the annuity,

(*c*) in relation to such a policy, references to the trustees or managers shall be read as references to the insurer,

and in section 25B(1) and (2) above, references to benefits under a pension scheme include any benefits by way of pension, whether under a pension scheme or not.

(4) In this section and sections 25B and 25C above—

"the party with pension rights" means the party to the marriage who has or is likely to have benefits under a pension scheme and "the other party" means the other party to the marriage,

"pension scheme" means an occupational pension scheme or a personal pension scheme (applying the definitions in section 1 of the Pension Schemes Act 1993, but as if the reference to employed earners in the definition of "personal pension scheme" were to any earners),

"prescribed" means prescribed by regulations, and

"regulations" means regulations made by the Lord Chancellor;

and the power to make regulations under this section shall be exercisable by statutory instrument, which shall be subject to annulment in pursuance of a resolution of either House of Parliament.

The new s 25B(1) refers to s 25(2)(*a*) and (*h*). The former relates to income and other financial resources. The latter refers to the value of any benefit which, by reason of the dissolution of the marriage, the party will lose the chance of acquiring—eg a spouse's pension or death benefit.

At the end of (1) are the key words, deleting 'in the foreseeable future' in relation to pension scheme benefits.

Very broadly, these provisions enable the court to order that part or all of a member's pension is to be 'earmarked' for his former spouse and paid to the spouse by the scheme. The court will also be able to order that lump-sum death benefits be paid to the former spouse (even where their distribution would normally be under discretionary powers). While ensuring that pension assets are always taken into account, the provision has the disadvantage that it cuts across the 'clean break' principle that has been part of divorce law since 1984. (However, for a 'clean break' see 3 below.)

The new s 25B(4) enables the court to order the trustees or managers of the pension scheme (who are referred to in the rest of this chapter as simply 'the pension scheme') if '*at any time* any payment . . . becomes due . . ., to make a payment for the benefit of the other party' but, by (5) the latter is not to receive more than would have been payable to the member *at that time* (author's emphasis, in both places). This seems to enable the applicant to receive the benefit of pension increases. Sub-section (6) makes clear that the payment can be less than the full amount due to the respondent.

It would appear that the pension would remain that of the original scheme member for tax purposes but this is not absolutely clear and may depend on further regulations.

Sub-section (7) enables the court to order compulsory commutation, and to include that sum in the earmarked rights.

Regulations provide for the variation of orders.

Third party rights

Although s 25C(1) refers to pension rights of the *member* in respect of lump sum arising on his death, subs (2) makes clear that the court can override the normal discretionary trust arising under the rules of the pension scheme, and direct that all or part of the lump sum death benefit be paid to the applicant, when it becomes due. It similarly provides that where there are nomination rights, the member can be ordered to nominate the applicant. Under sub-paragraph (*c*) a third party eg a child, can be disentitled from an interest in the lump sum (even where there is no discretion) in favour of the divorced spouse.

Whereas earmarking of a lump sum can defeat another dependent, it appears that earmarking of pension does not apply to a pension arising for a future spouse, although the member could defeat such spouse by transferring his full cash equivalent to a buyout policy—see para 2.2 below.

2.2 Transfers

Section 25D provides for the acquired rights to apply equally against a transferee scheme provided that scheme has been given notice (see below). Subsection (3) in effect provides that the transferee scheme may be a buy-out policy, and subs (4) provide that it may be a personal pension scheme (and defines pension scheme widely).

Presumably the member can still transfer his full cash equivalent to a buyout policy and, on maturity, choose a single life pension. The order would then direct the provider to pay part (deriving from his original scheme rights) to the divorced spouse. A potentially difficult provision is reg 5 of SI 1996 No 1676 that requires the pension scheme, if so requested by the member, to state the proportion of the estimated value that is in their opinion attributable to any contingent pension or allowance to which the spouse might have become entitled on the member's death.

A paper issued by the Lord Chancellor's Department while the regulations were in course of preparation, dated June 1996, stated that the proportion of a cash equivalent attributable to the spouse's pension should be identified in a 'broad brush' manner—it is difficult to see that this can be any simplification. Presumably one of the reasons for valuing a member's pension without the death benefit spouse's pension is because the loss of the latter is relevant to the other party in seeking general financial provision.

Interestingly, the paper mentioned that there would be no valuation of State benefits, and that the basic State pension would normally be supplied to the divorced spouse in his/her own right by reason of the substitution rules whereby the former spouse's national insurance record may be substituted. Although SERPS is not diverted, the loss would still be taken into account by the court, and the DSS Benefits Agency offers a pensions forecasting service from which a quotation of the notional capital value of the accrued net SERPS entitlement is to be available on request. Paragraph 29 of the paper makes clear that in the case of a partial transfer, the original scheme can only comply with the order to the extent of the reduced benefits, and yet the order does not transfer to the new scheme. This appears to tie in with s 25D(1)(*a*) which refers to *all* the member's accrued rights, regarding an order that *does* transfer. It also ties in with reg 7(1)(*b*) as the partial transfer would presumably be an event resulting in a 'significant reduction' in the benefits payable—hence the provision for notice mentioned below.

Not surprisingly, there does not seem to be an obligation upon a scheme to accept a transfer value that is subject to an earmarking order.

2.3 Administration expenses

Section 25D(2) authorises regulations to require pension schemes to provide information and also to enable them to recover administrative expenses both regarding the provision of information and the compliance with payment orders. The member will be entitled to some information at no cost, under the Disclosure Regs, but repeat information would be chargeable. Paragraph 35 of the Lord Chancellor's Department paper makes clear that this is the policy intention.

The pension scheme's costs are recoverable from the member, but at the time the member is unlikely to be in receipt of benefit and therefore the costs cannot be recovered by simply withholding the appropriate sum. There is likely to be room for argument about payment. So far as amount is concerned, reg 10 provides for assessment by the court if not agreed.

Interestingly, reg 11 in effect provides that if the trustees have made representations, the court when making a pensions adjustment order should take into account the practicability of effecting payment, having regard to the information supplied, and the administrative expenses—an obvious possibility being the impracticability of making small payments overseas.

2.4 Regulations

The main regulations are SI 1996 No 1676 (as amended by SI 1997 No 636 to take account of updated disclosure and transfer regulations, and to make minor improvements). Important practical provisions, however, are contained in an amendment to the Family Proceedings Rules 1991, effected by SI 1996 No 1674 and updated by SI 1997 No 637 which also contains a new form for the provision of information when applying for a matrimonial consent order. The latter insert together a new rule 2.70 regarding pensions, requiring a party to give all information concerning pension benefits including the most recent cash equivalent figure, and providing that a copy of the application be served on the pension scheme together with an address for service and also an address to which any payment would have to be made, and *where* that is the address of a bank etc, the account details (emphasis supplied, to indicate that there is no compulsion to provide bank account details although it is understood that a practice direction may be made).

By Rule 2.70(5) the pension scheme *may* within 14 days after service require the applicant to provide a copy of the affidavit supporting the application (emphasis supplied). Within 14 days of receipt, the scheme may file an affidavit in answer and, if it wishes, may require an appointment to be fixed by the court—presumably where there is likely to be a dispute as to the member's entitlement. Most schemes will wish to avoid any such involvement.

By Rule 2.70(8) the pension scheme can object to a proposed order, and the court may then require attendance or written details of the objection. Again, it is unlikely that schemes will wish to be involved. Presumably an objection would only relate to incorrect information or an impractical proposal. Sub-rule (9) then requires the party benefiting from the order (or an amendment or revocation) to serve a copy on the pension scheme.

SI 1996 No 1676 comprises the main regulations under the new provisions. Regulation 3 provides for values to be calculated on the cash equivalent basis—apart from pensioners, to whom that would not be relevant, and to whom instead reg 3(6) provides for any appropriate method of calculation. Regulations 3 and 4 have been updated to refer to the new Disclosure Regs, but the principle has not changed, *viz* that cash equivalent and transfer value information should be furnished to the member for the purpose of the court proceedings and that a reasonable charge may be made (save where the disclosure regs enable it to be obtained without charge—see the new reg 10A). The valuation date is to be within three months beginning with the date of the request but, surprisingly, the information need not be supplied until after the valuation date (but within ten days thereafter).

2.5 Notices

Where an order has been made, and subsequently the member transfers to another scheme or policy, the first scheme *must* give notice both to the new scheme and to the other party, within 14 days after the date of the transfer—reg 6. The notice to the new scheme consists of a copy of the court order and other particulars such as notices from earlier schemes—reg 6(3) as amended. The notice to the other party gives details of the transfer and the other scheme. It also has to inform the other party that the order is to have effect as if it had been made against the receiving scheme.

Notice to the other party must also be given where an event (other than transfer or market falls) has occurred which is likely to result in a significant reduction in the benefits payable under the scheme—reg 7. This is likely to be a very unusual event, and the thought of giving notice may not be uppermost in the minds of the trustees. It is not clear what loss the other party would suffer if notice were overlooked, or what sanction would apply. Contracted-out schemes sometimes make *partial* transfers to contracted-in schemes, eg retaining the guaranteed minimum pension (GMP), which would seem to be such an event; since 5 April 1997 these will be less frequent. It is unclear whether a member's decision to opt out of a scheme (as respects future accrual) would be such an event.

Interestingly, where the other party remarries, and the order ceases to have effect, or any particulars such as address or bank account have changed, *that party* is obliged to give notice to the pension scheme within 14 days. It seems unlikely that this will be uppermost in the party's mind at a time of remarriage. Presumably, if notice is not given, the member would have a claim against that party and not against the pension scheme. Conversely, reg 8(4) provides that where the particulars have ceased to be accurate and it is no longer possible to pay the other party (eg a move to an unknown address) the pension scheme may instead pay the member and be discharged to the extent of the payment. Reg 8A makes consequential changes where there has been a transfer.

If pension schemes do not have an appropriate system which records the existence of an order on the member's records, and which ensures that it is automatically reminded when a request for a cash equivalent is made, there is the likelihood that on making a transfer payment the scheme will not give notice to the receiving scheme, and will be left with the obligation to provide an earmarked pension but no money to pay for it.

2.6 Commencement

Regulation 3 of SI 1996 No 1674 provides that the rules are to apply to petitions presented on or after 1 July 1996 and that in respect of earlier petitions, it is as if the new rules had not come into force.

3 Splitting: Family Law Act 1996

The Family Law Act 1996, s 16, amends the above new 'earmarking' provisions to provide for pension 'splitting', but no commencement order has yet been made to bring these provisions into effect.

A Green Paper (Cm 3345) dated July 1996 indicated the difficulties that may arise on pension splitting and raised numerous questions for consultation. It was followed by a White Paper (Cm 3564) dated February 1997 which stresses the advantage of splitting in creating a 'clean break' but underlines that much work will be needed before legislation can be ready. It barely mentions the Family Law Act 1986, and in 1.14 refers to new primary legislation. The change of government on 1 May 1997 is unlikely to affect the principles within the White Paper as both parties have advocated 'splitting'. The new government may look to speed up the timetable.

A key point is the intention to split SERPS' entitlements. The Green Paper had indicated that the national insurance computer system will not be able to cope with this until, at the earliest, April 2000, and that is the target date in the White Paper, albeit see above regarding the change of government.

The new provision in the Family Law Act 1996 is therefore unlikely ever to be in force. It is very simple, adding paragraph (*c*) to s 25B(2) to provide that the court shall consider 'whether the order should provide for the accrued rights of the party . . . to be divided between that party and the other party in such a way as to reduce the pension rights of the [former] and to create pension rights for the other party'.

A new subs (8) is added to provide that where there is a willing recipient scheme, the trustees need not set up a benefit under their own scheme if they are able to make a transfer payment. This leads to the question whether the trustees will be empowered to make a compulsory payment to a buyout policy; it seems unlikely that this could safely be done without independent financial advice, and there remains a danger to both the adviser and the trustees that the other party would complain that the wrong provider had been chosen.

Sub-section (8) also provides that the court is not to have power to require a transfer if the scheme is unfunded (unless it is willing to make a transfer) or in prescribed circumstances. It appears that this will protect unfunded public sector schemes.

The White Paper indicates that the other party, for whom a benefit is to be set up, may be treated as a member (paragraph 3.14) but placed in a new category (4.13). No doubt there will be new disclosure requirements, and probably the right to a cash equivalent transfer. The paper proposes a *trustees* option whether to offer membership or external transfer (or the choice)—para 3.14.

The two significant advantages of 'splitting' are:

(*a*) a clean break can be made;
(*b*) the other party does not suffer loss of pension when the original member dies. Indeed, the other party would receive benefits at his or her own appropriate age whereas an earmarked pension is necessarily simply a diverted benefit paid to that other party but linked to the circumstances of the original member.

Paragraphs 3.4 and 3.5 of the White Paper suggest that earmarking will continue when splitting is in force, but that legislation will take powers to amend it or phase it out, or possibly continue it, according to experience. This ties in with 2.4/2.5 which suggest that splitting is not appropriate on judicial separation.

An interesting question is whether an applicant would be better off with an earmarked pension as it would appear that earmarking applies potentially to the whole of a pension in payment (if the court so orders) including the part accrued after the divorce order. By contrast, splitting would take the value at the date of the order (paragraph 2.12). It remains to be seen, however, whether the courts make earmarking orders to the above full extent.

The proposal on splitting is to treat the divorced spouse as a deferred pensioner with normal revaluation and indexation (paragraph 4.14). Both parties' pensions would count towards the Inland Revenue limits applicable to the scheme member (paragraph 4.23). This seems contrary to the policy that the member should have an opportunity to rebuild his own pension, and no doubt will be much debated before April 2000.

4 Scheme Benefits

Spouse's pension

On divorce, a member's spouse usually loses all prospect of a pension from the scheme on his eventual *death*. If a scheme is contracted out (Chapter 20, para 4 and 22, para 4) it must provide a pension (or protected rights) to a member's surviving spouse. There is no corresponding requirement in respect of divorced spouses.

The circumstances when the spouse's pension is payable are outlined in Chapter 20, para 4.2. If a widow has not attained age 60 (and, occasionally, even if she has) the pension may cease on cohabitation or remarriage. Similar provisions apply to widowers. Many schemes include the remarriage provision but few extend it to cohabitation.

Until the removal, with effect from 1 November 1986, of requirements relating to the excess over the guaranteed minimum pension (GMP) (Chapter 20, para 4.2), the balance of the requisite benefit above the guaranteed minimum could be paid to one or more dependents of the deceased member (although the relevant rule must have been approved by the OPB under s 36(8) of the Social Security Pensions Act 1975 and had to be discretionary). Most schemes that contained such provision will have retained it. It follows that where there has been a divorce, only this balance (in effect any scheme provision above the level of the GMP, necessarily accrued before 6 April 1997) can be paid to the first wife (but a former husband can receive more as widower's GMP accrued only from 6 April 1988), and even then the question of Inland Revenue approval must be considered (as mentioned below).

Apart from contracting out, rules sometimes incorporate discretion where the member and his wife are living apart at the time of cessation of employment and/or the time of his death. This discretion is usually matched by a discretion to deem another dependant to be his wife for the purpose of the scheme.

The Inland Revenue requirements for exempt approval (Chapter 17, para 3) do not permit the payment of a pension to a person other than a widow or widower unless that person was financially dependent on the member. It follows than automatic rule providing for divorced wives would not be permissible unless the requirement of dependence were included. However, a spouse in receipt of an 'earmarked' member's pension (see para 2 above) would, presumably be dependent.

Lump sums may arise on a member's retirement or death. The lump sums on retirement can be payable only to the member. In divorce proceedings it is therefore possible for the court to order the member to request payment of such sum (if it is by way of commutation of pension) and pay part or all of it to the other party. Lump sums on death are sometimes payable to the member's estate, in which case an order attaching the prospective benefit (if any) can be made, but are more usually payable to such of the member's family and dependants as the trustees select—but for proceedings commenced after June 1996 the court can override the discretion (see the commentary on s 25C in para 2.1 above).

In *Johnson v Johnson* [1982] 12 Fam Law 116, under the former law, a petition on the grounds of five years' separation was successfully opposed by reason of potential grave financial hardship for the wife. Medical reports indicated a considerably greater life expectancy for her, and she stood to lose an index-linked pension in widowhood that, at the time of the hearing, stood prospectively at nearly £2,000 per annum. The husband had no capital with which to mitigate the hardship, and his state of health precluded insurance.

In Scotland the pension rights which have risen during the period of the marriage are deemed to form part of the matrimonial property, Family Law (Scotland) Act 1985, s 10(5), and thus to be shared fairly between the parties. However, since this does not alter the rule of the pension scheme that disentitles the divorced spouse, the effect has been to require other assets to be transferred where available. Section 167 of the Pensions Act 1995, inserts into the 1985 Act various new 'earmarking' matters, principally regarding capital sum orders.

Chapter 24

Trusteeship

1 General

The task of administering a trust fund (that is a fund held by a trustee or trustees for the benefit of persons or objects other than, although possibly including, the trustee) is rarely required of a businessman until he establishes a pension fund. Pension funds are almost invariably held on trust, mainly for the following reasons:

(*a*) a trust is the normal means in English law of attaching to assets the rights and interests of a wide class of persons who are to benefit from them, including persons who may not yet have been born;
(*b*) the existence of a trust separates the assets from those belonging to the employer (and, perhaps his creditors);
(*c*) the law imposes strict obligations upon trustees, so that their conduct can be scrutinised by the court; contrast a contractual situation where warranties as to conduct would be required to offer the same protection;
(*d*) as explained in Chapter 17, para 1.2, the main tax advantages enjoyed by pension funds apply only if they are held on 'irrevocable trust'.

The first three of these reasons indicate that the concept of a trust antedates that of a pension fund. It does so by many centuries. As a result, the law relating to trusteeship arises from the experience of private family settlements. The duties of trustees are therefore strictly interpreted, in a manner to which the businessman (whose first priority may be practicality) will generally not be accustomed. Further, the concept of personal liability may be strange to an executive who has become a pension fund trustee in the ordinary course of taking over a new department within his employer company. A modern answer to this problem is discussed at para 8 below. The practitioner may well find it necessary to advise on this question of personal liability when the establishment of a scheme is first proposed.

On the whole the vehicle of the trust has adapted very well to pension matters. The two most important means of adaptation are, firstly, the provision of s 69(2) of the Trustee Act 1925 that the trust instrument can enlarge (or reduce) the powers conferred by that Act, and, secondly, the manner in which the power of revocation and resettlement (frequently found in family trusts) has been adapted to become the power of general alteration (sometimes fettered by provisos, and sometimes not, but always subject to the fiduciary duty mentioned in para 2 below).

The practitioner may find that the summary of various aspects of trusteeship set out in paras 2–6 below is of assistance when advising as to the administration of a scheme. Where appropriate, reference is made to provisions which, it is considered, can usefully be incorporated in the trust deed. Most of these are also referred to in Chapter 3 or 13. The questions of the appointment of trustees and the practitioner's relationship to them are considered in paras 7 and 9 below. Some relevant cases are outlined in para 10, and trustees' liability insurance is mentioned in para 11 (with some reference to indemnity clauses).

The existence of trustees' duties is no guarantee that they will be carried out. The 'Maxwell' scandal is outlined in para 12 below, with some pointers to inhibit a repetition.

The Pension Law Review Committee (para 12.2 below) recommended that trust law should continue to provide the foundation for interests arising under pension schemes but that some principles of trust law be modified for this purpose. The Government accepted this. Thus the standard rule of unanimity for trustees' decisions has been altered to 'majority' unless the scheme provides otherwise—see para 3 below and Chapter 25, para 3.2. The main area of major addition, to trust law in the Pensions Act 1995 is in the detailed sections on investment powers and their application (see Chapter 16, para 16). However, in numerous other areas there are changes, such as the appointment of trustees (para 7.2 below), the regulation of their appointments of professional advisers, their obligation to report delayed contributions to OPRA, their power to modify schemes for certain purposes of the Act etc—see Chapter 25 generally.

2 Fiduciary duty

The primary duties of a trustee are the preservation of trust capital and the application of that capital and its income in accordance with the trust instrument. The latter will describe the class or classes of beneficiaries.

Although the employer will, under normal Inland Revenue requirements, be an ultimate beneficiary in that a surplus on winding up a fund will usually be declared by the trust instrument to be held upon trust for the employer, it is not a beneficiary in the normal sense that is applied to, say, a remainderman who will take upon the death of the life tenant. The object of the pension fund, whether express or implied, will be the provision of pension and other benefits for employees and their dependants, and not the provision of a savings fund for the employer. In one sense, therefore, the employer will not be considered when a trustee has regard to the investment of a fund or its application as between different classes of beneficiaries (but regarding the former, see Chapter 16, para 16.4, for the new duty to consult the employer—subject to the exceptions referred to in para 16.1).

On the other hand a pension fund usually depends for the provision of its stated benefits upon the willingness and ability of the employer to continue its contributions. This willingness may be given the force of obligation by a covenant in the trust instrument between the employer and the trustees, but it is usually balanced by a provision for the cessation of contributions after due notice. Therefore, although the trustees will not include the employer among those to be benefited, they may feel that it is reasonable to pay some regard to the wishes of the employer where those wishes do not conflict with the trustees' duty.

There is no settled law as to where the balance lies (but see the reference to *Teacher's Retirement System of New York* in para 10.1 below). Some schemes include express provision for a refund of surplus to the employer, if requested, after a valuation (see Chapter 17, paras 9 and 10 for the Inland Revenue aspects, and Chapter 25, para 3.4, regarding the requirements under the Pensions Act 1995). Clearly where an employer is in liquidation, its employees have been dismissed and the undertaking of its business has been sold or wound up, the wishes of the liquidator are unlikely to carry weight with the trustees, since his actions will neither settle more funds upon them nor create more (or reduce the number of) beneficiaries. However, if a scheme has just been started and provides for substantial benefits in respect of past service, the possibility of paying those benefits may be wholly dependent on the future contributions of the employer. If the trustees are asked to agree some proposal of the employer which, while it does not conflict with the trust instrument, does require the exercise of their discretion in a particular manner, they may well feel it right to have regard to the employer's wishes but only as a means of protecting the interests of each class of beneficiary. The question is touched upon in Chapter 15, para 5 and Chapter 16. While the trustee may be anxious he can bear in mind the terms of s 61 of the Trustee Act 1925, which enables the court to excuse a trustee for the consequences of a breach of trust where he has 'acted honestly and reasonably, and ought fairly to be excused'. Nonetheless, the trustee cannot proceed blindly and without advice, hoping to be excused for honest but wrong administration. He must acquaint himself with his powers and duties, both those expressed in the trust instrument and those conferred by statute or the general law. He must be particularly aware of the positive duties imposed by the Pensions Act 1995.

A clear breach of the terms of the trust deed cannot be justified, and the favouring of one set of beneficiaries over another would, prima facie, be inexcusable. However, the peculiar nature of pension funds (mentioned above) may create circumstances where some action is essential and no guidance can be found in the traditional sources. It is in such circumstances that a trustee would normally apply to the court for directions but if he feels constrained from doing so (see below) and considers his actions to be justified and in the interests of the beneficiaries as a whole, he may receive some protection from s 61. There can be no hard-and-fast rule as to the extent of that protection.

An indemnity is often sought by trustees from the employer in respect of a proposed action. The question whether this protects the trustee should be considered carefully, for the existence of the indemnity suggests knowledge that the conduct was in breach of trust and may therefore militate against an exoneration under s 61. This could result in personal liability on the part of a trustee with right of recourse against an employer who might be in liquidation. Nonetheless, on the merger or winding up of pension funds, an indemnity from a substantial employer, such as a public company, may be of value in assisting trustees to take a decision, for example to permit an overall arrangement to continue but under a new constitution.

It is always advisable to include in the trust instrument an express provision that a trustee is not to be liable except for wilful conscious default and that, with that exception, he has a right of recourse to and indemnity from the trust fund. These may seem to be sweeping safeguards for the trustees, but they are no wider than those generally given in wills to solicitor-trustees and, although strictly construed, are of comfort to trustees required to make practical decisions. Although the trustee could always apply to the court for directions, he may be in a situation where such application would break a confidence and perhaps destroy a commercial opportunity created by the employer. On the other hand, there may be an occasion where he has little choice but to apply, for example where the unanimous approval of the trustees is required to an act of which he disapproves. To stand out may jeopardise his personal position in some other respect, whereas to resign in order to facilitate a breach of trust will not relieve him of liability.

'Wilful default' is mentioned, without definition, in the Trustee Act 1925, s 30(1) in relation to monies deposited with a broker (and others). The author follows *Re Vickery* [1931] All ER 562 in interpreting wilful default as consciousness of negligence or breach of duty or recklessness in the performance of the trust, albeit the decision has been criticised in its context. The earlier case of *Speight v Gaunt* (1983) 9 App Cas 1, not there cited, turned primarily on the reasonableness of employing an unsupervised broker, and hardly on the subsidiary issue of wilful default in connection with monies deposited. The test of prudent conduct was applied in *Lucking's Will Trusts* [1967] 3 All ER 726, but the facts did not fall within s 30(1) nor did the ratio relate to a true agent. It presumably remains open to the trust instrument to confer the wider indemnity (in which event there seems no reason to doubt the natural meaning of 'wilful default').

Note, however, that the Pensions Act 1995, now restricts the freedom to confer exoneration. Section 31 prohibits reimbursement from the pension scheme of civil penalties incurred by the trustees with OPRA, and creates a criminal offence for breach.

Exoneration is no longer available for breach of trust in the performance of investment functions—s 33(1). Exoneration in respect of delegated duties will depend upon proper selection of the delegate and reasonable monitoring—s 34(4) and (6). See also Chapter 13, para 3 and 16; and para 11 below.

3 Unanimity

In the absence of a contrary provision in the trust instrument, the normal rule relating to private trustee decisions, that is they must be unanimous, applied until 6 April 1997. (A technical exception was that a dissenting trustee could be compelled to concur in the sale of land held on trust for sale).

Since a pension scheme requires frequent decision-taking, it was normal to alter this rule and provide for decision by majority, subject to a quorum being present.

A sole corporate trustee would have corresponding provisions in its articles of association (see para 8.1 below).

The Pensions Act 1995, reversed the presumption so that decisions are by majority unless the trust instrument provides otherwise—see Chapter 25, para 3.2, for a fuller treatment.

4 Powers of delegation

The statutory power of delegation relates, in general terms, to the appointment of agents to transact specific business and not to the delegation of discretionary powers. Such powers can be delegated for up to 12 months by power of attorney, but the donor of the powers is liable for the acts of the donee—see ss 23 and 25 of the Trustee Act 1925, as amended.

Most large pension schemes can only operate if the trustees are able to delegate the day-to-day operation of the power of investment as well as many of the administrative powers. A well-drawn trust deed will enable such delegation. Care must still be exercised by the trustees in the choice of delegate and the establishment of reporting procedures.

See also the final paragraph of para 2 above.

The 'Maxwell' affair, outlined in para 12 below, has demonstrated the need for a cautious mandate procedure and the use of delegates of recognised standing.

The freedom to extend the power of delegation of investment powers is now restricted by numerous sections of the Pensions Act 1995, but principally s 34 (see Chapter 16, para 16).

5 Duty to invest

There are many ancient rules regarding a trustee's duty to invest. These arose from the need (mentioned in para 2 above) for fairness as between classes of beneficiaries and in particular those entitled to income and those entitled to reversionary interests. Failure to invest, or at least place moneys on deposit, might result in liability on the part of the trustee to provide the lost income.

Most pension schemes provide that trustees have the widest possible investment powers, including the power to purchase land and non-income-producing assets (such as commodities) or assets involving liabilities (such as shares that are only partly paid). There is usually also power to maintain cash balances, and perhaps to borrow.

Trustees previously needed to be aware of the insider trading provisions of the Company Securities (Insider Dealing) Act 1985 (albeit they might have been protected by s 7 if they acted on the advice of a person as there described) and Pt VII of the Financial Services Act 1986, both repealed by the Criminal Justice Act 1993 to implement EU Directive 89/592 EEC by amending and restating the law on insider dealing. The 1993 Act sets out the new provisions in Part V.

All except the largest schemes effect insurances and therefore include an express power to do so. Smaller funds may be wholly 'insured', in which event the actual investment will be a policy of some sort. Such schemes usually operate under a trust deed based on a life office draft (Chapter 13, para 2) containing special provisions authorising the payment of premiums or contributions under such policies. Such provisions should be drafted to take into account the requirement (in the Trustee Investments Act 1961, s 6 and the Pensions Act 1995, s 36) for diversification of investments (although each section does incorporate the saving words 'in so far as is appropriate to the circumstances of the trust [scheme]').

Section 34(1) of the Pensions Act 1995, confers the power of investment of an absolute beneficial owner, subject to any restriction imposed by the pension scheme.

6 Conflict of interest

The fiduciary duty described in para 2 above is inherent in the position of a trustee. It follows that his primary duty is to the beneficiaries or objects of the trust. This is so even if he has another capacity, eg that of employee, or even employer. Where a conflict of interest is apparent, he should seek advice—see para 9 below.

Nonetheless, although a pure trustee may not benefit from the trust, he may do so if he is also a beneficiary. To avoid doubt as to the position where the particular benefits may vary according to the exercise of a trustee's powers, it is common for the trust instrument to provide that such exercise shall not be questioned on account of the personal position of the trustee. Such provisions are subject to the general rule relating to the fiduciary exercise of the powers and perhaps may be effective only where the benefit (or its variation) is merely incidental to that exercise. The latter is probably also the effect of s 39 of the Pensions Act 1995.

7 Appointment, discharge and removal of trustees

7.1 Powers in the Trustee Act 1925

The question of personality and appointment of the initial trustees is touched upon in Chapter 3, para 7 and the power of subsequent appointment and removal in Chapter 3, para 3. It is common for the trust instrument of a pension scheme to add to the statutory power under which trustees (or their personal representatives) appoint their successors. The use of a deed for the appointment of a new trustee ensures formality and brings into force the (albeit inadequate) vesting provisions of s 40 of the Trustee Act 1925, but it is not essential. The new trustee should always be required to acknowledge the appointment, to avoid doubt as to his acceptance. If a deed is used, he will usually be a party to it.

Since the senior executives of a company are frequently appointed trustees of its pension scheme, and occasionally purport to resign that trusteeship when their employment ceases, a power of removal is often inserted in the trust deed to enable such resignations to be 'perfected'. In the absence of such power, a discharge can be obtained only under ss 36 or 39 of the Trustee Act 1925 or by order of the court. On the other hand, care must be exercised in the use of such power. In particular, its use to remove a trustee who stood in the way of a breach of trust would be a fraud on the power and might be void. It is for consideration whether to recite the reason for its exercise in the deed or other document by which the removal is effected.

7.2 Pensions Act 1995: Member-nominated trustees

Member-nominated trustees (MNTs) are a requirement of the Pensions Act 1995 unless scheme members approve an alternative proposed by the employer. This alternative, colloquially known as 'the Employer's Opt-out', can take any form ie it does not need to include member nominees or independent trustees, but it is only applicable if it is not rejected by the membership under the 'Statutory Consultation Procedure' defined in s 21(7) and set out in SI 1996 No 1216, Sched 1. Detailed changes to the regulations are made by SI 1997 No 786; as the procedures are crucial, these changes should be marked up before advising.

The MNT provisions are particularly well described in Leaflet PEC5-8/96 (24 pages) published by the Department for Social Security.

Exceptions

The provisions, being for the appointment of trustees, only apply to a 'trust-scheme' which means any occupational pension scheme established under a trust—but see below for the long list of exemptions under regs 4 and 6.

The provisions do not apply to a scheme with less than two members (bearing in mind that, save where s 125(4) applies, member includes pensioners and deferreds). Nor do they apply to a scheme that provides only death benefits or a scheme where an independent trustee has been appointed or is in place on the insolvency of the employer, under the Pensions Act 1995, s 22 or the predecessor of that provision, the PSA 1993 s 119.

The most common of the exemptions will be:

(*a*) unapproved (and non-statutory) schemes;
(*b*) relevant small self-administered schemes; this may simply be an ordinary 'small scheme' as described in Chapter 17, para 8

without any special voting or other requirements—the precise definition being in SI 1991 No 1614 as set out in Chapter 17, para 8. The cross-reference in the MNT regs is the definition in reg 2. An amendment, by SI 1997 No 786, adds an obscure variation as an alternative.

(*c*) industry wide schemes for non-associated employers;
(*d*) paid-up insured schemes.

Nominations

The requirements are contained in ss 16–21 (unless there is an opt out—see above). They provide also for member-nominated directors of a corporate trustee (MNDs). Sections 16 and 18 relate respectively to MNTs and MNDs, and ss 17 and 19 authorise the respective employer's opt-out. Where there is no opt-out, the MNTs and MNDs must be nominated in accordance with rules under s 20, being either rules proposed by the existing trustees to the membership under the above 'Statutory Consultation Procedure' or, if there is no such proposal, prescribed rules set out in Sched 2 to the above regs.

Sections 16 and 18 require member-nominees to be at least one-third of the trustees or directors, with a minimum of two (or a minimum of one if the scheme comprises less than one hundred members). The sections provide for the period in office (not less than three nor more than six years). Schedule 2, para 1, provides that nominees must be members unless the employer otherwise agrees. Similarly, if the trustees propose their own rules for member nomination, a non-member requires the employer's approval—s 20(5). However, a key difference between trustees' rules and the prescribed fall-back is that by the latter nominations are made only by *active* members (and require only two nominations which could lead to eccentric nominations)—Sched 2, paras 1(4) and 2(2). By contrast, a trustees' proposal would be able to include pensioners as nominators.

Statutory Consultation Procedure

The Statutory Consultation Procedure serves two purposes, being available either for the employer or the trustees:

(*a*) to be operated by an employer, if proposing an opt-out; or
(*b*) to be operated by the trustees if there is no opt-out, and they do not want the fall-back rules. (Where there is no employer's

opt-out the existing *trustees* must ensure that the MNT/MND arrangements are put in place).

In both situations the *trustees* have a particular question to consider viz, whether deferred pensioners should be included in the consultation—s 21(8). In the absence of a positive decision to include deferreds, the participants in the statutory consultation are the active and pensioner members. The trustees may choose some or all deferreds if they wish. For the initial consultations, in 1997, it appears to the author that few trustees have chosen deferreds, but that where they have done so they have excluded those whose interest is limited to a guaranteed minimum pension.

The key feature of the consultation is that it does not require a ballot (although that option is available). Instead, by Sched 1, para 6, members may be given a period within which they may object to the proposal, and are only balloted if at least 10 per cent of the members (or, if less, 10,000 eligible members) object. If such objections are lodged, the matter goes to a majority vote on a ballot.

Information

Schedule 1, para 3 sets out the information that must be given to members for the consultation. Sub paras (*a*)–(*b*) are alternatives, dependent upon whether there are individual or corporate trustees, and whether the consultation is by the existing trustees or the employer. In the latter, all-important, case the information is to be a statement of the fall-back position if the opt-out is not approved ie the provisions applicable to MNTs or MNDs.

Paragraphs 4 and 5 are relevant to trustee's proposed rules, but not to the employer's opt-out, except for 5(3) which requires information as to the proposed total number of trustees, the selection procedure, the period in office etc.

Paragraph 6 requires members to be informed of the objection/ballot arrangements.

Regulation 23 provides for adequate notice, and reg 22 provides for records to be kept by the trustees or the employer, as the case may be, of steps taken to comply with the regs.

Employer's opt-out

If the employer intends to propose an opt-out (Sched 1—see above), it must give notice to the trustees at the appropriate time, simply stating an intention to propose alternative arrangements—regs 9(1) and 15(1). If, as normally occurs, there are numerous subsidiaries participating in a group scheme, the employers can nominate a person (usually the holding company) to act for them, but if they do not do so they must act together—Sched 3, para 1(1)(*g*). The para is enlarged by SI 1997 No 786 to give trustees the power to nominate a representative employer where the employers omit to do so; to exercise their right, the employers (curiously) have to notify the trustees that they wish to be consulted—clearly an erroneous amendment that, hopefully, will be further amended.

Schedule 3 also applies where the employer is sole trustee, and by para 4 provides for the existing trustees to exercise the functions of an employer if the employers are all in liquidation or dead. There are also provisions, in para 5, for shorter periods of office to apply to a person selected to fill a vacancy.

Time limits

The obligation upon existing trustees to put in place MNTs and MNDs if there is no employer's opt-out has to be carried out within six months from 6 April 1997—regs 7(2) and 13(2). For schemes established at a later date, or first losing the exemption at a later date, the six months runs from the establishment of the scheme or the cessation of the exemption. However, the period is extended if, during the six months the employer gives notice of intention to propose an opt-out—sub-para (*d*) of each reg. The employer's notice ordinarily must be given to the trustees within one month from 6 April 1997 or, if later, from the establishment or first eligibility of the scheme—see definition 'permitted notice time' in regs 9(2) and 15(2) (there is no purpose in listing here the transitional provisions of Sched 4 which applied to notices given before 6 April 1997).

A key notice is to be given by the employer to the trustees (or the company, meaning 'trustee company') stating that the opt-out has been approved by the members and specifying various consequences. That notice must be given before the expiry of the 'approval period' defined in reg 9(3) or 15(3). Initially, the period expires, in most cases, on 6 October 1997. For a scheme subsequently established, it will be six months from when the provisions are first applicable ie normally six months from the establishment of the scheme. Where a *Relevant event* (see below) has occurred, the six months runs from the notification by the trustees to the employer of such event. In all other cases it is six months from the date when the employer notified the trustees of the intention to propose an opt-out, but such notification has to be at a 'permitted notice time' as defined in reg 9(2) or 15(2) which sets out numerous permutations including provision for second or subsequent notices after periods of six years.

Expiry

By reg 20, an opt-out (or special rules for nomination proposed by trustees) expires after six years, or on earlier approval of fresh arrangements (or on the scheme ceasing to be one to which the provisions as a whole apply).

Relevant event

The definition is in reg 20(2). This authorises the trustees, if they consider it appropriate (see below) to trigger provisions for fresh arrangements. There are three types of relevant event:

(*a*) the transfer of accrued rights of a group of members to another scheme of the same employer or in consequence of a financial transaction between the employers etc. Although reg 20(2)(*a*) labels the particular provision 'transfers without consent' it is not clear whether that label actually applies to the transfer or simply to the cross-reference where the event is described;
(*b*) a new employer participates in the scheme or an existing employer ceases to participate; or
(*c*) the participating employer becomes a subsidiary of another that does not participate.

To trigger fresh arrangements, there has to be a relevant event *and* consideration by the trustees that as a result 'it would be detrimental to the interests of the members of the scheme' for the existing trusteeship arrangements to continue. The trustees then give notice to the employer and six months later or (if sooner) on the 'opt-out failure date' as defined, the existing trusteeship arrangements, if they are special rules or an opt-out, come to an end. By reg

20(1), this does not affect the validity or term of appointment of any person who had been selected in accordance with those arrangements.

Miscellaneous Provisions

Section 16(7) provides that member-nominated trustees must have the same function as any other trustee (apart from provisions under an order of OPRA or on the insolvency of the employer).

An MNT or MND who was a member of the scheme when appointed must cease to be a trustee when he ceases to be a member—but by s 124 deferred pensioners are members so that this will only apply if the individual is the subject of a transfer and ceases to be prospectively entitled under the scheme. This provision will not apply if the employer has permitted non-members to be nominated.

Section 20(3) requires that a member-nominated trustee be eligible for re-selection at the end of his period of service. Section 20(5) provides that 'where the employer so requires, a person who is not a member of the scheme must have the employer's approval to qualify for selection as a member-nominated trustee' (or, by subs (6), an MND).

Sole corporate trustees who are *not ordinarily connected with the employer* are brought into the MND frame by reg 5.

The definition 'appropriate rules' which applies both to special rules to tailor the member nominations proposed by the trustees under the Statutory Consultation Procedure, and to the prescribed (ie fall-back) rules, is to be found in s 20. For the trustees' proposals, the authority is reg 8 or 14.

For MNTs where the scheme provides for an insufficient maximum total number of trustees, reg 11 authorises the existing trustees by resolution to modify the scheme accordingly. Presumably there is no equivalent for MNDs as the provisions would be governed by the articles of association.

Regulation 21 applies where insufficient nominations are received.

Statutory consultation is not invalidated where *afterwards* it is discovered that a requirement was not met but even on the most adverse assumptions it would not have affected the result. On analysis the text does not assist if the notice to members omits a material item of information ie the provision appears to assist only where a group of members may have received inadequate information or the like, rather than all members—Sched 1, para 10.

Section 20(5) is supplemented by the much clearer para 1(3) of Sched 2. This provides that a non-member may only be nominated if his nomination is approved in writing by the employer (or the employer does not require that provision).

Whereas statutory consultation involves pensioners, the prescribed rules do not—para 2(2) of Sched 2—and for MNDs, as brought in by para 3—but see below re Sched 3, para 4.

For an employer that is also sole trustee, para 3 of Sched 3 extends a number of time limits.

Paragraph 4(4) of Sched 3 enables pensioners to nominate member trustees if there are no active members. It would appear from regs 9 and 15 that an employer, before the expiry of a permitted notice time, may make more than one proposal eg if the first proposal is rejected, so long as time allows. The author offers this as a tentative conclusion, but it is stated to be so on page 9 of the above-mentioned DSS Leaflet PEC5.

Trustees who wish to propose that more than one-third of the trustees or directors be MNTs or MNDs (or more than two where that figure is applicable) must obtain the employer's consent—see the last three lines of ss 16(6) and 18(6).

An MNT or MND can only be removed by all the other trustees acting together—ss 16(3)(*b*) and 18(3)(*b*). These are not enabling provisions so that there would still need to be a power of removal, possibly exercisable by the employer or possibly by the trustees whose agreement is required.

If an employer has failed to implement the statutory consultation by the expiry of the relevant period eg initially by 6 October 1997, MNTs or MNDs must be in place within a subsequent six months—regs 7(2)(*d*) and 13(2)(*d*), and the definition 'opt-out failure date' in reg 2. A flow chart setting out the main limits is to be found in the Leaflet PEC5. While it does not cite authority, the above references will be of assistance. Interestingly, also without citing authority, on page 14 the Leaflet states that MNTs can be nominated under rules which fit the particular needs and circumstances of the scheme eg pensioner MNTs if there is a large proportion of pensioner members, or an MNT from each company location, or that nominations are made by a trade union or other staff organisation although it is difficult to see how this last provision can apply except where the nominators are members.

In general, it would seem unlikely that the trustees would

propose significant departures, in their special rules, from the prescribed rules, the main choice being whether to permit pensioners (or deferreds) to make nominations. If there is an existing arrangement, which may or may not comprise more than one-third member nominees, it is likely that the *employer* will propose an opt-out, thus leaving the trustees with the sole task of deciding whether or not deferred pensioners are to be consulted regarding that proposal (albeit once the consultation has taken place, if the proposal is agreed, they must give effect to it, and if it is rejected must give effect to MNTs/MNDs).

8 Corporate trustee

A corporate trustee may fall into one of the following three categories:

(*a*) a body having no special powers (although the question of its memorandum of association should be considered);
(*b*) a trust corporation;
(*c*) a custodian trustee.

8.1 Body corporate having no special powers

The majority of corporate trustees of pension schemes fall into the first category. The trust instrument usually provides that Pt III of the Trustee Act 1925 shall apply as if references therein to a trust corporation were references to any body corporate having power to act as trustee. The company generally has a nominal capital of £100 and holds no assets beneficially. Its issued capital is generally held by or as nominee for the principal employer (in which case the disclosure provisions of the Companies Acts in relation to its investments must be considered), and its directors are usually appointed by that employer. The directors are de facto the trustees of the pension scheme. Provision can be made, if required, for candidates to the board to be elected by members and then appointed under the articles of association.

Such a trustee has the advantage of never dying or resigning. Its bank mandates and investment authorities are simple. Its proceedings are governed by the well-understood provisions of the Companies

Acts. Its notepaper need not change (Companies Act 1985, s 305). It therefore provides a continuity which matches that of the pension scheme itself. The questions of quorum and majority decision will be addressed by the articles of association.

It is often stated that another advantage of such a trustee is that its directors are freed from personal liability. This proposition has not been conclusively decided in the courts. It may well be that the standards required of such directors would be identical with those required of personal trustees. Many trust instruments therefore provide that all the indemnities and safeguards afforded to personal trustees shall apply likewise to the directors of a body corporate that is trustee of the scheme.

8.2 Trust corporation

The term 'trust corporation' includes the Public Trustee, the Treasury Solicitor, the Official Solicitor, certain charitable corporations, corporations entitled to act as custodian trustee, trustees in bankruptcy and other persons. In the context of pension schemes it usually means a corporation entitled to act as custodian trustee under the Public Trustee Act 1906, whether or not so acting. Apart from bodies established by statute or Royal Charter, or authorised by statutory instrument, this means a registered company empowered by its memorandum of association to undertake trust business and having issued capital meeting the requirements laid down by regulation (at present a minimum of £250,000 of which at least £100,000 has been paid up in cash). Such corporations are able to act as sole trustee for all purposes (including the passing of title to land held on trust for sale).

8.3 Custodian trustee

Custodian trustees are rarely, in the context of modern pension schemes, appointed. Their trusteeship appears to be determinable only by the court. It operates in parallel with that of managing trusteeship, the managing trustees exercising all the normal powers of trustees. Occasionally, a trust instrument refers to a trustee as a custodian trustee when it is clear that something different is intended. No general guidance can be given as to this situation, but advice should be sought as to whether that trustee can exercise the normal trustee powers and how (if at all, other than by the court) it can be discharged. Clearly, it is not normally advisable to appoint a custodian trustee).

8.4 Replacement of individual trustees

The question has been raised in the occasional journal whether individual trustees can be replaced by a sole corporate trustee (not being a trust corporation—see para 8.2 above) where there had not originally been a sole trustee. Section 37(1)(*c*) of the Trustee Act 1925 suggests not. However, the Act is a consolidating statute and, applying *Re Turner's Will Trusts* [1936] 2 All R 1435 (CA), it appears appropriate to refer back to the Trustee Act 1893 which provided that the corresponding provision (s 10(2)(*c*)) was, by s 10(5), subject to any contrary intention expressed in the trust instrument. Sections in the 1893 Act contained provisions equivalent to s 10(5). The 1925 Act contained none, but provided, by s 69, that the powers contained in the Act were subject to any contrary intention expressed in the trust instrument. The argument is that s 37(1)(*c*) contains a prohibition and not a power and is therefore not capable of enlargement. It is the author's view that s 69 would be construed in terms of the provisions it replaces, so that the prohibition would give way to an authorisation in the pension scheme trust deed.

In practice, s 69 has been so interpreted by most practitioners.

Where land is held, it is probably not possible for the individual trustees to be discharged (the combined effect of s 37(1)(*c*) and of the Law of Property Act 1925 s 27(2)). There may be conveyancing techniques available in particular cases to mitigate the practical effect of these provisions.

9 Acting for employer or trustee

Under para 6 above it is mentioned that where a conflict of interest is apparent, the trustee should seek advice. Such a conflict may arise in connection with the normal administration of the scheme. However, it is much more likely to arise when the employer has a specific proposal (eg a takeover, or a merger of pension schemes etc) which can proceed only if the trustee is willing to implement his part of it. Since the proposal will have required preliminary legal advice, it follows that if the pension scheme solicitor's role is to be constructive, rather than merely responsive, he should endeavour to act for the employer. However, it will be in the employer's interest, if properly advised, to put to the trustees a package that is likely manifestly to be in the interests of the beneficiaries.

This conclusion is supported in other ways. For example, when the decision is taken to establish a scheme, or in connection with the decision to contract in or out of the State scheme (which is an employer's decision and gives rise to an employer's liability: Chapter 20, para 4.6), the practitioner will initially be consulted by the employer. This need not prevent him from subsequently advising the trustees so long as a conflict of interest does not arise. When acting for the employer he is likely to endeavour to construct a proposal that could be acceptable to the trustees, but where there is some element of doubt or where an indemnity is proposed (see para 2 above) the trustees will require separate advice as to the doubt or as to the scope of the indemnity. Sometimes that advice can be obtained by instructing separate counsel, but on occasion the need for continuing advice as proposals change will make it more appropriate for there to be separate solicitors, particularly if there is to be confidentiality regarding new proposals. The practitioner will also seek to avoid receiving such information from the trustees as might prevent him from subsequently acting for the employer, if likely to be requested to act for both.

The foregoing might suggest that trustees must always be wary of a proposal of the employer. This is not so. The trustees have a role which, as explained in para 2 above, has to balance the preservation of trust capital (and its application under the rules of the scheme) with the fact that in many cases the provision of benefits under the scheme depends exclusively (or nearly so) on the ability and willingness of the employer to make further contributions to it.

It follows from the foregoing that the lawyer may be acting for either party (the possibility of acting for the beneficiary is of course always present, but does not fall under the heading of this chapter). It is essential to establish which is the client and to advise whether there is likely to be a conflict between them. He could be professionally obliged to indicate a conflict but that has now been reinforced by SI 1996 No 1715 which requires the obligation to be stated in the lawyer's letter of appointment, and indeed that of the other professional advisers mentioned in s47 of the Pensions Act 1995—see Chapter 25, para 3.3.

10 Some pension fund cases

10.1 Job protection, overseas investments etc

The Mineworkers' Pension Scheme was the subject of proceedings in *Cowan and Others v Scargill and Others* [1984] 2 All ER 750, Ch D. The plaintiffs, the five trustees appointed by the employer, sought directions that the defendants, trustees appointed by the trade union, were in breach of their fiduciary duties in refusing to concur in the adoption of an investment plan. The defendants objected, firstly, to overseas investments, on the broad grounds of union policy that all available funds should be invested in the UK, and, secondly, to investments in oil, ie energy sources in direct competition with coal. Nonetheless they claimed to have no other consideration than the interests of the beneficiaries. The plaintiffs succeeded, the court giving a declaration rather than directions. While the reasoning of the judgment is entirely within established authorities, it conveniently restates them and declares them wholly applicable to pension fund trusts (p 764g). Of particular interest are the following points:

(1) 'The starting point is the duty of trustees to exercise their powers in the best interests of the present and future beneficiaries of the trust, holding the scales impartially between different classes of beneficiaries' (p 760f).
(2) Trustees must put aside personal views, eg about investments in South Africa or alcohol etc, to obtain the best price or the best investment (p 761b–e).
(3) While beneficiaries' (if all adult) strong views against certain investments may legitimately be followed, such cases are very rare. 'Plainly the present case is not one of this rare type . . . Subject to such matters, under a trust for the provision of financial benefits, the paramount duty of trustees is to provide the greatest financial benefits for the present and future beneficiaries;' (p 762a).
(4) The court approved the traditional standard required of a trustee to 'take such care as an ordinary prudent man would take if he were minded to make an investment for the benefit of other people for whom he felt morally bound to provide' (p 762b).

(5) Trustees have a duty to diversify investments (p 762f), all the more so in a very large fund (there were two funds of £3bn each here) (p 763d).
(6) Pension fund trusts are subject to the same principles as other trusts (p 764g). The interests of the beneficiaries are paramount. 'I can see no justification for holding that the benefits to them should run the risk of being lessened because the trustees were pursuing an investment policy intended to assist the industry that the pensioners have left, or their union' (p 763f).

The judgment cites an American case that had been mentioned in support of the theory that members' jobs were a relevant consideration, *Withers v Teachers' Retirement System of the City of New York* [1978] 447 F Supp 1248. There five New York pension funds agreed to purchase $2,530m unmarketable New York City bonds to stave off the imminent bankruptcy of the City, the TRS contribution being $860m. It was held that the trustees had been justified as acting in the best interests of the beneficiaries and not out of concern for public welfare or job protection since the TRS was vastly underfunded (with funds for only eight to ten years) and depended for its own eventual solvency on the ability of the City to make future contributions. The duty of 'undivided loyalty to the beneficiaries' (an American term) was stressed in citing this, and another American case which, while not binding in England, accords with the conclusion in the judgment. The Mineworkers' scheme was 'fully funded' (p 764h–j) by contrast with TRS which, together with the City, faced imminent disaster.

The defendants had put forward broad economic arguments for directing pension funds to 'real' investments, and to investments in Britain generally. While accepting that there might be a case for legislation, the arguments did not apply under the present law. 'Any possible benefits that would accrue to the beneficiaries under the scheme (as distinct from the general public) are far too speculative and remote' (p 767c).

At p 760g there is a very useful passage giving judicial support (albeit in passing) for the principle of investing with a view to capital growth as well as income. The point was not elaborated but it is worth mentioning the author's view that income has a special value in that it is actually received, while unrealised capital gain may not be obtained. Nonetheless in an expanding pension fund there is much to be said for seeking overall yield without excessive distinction between income and gain.

10.2 Appropriate fund on sale of subsidiary

The sale and purchase of subsidiaries is the subject of Chapter 11. It is there assumed that the contracting parties can make whatever arrangements they negotiate. Often the transfer value to come from the vendor's pension scheme will be determined within a narrow range by its trust deed or else by its actuary's certificate; in such cases the parties may choose to provide for a separate adjustment between themselves.

In the case of *The Imperial Foods Ltd's Pension Scheme* [1986] 2 All ER 802 Ch D, described in Chapter 11, para 12, the trust deed provided that 'the Seperated Portion shall be determined by the Actuary and shall be such portion of the Fund as shall in all the circumstances appear to him to be appropriate at the time the subsidiary company ceases to be a subsidiary . . .' (p 805b). The judge held, when contrasting two methods of valuation, that

> 'it is not my function to decide which of these two methods would be, in abstract terms, the more applicable . . . although I shall have some observations on the matter to make later on. Under the terms of the definitive trust deed the determination . . . is one for the actuary to find . . . and it is only if his certificate can be impeached that the court is called on to decide what should in consequence happen. It appears to me the principles on which a certificate of this nature can be impeached are well settled . . .' (p 810j).

In short, a valuation clause of that nature leaves the decision in the hands of the actuary, and his certificate can be impeached only if no competent actuary could have chosen that method, or some material factor was overlooked.

Nonetheless, obiter dictum, the court considered the various methods, accepting 'the principle in *Re George Newnes Group Pension Fund* [1969] 98 J Inst of Actuaries 251 that the function of an actuary in any situation which is not governed precisely by the provisions of the trust deed is to achieve the greatest possible degree of fairness between the various persons interested under the scheme'. Having stressed that it was not, in the *Imperial* case, for the court to decide, it unhesitatingly preferred the past service reserve method to the share of the fund. The latter apportions surplus (which there was in that case) or deficit. In an ongoing scheme funded preponderantly by the employer a surplus has 'no existence in reality, represents . . . what may be termed temporary surplus funding by the employing company' (p 812c). 'Provided that the company concerned is financially sound, and there is no question of a discontinuance of the fund . . .' (p 812f) the members' position is not dependent on the degree of surplus or deficit. The surplus contributions of the two subsidiaries had been made at the ultimate expense of the holding company (p 813d). In practice, the company may have been in credit, or strict balance or in arrears (the latter more likely resulting from adverse investment experience than deliberate underpayment) (p 812e). The implication is that within reason the employer can choose the pace of funding.

So far as refunds of surplus are concerned (to which the *Imperial* case did not relate) see also the observations at the end of para 10.3 below.

10.3 Exercise of powers, their purpose etc

The power to alter a scheme has been referred to throughout this book, its importance in the document establishing the scheme being mentioned in Chapter 3, para 15.

In *Re Courage Pension Schemes* [1987] 1 All ER 528 Ch D, the Committee of Management of three schemes had the exercise of the various discretionary powers formerly vested in the trustees. The judgment sets out a number of observations of great relevance to pension schemes generally. The schemes were heavily in surplus. The 'Company' as defined in the schemes was Imperial Brewing & Leisure Ltd' ('IBL'), itself a subsidiary within the Imperial Group. The Group was acquired after a takeover battle during which the three schemes were closed to new entrants. Some months later IBL was sold. The vendor proposed that, following an amendment to the schemes, it be substituted for IBL as the 'Company' and that on the sale a transfer be effected with only a small part of the surplus, to a new scheme to be established by the purchaser. The transfer would relate to current employees, leaving behind pensioners and deferred pensioners; the vendor's stated intention was ultimately to obtain the withheld surplus for its own benefit.

It was held that the particular type of substitution would 'manifestly alter the main purpose of the scheme and be ultra vires' (p 541j). The alteration clause contained a proviso to protect the main purpose, but the result apparently would have been the same without it for 'this is a restriction which cannot be deleted by amendment, since it would be implicit anyway' (p 537e). Even if the new clause could have been inserted, the court would not uphold the *exercise* of the power to substitute the new 'Company' in the particular circumstances (p 542g). The intention of the new holding company of the group (the vendor) to retain the surplus was 'foreign to the purpose for which the power to amend the Trust Deeds and Rules is conferred, and invalidates any exercise of that power' (p 542j). The new holding company had also proposed re-opening the schemes to new employees. The power to do so was held to remain, albeit at the discretion of the Committee.

At p 537f it was said:

> 'First, there are no special rules of construction applicable to a pension scheme; nevertheless its provisions should wherever possible be construed to give reasonable and practical effect to the scheme, bearing in mind that it has to be operated against a constantly changing commercial background. It is important to avoid unduly fettering the power to amend the provisions of the Scheme, thereby preventing the parties from making those changes which may be required by the exigencies of commercial life . . . Second, in the case of an institution of long duration and gradually changing membership like a club or pension scheme, each alteration in the rules must be tested by reference to the situation at the time of the proposed alteration, and not by reference to the original rules at its inception. By changes made gradually over a long period, alterations may be made which would not be acceptable if introduced all at once. Even the main purpose may be changed by degrees. This is demonstrated by *Thellusson v Viscount Valentia* [1907] 2 Ch 1, which concerned the Hurlingham Club.'

There was already a limited right to substitute a new 'Company'. It was said (p 541c) 'Where, on a reconstruction or amalgamation, substantially the same persons continue to be employed in the undertaking, then the substitution . . . is not only necessary and desirable but can properly be said to promote the main purpose of the scheme and not to alter it.' Here, however, the purpose was

> 'not to preserve the Schemes . . . for the benefit of those employed in the undertaking, but to prevent the Schemes from continuing for their benefit and to bring about an unnecessary dissolution of the Schemes, which would

not otherwise occur' (p 541e). '. . . the validity of a *power* of substitution depends on the circumstances in which it is capable of being exercised and the characteristics which must be possessed by the company capable of being substituted; while the validity of any purported *exercise* of such a power depends on the purpose for which the substitution is made' (p 542e) (emphasis supplied).

The judgment merits the closest study for a number of observations which, for reasons of space, are not quoted here. However, in connection with surplus (see para 10.2 above) it was stated that while surplus may generally derive only from employer's contributions (p 545f) it will

> 'only be in rare cases that the employer will have any legal right to repayment of any part of the surplus . . . [It] will normally require amendment . . . and thus co-operation between the employer and the Trustees or Committee of Management. Where the employer seeks repayment, the Trustees or Committee can be expected to press for generous treatment of employees and pensioners . . .'.

10.4 Exercise of powers by liquidator

Two contrasting cases were heard in December 1989. In *Icarus (Hertford) Ltd v Driscoll* Ch 1988 I 9674 [1989] PLR 1 the liquidator was authorised to exercise a discretion over surplus whereas in *Mettoy Pension Trustees Ltd v Evans* [1991] 2 All ER 513, Ch D he was not. While some of the conclusions in *Mettoy* are surprising this part of the judgment seemed to the author more likely to be followed than *Icarus*, and so it proved in *re Wm Makin & Son Ltd* [1992] PLR 177.

In *Icarus*, the scheme rules provided for surplus to be applied at the discretion of the Principal Employers but elsewhere provided that they act as trustee. It was held that the discretion was exercisable in the capacity of trustee. No comment was made whether a liquidator properly exercises a company's powers when the latter acts as trustee; that question does not appear to have been raised in the originating summons. The summons asked whether it would be proper for the company, in exercising its discretion, to determine not to apply surplus to increase benefits (for the balance went to the company, and thus to the creditors). The judge held that it would be proper. The task would involve three stages: firstly, a decision to exercise the discretion; secondly, the ascertainment of the relevant facts, and thirdly 'a decision made in good faith whether to apply the whole or part of the surplus to augment the entitlements' (p 9G of the transcript). 'Providing that any decision reached is bona fide, then that decision cannot be said to be improper, and in particular it would not be improper to take into account the fact that the Principal Employer is in liquidation and that there are creditors' (p 10F).

The *Mettoy* case contrasts with this decision. There, it was held, at pp 547–548, that if the discretion had not been fiduciary it would have been exercisable by the receivers, or by the liquidator if there had been no receivers. However, the result is different where the discretion is fiduciary:

> 'The exercise of a fiduciary power in the full sense vested in the company cannot be necessary for distributing its assets. Whether it may be necessary for winding up the affairs of the company is less clear. However the liquidator in this case would . . . be precluded from exercising the power because, if he did so, he would be in a position where his duties conflicted. As trustee of the power he would be under a duty to hold the balance between the interests of the beneficiaries under the pension scheme and the interests of the persons entitled to share in the assets of the company, namely its creditors and possibly contributories. As liquidator his duty would be to have regard primarily, if not exclusively, to the interests of the creditors and contributories. His position in that respect would differ from that of the directors of the company while it was a going concern, for they would be able to pay proper regard to the interests of the beneficiaries under the pension scheme and would be concerned to do so if only for the sake of the company's reputation as an employer' [p 548d].

The conclusion is repeated at p 562e where it was held that the particular discretion was a fiduciary power and could not be exercised by the receivers or by the liquidator. At page 549e the judge held that the court could ensure the exercise of the discretion by whichever of three methods seemed appropriate, viz the appointment of new trustees, the authorisation of representatives of the classes of beneficiaries to prepare a scheme of distribution, or by the court itself deciding the proper basis. Page 562f indicates that further evidence was to be heard before this choice was to be made. In the event there was an appeal which was settled between the parties so that the manner of exercise of the power did not call for further judgment.

In *Makin* the Judge had 'no hesitation in preferring the decision of [*Mettoy*]', page 182 at 13.

10.5 Trustees' duty to obtain full information

Stannard v Fisons Pension Trust Ltd [1992] IRLR 27, CA, cited with approval the unreported case of *Kerr v British Leyland (Staff) Trustees*, decided in the Court of Appeal on 26 March 1986, in which a decision had been held ineffective because the trustees had not carried out their duty to give a properly informed consideration to the claim (p 31, at para 36). In *Fisons* there had been a valuation in 1979 in which the company contributions had been assessed at 16 per cent of pensionable pay. By the time of a bulk transfer in December 1982 there had been a substantial rise in the stock market and a likelihood that the contribution rate could have been much reduced (as became the case on a subsequent valuation). The transfer was assessed by the trustees, with advice from the actuary, as an amount that took into account the 16 per cent rate, and was therefore lower than if it had assumed a smaller future company contribution.

At first instance, in *Fisons*, the judge had held that the trustees should obtain further evidence and assess, albeit not necessarily differently, the transfer value in the light of it. In the Court of Appeal it was held by Dillon LJ, at para 39 that 'it might materially have affected the trustees' decision in December 1982, if they had been properly informed as to the then current value of the fund and the implications of its value'. Staughton LJ affirmed that view (p 33 at para 65) but also stated that the decision was flawed on another ground, viz that the draft letter of advice from the solicitors mentioned an inappropriate rule and failed to mention the rule under which a wider discretion, or at least a plainer discretion, arose. The decision-making process was therefore defective for that reason also.

10.6 Employer's duty of good faith

A judgment of very wide potential implications was given in *Imperial Group Pension Trust Ltd v Imperial Tobacco Ltd* [1991] 2 All ER 597, Ch D. Here it was held that where a company had powers under a pension scheme, while it could look after its own financial interests, its right to give or withhold its consent to an amendment was, nonetheless, subject to an implied obligation of good faith to the employees. The obligation in full, is that the company may not exercise its right 'so as to destroy or seriously damage the relationship of confidence and trust between the company and its employees and former employees' [p 606j].

Good faith requires that the company considers each proposal when it is made, and does not say in advance that it would *never* consider whether to grant consent to an amendment increasing benefits (pp 607d–f). This rendered unlawful an alleged plan of (albeit denied by) the company, whereby members of an existing scheme were invited to transfer to a new scheme on the basis that there would *never* be amendments to award discretionary increases under the existing scheme, although certain guaranteed increases would apply under the new scheme.

There were three possible restrictions on the company's power. Firstly, it might be fiduciary, but this was not seriously proposed. Secondly, there might be an implied restriction that consent to an amendment was not to be unreasonably withheld; this too was rejected by the court. The third possibility was upheld, viz that a blanket refusal *ever* to consider the possibility of an amendment to award increases was a breach of the implied obligation of good faith. Instead each proposal must be considered at the time it is put forward in the light of the circumstances that then exist (p 607e).

Further, if the sole purpose of refusing an amendment (to provide increases) was, in the context of a closed fund which had no provision for ultimate return of surplus, the collateral purpose of pressuring members to transfer to a new scheme in which surplus could revert to the company, that would also be a breach of the obligation of good faith. The situation was urgent and the facts had not been adequately investigated, so that the judgment was given on hypothetical facts (pp 607h and 608f).

10.7 Benefits are earned by members

The cases cited at paras 10.5 and 10.6 above, and *Mettoy* cited at para 10.4, all refer to the rights under a pension scheme as having been earned, the members being not merely volunteers. *Mettoy* and *Imperial Tobacco* both refer to *Mihlenstedt v Barclays Bank* [1989] IRLR 522, CA. *Mettoy* cites the *Mihlenstedt* reference to members' rights having contractual and commercial origins (p 537g). *Fisons* refers to the *British Leyland* case (see para 10.5 above) which used identical language.

In *Mettoy* the fact that the beneficiaries under the pension scheme were not mere volunteers was one of the factors leading the judge to decide that the power to increase benefits, conferred on the employer notwithstanding that there were separate trustees, was nonetheless, in the particular circumstances, fiduciary (p 551j). In *Imperial Tobacco* it was stated that the members, far from being volunteers, had been given valuable consideration (the rendering of their services). This led to the implied obligation of good faith, since the employer was not conferring a bounty but was in a relationship of contractual origin (p 605j). In *Fisons* this aspect underlined the duty of the trustee to give properly informed consideration (p 31 at paras 34 and 36).

10.8 Information amendments may be effective

In both *Icarus* and *Mettoy*, cited at para 10.4 above, there had been announcements of benefit changes without corresponding formal amendments.

In *Icarus* the parties had acted on the basis of an announced reduction in accrual, when the State additional pension was introduced in 1978, with corresponding cancellation of the member's obligation to contribute. These announcements were not formally incorporated into the rules but the judge held that the parties were estopped from contending that any other benefit structure applied (p 5H of the transcript).

In *Mettoy* counsel for the company accepted that, whether by reason of an equitable estoppel or otherwise, provisions of certain booklets were binding on all parties (page 53b). The judge upheld this, stating that the issue of such booklets was common practice in the pensions field and that it would be 'inappropriate and indeed perverse to construe such documents so strictly as to undermine their effectiveness'. He cited an earlier case (*Re Gulbenkian*) which stated the duty to make sense of the parties' expressed intentions (pp 538b and c).

10.9 Failure of subsidiaries to execute a deed

In *Davis v Richards and Wallington Industries Ltd* [1991] 2 All ER 563, Ch D, a definitive deed and rules was to be executed by various parties including associated companies. None of the latter executed the deed.

The judge held that each of the associated companies that was still in the group and still contributing to the scheme was under an enforceable obligation to execute the deed. He then applied the maxim that 'equity looks on that as done which ought to be done' and held that want of execution by these companies did not detract from the efficacy of the rules (p 587e).

In *Richards and Wallington* there was also a question whether a trustee who had written a mere letter of resignation had in fact ceased to be a trustee. All the submissions were that the resignation was not effective (p 581a). The judge held to the contrary, firstly as a matter of construction (for the appointment clause actually referred to resignation), and secondly because the principal company had executed a deed without that individual's participation, on the basis that he had ceased to be a trustee, and since that company had the power to remove him, if (contrary to the judge's view) his resignation was not effective equity would impute to the company an intention to exercise its power of removal and would treat that power as having been exercised by the company's execution of the deed (p 583f).

10.10 Manslaughter—loss of pension

In *R v National Insurance Commissioner, ex parte Connor* [1981] 1 All ER 769, QBD, a decision disentitling from State pension a woman who had killed her husband was upheld by the Divisional Court. It is a principle of public policy that a person should not benefit from his own (serious) crime.

The woman's entitlement arose under the Social Security Act 1975 which was a self-contained code. Nevertheless, it was to be applied subject to the above rule of public policy. The judgment cited with approval (p 774e) an earlier case that noted that manslaughter is a crime which varies infinitely in its seriousness, amounting very nearly to murder at one extreme or to little more than inadvertence at the other. The earlier judgment did not decide that a person convicted of manslaughter would 'in any circumstances' be prevented from enforcing a benefit arising from the death.

In *Connor* the Chief Insurance Commissioner had appreciated that public policy was a reflection of the current public conscience, and was not static. There were no grounds to overturn the decision of the Commissioner that the widow was disentitled from pension by reason of the unlawful act of manslaughter. There had been evidence, decided upon by the jury, that the death had not been accidental. Presumably in the case of an occupational pension scheme it would be open to the trustees to reach a similar conclusion.

The Forfeiture Act 1982 includes, at s 4, specific authority for a National Insurance Commissioner to make the decision that was made in *Connor*. Section 2(4)(*b*) appears to apply to a pension scheme and enables the court to modify the forfeiture rule (the rule of public policy mentioned above) in respect of any beneficial interest in property that, before the death, was held on trust and, but for the rule, would have been acquired by the offender. The Act only applies to unlawful killing (but, by s 5, not to murder).

In effect, s 2 permits the court to redetermine any withholding of benefit, since it is to have regard to the conduct of the offender and of the deceased, to such other circumstances as appear material, and to the justice of the case. By s 2(3) the court can only make an order if proceedings are brought by the individual within three months of his conviction of the offence.

Connor was cited with approval in *R v Registrar General, ex parte Smith* [1991] 2 All ER 88, CA, where a psychotic double murderer, adopted at birth, was denied his apparently absolute right under the Adoption Act 1976 to a sight of his birth certificate as there was a very real danger of a prospective crime against his natural mother.

For a review of the public policy cases regarding civil rights of action in matters tainted with illegality, see *Euro-Diam Ltd v Bathurst* [1988] 2 All ER 23, CA.

11 Trustees' liability insurance

11.1 Extent of cover

It has become more common in recent years for trustees to consider insurance against their potential liabilities, although such insurance remains comparatively rare. There are several reasons for this rarity:

(*a*) few trustees are held personally liable for acts done on advice and in good faith (see para 2 above);
(*b*) most pension funds have sufficient assets to meet unexpected

modest claims, and the likelihood (when there is a modest loss) of a member claiming wrongful depletion of assets is remote;

(*c*) it is general for pension scheme deeds to include an exoneration provision on the lines mentioned at the end of para 2 above so that a trustee is not liable save for wilful conscious default—unless ss 33 or 34 of the Pensions Act 1995 apply;

(*d*) there is a general expectation that the employer, for whose management purposes the trust was established, will meet any legal costs, and there may be an express indemnity to that effect.

Nonetheless increasing awareness of pensions matters, fostered by current statutory changes and disclosure requirements, has aroused interest in insurance. Policies fall into three categories:

(*i*) reimbursement to the fund, whether or not a claim against the trustees is made;
(*ii*) indemnity to the trustees for their liability in the event of claim;
(*iii*) legal costs insurance.

The first of these heads applies whether or not the pension scheme deed contains an exoneration clause. It replaces funds that should not have been lost. To the extent that the employer bears the ultimate cost of the scheme, the insurance is for its benefit.

The great merit of the first type of insurance is that it is triggered by the trustees themselves; it does not require a claim against them to be made and therefore assists in the avoidance of publicity. It is likely to be the most costly.

The second head is clearly of comfort to the trustees. It may or may not provide for payment to the fund where the insured would have been liable but for an exoneration clause or the exercise of the court's discretion. Directors of a corporate trustee may be included in a Directors and Officers policy of the employer holding company.

The third head enables trustees to seek legal advice without the potential personal liability for legal costs while awaiting the court's decision on this liability. It is of value even where a deed specifically empowers defence of proceedings since there is usually a preliminary application (*Beddoe's* relief). Further, it enables a trustee to seek advice when he fears that he may be liable and is uncertain (regardless of the provisions of the deed) of the propriety of meeting the costs from the fund.

11.2 Period of insurance

It is essential to consider the period to which the insurance relates. It may cover acts done during the premium year, regardless of when the claim is made, or it may cover claims made (or circumstances coming to light) during the year, even where the acts done were committed prior to the insurance period.

A reimbursement policy will normally relate to matters coming to light during a policy period. Since no claim against the trustees is required, it is in order to trigger the insurance as soon as it is realised that a culpable mistake has been made.

Protection for particular trustees, however, requires that they be covered even if, after cessation of their trusteeship, the insurance is not renewed. It may not be possible to obtain this type of cover at Lloyd's (because syndicates alter), particularly in relation to a scheme that is winding up.

11.3 Payment of premiums

It is doubtful whether the trustees can properly pay from the trust funds premiums relating to their own potential liability unless expressly authorised in the original trust instrument, for it could hardly be a proper exercise of their fiduciary power to effect an amendment with that purpose.

With reimbursement policies, mentioned in para 11.1(*i*) above, some insurers split the premium so that the negligence element (which is very small if there is an exoneration clause) is paid separately by the employer.

Often the employer pays the whole premium.

11.4 Cost

At the time of writing, the type of insurance described in para 11.1(*i*) and (*ii*) above is included in the professional indemnity area where premiums have risen dramatically and reinsurance is often unobtainable to the underwriter. It may well be, however, that insurance for trustees will become the norm so that, particularly if limited to actual liability (ie a long stop where the exoneration clause does not suffice), premiums may be assessed for this type of matter separately.

One of the chief merits of the reimbursement policy is the ability to settle a matter without a claim against the trustees.

A problem may arise if insurance cannot be renewed on reasonable terms. It may be that the employer will be willing to extend an indemnity in such circumstances. It would seem more proper, however, where consciously the employer has not to date chosen to extend an indemnity, for such indemnity to be limited to para 11.1(*iii*), ie legal costs' cover. The directors of an employer company can properly incur on its behalf liabilities, or effect indemnities, only if to do so is in the company's interest. While giving effect to a pension scheme is likely to assist in the recruitment and retention of staff, and therefore be in the company's interests, the potential liability under an indemnity should be commensurate with the purpose that is being furthered.

12 The 'Maxwell' Affair

12.1 Background

The assets of several pension funds within the two groups of companies chaired by the late Robert Maxwell were heavily depleted during a short period before (and around) his death, on 5 November 1991.

Losses were so substantial that (subsequently) pension payments, even though a priority class, were due to terminate in a number of the funds. However, a short term Government loan was made available in June 1992, to enable payments to continue while efforts were made to trace assets.

Initial published figures suggest losses of the order of £400m from the pension funds with associated losses of £300m from the sponsoring companies. These losses appear to have arisen in two ways, *viz* share support purchases to keep up the quoted price of Mirror Group Newspapers plc and pledges of assets as security for loans to the sponsoring companies or their associates.

Neither of these operations appears to have been authorised by the trustees of the funds. Any such authorisation would, on the published facts, anyway have been unlawful in a number of ways, being a clear breach of trust where they were arranged for the benefit of the companies or their shareholders, and not for the pension scheme beneficiaries.

The operations were possible because a small group of individuals held mandated authorities in key areas. Further the custodian of the assets was the in-house common investment manager, Bishopsgate Investment Management Ltd and therefore perhaps less inclined to question unusual instructions.

Initial public knowledge derived from the hearings and second report (published 4 March 1992) of the House of Commons Social Security Committee. The Committee had been studying the operation of pension funds generally but turned to the Maxwell affair as soon as information began to emerge.

Bishopsgate Investment Management was an Occupational Pension Scheme (OPS) Member of IMRO (see para 51 of IMRO's submission to the Social Security Committee, dated 10 February 1992, available from IMRO). In creating the OPS regime IMRO had deliberately not made it onerous so that trustees could continue with their in-house advisers. Of the seven initial BIM directors three were Robert Maxwell and his sons.

A common investment fund was set up in March 1988, for six pension schemes of the Mirror Group and Maxwell Communications Group, 80 per cent of the assets being managed by BIM and the remaining 20 per cent by three other fund managers of which one was another in-house manager, London & Bishopsgate International Investment Management plc. It was said in evidence by the actuaries that the apparent thefts from the pension funds could have taken place just as easily without the existence of the common investment fund. It is plain from the evidence that procedures at the two in-house managers did not follow rigorous checks. The pooled fund therefore enabled a greater concentration of power although no doubt the same result could have been achieved by the appointment of the in-house managers to all the funds individually.

12.2 Pensions Law Review Committee (the 'Goode Committee')

The House of Commons Committee made a large number of recommendations, some of minor detail, others of major potential impact. The Government responded by announcing on 8 June 1992 a new Pensions Law Review Committee under the chairmanship of Prof R Goode QC, its terms of reference being:

'To review the framework of law and regulation within which occupational pension schemes operate, taking into account the rights and interests of scheme members, pensioners and employers; to consider in particular the status and ownership of occupational pension funds and the accountability and roles of trustees, fund managers, auditors and pension scheme advisers; and to make recommendations.'

The Goode committee was asked by the Government to report by around June 1993 and, if urgent changes are recommended, to issue interim reports to that effect. Its first consultation document was issued in September 1992.

The Goode Committee reported in September 1993 (Cm 2342), with 218 recommendations of which the leading ones, in the author's opinion, were the following:

(*a*) compensation scheme;
(*b*) member-nominated trustees;
(*c*) pensions regulator;
(*d*) minimum solvency requirement (amended by Government to minimum *funding* requirement);
(*e*) Pensions Act 1995 (building on trust law);
(*f*) more information;
(*g*) whistle blowers (auditors, actuaries);
(*h*) internal disputes procedure;
(*i*) simplification of Inland Revenue limits;
(*j*) alleviation of tax on surplus.

NB: Indexation: There was disagreement whether to require pensions to be 'indexed' (ie inflation proofed).

The Pensions Act 1995, is intended to incorporate items (*a*)–(*h*) above, and partial 'Indexation' (*viz*, on post-April 1997 accrual of pension). Chapter 25 mentions the White Paper that preceded the Act, and lists the chapters describing the outcome of the above recommendations.

12.3 Balance of power

Many of the questions raised by the Social Security Committee indicated a keen interest in the ownership of any surplus pension scheme assets. That question was raised before the 'Maxwell' affair and has remained a public issue. It is not directly touched by 'Maxwell' but is squarely within the remit of the Goode committee (see para 12.2 above).

The question only arises in respect of final salary schemes. It is not for this book to put forward a political answer. At present the question is addressed in Chapter 3, para 21 and Chapter 13, para 4. It is also touched upon in Chapter 17, para 9 and elsewhere. However, the author offers a mid-way solution whereby refunds to the employer would become more difficult (ie permissible only after leaving within the scheme a reserve for, say, five years' contributions) but the employer would retain the freedom to run down the surplus by a contribution holiday. This balance, one of a number that could be struck, reflects the inevitable fluctuations in the funding level of a final salary scheme and the source of the requisite balance for the solvency of the scheme.

Numerous other questions arise regarding the balance of power, as the above-cited chapters indicate. It may well be that the judge-made obligation on the employer (labelled the 'implied obligation of good faith') in the *Imperial Tobacco* case (see para 10.6 above) will enable the employer to retain the commercial control needed, for example, when a subsidiary is sold, while leaving the trustees with a measure of counterbalance. It is difficult to see how matters of this type, with endless permutations, can be fettered by statutory control while leaving freedom to transfer, in appropriate situations, funds that include a salary reserve, and therefore exceed the ordinary leaving service entitlements.

Chapter 25

Pensions Act

1 General

The Pensions Act 1995, arose out of the report of the Pensions Law Review Committee (the Goode Report) whose main recommendations are at the end of Chapter 24. Their implementation in the Act is mainly described elsewhere in this book, as shown in the following table, but the compensation scheme (and some lesser innovations) are described in this chapter.

Compensation scheme	para 2 below
Member nominated trustees	Chapter 24, para 7
Pensions regulator	Chapter 18
Minimum funding requirement (*originally called minimum solvency requirement*)	Chapter 16, para 17
Pensions Act 1995 (building on Trust Law)	Chapter 24, para 1
More information (Disclosure)	Chapter 16, para 6
Whistle blowers (auditors, actuaries)	Chapter 18, para 2.3
Internal disputes procedure	Chapter 16, para 18
NB: Indexation (decided by Government)	Chapter 16, para 3.2
Equality; Choice (added by Government)	para 1.1. below

The Goode Report was followed by detailed consultation documents issued by the Government, resulting in a White Paper (Cm 2594) published in two volumes in June 1994. Volume I stated that the Pensions Act 1995, would cover three areas: Security, Equality, Choice.

1.1 Security, equality, choice

The first, security, adopted in whole or in part 185 of the 218 Goode recommendations; in Volume II the White Paper listed each recommendation, together with the Government's response to it. See the table above, and para 1.2 below.

Equality

Equality was addressed in three ways, firstly by implementing the equalisation of State pension ages—Chapter 20, para 15. Secondly, by altering the requirements for contracting out to remove the ongoing accrual of unequal guaranteed minimum pensions (Chapter 20, para 4.1). Thirdly, an equal treatment rule was written into all occupational schemes not having one (Chapter 22, para 2.8).

Choice

Choice was addressed by a pledge to introduce greater flexibility in both occupational and personal pensions schemes, particularly in the options available at older ages and in the use of savings in retirement. This extension of choice resulted in enabling provisions in the Pensions Act 1995, for age-related rebates for contracted-out money purchase schemes (COMPs)—Chapter 2, para 9.4. A number of changes in Inland Revenue practice have been announced since the introduction of the Pensions Act 1995, to progress the implementation of flexibility, the latest being the issue of a consultative document in January 1997 on the possible desegregation of AVC benefits from main scheme commencement dates (which would tie in with the introduction for personal pension schemes in 1995 of an income withdrawal facility).

1.2 Security: affordability

The Goode Report struck a balance between tight regulation and the desire not to introduce such cost and complexity that employers would choose not to establish or maintain occupational pension schemes. The Government foreword to the White Paper also considered it important to strike such a balance. Many provisions in the Pensions Act 1995, therefore, were enabling provisions which were followed by consultation before the issue of regulations that took account of that balance. Nonetheless, the overall effect has been to introduce a significant compliance cost. Possibly the greatest cost, and yet the least pure result, is in the fourth item in the above table, the minimum funding requirement (MFR), as outlined below.

The Goode Committee were aware that in proposing an MSR (as it was originally labelled) there were technical difficulties in creating a precise solvency requirement, and that there were cost dangers in moving as far towards it as possible. Nonetheless, it was essential to their recommendations for two particularly significant reasons, the first being the importance of security for the pensions promise, and the second being the key role that the MFR plays in the compensation scheme (para 2 below). The Government recognised that there was an inevitable tension between a scheme funding basis that projects the returns on equity investments, and a solvency basis that looks at the cost of purchasing annuities (which are predominantly linked to the gilts market)—Chapter 16, para 17. It therefore moved the requirement further towards an equity basis, but probably too late to dispel first impressions on the part of:

(*a*) finance directors who were made highly aware, in and after 1993, of the volatility of the funding basis of a defined benefit scheme, and the possible cash flow consequence to the employer of a mismatch with the statutory requirement;
(*b*) scheme members, or more likely trustees, who following the original announcement of the Goode Report, probably received the impression that once the new requirement had been phased in, the solvency of schemes would be secure; even as proposed, this would not have been 100 per cent the case, but under the MFR the shortfall on a winding up would vary but in some cases might be very significant.

1.3 Compliance cost

The result when added to the number of compliance documents needed before or soon after April 1997, established an impression of cost and complexity, particularly for defined benefit schemes. Employers establishing new schemes are therefore more likely to choose defined contribution, or even the radically different Group personal pension schemes (Chapter 2, para 9.5). The first of these undoubtedly carries with it a significant financial simplicity, but unless combined with a hybrid arrangement it fails to address the needs of ill-health or other early retirement, and has a number of design disadvantages for both the employer and the members. Nonetheless, these are unlikely to be strongly perceived, and for some employers would anyway be outweighed by the 'certainty' factor.

While MFR and related provisions do not apply to defined contribution schemes, the significant areas of investment and trusteeship are regulated for such schemes.

Group personal pension schemes, which avoid both MFR and trusteeship, nonetheless are, in their present form, far from ideal for a large employer, but their design is being constantly improved and they are likely to be attractive in many cases. While the Pensions Act 1995, addresses some aspects of personal pension schemes, most of the compliance arises under the Financial Services Act 1986. There is a very real cost, but it does not feature in the direct pensions budget. Further, the purchase of annuities, even if postponed by income withdrawal, is an expensive feature whose cost is borne by the members.

It is significant that of the eight leading Goode recommendations, the most important, viz the compensation scheme, does not feature in the earlier chapters of this book. It is a new departure in UK pensions, and is outlined in para 2 below.

A number of other detailed areas regulated by the Pensions Act 1995, are briefly described in para 3 below.

2 Compensation scheme

2.1 General

A compensation scheme was the necessary political response to the 'Maxwell' affair (Chapter 24, para 12), since no amount of regulation can be sure to avoid fraud. It is of interest that, after a proportion of funds had been recovered, and guaranteed minimum pensions (GMPs) had been compensated by the restoration of SERPS rights, members and pensioners could expect to receive their entitlements under the Maxwell pension funds. However, recovery of assets took several years, by which time the Pensions Act 1995 was on the statute book.

The Goode Report recommended compensation, not reimbursement. The purpose of the compensation scheme is to ensure that if assets are stolen from a pension fund, members' entitlements should not be significantly affected. Compensation does not arise if, despite the theft, there are, in a defined benefits scheme, sufficient assets or, in either type of scheme, the employer is able to reimburse the fund (the Pensions Act 1995, creates an obligation for it to do so, over a period of time (unless there is a surplus) through the MFR mechanism or, on wind-up, through the deficiency regs). A defined benefit scheme does not receive compensation unless, after exhausting the employer's assets, the funding level has reduced below 90 per cent of the MFR. A fund in surplus, therefore, may not receive compensation despite significant theft.

These measures serve two purposes, primarily to reduce the potential cost (to *other* funds) of the scheme, and secondly to avoid 'moral hazard', *viz* lack of care on the part of the employer as to the security of the assets. The same purposes explain why the compensation fund does not meet an investment shortfall.

2.2 Compensation Board

The Government announced that the scheme will be administered by the Pensions Ombudsman with the support of a Compensation Board.

The Compensation Board is established by the Pensions Act 1995, s 78. Its constitution is set out in Sched 2, of which para 12 authorises regs to govern the exercise of its functions.

It is to prepare annual reports that are not to be laid before Parliament.

By s 80, the Board's decisions are final. However, on the application of an interested person, it may review its decisions if satisfied that there has been a relevant change of circumstances or that they have been ignorant of a material fact. Further, without such reason they may review any decision within three months of making it, and have power to extend that period.

2.3 Scope

The Pensions Act 1995, by s 81, authorises an application for compensation by a *trust* scheme if all the following apply:

(*a*) the employer is insolvent;
(*b*) it reasonably appears that a prescribed offence has resulted in loss;

(*c*) if the application is for a *salary-related* scheme, the assets have fallen below 90 per cent of the liabilities—in fact MFR, as applied by s 81(7);
(*d*) it is in all the circumstances reasonable.

Prescribed schemes can be excluded. By s 82, an application normally has to be made within 12 months of the employer's insolvency, but the Compensation Board may extend this period.

By s 83 of the Pensions Act 1995, compensation is limited in two ways:

(*a*) it is not to exceed 90 per cent of the amount stolen;
(*b*) in the case of a *salarv related* scheme, nothing is paid if there remain assets equal to 90 per cent of the liabilities, and if the assets are less, compensation must not exceed the amount needed to restore the assets to the 90 per cent level.

Where pensions cannot otherwise be paid, the Board may make payments on account to the trustees.

Interestingly, if the Board has surplus funds, it may distribute them amongst occupational pension schemes generally ie return excess levies. (For the method of funding the compensation scheme, see the last paragraph of Chapter 18, para 3—a levy on all occupational schemes).

All these provisions can be modified by regulation—s 86.

3 Some other provisions

3.1 Generally

The Act creates numerous items of new law. The practitioner is advised to study the contents list for the broad picture. It is not the purpose of this chapter to list all these items. Salient matters, however, may be of interest.

3.2 Matters affecting trustees

Section 32 provides for agreement by majority *unless the scheme provides otherwise*, and that where the majority provision is applicable, notice of decision meetings must, subject to any prescribed exceptions, be given to each trustee where it is reasonably practicable—it being an offence for any trustee to fail to secure compliance so far as he reasonably can.

Trustees are allowed to exercise their powers even though the result may bring them benefit as members of the scheme—s 39. The provision follows the recommendations of the Judge in *Re Drexel Burnham Lambert UK Pension Plan* [1995] 1 WLR 32 Ch D, and should not be taken to authorise a trustee to favour himself. The power must still be exercised properly, which means that the trustee benefits solely because he is in a class that it is proper to benefit.

Sections 42 and 43 have already been moved to the Employment Rights Act 1996 (ss 58 and 59) and provide that an employer must permit his employee remunerated time for performing his duties as trustee or undergoing relevant training. However, the sections do not go as far as to require the employer to make available any training, nor to require the trustees to obtain such training. It is simply a provision to assist them *if* they obtain training. The amount of time taken must be 'reasonable in all the circumstances'. Account has to be taken of the effect of the employee's absence on the running of the business.

An internal disputes procedure must be established in accordance with s 50, subject to any exceptions that may be prescribed (which by reg 8 means one-member schemes, and schemes where all the members are trustees)—see Chapter 16, para 18.

3.3 Professional advisers

Extremely important provisions are contained in s 47 and SI 1996 No 1715.

The provisions regarding auditors and fund managers have been mentioned in Chapter 16. The section provides that every occupational pension scheme must have an auditor an actuary and (where there are investments as defined by the Financial Services Act 1986) a fund manager, and that all these must be appointed by the trustees rather than being made available by the employer. DSS have consistently maintained that this does not prevent a dual retainer, and the regulations provide that the letters of appointment must state that notification of conflict of interest will be given to the trustees—reg 5(2).

The section does not oblige the trustees to appoint a legal adviser but does provide that if they rely on a legal adviser he must be their appointee. It is not clear whether this includes the provider of occasional or emergency legal advice, but the safer course will be to put in place a compliance letter of appointment. Regulation 5 makes other provisions regarding the letters of appointment, and reg 2 extends the section to persons giving one off advice on audit or actuarial matters, and to custodians. If counsel's advice is passed to trustees to assist them in exercising their functions, it would appear that a compliance appointment is required although some counsel disagree (being of the view that they are assisting the solicitors rather than acting as legal advisers to the trustees).

The penal provisions of the section are significant; trustees must have the relevant appointees in place.

3.4 Payment of surplus to employers

Sections 37, 76 and 77 are relevant where the trustees propose to make a payment to the employer. The first relates to an ongoing scheme, and the other two to a scheme in winding up. All three relate only to tax-approved schemes. SI 1996 No 2156 applies to them all but introduces no unexpected provisions, eg there has to be liaison with OPRA to check that no representations to it have been made—regs 6(2) and 9(2). For the main provisions regarding indexation of pensions in such circumstances, see Chapter 16, para 3.

3.5 Payment schedule for money-purchase schemes

Section 87, relating to money-purchase schemes, provides for a payment schedule to be agreed, and that it is an offence for trustees to fail to obtain it. Section 88 then requires them to notify OPRA of non-compliance with the payment schedule, being the parallel provision with the whistle-blowing duty of the trustees of a salary-related scheme under s 59.

3.6 Lien, forfeiture and bankruptcy

Sections 91–95 now regulate the above matters—see Chapter 13, para 3.26

3.7 Cash equivalents

Sections 152–154 provide for quotations of cash equivalents that are to be held for a guaranteed period which, by reg 6 of SI 1996 No 1847, is to be three months from the date of the member's application for the statement of entitlement. The new provisions are written into the PSA 1993, by these sections.

3.8 Penalties

It has been stated elsewhere that penalties have been introduced throughout the Act for matters that previously had no sanctions eg the disclosure regs. In addition section 155 substitutes a new s 168 into the PSA 1993, increasing the level of penalty that was already present in the PSA 1993, for breach of regulations under it.

Regarding criminal sanctions, see Chapter 18, para 2.4.

3.9 Commencement

Commencement Order No 10 (SI 1997 No 664) brought into force on 1 or 6 April 1997 almost all the remaining provisions of the Pensions Act 1995. The only significant omission appears to be ss 91(3) and 95, both relating to the interest of a trustee in bankruptcy, and awaiting valuation regs—see Chapter 13, para 3.26.

The penal provisions regarding whistle-blowing, s 48(7)–(13), and the supplementary provisions of s 48(2), almost appear not yet to be in force. This is in effect, confirmed by OPRA's guidance note (Chapter 18, para 2.3) which states, in its para 2.5, that 'Parliament has not felt it necessary' to bring its power to impose penalties under s 48 into force 'at this stage', and that professional bodies will deal with alleged failures through their own disciplinary machinery.

Chapter 26

Going privately administered

1 General

Most small pension schemes, or individual pension arrangements, are insured. Chapter 2, para 2 et seq describes the various approaches to this question. Chapter 17, para 8 describes the opposite approach, the small privately invested (or 'self-administered') scheme.

In a final-salary or money-purchase scheme (Chapter 8) the insurance policy is not a true insurance but merely a form of investment. There are many reasons for investing with an insurance company. The primary ones are likely to be:

(*a*) the need for a recommended rate of contribution;
(*b*) the need for investment management;
(*c*) the security given by 'guaranteed' policies or irreversible bonuses;
(*d*) the fact that benefits arising on death-in-service are true 'insurance' risks which (for a small group of lives) must be insured;
(*e*) the fact that most aspects of endowment or pension provision are first drawn to a person's attention by his broker and that he will rely on his broker for guidance as to the type of benefits that are generally considered 'normal';
(*f*) the fact that the life office will carry out most of the administration and the payment of pensions;
(*g*) the need for a package which has been approved by the Inland Revenue;
(*h*) the absence of custody problems (although care is still needed to guard against unauthorised surrenders);
(*i*) the fact that the package will include all the necessary documents;

(*j*) the assumption that once the scheme is established, it will continue without the need for further consideration.

All these reasons are valid, although the last two are often a little misleading (because the draft documents are so complex that advice in respect of them has to be sought, and because inflation or legislation may necessitate a re-examination of the scheme).

As a scheme grows in size, it is often possible to provide some services to it at a lower cost than applies under a life office policy. A revision of the arrangement therefore depends on the employer's ability to organise the necessary services. A half-way house is the managed fund (see para 2 below) but even this imposes a considerable burden on the employer.

It follows that the point at which it will be economical to change to private administration will vary according to the nature of the scheme and the ability or desire of the employer to increase its involvement. The cost of administration will be very small for a money purchase scheme (Chapter 8, para 6) limited to a few long-serving employees and conferred additionally to the State scheme (Chapter 20). At the other end of the scale, a contracted-out scheme (Chapter 20, para 4) with a large number of low-paid staff and final salary benefits (Chapter 8, para 1) will require full actuarial services even though the annual contributions may not (in absolute terms) be very large.

The decision to change cannot be taken until five aspects of the matter have received attention:

(*a*) it has been considered whether there are (or can be negotiated) surrender provisions in the policy governing the existing fund;
(*b*) an actuary (see para 4 below) has advised on the funds likely to accrue under the existing policy, the adequacy of them for the intended benefits and the rate of return required (for a given contribution rate) for private investment to match that performance.
(*c*) a consultant (who may be an actuary, a broker or a specialist consultant) has advised on the cost of providing the services at present supplied without charge by the life office;
(*d*) a solicitor has advised whether the existing trust permits or can be adapted to permit (see para 5 below) private investment;

(*e*) the client is confident that an investment manager and custodian can be appointed and monitored without strain on the trustees' personal involvement—see below.

It is outside the scope of this book to consider (*a*) to (*c*). The practitioner should, however, inquire as to the manner in which they have been considered and liaise with the other professional advisers.

Item (*e*) is the subject of Chapter 16, para 14. Specialist advice should be sought (perhaps from one of the above professionals but perhaps elsewhere) as to the way in which a selection will be made and the appointment subsequently monitored.

2 The managed fund

The term 'managed fund' has many uses. In pension matters it usually refers to a fund managed by a life office either individually ('a segregated fund') or on a unit basis, but not on the basis of applying contributions towards individual prospective benefits.

If the fund is too small to stand the strain that could arise from substantial death-in-service benefits, these are separately insured (often, but not always, with the same life office). Indeed, even a fully self-administered scheme will often insure its death benefits.

Very few schemes are set up with life offices as managed funds. The latter usually form a half-way house between 'insured' and privately administered stages. There are two chief reasons for choosing such a half-way house:

(1) The life office will continue to provide some of the services previously provided under the terms of the fully insured arrangement. In particular, it will normally provide regular actuarial valuations and may organise some of the administration connected with contracting out (Chapter 20, para 4).

(2) Some life offices quote low surrender values for their fully insured policies, but are more generous if part of the resultant fund is invested in one of their managed funds.

As to (1), the consultant will advise as to the amount of backup required and whether additional charges are made for the additional services. The position will vary considerably, as some managed funds will be solely investment media while others will offer complete packages.

As to (2), the matter is very much one for negotiation by the broker or consultant. Frequently a substantial proportion of the surrender value is left for, say, a minimum of five years in the managed fund.

The terms of the managed fund and the way in which administration charges within it are levied will require consideration, again mainly by the consultant.

3 The true private administration

In one sense, private administration is the oldest form of pension arrangement. It existed either as a pension paid out of current revenue (ie a pension of a particular amount) or as the right to the income (whatever it might be) from a particular estate.

However, in current commercial usage, the term refers to a fund which is administered by or on behalf of the trustees and not by a life office. Death-in-service benefits may still be insured.

Investment may be under the guidance of a merchant bank or a firm of stockbrokers. The larger funds have their own investment managers, or appoint several outside managers. As to the Financial Services Act 1986, see Chapter 16.

The powers of the trustees (see para 5 below) are of the greatest importance, since the contribution income will usually exceed pension outgo and it may be desirable to invest for medium or long-term gains rather than immediate income. The administrative arrangements are of equal importance. It is essential for the trustees, however wide their powers of delegation, to make adequate arrangements for reporting by the delegates as to the extent of the fund, its income and its outgo. The task of presenting this information is very skilled. It has to be considered in the light of the guidelines given to the investment manager and his reasons for particular investments. Generally it is better for the benefit reports to be considered at different meetings from the investment reports, and for the relevant executives to be present at the respective meetings.

Two questions for consideration are the requirements of the

Financial Services Act 1986 (Chapter 16, para 9) and the insider trading provisions of the Companies Acts (now to be read with the Financial Services Act 1986).

It is the privately administered fund that offers the most scope for the type of conflict of interest described in Chapter 24, para 6. On the other hand, it is just because a life office may have inflexible procedures, often causing great difficulty on the sale of a subsidiary, that some enterprising commercial decisions cannot easily be implemented except where there is private administration. In many other ways the privately administered scheme offers freedom to make intended arrangements. If an employee is sent to a tropical country but remains in the UK pension scheme (see Chapter 7) it may be possible to arrange an early retirement date. If the scheme is insured this either requires special negotiation with the life office or an acceptance that the benefits will have to be met partly on an unfunded basis. Private administration avoids the problem. Further, if a UK employee is permitted to retire early the life office may include a 'surrender' penalty for 'uplifting' the cash at an early date. Again, private administration offers complete flexibility.

4 Actuaries

The actuary is undoubtedly, for the general purposes of the scheme, the most important adviser where the arrangement is privately administered. Only he can advise whether the scheme is likely to become insolvent if it continues without change. The trustees are duty-bound (apart from the terms of the trust instrument) to seek regular reports from him and also to seek his advice if there is a substantial change in any circumstances on which those reports are based.

It may be thought that the auditor to the fund can advise on its solvency. However, his certificate only indicates the assets, liabilities, income and outgo. The actuary advises on the potential liabilities having regard to mortality tables, assumptions as to salary rises, investment experience, and other variables. The importance of these variables is so great that a considerable proportion of Chapter 8 has been devoted, in layman's terms, to some of them. However, where a scheme is insured it is to be hoped that the life office or broker will give some advice when changes in benefits are contemplated or changes in facts or assumptions occur. For a privately administered scheme, the actuary is the adviser in either such case.

Occasionally the actuary will be an officer of a life office who has undertaken private consultancy work. In Scotland, in particular, this has in the past been a frequent arrangement. In England it tends to arise only when an insured scheme becomes privately administered, and even then rarely.

The actuary is therefore likely to be an independent practitioner, usually a partner in a firm of actuaries, although increasingly an employee of a benefit consultancy company. He will be a member of one of the professional bodies and frequently also of the Association of Consulting (as opposed to employed) Actuaries. As with all professional advisers, it will be important to establish that his experience lies in the type of work for which his services are being engaged.

5 Are the documents a suitable vehicle?

It will already have been seen from Chapter 24, para 1 that the funds of a pension scheme will almost invariably be held upon trust. It will also have been seen (Chapter 3, para 15) that the trust deed will normally contain a power of alteration but that there may be fetters on its exercise and in particular a proviso protecting 'accrued rights'.

The power of alteration may not have been used since the establishment of the scheme. At the time that the scheme becomes privately administered, such power becomes of crucial importance, as the trust deed will rarely contain suitable powers of delegation and investment. Indeed, it may limit the application of trust funds to deposit with a particular life office. Unless such limitation can be removed, the proposal to administer the scheme privately may be impracticable (save perhaps by the introduction of a new scheme and the offer of a transfer to it).

Chapter 13, para 3 discusses the definitive trust deed under the headings commonly found to be essential or useful. It is suggested that each of these can be considered with the corresponding provision (if any) in the existing deed. The benefit structure is of less importance since it may remain unchanged for the time being, provided that the administrative provisions relating to benefits (eg whether pensions are paid in advance or arrear etc) are satisfactory.

Of the headings referred to, the power of investment is the most important as it is the subject of the change that is taking place in the scheme. While s 34 of the Pensions Act 1995, gives the powers of a beneficial owner, it is subject to any restriction within the pension scheme. The express power therefore should be in the usual general terms applicable to a family settlement that the trustees have the same powers as if they were absolutely and beneficially entitled to the trust assets. It should also specifically include:

(*a*) power to invest in land (to be held on trust for sale);
(*b*) power to retain cash balances (in current accounts);
(*c*) power to invest in non-income-producing assets;
(*d*) power to invest in units including those limited to exempt approved schemes and whether directly, or through a policy of assurance.

Several related powers should also be included, in particular:

(*e*) power to borrow;
(*f*) power to charge trust assets;
(*g*) power to effect insurances for the purposes of the scheme (eg for death-in-service benefits);
(*h*) power to underwrite and sub-underwrite (since the commission, assuming it is not trading income, will be exempt from tax under s 592(3) of the Income and Corporation Taxes Act 1988).

The list is not exhaustive. Nevertheless it should form a useful set of guidelines. The possible authorisation of financial futures and traded options should be considered (Chapter 17, para 1.1). If a merchant bank is to be appointed, or indeed any investment adviser, it should be given the draft first for perusal and comment. It should also be given a copy of the executed (amended) trust instrument so that it knows the limits of the powers. The fact that this has been done should be minuted. Further, the actual guidelines laid down for the investment adviser (which may be narrower than the trustees' full powers) should also be minuted. Such precision ought to be sufficient to avoid unauthorised ventures into speculative fields such as commodities or, alternatively, to negotiate recovery of losses from the advisers concerned.

The intended investment manager (and custodian if relevant) should supply draft agreements. The time needed to consider them, and to settle the above guidelines for scheduling to them, will be considerable (Chapter 16, para 14). Ideally at the selection stage drafts should be considered with each applicant but in practice this would probably involve the client in too much management time (and professional expense). The notification of success to the intended manager should therefore indicate that it is subject to completion of satisfactory documents.

Appendix

Glossary

This glossary includes only those terms most frequently to be found in documents or correspondence relating to occupational pension schemes. Where a term is referred to or defined in a statute, generally only one statutory reference is included.

Where relevant, references to chapters of this book are included in brackets.

The following abbreviations are used:

FA 70: Finance Act 1970
ICTA 88: Income and Corporations Taxes Act 1988
PA 95: Pensions Act 1995
PSA 93: Pension Schemes Act 1993
SSCBA 92: Social Security Contributions and Benefits Act 1992
SI 1996 No 1655: The Occupational Pension Schemes (Disclosure of Information) Regulations 1996
SI 1991 No 167: The Occupational Pension Schemes (Preservation of Benefit) Regulations 1991

Accrued rights This term is frequently used in connection with pension schemes. Nonetheless, its meaning is usually obscure. In particular, with a modern final salary, several meanings are possible (see the effect of salary increases Chapter 8, para 2). The term is defined for the purposes of PA 95(part I) by s 124(2) as if a member had left service.

Accrued rights premium A premium formerly payable to the State, in the absence of other approved arrangements, to guarantee certain benefits where a scheme ceased to be contracted out: PSA 93, s 55(6) (repealed).

Additional pension (formerly additional component) The earnings-related part of State pension benefits (Chapter 20, para 2): SSCBA 92, s 44(3) (*b*).

Administrator The term is used in connection with tax exemption (Chapter 17, para 1.4) and contracting out: ICTA 88, s 611AA, and SI 1996 No 1172, reg 1. The administrator was formerly the person or persons having the management of the scheme (and for contracting-out purposes, specifically such person or persons resident in the United Kingdom). ICTA now specifies the trustees (if they are resident in the UK).

Aggregate method One of the five basic methods now recommended (see **Funding methods**) for determining the employer's contribution rate; in effect the balance of cost as a percentage of member's earnings, after allowing for present assets; a variant of **Attained age method** or **Entry age method**.

Anti-franking Term for prohibition on absorption of GMP increases by other scale benefits (PSA 1993, Pt IV, Chap III).

Appropriate Scheme Certificate The contracting-out certificate for a personal pension scheme.

Approved scheme See 'Exempt approved scheme'.

Attained age method One of the five basic methods now recommended (see **Funding methods**) for determining the employer's contribution rate; in effect the cost (as a percentage of members' earnings) of future benefits assuming no change in membership.

Average salary scheme A pension scheme in which the benefits are calculated by reference to the period during which each level of salary has been earned (Chapter 8, para 5).

Barber judgment The seminal equal treatment judgment in the European Court of Justice (Chapter 22).

Basic pension (formerly basic component) The flat-rate part of pension under the State scheme (Chapter 20, para 1): SSCBA 92, s 44 (3)(*a*).

Board See 'Inland Revenue', and also see 'Occupational Pensions Board'.

Bonus credit Generally the prospective increase in pension granted ex gratia during the member's service. Defined as a form of 'supplementary credit': PSA 93, s 75.

Buy-out The purchase from an insurance company of an annuity (with or without dependant's rights) under the pension scheme; since 1 January 1986 a statutory option for most early leavers: PSA 93, ss 94, 95.

CEP See 'Contributions equivalent premium'.

Cash equivalent The amount of a **Buy-out** or transfer if arising under the statutory option of a post-1985 leaver: PSA 93, s 94.

Centralised scheme The term is applied to a scheme where more than one employer participates: SI 1984 No 614, reg 1(2) (now repealed); Inland Revenue Practice Notes 1R 12.

Closed scheme A scheme closed to new members which may or may not also be closed to further contributions.

COMBs Contracted out mixed benefit scheme (Chapter 20, para 4.8).

Commutation The exchange of pension for a single lump sum (Chapter 17, para 3.6).

Compensation scheme Colloquial term for compensation provisions administered under PA 95, s 81 (Chapter 25, para 2).

Contracted-in A term to describe a scheme that is not contracted out of the State pension scheme (Chapters 19, para 3 and 20, para 4).

Contracted-out See 'Contracted-in'.

Contributions Agency A branch of DSS that maintains National Insurance contribution records.

Contributions equivalent premium A premium sometimes payable to the State when a member of a contracted-out salary-related scheme leaves service after less than two years, to extinguish the member's right to a guaranteed minimum pension under the scheme or, for post-April 1997 service, to restore rights in SERPS (see Chap 20, para 4.5): PSA 93, s 55.

Controlled funding A method by which an insurance company may assess the required contribution rate for a fund without carrying out a full valuation.

Controlling director The term is defined in ICTA 88, Sched 23, para 5(5). Until 1973 no controlling director (as more restrictively defined) could be admitted to membership of an approved fund or scheme (Chapter 17, para 7).

Current unit method One of the five basic methods now recommended (see **Funding methods**) for determining the employer's contribution rate; in effect the cost for the one year following valuation (as a percentage of members' earnings) of the benefits which will accrue that year and the increases in past service benefits based on projected earnings at the end of *that year*.

DSS Department of Social Security.

Defined benefit scheme Usually means 'Final salary scheme' (Chapter 8, para 7).

Defined contribution scheme See 'Money-purchase scheme'.

Deposit Administration A description of one form of arrangement under which a life office handles the funds of an insured scheme (Chapter 2, para 4).

Employer-related investments Assets limited or prohibited for pensions schemes: PA 95, s 40 (Chapter 16, para 13).

Entry age method One of the five basic methods now recommended (see **Funding methods**) for determining the employer's contribution rate; in effect the cost of future benefits for members entering at a 'normal' age (or range of ages) as a percentage of their earnings.

Equal access The former legislative requirements for similar treatment of men and women in the rules relating to eligibility for membership of a pension scheme PSA 93, s 118 (now repealed).

Equal treatment rule Requirement for sex equality: PA 95, s 62 (Chapter 22, para 2.8).

Exempt approved scheme. The form of approval by the Commissioners of Inland Revenue that is necessary if a pension scheme is to obtain the four possible tax advantages (Chapter 17, para 1). Approval may be mandatory or discretionary (ICTA 88, ss 590 or 591) but generally will not be 'exempt approval' unless the scheme has been established under irrevocable trust (s 592).

Final remuneration The maximum permissible benefits payable under an approved scheme are calculated by reference to final remuneration. The term is defined in ICTA 88, s 612(1), as amended, as 'the average annual remuneration for the last three years' service'. The Inland Revenue under s 591, permit a number of alternative definitions (Chapter 17, para 3).

Final salary scheme A scheme in which the benefits are calculated on the basis of the employee's salary at or near the time of retirement (Chapter 8, para 1).

Finance Act 1956 policies Policies issued under the provisions introduced by the Finance Act 1956 and subsequently incorporated in ICTA 70, s 226 (now ICTA 88, ss 619 and 620) under which self-employed persons or persons not in pensionable employment may fund for their retirement with some of the tax advantages otherwise available only through an exempt approved scheme (Chapter 2, para 7). Policies issued under this provision are known as retirement annuity contracts and are sometimes referred to as 'self-employed policies' or 'self-employed deferred annuities'.

Funding methods The basic method set out by the Institute and Faculty of Actuaries in 1984 in a Report of a Joint Working Party, being (i) **Aggregate method** (ii) **Attained age method** (iii) **Current unit method** (iv) **Entry age method** (v) **Projected unit method**. Specimen descriptions are published in guidance entitled 'Pension Fund Terminology' (revised edn June 1988).

GMP See 'Guaranteed minimum pension'.

Guaranteed minimum pension The pension (or part of pension) accrued before 6 April 1997 by a member of a contracted-out scheme normally equal to that part of the State pension which was given up by virtue of the contracting-out arrangement. The widow of such a member will also have a guaranteed minimum: PSA 93, ss 13–17.

Hancock See Chapter 12, para 4.

Inland Revenue The Commissioners of Inland Revenue (PSA 93, s 181), the reference in ICTA 88 being simply to the 'Board' (ICTA 88, ss 590 et seq). The Board confer approval on schemes for the purpose of tax relief (Chapter 17). The relevant department of the Inland Revenue is the Pension Schemes Office or PSO (see Chapter 1, para 5).

Insured scheme A scheme whose contributions are all passed to an insurance company, the latter undertaking to pay certain (but not necessarily all) benefits (Chapter 2, paras 1–4; 4 and 8).

Interim trust deed The most common method of establishing a scheme; a relatively short deed declaring the trust and providing for a definitive deed to be executed at a later date and to contain detailed provisions (Chapter 3, para 2).

Irrevocable trust The normal *sine qua non* for exempt approval (Chapter 17.1): (ICTA 88, s 592 (1).

Life Office Insurance company conducting life (and usually pensions) business.

Limited Price Indexation Increases to pensions in payment and in deferment in line with retail prices index up to 5 per cent per annum: PSA 93, Sched 3, para 2(3), (6) and PA 95, s 51 (Chapter 16, para 3).

Limited revaluation premium A premium formerly payable to the State when a member of a contracted-out scheme left service before age 65 (60 for women), no accrued rights/contributions equivalent/pensioner's rights premium being payable; the scheme limited the subsequent increase of GMP to a maximum of 5 per cent per annum (Chapter 20, para 4.2): PSA 93, s 55(6) (now repealed).

Linked qualifying service Actual service under an earlier scheme (whether with the same or a different employer) which results in a transfer credit under a subsequent scheme (because a transfer payment is made from one to the other) and which is therefore taken into account (inter alia) for preservation purposes: PSA 93, s 179.

Long-service benefit The term is used in connection with preservation; it refers to the benefits payable to or in respect of a scheme member who attains the scheme's normal pension age: PSA 93, s 70.

Lower earnings limit The level of weekly earnings above which a member of a contracted-out scheme pays reduced national insurance contributions (it also approximates to the basic component of the single person's State pension): PSA 93, s 41; SSCBA 92, s 5.

LPI See Limited Price Indexation.

Managed fund An actual fund (as opposed to the insurance company's general business fund) units in which are referable to particular schemes whose investment is managed by an insurance company (Chapters 2, para 4 and 26, para 2).

Member Usually means current employees entitled to prospective benefits from a scheme, often pensioners as well (but not widows) and occasionally deferred pensioners. It is often defined by a scheme's rules. It is also sometimes defined for a statutory purpose, eg, PA 95, s 124 SI 1991 No 167, reg 3 (as amended).

Member-nominated trustees Trustees nominated by members under PA 95, s 16 (Chapter 24, para 7.2).

Memorandum The PSO and the former OPB (see Chapter 1, para 5) issued memoranda describing their powers and the manner in which they exercise their discretions (see, eg, Chapters 17, para 8, and 18, para 7).

MFR See Minimum Funding Requirement.

Minimum Funding Requirement: a level of solvency required for most salary-related approved pension schemes. It does not guarantee the benefits but does establish a funding requirement: PA 95 s 56 (Chapter 16, para 17).

Money-purchase scheme A scheme in which the amount of the employer's contributions follows a fixed contributions formula, and the amount of pension depends on the interest or bonuses earned by the fund (Chapter 8, para 6); also known as 'defined contribution scheme'; for 'money-purchase benefit' and scheme, see PSA 93, s 181.

New code The basis for approval set out in FA 70, now ICTA 88, Pt XIV, Chap 1 (Chapter 17, para 1).

OPB See 'Occupational Pensions Board'.

Occupational Pensions Board A body corporate (now dissolved) established by s 66 of SSA 73 whose main functions were to ensure compliance with the preservation and equal access requirements and to supervise contracting out (Chapter 1, para 5). Generally known as the OPB. PA 95, s 150.

Occupational pension scheme Generally used to refer to all pension arrangements other than the State (national insurance) scheme. Defined so as to include public service schemes (which are also defined therein) by PSA 93, s 1. See also 'Retirement benefits scheme'.

Occupational Pensions Regulatory Authority A body corporate established by PA 95, s 1, to regulate and enforce compliance with certain provisions of that Act. (Chapter 18, paras 1–4).

Old code The form (or forms) of Inland Revenue approval that preceded the new code established by FA 70 (now ICTA 88) (Chapter 17, para 5). All such approvals ceased to have effect on 6 April 1980 (Chapter 17, para 6).

Ombudsman See Pensions Ombudsman

OPAS Occupational Pensions Advisory Service A charity in receipt of grant under PSA, s 174. (Chapter 18, para 6).

OPRA See 'Occupational Pensions Regulatory Authority'.

Ordinary annual contributions Contributions of an employer or employee to an exempt approved scheme allowed for tax relief in the year of payment: ICTA 88, s 592 (6) as amended by Finance Act 1993, s 112.

PSO Pension Schemes Office. See 'Inland Revenue'.

Past service reserve A term formerly much used but having no unique meaning; generally referring to present value of all benefits accrued at the valuation date by reference to projected final earnings (the same as the standard fund, ie assumed balanced fund associated with the **Attained age method** and **Projected unit method**).

Pension Generally understood to mean a periodic payment beginning after cessation of the employment from which it is derived and continuing until death (or, occasionally, remarriage or forfeiture). For historical meaning, see Chap 15, para 2. Section 612(1) of ICTA 88 provides (without adding much illumination) that 'pension' includes annuity.

Pension business Premiums received by an insurance company in connection with an exempt approved pension scheme (where the life office liabilities "correspond" with the relevant liabilities of the scheme), an approved personal pension arrangement or an approved retirement annuity contract constitute pension business and may be paid into a 'gross' fund: ICTA 88, ss 431B, 438.

Pensioner's rights premium A premium formerly payable to the State, in the absence of other approved arrangements, to guarantee certain benefits of persons who have left service, where a scheme subsequently ceases to be contracted out: PSA 93, 55(6) (now repealed).

Pensions Ombudsman means the Commissioner appointed under what is now PSA 93, s 145 (Chapter 18, para 5).

Permanent health scheme A scheme under which salary continues until retirement age if absence is enforced through illness or accident (Chapter 2, para 8).

Personal pension scheme A scheme made available by a commercial provider for one or more (unconnected) individuals who choose to contribute, or require the DSS to contribute, to it: PSA 93, ss 1, 44.

Preservation Refers to the preservation requirements introduced by s 63(1) of SSA 73, now PSA 93, s 69 (Chapter 10, para 1).

Projected unit method One of the five basic methods now recommended (see **Funding methods**) for determining the employer's contribution rate; in effect the cost for the one year following valuation (as a percentage of members' earnings) of the benefits which will accrue that year based on projected final earnings.

Qualifying service Apart from general use in some schemes' rules, this term has a defined meaning for preservation purpose—see 'two years' qualifying service' in PSA 93, s 71 (7).

Registrar of Occupational and Personal Pension Schemes The registrar appointed under PSA 93, s 6 (Chapter 18, para 3).

Relevant benefits A defined term for the purpose of taxation: ICTA 88, s 612 (1). The definition is set out in full in Chapter 17, para 1.3. It is drawn so widely as to require the reporting to the Inland Revenue of all benefits (even if not formalised as a scheme) connected with retirement or death (other than certain accident risks). See also s 595.

Retirement annuity contract Meaning such a contract approved under ICTA 88, Pt XIV, Chapter 3. See 'Finance Act 1956 policies'.

Retirement benefits scheme A scheme for the provision of relevant benefits (other than a national scheme): ICTA 88, s 611. The charging (and exempting) provisions of ICTA 88 all relate to such a scheme. It is widely defined (Chapter 17, para 1).

Revenue See 'Inland Revenue'.

SEDA Self-employed deferred annuity. See 'Finance Act 1956 policies'.

SFO Superannuation Funds Office. Former name of PSO (qv).

SORP Statement of Recommended Practice regarding pension fund accounts (Chapter 16, para 11).

SSAP 24 Statement of Standard Accounting Practice 24 regarding treatment of pensions in company accounts (Chapter 16, para 11).

Salary sacrifice An agreement whereby remuneration is reduced and pension is increased—see Inland Revenue practice notes IR 12 (1991) para 4.9.

Scheme See 'Occupational pension scheme' and 'Retirement benefits scheme'.

Section 208/222/379/388 scheme See 'Old code'.

Section 226/226A policy See 'Finance Act 1956 policies'.

Self-adminstered scheme A retirement benefits scheme whose assets are not administered by a life office (Chapter 2, para 5).

Self-employed policy See 'Finance Act 1956 policies'.

Self-invested scheme A retirement benefits scheme of which a large proportion of the assets are invested in the employer (Chapters 2, para 5 and 17, para 8); for restrictions see Chapter 16, para 13.

Share of the fund A term having no unique meaning but generally applied to the proportion of the fund equal to the proportion of liabilities represented by the particular members' deferred pensions assuming an immediate discontinuance, ie dividing the whole fund (whether in surplus or deficit) in the latter proportion.

Short service benefit The benefit to which a member falling within the preservation requirements (Chapter 10, para 1) must be entitled (whether for himself or others) on leaving service before a scheme's normal pension age: PSA 93, s 71(2).

Small scheme A scheme with a small number of members (usually fewer than 12) that is self-administered (Chapter 17, para 8).

Statutory scheme Section 596 of ICTA 88 exempts relevant statutory schemes from the charging provisions of s 595. The term is defined in ss 611A and 612 and means a retirement benefits scheme set up by statute or regulation or approved for the purpose by a Minister or government department and, in effect, registered by the PSO.

Stock lending The passing of stock temporarily to a third party (and, if done correctly, in exchange for security).

Superannuation Funds Office See SFO.

Supplementary credit The term used in connection with preservation to describe a special increase in prospective pension. It includes bonus and transfer credits (as well as another credit known as purchased credit): PSA 93, s 75, and SI 1991 No 167, reg 4.

Transfer credit Defined by PSA 93, s 181, and meaning briefly the rights of a member arising by reason of a transfer from another scheme. The provision of a transfer credit extinguishes the right to short service benefit from the previous scheme: s 73.

Transfer premium A premium formerly payable to the State by trustees of a contracted-out scheme in certain circumstances: PSA 93 s 55(6) now repealed (Chapter 20, para 4.5).

Trustees' report. A colloquial term for an annual report to members, accompanied by fund accounts and other information: SI 1996 No 1655, reg 6.

Twenty per cent director A director, who, either alone or with associates, controls 20 per cent or more of the share capital of the company. For full current definition, see Chapter 17.7.

Upper earnings limit The maximum weekly earnings (or part of earnings) on which National Insurance contributions are payable by an employee and additional component of State pension accrues: SSCBA 92, s 5.

Whistle-blowing duty of professional advisers (and in one respect trustees) to notify OPRA: PA 95 ss 48, 59 (Chapter 18, para 2.3).

Index